french theory in america

edited by
Sylvère Lotringer
and **Sande Cohen**

french theory in america

Routledge   **New York London**

Published in 2001 by
Routledge
29 West 35th Street
New York, New York 10001

Published in Great Britain by
Routledge
11 New Fetter Lane
London EC4P 4EE

Routledge is an imprint of the Taylor and Francis Group.

Printed in the United States of America on acid-free paper.

Library of CongressCataloging-in-Publication Data

French theory in America/edited by Sylvère Lotringer and Sande Cohen.
    p. cm.
  Includes bibliographical references and index.
  ISBN 0-415-92536-3 ISBN 0-415-92537-1 (pbk.)
  1. Philosophy, French 20th century. 2. French Intellectual life 20th
century. 3. United States Civilization French influences. I. Lotringer,
Sylvère. II. Cohen, Sande.
B2421 .F75 2000
194 dc21   00-035312

10 9 8 7 6 5 4 3 2 1

Contents

Introduction:
A Few Theses on French Theory
in America

SYLVÈRE LOTRINGER AND SANDE COHEN

"French theory" is an American invention, going back to at least the eighteenth century, and no doubt belongs to the continuity of American reception to all sorts of European imports, an ongoing process.

This process turns what the French call "thought" *(pensée)* into what Americans call "theory" and so pertains to strange psychopolitical facts about America. It may well be that most Americans actually believe in only two modes of thought—utopianism, expressed in versions of an "American exceptionalism" and which perforce includes "apocalypticism"; and legalism, or reliance on the intellectual patterns of law. Utopianism and legalism deny philosophy and nonlegal "theory" much leeway to arbitrate disputes, or even to address criticism; could it be that criticism, of all kinds, grafted itself to "theory" in America as a way of slipping out from under utopia and law? Be that as it may, the reception and dissemination of recent French "thought" into "theory" is irreducible to the vicissitudes of utopia and law, with their never-ending problems of discipline, boundary, propriety. In geologic terms, utopianism and legalism are like two gigantic plates tightly poised against each other, each attempting to slide past the other; French theory can be compared to the tension formed at the boundary of the two, which sometimes builds and at other times is released. As Webster's dictionary puts it, theory is something that is not "conclusively established or accepted as the law," and, in this sense, it is undoubtedly fortunate that French thought became American theory, freeing up, like faultlines, the interstices among belief, judgment, facts, and principles. The first thing to say about French theory in America is that it provides new senses of art, philosophy, and science "outside" reigning American ideas and writing.

That such theory has often been rejected by the existing disciplines of academic institutions, especially history and philosophy departments attempting to protect the archaicisms of linearity and "clear and distinct" ideas, is both a fact of recent history and evidence of a structure that French theory set out to contest. We have been saturated by the invocation of repressive ideals against French theory—the ideal

of regulative truth, the ideal of form fits fact, the ideal of metanarrative social co-
hesion, the ideal of language transparency. Given these ideals that derive from utopia
and law, we think French theory will have a long and noble future in America.

In terms of understanding the present configuration of forces in relation to
French theory, first consider the "beginnings" of French theory in America, or at
least as humorously evoked in the spring of 1997 by Arthur Danto during a panel
at the Graduate Center, New York. As an aside, Danto offered that the "Schizo-
Culture Conference" organized by *Semiotext(e)* in 1975 at Columbia University,
which included papers by Gilles Deleuze, Félix Guattari, Michel Foucault, and
Jean-François Lyotard, was an event totally out of sync with American thought:

> I was there. In fact, I was a speaker. For some reason I was put in the same
> slot that first evening as Lyotard, a man who has what I think of as the *true
> gift of incoherence*. The rest of the French have been trying to achieve it, but
> he was born with it, like perfect pitch.

Danto's deft aestheticization of "incoherence" is worth quoting more fully:

> Lyotard spoke in French, and there was a table with three people whose pur-
> pose was to translate what Lyotard was saying . . . and they couldn't agree!
> finally, they would say, "Well, we think this is what he means . . ." The three
> interlocutors were trying to convey to us, knowing that it was hopeless, that
> we should have tried to understand on our own, even if we didn't know
> French, what Lyotard was trying to say.[1]

Danto was boggled by the mixtures of thought that were not coded from
speaker to listener ("couldn't agree . . .") and of potential misrepresentation, a
disturbance of "rational" communication carried out by speakers-in-charge whose
own discourse was not attributable to a subject or to any speaker's intention. In
this "breakout" of discourse mixed with collective bargaining, the expertise expected of experts, a proliferation of "ex's," instead of correct attribution to
intention/listeners, gave way to an *event*—the visibility of commentary "on" overt
content dissolved and discourse opened onto other groups in emergence and a
plethora of figurations.[2] Danto's recollection in 1997 expressed a generalized distrust of indirect free discourse, which, in *A Thousand Plateaus*, Deleuze and Guattari called a language that goes "from saying to saying . . . voices in a voice . . .
no clear distinctive contours . . . shifting distributions within discourse."[3] The
main effect of indirect free discourses: to dissolve boundaries of representation.
Unable to proceed with the consumption of the purported recordings (discourse)
in the *aporias* between the speaking subject (who is supposed to be epistemically

responsible: "I am saying to you that . . .") and grammatical subject (which detaches from speakers), our scholar became fettered by discourse that could not be controlled. In the 1966 colloquium at Johns Hopkins University, often said to have been the real beginning of French theory in America, Jacques Derrida could postulate that with language, repetition, not the subject who speaks, is original. A present enunciation—"I am dead"—really gives, he added, ". . . the condition for a true act of language [that] is my being able to say 'I am dead.'"[4]

We make these comments as a warning: requesting from French theory a unified, all-embracing model for criticism, especially one that would lead to a goal for discourse, is a mistake. French theorists made language and representation a problem in specifying any sort of goal. There was some consensus, however, that language is inseparable from "semantic tensions and uncertainties," to borrow a phrase from Jean-Jacques Lecercle, coextensive with language and event, connected in the most diverse ways to other collective agencies of enunciation. Paul de Man, in agreement with Deleuze over the *terror* exercised by order words that arrest, on the spot, wayward and errant sense, would have said that the discourse uttered by someone called Arthur Danto manifested the very terror it objected to, even if mixed with erudition and genuine puzzlement.

French theory in America comes with some baggage. Arguably the most intellectually stimulating series of texts produced in the postwar era, joining visible public facts (e.g., the tribulations of capitalism) with experimental criticism (e.g., *Anti-Oedipus*'s mixtures of theory, philosophy, social science, and searing polemic), French theory pressured every concept of representation, surpassing the critiques made by existentialists, structuralists, Marxists, feminists, and multiculturalists. This French theory is also now both being absorbed and being disdained.[5] We worry about the academicization of French theory, achieving some dominance in one area, derided in others—the kind of sorting-out processes keenly examined by Bruno Latour (see Elie During's and Mario Biagioli's essays in this volume on questions of disciplinary identity, on French theory's provocation of boundary questions). History, economics and political science have labored to make themselves immune from theories that criticize capital, just as in the areas of art and film, as covered in this volume by Sylvère Lotringer's, Kriss Ravetto's, and Alison Gingeras's essays, French theory has been welcomed and sometimes turned into an exclusion discourse (the case of Lacan). It may turn out that in the arts one can most acutely perceive the tribulations of French theory in America. Why? As other writers in this volume suggest, the contemporary fury over the writing of art history, with all sides having dovetailed on *recoding* or *capturing* art history for a number of purposes (commercial, academic), indicates that French theory intersected with the postwar expansion of the *concept of culture*, especially signaled in America by the intractability of capital combined with the emergence of pop culture. The concept of culture has expanded to the point where it doesn't mean anything. The arts, including the "fate" endlessly pronounced on literature, have proliferated exactly at the same time that French theory took up the challenge that culture itself was veering toward extinction, a thesis propounded by Claude Lévi-Strauss and others in the 1930s and '40s. One of the most well-known books of French theory, Lyotard's *The Post-Modern Condition*, gave a technical analysis of the concept of postmodernism and concluded that information was more politicized than ever, but that the arts, or language games without end, "deny the solace of good forms" and so might enjoy a proliferation of new effects that would render a sense of *making culture* in the face of the dissolution and shattering of "the modern."

Perhaps we can suggest the following theses about French theory. We understand the synthetic "point" of this theory/thought as the *permanent suspension of representation* (see the essays by Derrida, Gaillard, and Cohen, herein). Most often, to represent means to settle, answer, resolve, and control the represented—the experiences of the world put in their "right" place. Instead, representation as conceived by French theory was turned to entirely critical and productive purposes—to make thought experiments. Instead of treating writing and books as conclusive models, books and writing were encouraged to support the idea that "there is no difference between what a book talks about and how it is made."[6] This first thesis can be stated as follows: Where modern communications theory has incessantly postulated positive outcomes from its models (consensus, agreement), in essence promoting social reconciliation, French theory subsumed concepts of communication in notions of *signification* and *contestation*. As there are no metanarratives that can be appealed to without becoming ideological, the turn to signification and contestation involved analysis of society's modes of writing, its ability to, as Barthes put it, "naturalize the unmotivated," tying the economic to the psychological ("doxa"), linking the academic to the represented as one variegated semiotic machine, some parts of which work, some of which work by not working (e.g., psychology and its subjects). In America, criticism and construction of models of language edged out questions of historical consciousness, at least for a while (Andrea Loselle gives a strong reading of this in her essay here on "new historicism"). Theories of signification sprouted, each moving aside the primacy of consciousness. This explains how, for example, Merleau-Ponty's work, with its emphasis on phenomenology and gestalt psychology conceived as the road to sensory and cognitive security, came to be considered dated. As Donald Theall points out in his paper here, McLuhan's *The Mechanical Bride* (1951) and Barthes's *Mythologies* (1957) helped to inaugurate semioclasm and undo the phenomenology of perception. Merleau-Ponty's belief that "lived experience" was "present" in Cézanne's paintings—"the impression of an emerging order, of an object in the act of appearing, organizing itself before our eyes"—was perhaps the last attempt to connect presence and sense.[7] Phenomenology, existentialism, Marxism, and psychoanalysis failed to give what language cannot give—a condition of security for meaning. There are meanings whose foundation is so *genealogically* complex that it is not possible to speak of language as the proper mode of representing *the everything* (see Baudrillard's essay, herein). Collectively, what French theory said was that meaning is probably a red herring, a repressive ideal, as signification is local, partial, precise; neither language nor consciousness can be relied upon to achieve understanding of totalities that are themselves always partial and fragmented. So while "meaning" remains the object of the goal of possessive understanding, other types of writing and thinking cleared the way for other goals. In this sense, many French theorists were read in America as abandoning enlightenment and utopia, since these theorists emphasized tactics and strategies of representation that are not based on the resemblance of representations to what they represent—the opinions of passive habit, transcendental stupidity, and subject/institutional mergings. If the earliest writings of French theory focused, then, on language, where Barthes could insist on the proximity of language as such to fascism, later writers such as Baudrillard and Virilio took this to heart and argued that only writing that itself becomes radicalized has any chance to offset the pull of institutions and reliance on a few super-words, invariably misleading. Such words as *truth*, *history*, and *value* may well be indispensable, but French theory tried to do without them as much as possible.

In short, what French theory brought to America was a politics in *language*, famously borrowed from Bakhtin and so many others. Politics in language means the scuttling of any discursive mode that refuses to account for its "implicit presuppositions," its despotic significations turning language into a command system that keeps saving representation despite the latter's ceaseless dissolution—books, newspapers, radio, TV, Internet: each plays the role of simplifying. What Foucault called the "discursive regime" (big or small, local or not) always opposes proliferation by discourses that might disorganize the going "common" and "good" sense; hence Deleuze could argue in *Difference and Repetition* that the only "proper" response to the proprieties of representation was *superproduction*, or writings that strive to change the very function of concepts from integrative devices to concepts that add onto other concepts at places and junctures that simply make more thoughts. It seems to us that the American style of *discounting* language is itself already "French," although we acknowledge a high degree of ambiguity about this phenomenon.

A second thesis concerns subjectivity. Beginning in the late 1960s, the writings of Lukàcs and the hegemony of Frankfurt-style criticism inadvertently made for a positive reception in America to some aspects of French theory. By the time of *Anti-Oedipus* (1972), the Frankfurt school reliance on refurbishing subjectivity from the rubble of Nazism and Fascism came to be a forum of *political correctness* and was seen by some American and French writers as obsolete, even reactionary. The synthesis of Marx and Freud, emphasis upon political consciousness and the ego-in-resistance, proved unworkable, a throwback to conditions of criticism already surpassed by capitalism. Here the American writer Norman O. Brown foreshadowed American receptivity to French theory (and which Donald Theall brings out in his essay on McLuhan, or the case of Canada). His *Love's Body* (1966) argued for a different sense of subjectivity, not riveted to representation or the politics of the "good image."[8] French theory broke apart the previous Americanization of German synthesis, in which negation of the existing realities was to lead, through self-consciousness, to political import and sense. A way of gauging this change is to note that recent French theory, Jacques Lacan excepted, turned away from all *theories of lack* (and law and signifier, as *Anti-Oedipus* stressed), shifting from what Terry Eagleton called the very job of (politically correct) criticism: "to explain the ideological necessity of . . . *the unconsciousness* of the work [text, object]—that of which it is not, and cannot be, aware." Criticism leads to a higher moralism because criticism is *corrective*[9]—the unconscious vanquished. French theory set these ideas aside. Instead, pursuing what the literary critic Gérard Genette called "an active disavowal and an immanent refutation of the insipid—and impotent—aesthetic of resemblance," it did not try to salvage or rehabilitate the subject, especially the subject's capacity for identification. Rather, French theory pursued the idea of *moleculating agents* who "remain in disjunction," affirmatively, as in Beckett's *Molloy*.[10] It seems to us that many American writers and artists wanted to increase their distance from the demands of resemblance; in place of a better historical self-consciousness that would dovetail with an equally improved subjective moral sense, French theory moved to Nietzschean paths, suspending identity whenever it showed itself, insisting on readings and interpretations that are less *accumulative* (of sense, of history) than they are *incessant* in posing problems. Hence the accusations that French theory is "scientist and aesthetic." Lyotard's emphasis strikes us as appropriate—the way to suspend binarism and the logic of the least negative (affirmative based on a silent negation) is to make writing itself "a mask without a face," more like a precise and analytic hit-and-run activity than a monument to representation.

In relation to language and notions of the subject, our third thesis concerns negative schizophrenia as a general social condition. This concept means negations of all kinds are interpreted into the System, all of life capitalized. New collective agencies have been unable to productively change the language or anything else. The behaviorism (e.g., demands for security) associated with capital is more "natural" than ever, making French theory dissident in relation to ordinary cultural and political criticism. Deleuze and Guattari turned capitalism into the triumph of zombies. "Writing has never been capitalism's thing," they wrote, for capitalism "is profoundly illiterate . . . [it] overcodes . . . and induces a fictitious voice from on high . . . transcendence of the despotic signifier . . . axiomatic . . . and regulated."[11] Lyotard rendered capital in the anti-identity of voracity, an appetite, as in this blast:

> Capital makes us tell, listen to and act out the great story of its reproduction, and the positions we occupy in the instances of its narrative are predetermined. [Capitalism] is subtle. It does not just stamp out little stories; it also asks for them. It does not automatically send innovators into exile; it sometimes grants them patents and subsidies . . . And whilst it is true that it puts us under house arrest in its narrative instances, it is also true that it requires us to change places.[12]

Baudrillard rendered capital as extermination of difference, and its endless reproduction as simulacra. All in all, French theory asks us to consider capitalism as both "normal" and "schizo," asocial and nihilistic to be sure, and here Foucault's work infuriated everyone in the 1960s because it was both anti-Marxist and anticapitalist. Foucault never ceased arguing that the labor of criticism and art had to rise to the occasion of capitalism's challenge and thus conceive of criticism and art as an event in and of itself; to the terror of capital, words and subjective feeling, the contemporary writer/artist had to be a constructivist, an inventor of relations on-the-spot, making events or what Deleuze and Guattari might have called "joy-flights" of critique, texts that managed to work up the normal schizophrenia of us all into celestial, celibate and paranoid documents that allow new moves. In short, the subtitle of Deleuze and Guattari's major work—*Capitalism and Schizophrenia*—managed to help Americans understand that the dominant modes of conceiving history and subject were inadequate to the violence and terrorism of capitalism.

Our fourth and last thesis has to do with the reception of Nietzsche's texts in America, traveling on a French ticket. The French didn't effectively turn to Nietzsche until they were finished with Hegel, who had reentered modern French thought with the writings of Alexander Kojève in the early 1930s. After making the concept of a historical dialectic murky and opaque, which it properly is, Kojève wagered that the master-slave couple would retain its governance as a model for intersubjectivity. The French Nietzscheans, notably after the publication of Deleuze's *Nietzsche and Philosophy* (1962) and *Semiotext(e)*'s 1978 issue on

"Nietzsche's Return" (as well as essays that appeared in *Boundary* 2, et. al.), set aside the master/slave model with its mutually assured destruction in the form of a competition over recognition. They opted for an intellectual "emancipation from the law."[13] Nietzsche was invoked to contest the *antiproduction* of recoding and reterritorialization, which today effectively means the university's (museum's, etc.) affirmation of negation (what one lacks, what one needs, what one has to have, etc.). To the linearity of historicism, which turned existence as such into the evolution of survival and recognition, endowment and debt, Nietzsche's texts came to America already quasi-antihistoricist. It may well be that one of the great effects of French theory in America will have been making belief in the autonomy and majesty of history, metanarratives, anarchistic.

All in all, from Jacques Derrida to Helène Cixous, ideas and texts that were nearly eliminated in the American political correctness of the 1970s and after, ideas that asserted the *inseparability* of politics, writing, and representation, were reinstated by the French use of Nietzsche. Many intellectuals, writers, and scholars still find this horrifying.

Finally, some remarks are in order on the false impression of "unity" to French theory. We are well aware of right-wing uses of Baudrillard's arguments. It is a short step from some of Baudrillard's provocations to intellectual deep freeze, but that also makes his work provocative and dangerous. One also notes that at the 1975 conference mentioned above, Lyotard publicly asked Deleuze and Guattari as well as Foucault, present in the audience, to take up the questions posed by his *Libidinal Economy*, soon to be recast as *The Differend*, questions as to how intellectuals could adhere to a "master discourse" and still claim to offer alternatives to writing's inclusive disjunctions (e.g., adherence to unexamined concepts). Lyotard challenged how any "magisterial discourse" can do anything but externalize itself in concepts. At the time, these thinkers demurred and walked away from the room: there was never any "unity" to such French theory, even among those who were close to each other. Foucault, for example, did not go in for direct critiques of institutions, but he did analyze power transformation that used institutions. And yet in some academic quarters his writings are associated with a version of the will to power that reduces both concepts, will and power, to "arbitrarily . . . engage in the invention of 'truth'" a serious reduction and misrepresentation of Foucault's position. There is too much such misrepresentation or politics already lodged in writing, as writing.[14] Further, Deleuze and Guattari always emphasized a *generosity* of critique, often forgetting a critic's reductive arguments if they could extract a bit of a concept for more intellectual labor. Thus, neither in France nor in America is there "unity," but there are a number of astonishingly smart readings of the most diverse "plateaus" or interconnections of word/thing mixtures. We believe, in this regard, that the last French theorists will be American because we are convinced that Americans will keep finding in the overall unpacking of "differences" provided by French theory powerful means to counter law and utopia, or other such satisfactions of negative schizophrenia.

Some of the papers in this volume were first given as conference papers in the fall of 1997, one at New York University, the others at the Guggenheim Museum and at the Drawing Center, New York. We hope these essays addressing the legacy of French theory in America will go some way toward raising problems that are as undeniable as they may be intractable. We wish to thank Tom Bishop of New York University, William Germano at Routledge (nice cover, too), Ann Philbin at the Drawing Center, and everyone who encouraged this project. Sande Cohen wishes to thank F.S. Chang for her generosity.

Notes

1. *Theatre*, v.8, #1, 1997.
2. For the notion of event as used here, see Tom Conley's essay "Afterword: The Events and Their Erosion," in Michel de Certeau, *The Capture of Speech and Other Political Writings* (Minneapolis: University of Minnesota Press, 1997), p. 177.
3. Gilles Deleuze and Félix Guattari, *A Thousand Plateaus* (Minneapolis: University of Minnesota Press, 1980), pp. 76–79.
4. Jacques Derrida, discussing Roland Barthes' essay "To Write: Intransitive Verb?" in *The Languages of Criticism and the Sciences of Man*, edited by Richard Macksey and Eugenio Donato (Baltimore: Johns Hopkins University Press, 1970), pp. 155–56.
5. Sometimes French Theory induces apoplexy. See the nearly hysterical rejection of it in J. Appleby, M. Jacob, and Lynn Hunt, *Telling the Truth about History* (New York: Norton, 1994), pp. 209–10.
6. Deleuze and Guattari, *A Thousand Plateaus*, p. 4.
7. Maurice Merleau-Ponty, *Sense and Non-Sense* (Chicago: Northwestern University Press, 1964), p. 14.
8. Norman O. Brown, *Love's Body* (New York: Vintage, 1966), p. 109.
9. Stanley Aronowitz's *The Crisis in Historical Materialism* (New York: Praeger, 1981), p. 262, was an American version of Eagleton's assertions; in Aronowitz's terms, French theory might help with "self-critique by the artist" while "real theory" belongs to Marxism.
10. Deleuze and Guattari, *Anti-Oedipus*, (Minneapolis: University of Minnesota Press, 1977), p. 77.
11. Ibid., p. 240.
12. Jean-François Lyotard, *The Lyotard Reader*, edited by Andrew Benjamin (London: Blackwell, 1989), p. 140.
13. Gilles Deleuze, *Nietzsche and Philosophy* (New York: Columbia University Press, 1983), p. 136.
14. Allan Megill, *Prophets of Extremity* (Berkeley and Los Angeles: University of California Press, 1985), p. 192.

1

Some Views From France

Deconstructions: The Im-possible

JACQUES DERRIDA

Perhaps this time I will add an English subtitle to my French title, which Tom Bishop just pronounced for this conference whose posters have advertised, with a remarkable painting by Mark Tansey, that it would be given in French. The English subtitle will be the following. I pronounce it as best I can and you will understand it how you will: *Falls.* Or to return to French at its most untranslatable: *comment tirer un trait.*

It is autumn. Autumn for me is the season of the gracious hospitality of NYU, which always welcomes me "in the fall" and always welcomes a visitor immersed in his own gratitude. Last spring, in Paris, once again in friendship, Tom Bishop extended an invitation to attend a conference here, and he made it clear that my proposal, whatever freedom he would grant me, as he always so generously does, should be inscribed within a series of retrospective, if not melancholy, reflections on so-called French theory in America over the last twenty years. This is the theory that has, and I quote, "massively penetrated the American university and the American art-world"—thus runs the beautifully illustrated poster that I will shortly say a few words about. Well, last spring, before I answered Tom, I must have said to myself, someone in me must have instantly said: *impossible.* I will not talk on this impossible subject, whether because it is not feasible in an hour, or because, in a thousand different ways, here and there, and here often enough, we have already said so much about it. This inexhaustible subject has exhausted even us. It is becoming more than a *topos* or a common place: it is becoming a genre. It has its rites, its theater, its unavoidable characters, its laws, its law of genre. And since we mention law of genre and French theory over the last twenty years, allow me to remind Tom, and myself, that twenty years ago, in 1979, I think, the first conference that I attended here was entitled "The Law of Genre." Already there was a superb poster, which you can admire in the French department. At that time, the poster did not yet show me in the process of getting ready for a fall, on the point of sinking into some abyss, mimicking a scene from the well-known detective novel *The Death of Sherlock Holmes:* Moriarty connected by some dance to a well-known partner, "Derrida queries de Man," whom I am dragging or who is dragging me toward, toward what? The falls, precisely, in the fall. But a fall at the edge of a waterfall, a torrent. Falls. A fall at the edge of falls in the fall. As you have noticed, the landscape, the rocks are saturated with inscriptions, letters, hieroglyphs, a sort of text in stone: a somber and autumnal landscape, waterfalls like Niagara Falls. All of that is falls, false. This is the subtitle that I would give to the painting. Falls in the fall of the falls which remain at the edge of the falls, thus at the edge of itself, transfixed, photographed as in freeze-frame, in the imminence of a fall that does not come to an end, that in the end does not take place. Falls. Thus the fall will not take place, you see, there it is still. In any case, by all appearances, we are surely at the edge of the fall, as ever, as we have been from the beginning, but gripping the edge just enough to provoke the impatience, or the desire mixed with concern, of those observing this bizarre ballet, a dangerous *pas de deux*, and who no longer even know what they want. Like graffiti on the wall, this painting remains unreadable, somber as an autumn night, blue, blue-black, in the fall. For if in the end we ended up falling, things might fall out right. And no one knows who might get the upper hand, indeed raise himself up in the fall, from the very fall. Falls. I do not know what Mark Tansey meant to tell us; perhaps he himself does not know, and the only time we met, during a breakfast at the French Embassy, we hardly said a word to one another; I forgot to ask him what he meant to say, what he expected from all these Frenchmen that he puts on stage. In the shadow of this painting, next to Barthes, another representative of French theory, who they will talk to you about on October 27—next to Barthes I appear on this other painting entitled *Mont Sainte Victoire*. Because of this title and, to be sure, because of the fact that I find myself between Barthes and a bearded French veteran of the last war, we are in the French memory of Cézanne; the word *victoire* belongs to a landscape of war, but a war of the past, the first World War, and this surpassed war of the past, this victory both archived and pregnant with catastrophes to come, from the Treaty of Versaille to the Second World War, is perhaps an allegory of French theory in America. A victory pregnant with a menacing future. In any case, already or once again in *Mont Sainte Victoire*, whose reproduction you have just seen, I am put or see myself put on stage at the edge of an abyss, but this time a little like a tree at the edge of a river or lake, a reflective watery surface, wherein my image seems to have fallen to reflect itself before me, while I remain still on the edge, like a tree whose branches continue to grow. But the image that is reflecting me in the water is deformed, deforming: I am an other. You see, I would have preferred to run away or to talk around Tom Bishop's impossible proposition. And instead of talking to you about French theory in America over the last twenty years, I would have preferred to spend more than an hour

reflecting on the desire and the work of Mark Tansey, who has me either danc-
ing dangerously at the edge of a waterfall, or growing like a tree, but still at the
edge of somber and menacing water, to the bottom of which, in the autumn, in
the fall, I could sink. In the fall, into the falls, falling down into the false. Of
course I will not do so, I mean, I will not speak of these simulacra any longer.

I could have, because this painting—seen in a certain light, of course—these
paintings say everything, metonymically, that there is in my opinion to say, think,
interpret, or overinterpret, about French theory in America over the last twenty
years, at the edge of which all the equivocations and ambivalences can transfix
or immobilize themselves as in a freeze-frame. Naturally, when I foolishly proposed the title in the plural, "Deconstructions: The Im-possible," I did not just
let speak, like a symptom, the spontaneous recoil that the program inspired in
me: talk on this subject, pretend to talk on it? Again, no, impossible. Rather, I
meant something else that I will try to explain.

After the fact, thus after having improvised this title, "Deconstructions: The
Im-possible," in my proposal to Tom Bishop, I realized that—so as not to play,
not to deceive, once again at the edge—I had inscribed the word *deconstruction*
in a title, undoubtedly for the first time in my life, in more than thirty years.
And for the first time I had announced that I was going to talk, without subterfuge, about this thing and this name, this name in the plural of course, and
in quotation marks, mentioning the name rather than using it, referring to it: to
the effects of this name rather than to some improbable thing itself. Deconstruction in the singular does not exist and has never presented itself as such in
the present, and the plural signifies first and foremost this: the open set of effects
that one can, here or there, in the world and in America, associate *with*, invest
in, love or hate to death under this name. The impossible is already this: identifying in the singular something that may present itself, that may be accessible
as deconstruction. But I thought that, out of courtesy and a taste for hospitality and gratitude, I should talk as directly as possible, straightforward, without
ruse or subterfuge, about this word *deconstruction* and what has happened to it,
what has happened through it, with it, in spite of it, in this country and, above
all, over the last twenty years.

First, allow me another preliminary reflection on this number, this sequence:
twenty years. Why not thirty years, why not ten? I take this number quite seriously. Why twenty years? Twenty years ago the massive penetration that the poster
mentions had already begun. It had been going on already for at least ten years.
Ten years of penetration before twenty more years of penetration, that is a long
time. It is long for a pleasure or for a suffering, or for a suffering at the edge of
pleasure, or the opposite, and yet it is indisputable. Things had begun around
October 1966, in the autumn, the fall, the date that classic historiographers gen-

erally record. In October '66, the marker, the quasi-event, would be, would have been the famous autumnal conference in Baltimore at Johns Hopkins University that some have interpreted as the end of structuralism and the birth of poststructuralism, a purely American notion, moreover, as you well know, which I do not care for, and which I am eager to maintain as suspect and problematic; nevertheless, more than thirty years ago, the symbolic or symptomatic moment of this conference of 1966, in which I had the privilege of participating with my elders—Hyppolite, Lacan, Barthes, Vernant, Goldman, et cetera—will have marked the beginning of what some will call, depending on the figure, the desired trope: penetration, invasion, reception, welcome, alliance, assimilation, incorporation, injection, grafting: the transformation in America of this thing come from France and for which one created the name and the concept of "theory," yet another purely American word and concept. In France, "theory" does not have an accredited conceptual equivalent any more than poststructuralism does. So why point out this difference of a decade between the thirty years I have just recalled and the twenty years alluded to in the title of this series, French theory over the last twenty years? Because from the beginning of the nineteen seventies, as far as deconstruction in the plural is concerned, they were already beginning the prognosis, indeed the diagnosis of the fall, its decadence and decline. They were already saying that it was damaged, that it was going over the dam. Falls, falling down, dead. The word they used was *waning*, on the wane. This was the mantra or the wishful thinking of the times. Falls: is that not the fall, decadence from the start, already in the nineteen seventies? In German *fall* means "case." Fall, such is the case. Make no mistake. It is over.

The end is approaching, the time of the end keeps approaching, but that was already yesterday. And it has not stopped. This diagno-prognosis has not stopped resounding and echoing. I could give you a thousand examples, exhibit an entire dossier of references, but we do not have the time, and what is the point? In any case, it was and still is for me a source of astonishment and endless entertainment, as well as a subject for historical reflection, from at least two points of view: that of the diagno-prognosis, that is, the death notice, and from the point of view of the thing whose fall and then death one announces.

First, from the point of view of the diagnosis and prognosis. What happens when a fall does not stop? Falls and falls and falls in the falls from the beginning. Isn't this just like an inaugural fall or an original sin? The origin of sin or evil begins with the fall. And what happens when a death notice is rehearsed day after day for the same death in the same newspaper? Even for Diana it did not last so long, a week, two weeks (already an exception), and then it's over. What is dead is dead. The fall takes place once, and it's over. But when it comes to the end of deconstruction, of French theory, the fall lasts, it repeats itself, it keeps insisting, it keeps multiplying. Falls. Perhaps it is this suspended imminence, this suspense of the fall, the fall into the falls, that Tansey wanted to represent or immobilize or transfix in his painting. Like an instrument panel, perhaps he wanted to register the fall or the imminence of the fall, or the desire for the fall, in the spectator. It lasts and lasts endlessly. And the spectator, the one who watches without exerting any effort, and who grows impatient, who would like to get on with it, who wants it finally to fall, will say to himself: How long can this last! And the longer it endures, the harder the fall. But it lasts too long, it's not possible, it's intolerable, unbearable. It's impossible.

Secondly, from the point of view of the thing one is talking about, for example, a moribund deconstruction, we can ask ourselves what it means to begin, when all is said and done, from the very start by declining and deceasing, by wearing the joyful color of mourning, mourning for oneself, as the best protection against aging, even to the point of appearing invulnerable to the usual rites of fashion, the rites of passing, that the sociologist and historian of ideas or intellectual fads know so well. Regarding the question of fashion, longevity, or death, the question of an originary fall, I was saying to myself a little while ago as I came here that perhaps I envied the few French compatriots who have recently been shelved and swiftly classed in what one calls "the new French thought." You know, the incredible artifact, editorial or academic, that they swiftly immortalize on the market after having announced in advance that this *bricollage* was *new* in order to ensure that the advertisement escape no one. At all costs, this novelty should become the new fashion. Well, I confess, I envy the ins and outs of this new French thought, for I am just about sure, and I am ready to bet on it, that they would not announce, that they will never announce the death of some new French thought. It will have been born immortal, deprived of any possibility of dying from its very first day. So, what can this mean: to be immortal from birth? You can perhaps guess. It is quite the opposite of the decompositions that would threaten the French theory associated with the deconstructions that I would like to speak to you about this evening.

Perhaps it is a certain impatience with the rebounding longevity of this thing that does not cease to fall and fall out so well, perhaps a feeling of impatience or resentment, that makes so many academic spectators sigh, so many idle passersby, feeling annoyed, say: This is not possible. There, again, impossible. But it is these people who are impossible. That would thus be one possible sense of the word *impossible*, but it does not interest me very much, and as you suspect, it is something else that I have in mind by the title "Deconstructions" in the plural and "the Im-possible" as two words.

I fear that I will disappoint those who in reading the title may have come, mouth watering, to see someone contritely admit to the failure of a whole project, a whole lifetime, and confess with a tear in his eye:, "Contrary to what I had thought or tried to make others think, I must recognize that deconstruction is impossible. Please forgive me, that was a faux pas." I just asked for a grand pardon, and now I must beg your pardon for not begging pardon.

I thus arrive at my subject. And instead of yielding to the temptation, a legitimate one, moreover, of a history, a sociology of ideas or currents or modes, I still have the desire to work and to speak to you about what is at work, hard work, about what endures, in the way of deconstructions, and about what works deconstructions through and through, in the very body, at the very brink, of the impossible—or through the impossible. The preceding remarks were not intended to speculate in specular or narcissistic fashion, self-indulgently, in a watery mirror, on the indefatigable longevity of deconstruction, which I never did believe in. I believe only in death and in death precisely as impossible, for which reason I am obsessed with, curious about, and convinced of mortality. Rather, it was a matter of preparing a reading of this dash that I thought it necessary to draw right in the middle of the word "im-possible," of the im-possible. Perhaps there we find the reason for signing this autumn evening with the word *falls*, and of giving to a painting as blue as the falling of water its true title, *falls*. It is not a question of crossing out deconstruction with one stroke, nor of finding in deconstruction or deconstructions features tired and drawn from a too long career, over the course of which one would have taken too much pleasure in penetrating a culture. Rather, it is a question of doing justice to a trait, a hyphen, a joining and thus a separation, a dash drawn in the heart of the impossible. In other words, this im-possible is everything but impossible; in any case, it calls for another reflection on what possible, power, potentiality, dynamic, *dynamis*, "I can," "I can be," and "maybe" all mean. And the entire business of deconstruction seems to me more and more concerned precisely with deconstructing, with all its consequences, this semantics of the possible inherited from Greco-Christian, indeed biblical, thinking: the possible opposed to the impossible, the possible as virtual opposed to the actual or the act, the possible versus the real, *dynamis* opposed to *energeia*, and so on. There you go, and so now I begin, and since I have been invited to, I will improvise a historical periodization.

From the beginning, from the first decade, of which I spoke a little while ago, there existed a certain Americanization of a certain deconstruction, the one in any case that I was trying to put to work by that name. By Americanization I mean a certain appropriation: a domestication, an institutionalization, chiefly academic, that took place elsewhere in other forms as well, but here in a massively visible fashion, I mean, in this country. What they asked me to speak about tonight is this Americanization. From the first decade, it rested on the supposition of what I would call the becoming-possible of that which was already taking the form of the impossible. What does this mean? That often, here and there, most notably in the domain of literary theory and literature departments preoccupied in the first place with the concerns of reading and interpretation, with the method and epistemology of literary criticism, in all these places critics took pleasure in drawing on these texts or discourses that had apparently come from France and were identified as examples or paradigms of deconstruction—in drawing from these texts, borrowing from them, translating, transporting *possibilities* and *powers*. That is to say, organized bodies of rules, of procedures and techniques, in a word, *methods*, know-how applicable in a recurrent fashion. One could even formulate or formalize (and I applied myself in this way at first) a certain consistency in these laws which made possible reading processes at once critical and critical of the idea of critique, processes of close reading, which could reassure those who in or outside the wake of new criticism or some other formalism who felt it necessary to legitimize this ethics of close reading or internal reading. And among the examples of these procedural and formalizing formulae that I had proposed, and which were circulating precisely as possibilities, new possibilities offered by deconstruction, there was the reversal of a hierarchy. After having reversed a binary opposition, whatever it may be—speech/writing, man/woman, spirit/matter, signifier/signified, signified/signifier, master/slave, and so on—and after having liberated the subjugated and submissive term, one then proceeded to the generalization of this latter in new traits, producing a different concept, for example, another concept of writing such as trace, *différance*, gramme, text, and so on. Or to take another example: the privilege granted to the self-contradictions or the performative contradictions of a discourse, contradictions that could furnish a strategic lever in the consideration of marginalia, a minor text, a brief essay, a bizarre footnote, a symptomatic phrase or word, in order to dislocate and destabilize the autointerpretive authority of a major canonical text. For example, Rousseau's *Essay on the Origin of Language*, or the word *pharmakon*, the "supplement," "hymen," or a minor text of Kant such as the *Parergon*. Although I am the last to find this useless, illegitimate, or contingent, I would say, nevertheless—I was already saying—that this slightly instrumentalizing implementation tended to reduce the impetus or the languages, the desire, the arrival so to speak, the future, of deconstructions, and might well arrest them at the possible: that is, at a body of possibilities, of faculties, indeed of facilities, in a word, a body of easily reproducible means, methods, and technical procedures, hence useful, utilizable; a body of rules and knowledge; a body of theoretical, methodological, epistemological knowledge; a body of powerful know-how that would be at once understandable and offered for didactic transmission, susceptible of acquiring the academic status and dignity of a quasi-interdisciplinary discipline. For deconstructions migrate, hence the plurality, from philosophy to literary theory, law, architecture, et cetera. From this standpoint, although this movement, contrary to what its enemies have always claimed, remained in the minority and under attack, deconstruction was becoming or risked becoming not only possible in the sense of "feasible" but practical: a practical theory, a practical praxis, giving rise to instructions, evaluations, legitimizations, and to signs of recognition. *Possible*, deconstruction was becoming not only an act, an activity, a praxis, but it was becoming practicable, and, as they say in French, practical, in the sense of easy, convenient, and even salable as a commodity, as merchandise. Editors and university presses never spat on it, even at the most difficult moments, even at the most reactionary universities such as Cambridge, where an entire pack of dons, foaming at the mouth, spat on the deconstructionists; moreover, the word *deconstructionist*, yet another American invention, designates precisely this adaptation of deconstructions to a possible praxis, a quasi-doctrine that is teachable, institutionalizable and reproducible. And that is the case most often made against deconstruction, either from the point of view of a frightened conservatism, or from the point of view of a leftist activism that had an interest, to be sure, in leaving a certain political code undisturbed. The paradox of this situation or this phase that began, I repeat, after the first decade, is that what we were then trying to appropriate by making it possible, that is, functional and productive, was in any case that which had already shown itself explicitly as impossible, as the im-possible, in discourse, writing, or teaching that interested me personally and in which I found myself involved. I could show you, but I can develop this topic no further on account of time constraints and because I want to get beyond this phase we have come to.

Here are three brief and schematic arguments on the topic of this phase, which was more than a phase and which was already resistant to periodizations. First, very quickly, it was shown that *deconstruction*, if this word has a sense that does not let itself be appropriated, was indissociable from a process and a law of ex-propriation or ex-appropriation proper that resists in the last instance, in order to challenge it, every subjective movement of appropriation of the following sort: *I* deconstruct, or *we* deconstruct, or we have the *power* and the *method* that make it possible. Deconstruction, if there be such a thing, happens; it is what happens, and this is what happens: it deconstructs itself, and it can become neither the power nor the possibility of an "I can." I insist here on the "it happens" because what I would like to make clear later on is this affirmation of the event, of the arrival or the future at the beating heart of a reflection on the im-possible.

Second, early on, all the motifs that we tried to possibilize or make possible, but only to a certain point, and this success is not negative—all these motifs became reading techniques or techniques of interpretation, such as *différance*, the undecidable, the supplement, the pharmakon, the parergon, and so on. These are not only names, but if we wanted to nominalize them, there would be fifty or so of them. All these motifs became possible and made many decodings and many texts possible. But these motifs also mark, precisely, the impossible, the limit of the possible. And this appeared quite clearly from the beginning. All quasi-concepts or quasi-transcendentals at work in deconstruction are inconceivable impossibilities, inconceivable concepts of neither/nor: the trace is neither present nor absent, the specter (which appears much earlier than *Specters of Marx*) is what is neither living nor dead, the parergon that is neither sensible nor intelligible, neither/nor, et cetera.

Third: already, from this quasi first decade, it is often literally a question of the conditions of possibility as conditions of impossibility. A law of contamination compromises and renders impure, without absolute rigor, the very thing that it makes possible. It is everywhere insistent, particularly in *Signature, Event, Context*, or in *Limited Inc.* concerning the performative. What makes a performative possible, what makes it successful or felicitous, as they say in the language of speech act theory, what makes the performative possible is that which threatens it, which threatens its possibility, and thus which renders its purity impossible. And the risk of the unfortunate case, of infelicity, a risk that must remain always open, this is what makes possible and gives the performative event a chance, but instantly renders its purity and its pure presence as performative impossible. This schema was in fact already generalized, but I cannot develop it further here for lack of time. This recurrent expression of the conditions of possibility as conditions of impossibility did not fail to signal some major stakes, namely the shock delivered to hardly calculable consequences. Naturally it is a question here of the calculable and the incalculable. Shock, indeed a trauma, which it is necessary to register within the classical philosophical concept of possibility, in the style of the Kantian transcendental critique devoted to the search for the conditions of possibility, in the canonical expression of Kant. For all these reasons, what thus was happening in the so-called first decade should or should have resisted, did resist in fact, a sort of possibilization, this facilitating practice which was a certain, particularly American, institutionalization. Luckily, in this country and elsewhere, there were studies that measured up to this resistance, and in paying them tribute I would very much like to avoid reducing, simplifying, or homogenizing them as their detractors have all too often done.

I am now going to try to deal more directly with my subject and take up the sequence of the last twenty years from the point of view of this possibility of the impossible. It just so happens, and this is no coincidence, that all my work these last two decades have made of the impossible their privileged theme, and of the very experience of the event—the sense of "possible," "experience" and "event" being different, having evidently changed—the very focus of their formalization.

Since I cannot here reconstruct all the *topoi* and movements of these demonstrations over the last twenty years, you will allow me to propose, hypothetically, an emphasis and a taxonomy. The emphasis would concern a past periodization that I don't quite believe in, that lacks rigor in my opinion, but is not totally insignificant. In other words, it would possess, without being rigorously either true or false, a certain appearance in its favor, and an appearance that we should take account of. It just so happens that what some—not myself, above all not myself—have thought to fix or actively identify by the name of "ethical or political turn" in deconstructions in fact dates from the time when this thematics of the impossible became preponderant or massively insistent. The timing of this supposed, presumed turning point is not by accident and should give us pause. Now of course I do not believe, and I explained why, that there ever existed such an ethical, political turn: in the first place, because what others find reassuring in texts thus designated (e.g., but allow me not to list them all here: *Force of Law, Ethics of Discussion, Other Heading, Specters of Marx, Politics of Friendship*) had been in the works for a very long time; in the second place, these texts that people like so much to read and think about, and the concepts therein of responsibility, decision, justice that organize them, are anything but reassuring to those who wish to reassure themselves in ethics and politics. That said, it is not entirely false, if it is not true either, that the explanation with these classical figures of ethics, law, politics, responsibility, decision, and so on begins to gain a kind of immediate visibility, a kind of pedagogical insistence, that they did not before possess to the same degree. Above all, and here are the principal stakes of the conference I have been wanting to get at, this ethico-politico-juridical, indeed religious, phenomenality, this opening is indissociable from its very key, namely the urgency to reflect otherwise on the impossible. There you have it as for the emphasis or periodization.

As far as the taxonomy is concerned, the classification of themes and concepts, I am going once again to pretend to paint them before your eyes and to disentangle them from each another when they are inexplicably intertwined and in motion: they are just so many figures of the impossible. There you have the essence of what I wanted to say tonight: figures. These figures, I give them a few names, about a half-dozen names, in a list by definition open-ended. They are the figures of invention, the event, the gift, the pardon, the aporia of decision, and the "perhaps."

In the brief analysis that follows I will content myself with running along the edge that forms the union and the separation of the possible and the impossible, the dash between them—the im-possible as possible or the possible as im-possible—a hyphen, an impossible that is not simply negative and that questions the *as*, the phenomenological *als*, possible as impossible.

I begin with invention, invention in art, in literature, as well as technical invention, technoscientific invention or the invention of the other. For it is by working through this terribly equivocal concept of invention that I attempted, more than fifteen years ago, to formulate this intriguing intrigue between deconstruction and the possible as im-possible. The only quotation I will allow myself this evening comes from an essay on invention, "Psyche or the Inventions of the Other," and reads as follows:

> Deconstruction at its most rigorous has never presented itself as a stranger to literature nor, above all, as something that is possible. It loses nothing in admitting itself to be impossible, and those who would too quickly rejoice over it lose nothing for waiting. The danger in the task of deconstruction would rather be its possibility, the danger of becoming an available body of regimented procedures, of practical methods, of accessible paths. The interest of deconstruction, of its force and its desire [and I underline the word *desire* for reasons which will become apparent later], if it possesses any, is a certain experience of the impossible, experience of the other as invention of the impossible, in other words, as the only possible invention.

What is the aporia here in its driest, most abstract form? Well, in whatever domain it may be, an invention that could only invent what it is possible to invent would invent nothing. Let's suppose the historical analysis of a paradigm in the sense of Kuhn or an episteme in the sense of Foucault, some "themata," or as they say, an historical analysis of givens, a configuration that explains that at a certain moment an invention was made possible, that it became practicable under certain conditions, technical, economic, social, psychological, scientific, et cetera. According to this analysis that I hold to be necessary and, to be sure, legitimate, and which we must push as far as possible, the invention of this possible will have done nothing but make explicit, reveal, deploy that which was already there, potentially, programmatically in reserve. And of course what then appears as an invention whose responsibility and initiative are attributed to the creativity of the inventor or inventors, this "invention" will have invented nothing. In other words, for an invention worthy of its name to be possible, it must invent the impossible, that which appears as impossible. And to invent the impossible, it must do otherwise than deploy the potentialities that a subject or a community of subjects could posit as properly their own: their powers, their know-how, their force, their *Vermögen*, their *Möglichkeit* proper. I use these German words because I would like to come back to them at the end. Hence the conclusion I thought it necessary to draw in "Psyche or the inventions of the Other," namely that invention, if there be such a thing, must always be invention of the other; a double genitive. That invention may not be possible except as impossible and come from the other, indeed from the other irreducibly other than myself, does not mean that the aporia prohibits invention and that there does not exist such an event worthy of its name. To the contrary, this means that the event of invention, if there be such a thing, can never present itself as such to a theoretical or observing judgment, to a historical judgment of the observing sort, a determining judgment, permitting itself to say: invention exists, it presents itself, it falls to this subject, to this community of subjects capable of claiming it as their own, of reappropriating it for themselves. Invention as the invention of the other is not possible except as impossible, as exceeding the observing reappropriation of whoever would be tempted to say: I, we, have invented this or that. And to paraphrase what I was at that time trying to show, I would say that if invention is of course still possible, if it is the invention of the possible, then invention would conform to its concept, to the dominant traits of its concept and word, only insofar as invention, paradoxically, invents nothing: when the other does not appear in it, when nothing comes to the other and from the other. For the other is not the possible. It would thus be necessary to say that the only possible invention would be the invention of the impossible. "But the invention of the impossible is impossible," objects another. Indeed. But it is the only thing possible, it is the only possibility. An invention must announce itself as the invention of what did not seem possible, without which it does nothing but make explicit a program of the possible, in the economy of the same.

In the seminars or texts that began exactly twenty years ago in 1978, even if some of them were not published until later, I had tried to formulate an analogous aporia on the topic of the impossible possibility of the gift or the pardon. To put it once again in the driest, most formal, most economical way possible, a gift must break precisely with every economy to be possible. It must remove itself from every horizon of exchange, restitution, and retribution, and even from any recognition, any gratitude. Which means that if the gift appears, if it is determined as gift, whether from the side of the receiver or the side of the giver, if it presents itself phenomenologically as gift, as such, it is instantly destroyed. For then, no matter how symbolically, it is dragged into the circle of exchange, into compensation, reciprocity, et cetera. Thus the gift can never be possible as present. There is never anything that can represent itself as gift to consciousness, to the determining judgment or some such teleology. This does not mean, as some have too hastily concluded, that I do not believe that gift giving ever takes place. I say only that these events, if they take place, must appear as impossible, must exceed in any case any possibility of appearing and of presenting itself in the present as such to a consciousness or even to an unconscious. In other words, here we see the introduction to an unparalleled aporia, an aporia of logic rather than a logical aporia; here we see an impasse of the undecidable through which a de-cision cannot not pass, through which a responsibility must pass, and which, far from paralyzing this new thinking of the possible as impossible, rather puts it into motion. This aporia ensures it its rhythm and breathing, systole/diastole, syncopation, pulse of the possible/impossible, of the impossible as condition of the possible. And from the very heart of the impossible, one would thus hear the pulsing drive of what is called deconstruction. The condition of possibility would thus give one chance as possible but by depriving it of its purity. And the law of this spectral contamination, the impure law of this impurity, is what one must never cease reelaborating.

For example, a promise must be able not to be kept. And this in the end con-cerns the means of the performative, too—well, the possibility of failure, of in-felicity, is not only inscribed in the preliminary risk, not only in the condition of possibility of the success of a performative (and the gift is also a kind of per-formative). A promise must threaten not to be kept, to become a threat even to be a free promise and even to be successful; it must continue to mark the event, even when it succeeds, as the trace of an impossibility, sometimes its memory and always its haunting. This impossibility is not the simple contrary of the pos-sible. It supposes and also gives itself over to possibility, traverses it, and leaves in it the trace of its removal. There is nothing fortuitous about the fact that this discourse on the conditions of possibility, at the very place where its claims are haunted or tormented by impossibility, can spread to all the places where per-formativity, indeed pure factual history (beyond every performativity or perfor-mative power), would be at work: the event, invention, the gift, the pardon, hos-pitality, friendship, the promise, the experience of death, et cetera. By contagion and without limit, it contaminates in the end every concept and undoubtedly the concept of concept.

To give without the hope of knowing, recognizing, seeing my gift recognized or reciprocated by some sign of recognition or gratitude, I must do the impos-sible without knowing it, without knowing, beyond all knowing. The event, this event here, if there be such a thing, is not the actualization of a possible, a sim-ple passing to the act, a realization, an effectualization. It is more than a perfor-mative. The event must announce itself as impossible or its possibility must be threatened.

When I say *must* it is meant to indicate that there exists here as well a neces-sity, a law. We must rethink this relationship, this hyphen or union between the possible and the impossible. You have seen that this impossibility of the gift is not negative. In spite of its terrifying aporia, it seems to prohibit any gift from presenting itself or appearing possible, to give itself up to be known; well, the desire of the gift, the thinking of the gift, beyond the knowing of the gift, does not give up, and does not give up on the impossible. It is the experience of the impossible that makes it so that I never give, that I can never say with assurance or complacency: I give, it is I who am giving. But what I give is in a way given always as the event of which I spoke a moment ago: in the name of the other, as the gift of the other. And I am trying at this very moment to deploy the same logic on the topic of the pardon, which moreover it is already a question of at the end of *Given Time: Counterfeit Money* concerning Baudelaire.

I purposely more than once underlined the word *aporia* in the exposition of the two examples I just gave: invention as event, the gift. I did so for several reasons: first to indicate, I cannot do more here, that this thinking of the aporia, the nonpassive endurance of the aporia—which I systematize, recall and also project in the book bearing the title *Aporias*—shows the affinity between the possible and the impossible, the principle of ruin and chance, a chance that is given, but also the forms and the political stakes of this aporia. Second, this reflection on the aporia is very different, to say the least, from that of Paul de Man who often uses the word *aporia* and predicament, but in a space much more linguistic or rhetorical than I do myself: the reflection on the aporia as aporetical experience of the event that I propose remains marked by this questioning of logocentrism, liguisticism, and rhetoricism, which was the ABC of deconstruction thirty years ago. I mark this difference from Paul de Man and do so today mostly because I did not want to do so at a time when it would have been indecent and overinterpreted by de Man's pack of enemies that I wanted nothing to do with. Finally, the choice of Tansey's painting, *Derrida Queries de Man*, marks an apostrophe of this genre on the edge of the abyss. And if the aporia was not circumscribable as an effect of language or rhetoric, the same question, the same query could be addressed to Lacan precisely on the topic of the impossible, of what he himself calls the impossible. The book that bears the title *Aporias* extends the possible as impossible also to love, friendship, the gift, the other, witnessing, hospitality, and so on.

In recalling its many stages, it is undoubtedly here that the logical trajectory of this deconstruction of the possible is assembled or formalized in the most explicit fashion. But in questioning the Heideggerian discourse on death, on its possibility as *(als)* impossibility, this trajectory is closest to a meditation of death. Thus Heidegger defines death: the possibility of an impossibility. The analysis then leads one to call into question the phenomenological authority of the *as such*, precisely, concerning the possible *as* impossible. The as, the *als*, signifies that possibility is *at the same time* unveiled and penetrated by the impossible. This is not merely paradoxical possibility, a possibility of the impossible: it is possibility *as* impossibility. This possibility as impossibility, this death as the most proper possibility of Heidegger's *Dasein* as much as its most proper impossibility, there we see it at the same time "unveiled" and unveiled by Heidegger's "penetrating" advance.

But here at least we have the schema for a possible/impossible question. What difference is there between, on the one hand, the possibility of appearing *as such* of the possibility of an impossibility and, on the other, the impossibility of appearing as such of the same possibility? And it is in the aporetical logic of this necessity that we thus come to think a kind of law of impossibility. For example, if one must endure the aporia, if such is the law of every decision, of every responsibility, of every duty without obligation, then the aporia cannot ever be simply endured *as such*. The ultimate aporia, I would say, is the impossibility of the aporia *as such*, the impossibility for it to appear *as such*, phenomenologically. And the reserves of this statement appear incalculable: it is uttered and reckoned with the incalculable itself.

I come now to our last theme, decision, without which indeed there would be neither responsibility nor ethics, neither rights nor politics—with or without an ethical or political turn. The aporia of which I am speaking, the non-passive endurance of this aporia—well, not only is it not negative, not only is it being in paralysis at an impasse (for the etymological figure of *aporia* seems to say "dead end," "nonpath"), but it is, when understood in a certain way, the condition of possibility of everything it seems to make impossible. How does one schematize the possible decision as impossible, such as I try to elaborate it in diverse places and above all in *Specters of Marx, Politics of Friendship*, most notably against the decisionism of Carl Schmitt? A decision, as its name indicates, must interrupt, cut, rend a continuity, the fabric or the ordinary course of history. To be free and responsible, it must do other and more than deploy or reveal a truth already potentially present, indeed a power or a possibility, an existent force. I cannot decide except when this decision does more and other than manifest my possibilities, my power, my capacity-to-be, the predicates that define me. As paradoxical as it may seem, it is thus necessary for me to receive from the other, in a kind of passivity without parallel, the very decision whose responsibility I assume. What I decide for the other, he decides as much for me, and this singular substitution of two or more than two irreplaceable singularities seems at the same time impossible and necessary. This is the sole condition of possibility of a decision worth its name, if ever there were such a thing: a strangely passive decision that does not in the least exonerate me of responsibility. Quite the opposite.

And you have undoubtedly noticed that for all these "impossibles"—invention, the event, the gift, decision, responsibility, et cetera—I always cautiously say, "if there be such a thing." Not that I doubt that there ever were such a thing, nor do I affirm that it does not exist, simply if there be—this is why I say *if there be* such a thing—it cannot become the object of an assertive judgment, nor of an observing knowledge, of an assured, founded certainty, nor of a theorem, if you like, nor a theory. There is no theory on this topic. It cannot give rise to a theoretical proof, to a philosophical act of the cognitive sort, but only to testimonies that imply a kind of act of faith, indeed an act of "perhaps." Perhaps. Nietzsche says, and I quote him in *Politics of Friendship*, that the philosophers of the future will be the thinkers of the "dangerous perhaps." Philosophy, in its Hegelian form, has always tried to disdain or ridicule the category of "perhaps." The "perhaps" would be for the classical philosopher an empirical and approximate modality that the philosopher should begin by being right about. It would be incompatible with the thinking of the necessary and the law. Now without wanting to *rehabilitate* this category or this modality of "perhaps"—I say *perhaps* rather than *maybe* in order, precisely, to liberate this reference to the event, the happening, from the thinking of being—I would be tempted to see in it only the element itself in which a possible/impossible decision always takes place, if it takes place. A decision must be exceptional and incalculable; it must make an exception; a decision that does not make an exception, that does nothing but repeat or apply the rule, would not be a decision. And perhaps the haunting of the incalculable exception could here indicate the passage, if not the way out. I say *the haunting* because the spectral structure is here the law both of the possible and of the impossible, and of their strange intertwining. The exception is always required. And the same goes perhaps for this stubborn "perhaps" in its modality, which is elusive but irreducible to any other, fragile and yet indestructible. Reflecting on the "perhaps," a reflection on the "perhaps," perhaps gets under way the only possible reflection on the event.

When the impossible is made possible, the event takes place—possibility of the impossible—and here it is, incontestably, the paradoxical form of the event. If an event is possible, that is, if it inscribes itself within the conditions of possibility, if it does nothing but make explicit, unveil, reveal, accomplish what is already possible, then it is not an event. For an event to take place, for it to be possible, as event, as invention, it must be the arrival of the impossible. There we see a poor proof, an evidence that is nothing less than evident. It is this evidence that will have never left off guiding us here between the possible and the impossible, and that often drove us to speak of conditions of impossibility.

Without concluding, I conclude on a note that might seem slightly theological if one lends his guard to it, but which is intended here to call upon, for thinking, the impossible possible and the more than impossible, and more than a language. Already the word *fall*, *Fall*, resonated in more than one language, and deconstruction has always been defined precisely in its irreducible plurality— "Deconstructions: The Im-possible"—as more than a language. I recall having said one day that if, God forbid, I had to provide a minimal definition of deconstruction, it would be "more than a language"; that is, several languages, more than one language, more than language. However, how can the "more than a language," more than language, resonate here with the more than impossible impossible? In German, *Mögen* means to love, to desire, before it means "to be able" and before *Möglichkeit* means possibility. And that's why I emphasized the word desire a little while ago. In his "Letter on Humanism" and elsewhere, Heidegger adopts this meaning of *Mögen* as desire and love rather than as possible, the possible traditionally opposed to the real, or to the act, the actual, just as the virtual or a dynamic is opposed to its realization, to the *energeia*, the energy of the act. A total rereading of Heidegger's thinking on *Mögen* and *Vermögen* becomes necessary—which I should try to connect one day to what I have often analyzed in the work of Heidegger: the rapport between *Möglichkeit* and *Unmöglichkeit*, particularly in the aporia concerning death. With that in mind, let me recommend to you my friend Richard Kerney's book, which goes back to 1984, entitled *Poetics of the Possible*, which takes a keen interest in the story behind this *Mögen*. Here one should reinterpret the propositions in the "Letter on Humanism" that situate the *Mögen* as love or desire, not as power before being or before essence, beyond the being and essence that precisely desire gives rise to, and gives to the other, where being is not or not yet is. For lack of enough time to do this work here, I will simply cite a few words from Heidegger's "Letter on Humanism," some sentences that I had not previously given my full attention but deserve a closer look. Heidegger says the following: "to take charge [*abnehmen*] of a 'thing' or a 'person,' *das heisst sie lieben, sie mögen.*" That means to love them, to desire them. He goes on: "This *Mögen*, if one takes it more originarily [*bedeutet ursprüglicher gedacht*], means *das Wesen schenken*, to make a present of the essence." We have to reread the entire passage, and I will quickly reread it in translation:

> The power of desire and that thanks to which something properly has the power of being, this power is properly the possible, that which the senses propose in desire. Through this desire, being can think that something, desire makes it possible. Being as desire which accomplishes itself in power is the possible [*Mögen*]. Insofar as it is the element, the quiet force of loving-power, i.e. the possible. Under the sway of logic and metaphysics, our words possible and possibility, actually, are only thought in opposition to reality, that is, through an interpretation which is determined metaphysically, a metaphysical interpretation of being conceived as *actus et potentia*, an opposition which we identify as the one between *existentia* and essence, and *essentia*. When I speak of the quiet force of the possible [*die stille Kraft des Möglichen*], I no more mean the possible as *possibilitas* than I do *potentia* as *essentia*. I do not mean the possible as only a represented *possibilitas* of an *actus* of *existentia*,

but rather the being itself which, desiring, has power over thinking and thereby over the essence of man, i.e. over the relation of man to being, etc. To be capable of doing a thing here means to keep it in its essence, to maintain it in its element.

I would have to say much more to follow and question this text by Heidegger, but I simply wanted to quote it here as a way of pointing out its necessity. For the moment, what I would like to keep in mind about this other way of thinking of the possible is that emphasizing the affinity between the possible and desire or love according to a desire to give, and to give what is, according to a giving which does not have and is not that which gives and cannot present itself as such, this does not amount to the act of a subject. Indeed the thinking of such a possible is inseparable from an experience of the impossible, of that which is not possible. What is not is not possible as an act, a reality, or a present object of knowledge possible according to the classic philosophical determination of the word *possible*. Such a possible gift must therefore endure every aporia of the impossible evoked earlier. Henceforth, the im-possible—there you see the dash I wanted to draw, the stroke I wanted to make—the impossible is no longer the negative of the possible, dialectical or nondialectical, but it is at the same time more impossible than the one we discussed and nevertheless possible as the more than impossible. More than one language is more impossible, more than impossible.

Angelus Silenus says this very well in German in his "Cherubim Pilgrim" when he names God, in any case when he names the impossible or the more than possible. He writes, "*Das Überunmöglichste ist möglich.*" He says it as much of God as of nothing. Becoming God as becoming nothing. I quote: "*Nicht wer den ist Gott werden.*" To become nothing is to become God, it is God-becoming. In a recent text, I tried once again to join a thinking of the possible impossible, more than impossible, to the strange adventure in thought or in Western mysticism that others call in such a problematic way "negative theology." Without coming back here on the political perspective that I suggested for this Greco-Christian theology and its limits, I will rather conclude this evening by emphasizing how this becoming nothing as God-becoming, which seems in fact impossible, is more than impossible, the most impossible possible, possible because more impossible than the impossible, if the impossible is simple negative modality. This seems strangely familiar to what we call deconstructions. These are not methods or techniques, not programs or procedures deploying powers or possibilities, but the very experience of what happens, of what arrives as event in the figures of the impossible possibility of impossibility: in the gift, the pardon, the yes, decision, witnessing, hospitality, et cetera. And perhaps death. Perhaps.

With regard to the "perhaps," moreover, there exists a theological vein, in the work of Böhme, Bruno, Nicholas of Cusa, that defines God not as being—and precisely for which fact they break with what Heidegger calls the "ontotheological tradition"—but defines God as "before" and outside of being, *without being.* They define God as "perhaps." God is the perhaps. According to a potentiality or a *dynamis*, a *posse* they call it—the word is theirs—a *posse* that no longer depends on the metaphysical definition of the possible, a *posse* that is "before" being and that no longer is what a dominant tradition in philosophy calls the possible. A *posse.* God as perhaps. Then the becoming nothing, the becoming other than being as becoming God, becoming *(werden)* as engendering or invention of the other, from the other, there you see what according to Silenus Angelus is possible but as still more impossible than the impossible. And here the more, *über, Das Überunmöglichste ist möglich,* this *über* is over and beyond, and signifies an absolute heterogeneity between two qualities of the possible. That which is possible as impossible is not so according to the same region, the same regime of the possible. There it stands as an interruption in the traditional sense of the word "possible." There is a changing of gear in the thinking on the experience of the possible, the traditional sense of possible, which nonetheless continues to signify within us, as we think, "possible." And in the three verses which I will read aloud and translate to finish up, the *über* of *überunmöglichste* signifies, can signify, perhaps "the most" as well as "more than," more impossible and more than impossible, otherwise than impossible. The most impossible becomes more than impossible, otherwise than impossible.

> Das überunmöglichste ist möglich
> Du kannst mit deinem Pfeil die Sonne erreichen
> Ich kann mit meinem wohl die heilige Sonne bestreichen

> The most or the more than impossible is possible
> You cannot with your arrow reach the sun
> But with my own at the eternal sun I take aim

The arrow of the possible impossible, this arrow that takes the sun in its aim, will they say that it must fall back to earth, that it desires the fall? In any case, this arrow to the sun, this arrow lights up a whole other landscape in a whole other light than that of autumn or the falls. And that is what I called, in my French title, drawing a dash or an arrow.

Translated by Michael Taormina

Europhilia, Europhobia

JULIA KRISTEVA

Allow me a confession: I love your country. If I were to die tomorrow, I think I could say today that I have lived the best moments of my personal and professional life here, on the American continent. I love its immensity, this landscape that seems to open toward an unknown promise, the naive and sometimes brutal freshness of its inhabitants, always entrepreneurial, rhythmical, and "jazzed," the speed and the simplicity of your streets and of your academia.

Still, initially there seemed to be no predestination in my affection for America. It is perhaps useless to tell you that in my native Bulgaria, after the war, Uncle Sam was not in fashion: we hardly even appreciated the American milk powder that was sent to our schools; we used to mock the American cult for Coca-Cola that the communist propaganda described as a drug, and we used to dislike America profoundly for the Korean War.

When I arrived in Paris, the war in Vietnam was at its climax, and we used to protest against American bombardments. It was then that René Girard, having attended my first presentation of Bakhtin in Roland Barthes's seminar, invited me to teach at the University of Baltimore. I could not see myself collaborating with the "cops of the world," and despite the dialectical advice that I got from my professor, Lucien Goldmann, who used to say, "My dear, American imperialism has to be conquered from the inside," I honestly did not believe that I could do that. So, I remained in France. It was 1966. Several years later, in 1972, I met Professor Léon Roudiez from Columbia University, at the Colloque de Cérisy on Artaud and Bataille. That's how I made my first trip to New York in 1973, and ever since I have been a visiting professor in the department of French of this university, which, without improving the quality of my English, has at least helped me in making many friends and accomplices in the very special context of the American academy. Here are some of these friends: Tom Bishop, Michael Rifaterre, Donna Stanton, Toril Moi, Kerry Oliver, Alice Jardine, Teresa Brennan, Nancy Miller, Ann Caplan. Unfortunately I do not have enough time today to also speak about the numerous students that I have had the great opportunity of working with, some of whom are teachers today, or writers such as Philip Roth and Barbara Salomon, psychoanalysts such as Otto Kernberg, Peter Neubauer, and Allen Roland, whom I had the privilege of meeting later on.

Of all this experience, which I cannot résumé here tonight, and about which I have written in my book *Les Samourais* (Fayard, 1990), I would simply like to bring to you two symbolic images that have become inseparable from my psyche and that will perhaps give you a sense of what my attachment to the United States means.

The first one is a tiny amateur photograph, in black and white, that Léon Roudiez took of me, and which shows me with my long student hair, on the ferry that took me to the skyscrapers of Manhattan. Since I do not have a picture of my arrival in Paris, this one is for me the only and the best proof of my renaissance in the "free world." You can see this picture in *Kristeva Interviews,* a book edited by Columbia University Press. I therefore wish to take this opportunity to also thank Columbia University Press for its loyal complicity, due to which my work became accessible to the English-speaking public all over the world.

My second image is that of my apartment on Morningside Drive, which dominates Harlem Park, and where I usually stay when I teach at Columbia, a place invaded by this unusual American light, dazzling and inviting at the same time, where I wrote pages that are dear to me from *Histoires d'amour/ Tales of Love* (1983) and *Soleil Noir/ Black Sun* (1987), a place that remains in my personal mythology a space of happy solitude.

When Philippe Sollers and I decided to devote a whole issue of *Tel Quel* (71/73, fall 1977) to New York, very many were surprised. What came across in that issue was a praise of American democracy, as opposed to French centralization, so hierarchical and *jacobine.* It was actually an acknowledgment of what seems to me to be the most important quality of American civilization, which also explains the enjoyment that I have with my freedom of work in the American academy, namely, its hospitality. I have to include in the designation "American" your Canadian neighbors to the north.

By *hospitality* I mean the ability that some have to offer a home to others who do not have one or lack one temporarily. Running away from communism to France, I did not encounter this hospitality over there, although France has given me my French nationality, for which I will always be grateful. Paralyzed in its administrative and cultural tradition, and at the same time trying to free itself from this, my adoptive country promotes stunning innovations such as the artistic, philosophical, and theoretical avant-gardes that have seduced me, and have made its glory abroad, while, at the same time, promoting a violent rejection, if not hatred toward these innovations. On the contrary, America seems to me to be a territory that welcomes hybridization and even encourages it, perhaps excessively, but I will get back to this later on.

However, this is indeed a French woman that you are meeting here, or perhaps, a Frenchified European, the very essence of what *francité*, "Frenchness" means. This often comes as a surprise to the French themselves who, obviously, do not see in me one of them. Sometimes, after listening to you, here in America, discussing passionately my work as part of French theory, I am even tempted to take myself for a . . . French intellectual. This has also encouraged me at times to think about settling in America, or more precisely, in Canada, which is more European and Francophone, all the more so when I feel the xenophobia of that old country of mine hurting me.

In this modern world of ours, in this "new world order," we seem to lack a positive definition of what it means to be human (not in the sense of "human species," but rather in terms of "human quality"). We are sometimes forced to ask ourselves what humanity is all about when we have to confront "crimes against humanity." My own experience, though, makes me think that the minimal definition of humanity, the zero degree of humanity, as Barthes used to say, is precisely hospitality. The Greeks were actually right when they chose the word *ethos* to designate the concept of "choice," "the choice" between good and bad, and all the other possible choices, and that gave rise to the notion of "ethics." Originally, the word *ethos* (hence "ethical") meant "regular stay," "animal shelter," finally leading to "habitat," "habit," and "character" as *characteristic* of an individual and of a social group.

I would therefore say that offering shelter, opening your door, your academia, your publishing houses, your way of thinking, your professional and personal preoccupations to the life and work of a foreigner, in other words *hospitality* of the kind that you have offered me, is the zero degree of *ethos*. America is for me this moral stand that today becomes essential, and also problematic, especially now when massive migration forces us into an encounter with the "other," requiring from us adequate standards of morality and legislation. Whatever your ostracisms and difficulties with foreigners, here on American soil I feel a foreigner, just like all the other foreigners. And I believe that together we can build something from this solidarity because we all belong to a future type of humanity that will be made entirely of foreigners/strangers that try to understand each other.

Your hospitality toward me was first and foremost hospitality toward my ideas and my work. When I started here—and I've continued to do so—I tried to bring to you a cultural memory, French, European, as a mixture of German, Russian, and French traditions: Hegel and Freud, Russian formalism, French structuralism, the avant-gardes of the "nouveau roman." and *Tel Quel.* You may have felt at times that my "migrant personality" was less "Frenchy" in the strict and sometimes arrogant and despising sense of the word, and that through the foreigner that I am, you, as foreigners, can also have access to this French and European culture that is sometimes so inaccessible and jealous of its purity.

Also, part of my work has resonated in a special way here and has further developed in a direction that I am most pleased with, and which encouraged me to go on. Sometimes the images that you send back to me, of myself and my work, surprise me, and I have difficulty in recognizing myself. But I have never had and will never acquire a taste for polemics, partly because I am convinced of at least one thing: either these interpretations go against me in a useless way and will consequently exhaust themselves in the process (for example, some activist and "politically correct" comments), or they are part of a more personal quest of the American men and women, original and innovative, who assimilate my work into theirs at their own risk, which may well be, after all, just a wonderful way of practicing this hospitality that I have been talking about. The whole idea of "transplanting" or "hybridization"—isn't it meant to generate unexpected consequences, the very opposite of cloning?

I will allow myself now to get back to some of the main themes of my work that have been under extensive debate, only to make a few points.

1. *Intertextuality* has always enjoyed tremendous success: it's an international "star," some would say, *une tarte à la crème*. An idea that I developed starting from Bakhtin, this concept invites you to read a text as a crossing of texts. Very often, in the formalist or structuralist visions this has been perceived as a return to "citations," or to "source." For me it is mostly a way of introducing *history* to structuralism: the texts that Mallarmé and Proust used to read, and which nourish *Le Coup de dés* and *à la Recherche du temps perdu,* allow us to introduce in the laboratory of writing Mallarmé's interest for anarchism, for example, and Proust's interest for Zohar's Jewish mysticism and for the *Affaire Dreyfus.* Also, by showing to what extent the internal dimension of the text is connected to the external context, we may have the revelation of the inauthenticity of the writing subject. The writer is a "subject in process," *sujet en procès,* a carnival, a polyphony, forever contradicting and rebellious. The apparently poststructuralist theme of intertextuality also started an idea that I have been trying to work on ever since, especially in my books from 1996 and 1997, namely that of the connection between "culture" and "revolt."

2. The distinction that I have set up between the *semiotic* and the *symbolic* has no political or feminist connotation. It is simply an attempt to think of "meaning" not only as "structure" but also as "process" or "trial," by looking at the same time at syntax, logic, and what transgresses them, or the *transverbal.* I refer to this other side of "meaning" as *transverbal* because calling it *preverbal* could cause some difficulties. The semiotic is not independent of language, but underpins

language, and, under the control of language, it articulates other aspects of "meaning" which are more than mere "significations," such as rhythmical and melodical inflections.

Under the influence of Freudian distinctions between "the representations of things" and "the representations of words," I try to take into consideration this double nature of the human mind, especially the pulsional and biological constraints of meaning and signification. This because indeed *in the beginning there was the word,* but before the *beginning* there was . . . *the repressed.*

I am personally convinced that the future of psychoanalysis lies in this direction, namely that of the approach between the translinguistic logic of the unconscious and biological and neurobiological constraints. At the *Institut du Vivant,* at the University of Paris, we try to bring biologists and psychoanalysts closer in their work. Unfortunately, those implications of my notion of semiotic are not as much part of the North American understanding of it. This gives me the opportunity to say that, at this point, our collaboration with American psychoanalysts is not very fruitful. Except for some repetitions of the Lacanian discourse that are being promoted less in clinics and more in departments of literature, American psychoanalytical organizations are barely interested in French Freudian research.

Our basic preoccupations, that is, the opening of psychoanalysis to biology and its more active involvement in social politics, which we hope will revitalize contemporary psychoanalysis in the long run, do not seem to appeal to our American colleagues. In North America, it seems to me, there is right now a sort of anti-Freudian, "revisionist" trend, which is not only a protective retreat in a supposed tradition, but also a sort of normative psychology of the ego instead of a close analysis of Freudian texts. We hope that the recent designation of Otto Kernberg, who is very much aware of the recent evolution of French psychoanalytical research as head of the IPA, will change this state of things.

This "semiotic" transverbal side of our research is connected to the archaic relation between the mother and the child and allows me to investigate certain aspects of the feminine and the maternal in language, of what Freud used to call "the black continent" or Mycenaean (after the name of the Greek civilization that preceded the civilization of classical Greece). This "other logic" of the feminine and the maternal, which works against normative representation and opposes phallic representation, both masculine and feminine, is perhaps my own contribution to the effort of understanding the feminine as connected to the political via . . . the sacred.

I am convinced that this *fin-de siècle* which seems to be so much in need of religion is actually in need of the sacred. I understand the sacred to be the desire of human beings to think, not in the sense of calculus, but rather in the sense of a need for fundamental questioning, which distinguishes us from other species and, *a contrario*, approaches us to them. This human characteristic that we call *le sens du divin et du sacré*, "the sense of the divine and of the sacred," lies for me, writer, psychoanalyst, and semiotician, at the basis of the emergence of language. The semiotic, with its maternal ties, seems to be the furthest point we can reach when we try to imagine and understand the frontiers of the "physis." By understanding the semiotic "as emergence of meaning" we can overcome the dichotomies of metaphysics (soul/body, physical/psychical). This could also be a way of telling you that my preoccupation with the sacred is, in fact, antimetaphysical and only consequently feminist. If I am indeed passionately attached to the recognition of women in social, intellectual, and political life, this is only to the extent where we, as women, can bring a *different attitude* to the ideas of power and meaning. This would be an attitude that takes into consideration the need for survival of our species, and our need for the sacred. Women are positioned at this crossroad.

3. *The abject and abjection* are concepts that I developed starting from my clinical experience when facing the symptoms that I call *nouvelles maladies de l'âme* ("new maladies of the soul") [Fayard, 1993]) where the distinction between "subject" and "object" is not clear, and where these two pseudo-entities exhaust themselves in fascination and repulsion. Borderline personalities, and some depressive personalities, can be described starting from this psychical basis, which is also reminiscent of an archaic state of communion with the maternal holding, the mother being the first "ab-ject." Artists such as Picasso and de Kooning obviously know something about this.

Parallel to the concepts of abject/abjection, I first tried to understand the complex universe of a writer such as Céline, master of popular fiction, of the argot, carrier of exceptional emotion who, instead of taking the cathartic road of abjection as religions do (and I believe any religion is in fact a way of purifying the abject), insists on following imaginary abjections that he then transfers to political realities. His anti-Semitism and his abject compromises with Nazi ideology are expressed in his pamphlets that I tried, among the first, to read without fear, as an analyst.

My adventure on the very dangerous territory of abjection (and I hope you agree with this) has brought me many alliances. Many American artists, and in fact, artists from all over the world, have recognized themselves in the experience of the abject, which is close to the psychotic states that they encounter in the process of artistic creation. But this adventure has also given me the sharp reaction of journals such as *The Nation*, which stated that if I chose to analyze Céline, it was only to excuse him, as if trying to understand means necessarily trying to forgive. That was one of the most radical rejections of my work, due to misunderstanding, which I personally perceived as a partisan excommunication that targeted the very idea of thinking.

This excommunication seems to me to be the tragic version of a more recent event, the latter more comic than tragic, which came from the pen of a rather noisy person in your university [New York University] who thought he was "exposing French impostors" by rejecting our "pseudo-scientific models" when we know that, in fact, there has never been a question of "model-ization," but only of metaphorical transfers.

4. *Strangeness/Foreignness*, is, as I am sure you know, something dear to my heart. *Etrangers à nous-mêmes (Foreigners to Ourselves)* [1988] gave me the opportunity of outlining a history of foreigners, their actual destiny, and the way in which they are perceived in the West, and also to state my position in this debate, a position that again seems to be accepted with some difficulty. First of all, I believe that in order to fight the state of national depression that we have in France (and in other countries as well) as a result of globalization and of the influx of immigrants, and also in order to oppose maniacal reactions to this depression (such as that of the Front National), it is important to restore national confidence. This has to be done in the same way in which we sometimes have to restore the narcissism or the ideal "ego" in a depressed patient before proceeding to the actual analysis, that is, to the dissolution of his system of defense and resistance.

I am convinced that, in the next century, the cosmopolitan society that we have been dreaming of ever since the Stoics and throughout the Enlightenment will not be possible in the utopian shape of the "melting pot," universalized and "uniform-isized" by the market, the media, and the Internet. At most this will lead to a more or less conflictual cohabitation of nations and of various social groups that will live *with* and *against* each other. A certain amount of respect for "national identity" and support for the idea of "general interest," *intérêt géneral* (see Montesquieu), this combination will have to replace the excesses of contemporary globalization.

Two Types of Civilization

You may have noticed that with the above-mentioned elements of our *interface* I have chosen to discuss the things that unite us and the ones that divide us. Without getting into further details about my work, I would like to take this opportunity to distance myself from this personal research in order to understand the wider cultural and political context in which we work.

The collapse of the Berlin Wall in 1989 enhanced the difference between two types of culture, a difference that, earlier, your *hospitality* had partially stopped me from noticing. I want to make it clear from the start, and in order to avoid any misunderstanding, that I am referring to *two visions of freedom* that democratic societies have elaborated and which we, unfortunately, do not cherish enough. I am speaking of two visions of freedom that rely on the Greek, Jewish, and Christian traditions, and which, in spite of the horrors and difficulties they have encountered (I only wish to remind you here of Mme Roland on the scaffold saying, "Oh, freedom, so many crimes have been made in your name!"), these two visions of freedom remain our most important achievement. These two visions of freedom are, nevertheless, essential and compatible. They sometimes are, as it is the case now, opposed, if not at war.

Kant, in his *Critique of Pure Reason (1781)* and his *Critique of Practical Reason* (1789) defines for the first time something that other people must have also experienced, but were unable to articulate, namely the fact that freedom is not, negatively speaking, an absence of constraints but positively speaking the possibility of "self-beginning." Thus, by identifying freedom with the ability to "spontaneously begin," Kant opens the way to the praise of the enterprising subject, to the initiative of the self, if I am allowed to transfer his "cosmic" thinking to a more personal level. At the same time, he subordinates the freedom of reason, be it pure or practical, to a cause, divine or moral.

I will expand by saying that, in a world more and more dominated by technology, freedom becomes the capacity to adapt to a cause always exterior to the self, but which is less and less a moral cause, and more and more an economic one. In the best situation the two operate at the same time. Along this line of thinking, which is favored by Protestantism (I refer here especially to Max Weber's work on the connection between capitalism and Protestantism), freedom becomes the freedom to adapt to the logic of causes and effects. Hannah Arendt would say "to the calculus of consequences," the logic of production, of science, and of the economy. To be free would be then to be able to profit from adapting to this logic of causes and effects, and to the economic market.

The logic of globalization, and unregulated free market capitalism, known in Europe as liberalism, are the climax of this kind of freedom. The supreme cause (God) and the technical cause (the dollar) are its two coexisting variants, which guarantee the functioning of our freedom within this logic of instrumentalization. I am not denying here the benefits of this freedom to adapt to the logic of causes and effects that culminates in a specific way of thinking, which is calculus thinking, and science. I consider this vision to be crucial for our access to technology. American society seems to be well adapted to this kind of freedom. However, this freedom is not the only one.

There is also another vision of freedom that emerges in the Greek world, at the very heart of its philosophy with the pre-Socratics, and which develops in the Socratic dialogue. Without becoming subordinate to a cause, that is, previous to the concatenation of Aristotelian "categories" that are already a premise for scientific and technical thinking, this fundamental freedom relies on *being* and, moreover, *on the being of language that is being delivered (l'etre de la parole qui se livre),* which delivers to itself and to the other, and thus sets itself free. This liberation of the being of language that occurs between the self and the other was emphasized in Heidegger's discussion of Kant (in a 1930 seminar "The Essence of Human Freedom," published in 1982; French translation, 1987). This inscribes freedom into the very essence of philosophy as eternal questioning, before philosophy became fixed, philosophy's initial fixation, in the succession of causes and effects, and the ability to master freedom and philosophy.

I would like to assure you—don't be afraid—that I will not go too far in this debate that I have already oversimplified over the two visions of freedom in Kant and Heidegger. What I am interested in is to discuss, in the context of the modern world, this second conception of freedom, different from the logic of technique that culminates in savage consumerism, as manifest in the being of speech in the presencing of the self to the other.

I hope you understand the connotations of this kind of freedom. The poet is its main custodian, together with the libertine, who defies the conventions of social causes and effects in order to bring out and formulate its desire for dissidence; and the analyst, too, in the experience of transference and countertransference; and the revolutionary, who places the liberties of the individual above any other convention. This is the foundation of human rights, and the slogan of the French Revolution, Liberty-Equality-Fraternity *(Liberté-Egalité-Fraternité),* which at the time reinforced the ideas of the English habeas corpus.

But I would like to come back to our reality. We are on our way toward building a European Community in spite of all the difficulties that we cannot ignore. In this often chaotic European assembly the voice of France, which sometimes finds it hard to make itself heard, still finds allies in other socialist governments and in the public opinion of various countries, all of them deeply attached to their cultural tradition in order to build a social Europe *(une Europe sociale).* We try to promote a type of society that is not exclusively that of liberalism, often identified as the American model. Our requirement for this cultural difference is not only due to the fact that we belong to a tradition and memory which may be older, more refined and more sophisticated, et cetera., because it originates in the Old World. It is rather due to the fact that we have a different vision of freedom, namely one that privileges the individual singularity over the economic and the scientific. When the French government insists on our solidarity in opposition to liberalism, we have to understand this to be a need for recognition of those different experiences of freedom.

Still, we are fully aware of the risks that may come with such an attitude: ignorance of the contemporary economic reality, excessive union demands, an inability to take part in international competition, idleness, backwardness. This is why we need to be alert and always remember the new constraints of our technological world, of causes and effects. But at the same time, we can easily see the advantages of this other type of freedom. That mainly Catholic European nations such as France, Italy, Spain, and Poland aspire to this alternative type of freedom, which is an aspiration rather than a fixed project, is driven by real concern for the singularity and fragility of each and every human life: the poor, the disabled, the retired, the ones who rely on social benefits. It requires special attention for sexual and ethnic differences, men and women, considered in their singular intimacy rather than as simple group consumers. The consequence of this is the fact that some leftist movements and governments in Europe, socialist and communist, are often associated with charitable causes, Catholic, for example, in their desire to build a world on other principles than those of consumerism. We witness in Europe the emergence of a new and surprising alliance between the humanitarian side of the Catholic Church, which is often criticized for its conservative attitudes toward sexuality and human reproduction, and the most exigent scientific and union circles. The basis of this convergence lies in the belief that there is this alternative vision of freedom to struggle for.

In our postmodern era, economic and technical performance may not always be a guarantee of human freedom, as was the case at the advent of capitalism. From this perspective, the main characteristic of European culture could well be (and you may find some of the French terms difficult to translate in English) its emphasis on the intimate, the particular, the art of living, taste *(goût)*, leisure *(loisirs)*, pleasure without purpose *(plaisir pour rien)*, grace *(grâce)*, the incidental *(le hasard)*, playfulness *(le ludisme)*, wastefulness *(gaspillage)*, our "damned side" *(la part maudite)*, or, to cut it short, freedom as the essence of "the being in the world" prior to any "cause." Can we preserve this as a general human value? This still remains to be seen, since we are overwhelmed by the maelstrom of our calculus thinking and our consumerism. The only counterpoint to this seems to be the rebirth of religious sects for which the sacred is no longer a permanent quest, as the very concept of human dignity would require, but a subordination to absolute causes and effects, which means that the religious alternative is a nonreliable counterpoint. It is therefore rather unlikely that this alternative vision of freedom that I am trying to rehabilitate today can become more than an aspiration, but the dice are cast, and this is our bet.

In this perspective I would say that even the so much criticized *étatisme* (the power of the French state) works in favor this logic of opposing solidarity to liberalism. In France, some of our political groups on the right pretend not to understand this, and explain the recourse to the power of the state as a solution to some of our economic problems (such as the rate of unemployment with the young), as backwardness and need for assistance. The reality is different, though. The state currently tries to decentralize itself while purging itself of its old complicity with the Nazi regime of Vichy, a complicity long under cover, even during the presidency of François Mitterand. The trial of Papon (which is less of Papon as an individual and more of Papon as a symbol of the regime of Vichy) is going on, whatever the difficulties, and one hopes that the state will be reborn with a new amount of credibility. This, we hope, will allow it to continue aspiring at this solidarity, so necessary to the weak who still need to rely on the help of the *res publica*. Thus the republic, which is in the process of being reborn not as a symbol of centralization but as the expression of popular will, will ensure the existence of pluralism within the framework of a united nation. This will be another version of the nation-state, decentralized and respectful of individual rights while, at the same time, unifying and protective. This is perhaps the best antidote to the national depression of which the National Front seems to take advantage.

From this perspective, the participation of France in the European Community will consist of its support for European socialists and the public opinion at large for the enhancement of their role as messengers of this alternative version of freedom and humanism. I could put this differently. The French plural left is proof that the French people still see themselves as the carrier of the ideals of the French Revolution, whose message is fairly simple: the disadvantaged and each one of us can live better, and this better life is not only a better economic calculus, but a better concept of human dignity. Moreover, it is possible to satisfy this need for the freedom of the self not only in the church and in our private lives, as you do here in America, but also in our public lives.

I have been speaking for a long time now, although, I feel, still briefly, about the political implications of this European vision of freedom, a vision that is deeply ingrained in our *social experience* as well as in our *way of thinking*. Isn't this the reason why part of the American academy has supported our work? In your own attempt to oppose the economic, political, and academic "establishment" of American society, you have perhaps noticed in our work this side of our freedom that often takes the form of political contestation, but which is fundamentally more than that: it is a way of being that reveals itself in the act of revolt. In fact, politics *strictu sensu* can also be seen as the betrayal of this freedom of thinking. This is why, in my last two books on the culture of revolt (Fayard, 1996, 1997), I, discuss the idea that political revolution (the French Terror of 1793 and the Russian Revolution of 1917) can be seen as the stifling of revolt in the sense of free questioning and permanent restlessness. The horror of totalitarianism, which took over the idea of revolt only to transform it into a deadly dogma, hasn't managed to compromise entirely the possibility of thinking as revolt, as a part of our political experience, and not only of our spiritual life. In this respect, it seems to me that you have developed Francophilia. or Europhilia, or rather an interest in Continental philosophy, as a way of protesting against the limitations of consumerism and American positivism, and that you have relied on our research and on its theoretical and ethical foundation.

Still, the deformation imposed by "political correctness" has hardened the political implication of the philosophy that exists in our work but as an implicit dimension of our way of thinking. Some of our American readers simplified them, others forgot them. What was neglected by this attitude was *the working through of thinking* just as Freud used to speak of *the working through of dreams.* This is "unconcealed" thinking in the Heideggerian sense, the "disclosure" of thinking according to Hannah Arendt, a thinking that opposes calculus thinking. In this way thinking finds a source in fiction and therefore in the sensitive human body, "unveiling" a "third type of cognition" as described by Spinoza, by free association, and transference in psychoanalytical experience.

Those who ignore or reject this kind of thinking develop a real Francophobia and Europhobia, in fact, fear of Continental philosophy. This is not only their way of reacting to their fear of being "colonized" by some "French stuff" that would put a barrier between them and the simple and practical nature of things. This reaction is much more serious and much deeper. When they are not simply limited promoters (and victims) of political obscurantism, I would give credit to our opponents for simply sharing in the belief in that first type of freedom that I have already mentioned. They subordinate the unfolding of thinking to the calculus of causes and effects. You may end up with two consequences of this attitude: either you adopt a scientist's attitude, "scientifically correct," and then you become Freudian revisionists and you discredit psychoanalysis, or you adopt a politically correct militantism, and we become mere servants of a minority cause, noble at first, but which degenerates in a new dogma, a limited revindication that works against the working through of thought.

On the contrary, far from being exhausted, this drive for freedom in our thinking continues to grow in France. In order to convince you, I'll give some examples.

This is visible in the ever-increasing emphasis on the speaking subject in the humanities. This does not mean that objective facts are ignored, but, quite on the contrary, that by taking them into consideration, the researcher is much more subjectively involved in their interpretation. In France, we will soon initiate a national debate on the role of human sciences along this idea of "facts and interpretations." It goes without saying that the part played by psychoanalysis in this is crucial.

Also, and this is undoubtedly the result of the psychoanalytical perspective on human beings, the imaginary *(l'imaginaire)* is more and more perceived as an essential component of our psyche, and as the place where this other version of freedom that I am trying to rehabilitate today emerges. We are alive precisely because we have a psychic life. This life is our intimacy *(for intérieur)*, which allows us to shelter inside and outside attacks on our being—psychological and biological traumas, as well as social and political external aggression. The imaginary transforms them all, sublimates them, works for us and keeps us alive. Which imaginary? Well, precisely the fantasies that psychoanalysis works with. Literature welcomes our loves and insomnia, our states of grace and crisis. Religion opposes liberalism and its logic of causes and effects by adding this supplement of the "human soul." In the modern state of human science, thinking is now ready for a fruitful and critical encounter with this religious imaginary, and not only for its condemnation. Religion also becomes analyzable. Here, too, I believe, French theory can make its contribution.

I have insisted a lot on the Greek and French origin of this type of freedom that, in my opinion, underpins what I call "French theory." Still, nobody has the monopoly over this vision, neither the Catholic nor the Protestant worlds. They both have an equal potential for dealing with these problems. Also, I believe that the idea in Judaism of "being chosen," although different from the idea of freedom that I have tried to outline here, makes a person coming from this tradition particularly capable of restoring what we lack so much: an interaction of these two versions of freedom—liberal and solidarian, technical and poetic, causal and revelatory.

At the beginning of this conference, when criticizing the resurgence of French nationalism, I pointed to the fact that this intimate and solidarian type of freedom is indeed a difficult if not an impossible choice. Still, this is the challenge that socialist France is ready to face, and this is in the long run the challenge that Europe as a whole is willing to take. It is a challenge that I am also willing to take.

To this, America, the America that I love, an America that has silenced all its opponents, risks becoming a fourth Rome, after Byzantium and Moscow. In this new economic order, America imposes a financial, economic, and cultural oligarchy under the label of liberalism, a liberalism that excludes or puts at risk an important dimension of human freedom. Other civilizations have other visions of human freedom. They also need to be heard in this global world and to be allowed to bring their own correction, through diversity, to this new global vision of freedom. The diversity of cultural models is the only guarantee for this humanity that I referred to in the beginning of my lecture, a humanity that we describe as hospitality for lack of a better definition. But hospitality is not only the simple juxtaposition of differences, with one model dominating all the others and pretending to respect the others while being indifferent to them. Quite the contrary, hospitality suggests a real attempt to understand other kinds of freedom in order to make every "way of being" more multiple, more complex. The definition of humanity that I was looking for is perhaps precisely this process of "complexification."

In this sense, understanding (or lack of understanding) for a European alternative could prove to be a decisive step. The creed of French moralists is well known: If God did not exist, we would have to invent Him. I would paraphrase this by saying, if Europe did not exist, we would have to invent her. This is to the interest of our plural world, and to the interest of America. Whatever the economic and diplomatic competition between the Old and the New Worlds, the need to overcome Europhobia is obvious, and intellectuals should be the first ones to do so. The most urgent and the noblest mission of French theory is, after all, that of drawing attention to human diversity in its experience of freedom. French theory is just another experience of freedom.

For a Political Roland Barthes

FRANÇOISE GAILLARD

I would like to limit what I have to say tonight to a single confession: I miss Roland Barthes. I would like you to understand that this confession is a judgment of our times in which a voice like Roland Barthes's no longer makes itself heard. We have symptomalogists, moralists, and "imprecators" (I am speaking only of those who express themselves in the French media), but where is that critical vigilance that made thinking an exercise in radicality and, in relation to politics, an exercise in intelligence? But I cannot limit myself here. I see I will therefore be obligated to enter into the reasons for my nostalgia with you. Of Roland Barthes, I would like to be able to say what one of his students, who is none other than Jacques Alain Miller, wrote about him:

> It was definitely a joy to meet each week with someone who demonstrated that in all and nothing, everything has meaning, that not everything is a veiled message of being, but that everything makes up a system, gets articulated, and is not foreign to anything human, for in his eyes, the human was like Saussure's language. He took this postulate seriously, and carried it out to its utmost consequence. Powerful in its operation, corrosive, the nature of which makes a philosophy student's being-in-the-world vacillate. Hence the fever with which I read the unforgettable *Mythologies* for the first time.

As for me, unfortunately, I was not one of his followers from early on, a regular at his seminar, and therefore was not accorded the honor of being at those gratifying weekly meetings out of which have come so many texts. I think that I have made up for lost time, though, for it has now been almost twenty years that I have been attempting to communicate to my own students this joy. For, of all the numerous writings that have come out of what one customarily calls the glorious thirty—those thirty years of extraordinary effervescence in thought (1950–1980), right before the bell was tolled by the censors of 1968 thinking—

Roland Barthes's books, or at least a large part of them, are those that have aged the least. And the intellectual pleasure is still the same, to read and to reread them.

My personal knowledge of Roland Barthes, our friendship and the affinity in thought that ensued, all started in the commotion of the first grand show on semiology organized by Verdighone in Milan. The year was 1972. My intellectual interest, however, goes back further; the tattered copy of *Mythologies* that I still read, simply for the pleasure of savoring in pure critical thinking, was given to me by Lucien Goldmann. It used to be his. In keeping with the spirit of intellectual generosity that we have acknowledged in him, he had wanted me to share in his enthusiasm. The linking of these two names may surprise some, especially since Lucien Goldmann is somewhat forgotten today, and yet it makes sense. At the time of *Le degré zero de l'écriture*, Roland Barthes was interested in realism and bourgeois writing. It was in vogue at the time. And, just like Sartre, may I add, he did not want to leave historical territory to vulgar Marxists, all those who, in keeping with the old work by Plekhanov, *Art and Social Life*, thought of the relationship between literature and history in terms of simplistic determinism. This was also Lucien Goldmann's concern, and Georg Lukàcs's before him.

Roland Barthes, however, played the game differently. In order to avoid the pitfalls of mechanical causality, he blatantly sidestepped Marxist theory—just as he would continue to do with every other system of thought with which he flirted. It was in those days that he invented a notion that allowed him to place literature at the junction of the subject and history; he called this notion *écriture*. Difficult to define, what can I say about it, other than it is the critical moment at which a subject's historical destiny asserts itself? The *subject* and *history*: here Roland Barthes holds both ends of a rope that he will never let go—despite what some may think. The subject, not as a biographical or psychic reality, but as an instance without any affective or personal attachment, just an instance of crystallization of meaning; history, not as positive data or an originating referent back to which everything must be linked, but as a genealogical process that explains, by relativizing it, the meaning of the meaning on which a tribe agrees, and the value of the values to which it adheres. In this time, in what is unfortunately our present time of referring meaning and values to nature, we would once again like to hear that voice that was constantly telling us, "nothing is natural, everything is genealogical."

Roland Barthes's entire thought process is summed up here, in these progressive shifts in meaning to which he subjected knowledge and theories, for the simple pleasure of pure thought. His intellectual journey is here as well. Roland Barthes, as we know, never settled; he never confronted, either, admitting himself that he always took oblique paths. What must be understood, however, is that he never sought to conquer a position, be it theoretical or ideological, and it is precisely for this reason that his discourse is not a discourse of control. The dynamic of his work is tactical, not strategic, as he himself stated. And indeed, for him, in situating something there was always the question of shifting, never of occupying a place. Shifting what, you may ask? Shifting acquired notions, recognized values, received ideas; in short, shifting conventional meaning (*doxa*). Even in the prime of his association with semiology, he was not a man who adhered to a system. In which system could one pretend to confine reality? He was too much a writer not to have known that reality is uncontrollable. At the time, this attitude both seduced and disconcerted. Undoubtedly, this explains the unusual reception of his texts. At the core of his work hovered a never formulated question: what use (other than aesthetic or hedonistic) to make of it all? Of course there were the semiological elements, and the diverse contributions to "narratology," but we felt that the essentials were elsewhere. The problem was knowing where. Even *Mythologies* came to be read in France only for its flavor (*saveur*), and abroad for its informative value (*valeur*) on those strange people called "the French."

Only publicists and those in the media continued to see how to put to good use, albeit in reverse, that which had once been the motivating factor: *disalienation*.

Roland Barthes's entire collected works are in effect a little machine constructed against all forms of intellectual alienation, and as a result, against all the effects of political resignation that they entail.

And this man who claimed to have not had a strategy managed to inscribe the dynamism of his work into a permanent process of reappropriating meaning. Without this process, there is only fatalism and submission to an order of things against which we can do nothing, be it globalization, market law, or some other transcendental specter that will invent for itself, only to then submit to it, our post-political era.

Undoubtedly against all expectations, I will therefore plead for a political Roland Barthes.

Although I did not have the same privilege as Jacques Alain Miller, I would nevertheless like to share with you a personal memory of Roland Barthes as well as read a fragment, for it seems to me that both are likely to explain the singular place that this man occupied in intellectual circles, and in the life of the mind, and why from the outset I had put forward that today I (we) miss him terribly.

Let us begin with the memory. Yielding to the pressure of a student body that was not able to share in the almost intimate nature of his normal seminar, Roland Barthes had opened up what I have some difficulties referring to as his teaching to a large audience. During the opening session, where he found himself alone on the stage of the small theater that the EHESS [the School for Advanced Study in the Social Sciences] had placed at his disposal, he read, in his beautiful deep voice, a text by Bertholt Brecht, entitled *The New Year Address to the German Nation.* He then began to comment upon it. I suppose that many had come with the expectation of a follow-up to *Elements of Semiology.* Undoubtedly they were hoping to leave with a few solid concepts in their knapsacks, their theoretical ration of combat for the week. What they received was what may be the most beautiful lesson in citizen exercise of conscience and political thought. Here the unusual layout of Brecht's text must be mentioned. The page is divided into two columns. The column on the left reproduces, word for word, the speech Hitler delivered to the German nation on New Year's Day 1933. In the right-hand column is Brecht's text, a sort of reading between the lines of the official speech. It is something that situates itself somewhere between purely linear translation and exegesis, between decoding and interpretation. For example, beside the führer's statement, in which we hear the hysterical orator's voice hammering out "the Reich is Peace," Brecht simply writes, "the Reich is War." His point was made.

The effect is devastating, much more so than any direct written refutation or traditional political speech of denunciation would have been.

This act by Brecht pleased Roland Barthes, who was wary of confrontation and of the war of discourses. In his eyes, the two were merely bouts of paranoia and dogmatic violence, both of which closed the door on intelligence and blocked access to the intelligibility of things. To denunciation, which was always violent, he preferred demythification. And, empowered by Brecht's lesson, which was one of his oldest and most constant inner references, he always worked to separate the meaning from the assertive arrogance of a political, ideological, or mythological speech, in order to expose it in all its fragile nudity and relativity. This was his way of writing his entire work into the political arena, without being obligated to pass by militant babble that, in a way, horrified him by its repetition, its stereotypes, and its fixed terminology from which reality had long since evaporated. He would often doubt, though, that this was enough. In a passage entitled "Brecht's Reproaches to RB," he worries about his relationship to politics—politics that, as he tells us, were a constant worry in his life, "All my life, I've worried myself sick about politics. I infer from this that the only Father I knew (that I gave myself) was Father politics." Was Brecht one of the incarnations of this father? The fact remains that in the passage "Brecht's Reproaches to RB," the latter defines himself as being "the historical witness of a contradiction: that of a sensitive, avid and silent political subject," adding, "these words must not be separated." No, we must not separate them. We know that silence is the worst reproach that one can level at intellectuals suspected of indifference or resignation. There is nothing of the sort for Roland Barthes, and the silence for which he blames himself has nothing to do with the clerics' betrayal that Julien Benda speaks of. To his contemporaries, Roland Barthes was capable of seeming silent on political matters only because he never expressed himself, as least not in his *écriture,* on "political" topics. This is a shortsighted vision of things. It is evident that for Roland Barthes, sensitivity and responsibility with regard to politics did not follow the traditional paths of direct intervention, petitions, or counter-speeches. Roland Barthes or the anti-Sartre! This does not mean that they did not exist, however. His method was demythification or reversal. "Often," he will say in *Mythologies,* "politics is in the final touch *(pointe finale)."* Nothing could be more true. It is precisely the moment at which Roland Barthes turns the evidence of a social habit (drinking wine), a received idea (on Martians), or an image (the cover of an issue of *Paris Match*) inside out that the political stakes reveal themselves. And this process is just as caustic as Brecht's!

This conception of the critical intellectual's role is undoubtedly less resounding than the one we are used to, but perhaps it is more efficient in the end, for it does not link critical attitude to a world vision, an ideology, or a belief—in short, to a dogma. In any case, the story of these last twenty years leads us to believe this. We do indeed notice that when an intellectual founds his criticism on an ideology, it suffices that that ideology collapse for the entire critical horizon to be swept away (some believe this is nowadays the case for Marxism). And it is in the void of this massive cleansing, that discourses on the reconstruction of norms and values arise. This is where we find ourselves at present, in a reactionary period.

We are now in the age where values are simply accepted as evident, given by nature. Indeed, we now see that along with the ideological base on which it had founded itself, the critical position was also carried away by the winds of historical reversals. And today, what replaces the critical intellectual is what I would call the reactive intellectual: one who is moved by feelings of indignation, emotion, or sympathy. But precisely what Roland Barthes was teaching us was to be wary of such reactions that serve only to maintain an axiological solidarity with that which had provoked them. "Reactivity" does not vacate a space of thought. On the contrary, it etches itself into it. It depends on it.

Roland Barthes taught us the virtues of shifting, and he did so in two ways: by shifting position, and by incessantly shifting the cornerstones of meaning so that meaning eventually reached the point of oscillation where it would vacillate the certainties that had founded it.

No matter what he could have said or thought, what he called his tactic, which consisted of perpetual shifting, once put to use, revealed itself to be a formidable strategy. For without openly declaring war, with all the drum rolls and trumpet sounding which come with such a declaration, it destabilized every discourse of accepted obviousness *(évidence)*—those dictated by common sense (which is never more than an idea that an interest group makes up for itself, at any given time), as well as those dictated by good conscience. This silent tactic aimed continually at impeding these discourses from setting (setting, as in when one makes Jell-O) and stopping us from being taken by them. It is unfortunate that this tactic was abandoned by today's thinkers under the pretext that it contributed to maintaining a generally suspicious climate that favored nihilism. This reproach, in my opinion unfounded, was addressed at almost all those whose theoretical work and whose philosophical reflection illuminated those thirty years of unchallenged reign of the social sciences concerned with tackling ideologies as meaning, that is to say the functionality of discourses as well as their functioning. *Decompose* is not exactly *deconstruct*. Although in both cases it is a question of attacking discourses, neither the method nor the goal are entirely the same. *Decompose* for Roland Barthes stands in opposition to *destroy*. Destroying is a violent act that supposes that the one who does it holds a position of exteriority. One can only destroy from a place (be it geographical, or, in this case, ideological) outside of the target. We drop bombs from airplanes; we destroy a social order from a revolutionary ideal or from a utopia that is at the same time a radically different conception of both order and social issues. Therefore, in choosing destruction, it is not violence that bothers Roland Barthes, but the illusion of exteriority that comes with it. He does not believe that apart from revolutionary situations, which is far from being the case for our Western democratic societies, there exists an outside place from which to launch an offensive.

"In short, to destroy, one must be able to jump. But jump where? Into which language? Into which place in good conscience and in bad faith?" In fact, despite his warm feelings for those who were playing at cultural revolution in their offices at the Seuil publishing house, he always thought that in democratic societies the bourgeoisie was a total fact *(fait total)*. His lack of enthusiasm upon his return from a voyage to China with his friends from *Tel Quel*, aroused doubts at the time as to his avant-gardism. This was due, however, to the fact that he saw with lucidity, and with an undoubtedly disturbing realism, that in our societies there was no out from bourgeois consciousness, whatever the illusion the classical critical intellectual could maintain. What are we to do? Allow one system of thought *(pensée unique)* to reign, all the while moaning and groaning? An attitude of which we see too many examples today. No, Roland Barthes proposed something completely different: "decomposition." Let us listen to what he has to say:

> Let us admit that at present the intellectual's (or writer's) historical task is to maintain and to accentuate the decomposition of bourgeois consciousness. We must therefore keep in mind all its precision; this means that we must voluntarily feign remaining inside this conscience and that we will ruin it, cause it to cave in, cause it to collapse on the spot, just as we would do to a sugar cube by soaking it with water.

It is evident that this entails some risks: "by decomposing, I accept to accompany this decomposition, to decompose myself, as I go along."

In a way this was Roland Barthes: an agent of decomposition more than a deconstructor. He was also a formidable fermenting agent for thought, however. Roland Barthes, an intellectual bacteria (*intellectuel bactérien*)? Why not? It is a subspecies about which we do not think, and yet, of all the species that make up the critical intellectual family, it is perhaps the liveliest and the most resistant form in unfavorable climatological conditions. In order to draw out the metaphor, I will say that Roland Barthes precipitated the decomposition of the cadavers of our societies' cultural and ideological consensus, while at the same time making the often soft dough of our minds rise. The two acts have something profoundly Brechtian in them, and they are both profoundly political.

This fairly abrupt affirmation may be surprising, but it is enough that we stop and reflect on it to see just how closely the question of meaning is tied, for Roland Barthes, to that of political consciousness. If indeed, a person no longer has access to the understanding of what he or she is living, seeing, or receiving from his or her world, that person's political conscience cannot awaken. It atrophies in much the same way as does an organ that is no longer used. The person is acted upon and is no longer the actor. He or she is, as said Brecht quoted by Roland Barthes, "the political object" and not "the political subject." We see this today in the loss of meaning that is leading our fellow citizens to fatalism, which is precisely the flip side of a political attitude. The result is a form of resignation, dotted with moments of emotion: the massacres in Rwanda, the death of the Princess of Wales, everything is lived in the affective mode; everything is felt as if it were a natural disaster, an act of God. And yet, had Roland Barthes not denounced nature's alibi enough, even down to his semiological works?

The constant worry of giving everything meaning and continually asking himself about the meaning of things, even the most "insignificant," as everyday speech says when speaking of unimportant things (though wrongly, for these things are also steeped in meaning), is perhaps the idiosyncratic trait that made Roland Barthes, who worried about being "a bad political subject," unparalleled in awakening political consciousness. It is precisely by demonstrating "on all and nothing that everything has meaning" that he made everyone both curious with regard to meaning and to the system that had produced it, and suspicious with regard to its stakes. Does political consciousness itself (in the larger sense of the word) not commence precisely with this curiosity and suspicion? When I evoked the opening session of the public seminar where Roland Barthes read, and analyzed in an almost Brechtian fashion the text by Brecht, I had announced my intention to remind you of a fragment from *Roland by Roland Barthes*. It seemed to me, despite its appearance of frivolity, able to show just what a master, in both learning and exercising thought, this man who never claimed to be a "master of thought" (*maître à penser*) was. The fragment is called *What does it mean?* "It is a constant (and elusive) passion to affix on every fact, even the most minute, not the child's question: why? but the ancient Greek's question, the question of meaning, as if every thing quivered with meaning: what does that mean? We must at all costs transform the fact into an idea, a description, an interpretation, in short give it another name." Would it not be precisely because Barthes had developed in himself that rare capacity to put, as a common factor, before every fact, every event, every statement, the question "What does it mean?" that he joined contemporary criticism to the ancient Greek invention of that way of political life that requires both autonomous judgment and powers of criticism, the city? Roland Barthes does not say it, but we dare to formulate this hypothesis in his place. If our democracies owe this invention—the city—to the ancient Greeks, they must also be indebted to Barthes for the mode in which to ask questions that have made us possible. And this should lead today's thinkers to reflect on the fact that perhaps democracies cannot live outside of the questioning of meaning. What does it mean?—a question that each citizen must ask himself as a morning prayer.

This used to be Roland Barthes's question. I am afraid that it is no longer theirs. Therefore, I would like to read to them the continuation of the fragment that Roland Barthes seems to have written, not without humor, especially for our era which, by turing away from meaning, denied itself access to the intelligibility of the historical movement that is carrying it away: "This mania [that of giving everything meaning] does not distinguish triviality: for example, if I notice—and I hasten to do so—that in the country I like to pee in the garden and nowhere else, I immediately want to know what does that mean."

Perhaps it will now be better understood why I started off by saying that I miss Roland Barthes.

It is true, I dare to admit, that there is not a day when I am not seized by some sort of rage before a new manifestation of this denial of thought that we refer to as the return of morals. Who does not see that this noble designation quite simply conceals the return of conservative conscience? Therefore, I miss Roland Barthes. I thought of him again one day in April when all the television stations had called a truce on the ruthless war on viewer ratings that they usually wage. They had united to sensitize (we no longer say inform, and rightly so, for now we only address sensitivity—sentimentality would be more appropriate—and not understanding); it was a question of sensitizing the French to this terrible illness that they often do not dare to look in the face: AIDS. We were given a long, moving presentation by our own Line Renaud, whose tears made her voice tremble, followed by ten seconds accorded to Professor Luc Montagnier, who had discovered the virus. Perhaps it was seeing the image our venerated L'Abbé Pierre, our guru of charitable acts, with his missionary's beard only scarcely fuller than in the past, surge up on the screen, that once again that evening made me regret so painfully the loss of a voice never abused: "I worry about a society which so avidly consumes signs of charity that it forgets to wonder about its consequences, its uses and its limits. I am beginning to wonder if the ever so beautiful and touching illustrations of L'Abbé Pierre are not the alibi that a large part of the nation uses as an excuse, yet one more time, to substitute with impunity charitable signs for the reality of justice."

That was in 1954, and intellectuals did not then belong to that small part of the nation that had always preferred treating social injustices with humanitarian potion and charitable plans than with political eradication. And yet, Roland Barthes was not an adversary of moral attitudes or of ethical motives. The word *ethics* he had dared to link to the word *politics*. He was almost embarrassed for having done so; that is how great the audacity of it seemed at the time. That was in 1975. And, just as every time that he advanced, against each intellectual mode, an idea that was dear to him, he took refuge behind his so-called naïveté. The fragment is entitled *Politics/morals*: "It is a simple thought, that comes back to me often, but I never succeed at formulating it (maybe it is a silly thought): are there not always ethics in politics? That which founds politics, the order of reality, the social reality of purescience, is it not Value? In the name of what would a militant decide to . . . militate? Political practice, tearing itself away from precisely all morals and psychology, does it not have an origin that is . . . psychological and moral?"

The question of politics cannot hedge that of ethics, which it meets at least twice along the road: a first time in the form of the foundation of the values defended by the militant, a second time in the form of the foundation of the militant acts themselves. Roland Barthes was clearly conscious of this. But by recalling politics to its double ethical dimension, what he was trying to do was to reposition politics on the ethical horizon, and not, as is the case today, make ethics the substitute for politics. For the present return of ethics, far from translating a new awareness of the necessary ethical dimension in politics, in reality serves as the hallmark of its deficit. The locus where, not so long ago, intellectuals decided the fate of truths now only features humanitarian aid or humanitarian interference. Viewers were able to measure the opposite effects of such a substitution, on the same evening in April. Imagine their stupor at seeing L'Abbé Pierre, the man of all good causes, decree with the serene assurance that quasi-sainthood brings, that the only way of protecting oneself against AIDS was faithfulness. He could just as well have said abstinence, the commotion would not have been greater.

The public was no longer with him. It no longer understood. It felt betrayed. We even heard booing in disapproval. L'Abbé Pierre was, however, faithful to his original commitments and to the values which upheld them: a certain Christian conception of mankind and life. It was the public who had not known how to (or had not wanted to) discern the profoundly Christian foundations of an exemplary charitable action, it was the public who thought him inane until his inanity was related back in such a visible way to its ideological, or in this case religious, presuppositions. The misunderstanding was their fault. We assess this anecdote according to the social function of "ethicism." By this neologism, I mean morals that have become ideology. It serves to cover up with that consensual veil that is the good the divergences in both motivations and aims of "good" acts. Ethicism works just as well upstream for draining down into the bed of morals the uncoordinated demonstrations of a need for action, as it does downstream, for it presents all the acts born of a real, albeit confused, need for social engagement seen solely from the angle of their moral sense and value. The result is that the divergences in interests and the differences in ideological positions between social actors find themselves completely masked. They too see themselves cut off from everything that could give them access to the motive of their actions. Is this not the feature of alienation? But the word today rings hollow.

Only one term seems to bring life to the body social: *love of good.* Ethicism produces consensuality, but one should not forget that it is also its product. What does this mean? Something quite simple. In our fin-de-siècle that has seen all its strong values inherited from Marxism and utopian socialism carried away by the winds of history, it seems that all that remains is to reconstruct the edifice of our social axiomatics on the evidence of good. Ethicism bases its whole effectiveness on the feeling that there is something of an evidence and, for our disoriented society, that the most evident of all the evidences is the notion of good. But is this not what should make us, readers of Roland Barthes, start thinking? He never stopped fighting against evidence—and here we come upon his faithfulness—he never stopped fighting it, I was saying, not because of a singular disposition that would have pushed him to a paradox, but because he saw in evidence the underhanded and therefore, paradoxically, most violent form of intellectual and moral servitude. We are all familliar with the fragment entitled *Violence, evidence, nature.* I cannot resist the pleasure of reading it in its entirety, not to comment upon it, the text speaks for itself, but for you to hear it: "He could not shake the gloomy thought that real violence stemmed from saying 'It's self-evident': that which is evident is violent, even if this evidence is represented gradually, liberally, democratically: what is paradoxical, what does not fall under meaning, is less, even if it has been imposed arbitrarily; a tyrant who would promote his preposterous laws would be, all things taken, less violent than a mass which would content itself to stating what is self-evident; in short, the 'natural' is the final outrage."

Roland Barthes sought to drive out the evidence from the cover of our social myths, despite whatever kind of support it had, "an article in the press, a photograph in a magazine, a film, a show, an exhibit." The natural for Roland Barthes was the most formidable form of both intellectual deception and social alienation. Indeed, it puts an end to criticism, as it does to every other vague impulse to act. For, against that which imposes itself under the cover of nature, there is nothing left to do but to throw our hands up. And when we throw our hands up, injustice and lies await us at the end of the road. To take as evident knowledge what is merely a fact, or a cultural effect, and you condemn the old Dominici without proof, solid in the intimate conviction forged by cultural, often bookish, prejudices about the psychology of peasants. Offer as evidence the image of a young black man dressed in a French army uniform saluting the flag, and you erase in one fell swoop the history of both colonization and struggles for autonomy, only to benefit the natural consubstantiality between the peoples of the French empire and the people of France. And you understand nothing either about photography (*La Chambre claire*) or about love (*Fragments d'un discours amoureux*).

Translated by Diane Barbaric

From Radical Incertitude, or Thought as Impostor

JEAN BAUDRILLARD

The problem is how to give up on a critical thought that is the very essence of our theoretical culture, and belongs to a history and a past life. Instead of making a determinist analysis of a deterministic society, can one finally make an indeterminate analysis of an indeterministic society, a fractal, stochastic, exponential society of critical mass and extreme phenomena—a society entirely dominated by the relationship of uncertainty?

This has nothing to do with metaphor and the abuse of "scientific" metaphors—that is to say, wondering whether it is legitimate to extend to other domains a principle of indetermination and incertitude coming from elsewhere. Rather, we should ask: What about quantum physics, fractal physics, and catastrophe theory? What about the radical principle of uncertainty in our universe, in the human universe, in the moral, social, economic and political universe? The problem is not to transfer concepts borrowed from physical, biological, or cosmological science into metaphors or science fictions, but to transfuse them literally into the core of the real world, making them suddenly appear in our real world as nonidentifiable theoretical objects, as original concepts, as strange attractors—as they simultaneously are in the cosmos and in the microcosm, which they revolutionized, but also our macrocosm, in our relative universe and in our linear history that they now are in the process of revolutionizing, of reshuffling in the same way without us being really conscious of them.

Our conventional universe made of subject and object, means and ends, true and false, good and bad—all of these regulated oppositions no longer correspond to the state of our world. The normal dimensions of our so-called real world, including the dimensions of time, space, determination, representation, and also of critical and reflexive thought, are all deceptive. The entire discursive universe around us—psychology, the social, and the mental are all deceiving: they still operate in a Euclidean dimension and at present there is almost no theoretical perspective left on this normal universe that became quantic without us being aware of it.

All these concepts coming from elsewhere—from the confines of uncertainty and the indetermination of the object, from calculus—concepts at once "scientific" and fictional, are not to be taken metaphorically, as the human sciences are eventually doing, and scientists themselves when they extrapolate their intuitions to fit the human dimension. These must be at once transferred literally and conceived in the two universes. Uncertainty, fractals, catastrophic form, the relationship of incertitude, the indetermination of subject/object are not the privilege of science; they are active throughout the social order, on the order of the events, and we cannot assign a priority between the conjectural order of science or the subjective order of morality and history. It is part of uncertainty that we cannot tell whether scientific intuitions secretly belong to a society at a given moment in history. All of this makes a simultaneous irruption and one must deplore the impotence of our thought and incurably determinist discourse confronted with this revolution of our material universe. It is up to us to entertain a radically different philosophical vision of this situation: the nonmetaphorical use of scientific concepts doesn't carry with it an effect of truth because there is no longer a definition of this science just as there is no longer a definition of our real world.

Henceforth it is no longer the human that conceives the world; it is the unhuman that conceives us. We can now only grasp ourselves from an omega point exterior to the human, from objects and hypotheses which play the role of strange attractors. We are no longer about discovering, but about being discovered. Critical thought has already flirted with this type of object, at the limits of the human or the inhuman—with archaic societies, for instance, questioning Western humanism. Today we must look beyond critical thought; we must look elsewhere, toward objects that are much more foreign to us—carriers of a radical incertitude upon which we can no longer impose our own perspectives.

Therefore, it is not a metaphor when theoretical thought incorporates the notion of uncertainty, antimatter, black matter, viruses, critical mass, or when it incorporates biology, micro-physics, and cosmology. Critical thought still presumes a subject that explores the world from the privileged position of the subject and language (even though, according to Jacques Lacan, it is language that thinks the subject), but mutual and simultaneous correlations are at work in every area of the same principle of uncertainty. Homologies reinforce each other without any other definition or verification than this convergence in which it is not one of truth that is involved, but of a kind of objective thought, a thought of the object in which the subject is irrelevant. We certainly shouldn't trust the subject if we want to escape truth. We should trust the object and the filter of the object, in particular the theoretical filters of all these new objects that have cropped up from beyond our horizon.

It is the end of the anthropic principle, denial of any anthropy, and at the same time all entropy—entropy being the only banal destination, and the unique ends by inertia left to matter in the (mysterious) absence of antimatter, and to the human itself in the absence of the inhuman. Now we are going more and more rapidly toward the radical elimination of the inhuman, toward an anthropological fundamentalism whose aim is to subject everything to the jurisdiction of the human. We are moving toward a generalized homogenization and a totalitarian humanism. And this with the best intentions in the world, under the sign of the human as a single thought; under the sign of human rights extended to children, animals, to nature and to natural elements, and to all the other species; under the sign of a rehabilitation of moral and anthropological promotion; under the sign of universal ecology, spearheading the universal colonization and the final annexation of the single thought of the human. We can't denounce emphatically enough this enterprise of planetary integration meant to exterminate the inhuman in all its aspects, everything that until now escaped humanitarian control, this domestication imposed under the sign of the law and the forced recognition of every foreign and strange reality—extreme peripeteia of human imperialism, humanism, and humanitarianism (in the end, they are all identical) by means of which we are depriving ourselves of any thinking, any thinking of the inhuman as such, because this thinking could only come from the inhuman. It is only from the point-of-view of irreducible objects that we can have a vision of ourselves. Except for a major event, a positive or negative catastrophe, except for a radical alteration of our point of view and the inversion of the present movement, it certainly looks as if nothing will oppose the banal destiny of thought and energy degrading toward their lowest forms, which seems to be our own. Our only hope lies in a criminal and inhumane kind of thought. Thought itself must participate in this convergence, become exponential, mutate, escalate in power in relation to critical thought. Thought must become a critical mass just like the system itself. No longer is it a question of making the system contradict itself, forcing it to experience a crisis as happened to critical thought (and yet we know that today it's regenerating itself in the spiral of the crisis), but engage it through failure, collapse, and catastrophe. We must destabilize it through the instillation of a viral kind of thought. Through infiltration and injection, this viral thought will become virtual and exponential, entirely hooked on uncertainty, on the fractal, on the chaotic, on chance and microscopic gradations, that is on an inhuman thought. This thought coming from beyond, from the inhuman, is a thought that can only be conceived through the inhuman.

Thought and consciousness may already be in us a form of the inhuman, an appendix, an excrescence, a luxurious dysfunction that infringes upon the entire evolution by suddenly becoming conscious of it, falling back upon itself—

transfixed by its own image? Far more than the living mass, does not the neurological development of the brain already constitute a critical threshold, a critical mass in the eyes of the species and of evolution? So why not play the game to its very end, push the process and precipitate other chain reactions, other forms—those of alterity, of an objective fate that can't even be conceived at this point?

Two parts: one physical, one metaphysical. The world's definitive uncertainty, its unpredictability. Thought's final uncertainty: in what way is it an extreme and exponential phenomenon? In what way is it part of the world's uncertainty, of the critical mass that makes the world tumble into uncertainty?

Terminal uncertainty makes exchange impossible, having no equivalence in any other language. The world has no equivalence in its totality. Actually, it is the very definition of the universe: something which has no negotiable equivalent, no exchange, no double, no representation, no mirror. A mirror would still be part of the world. There is no verification and no proof: this is the radical uncertainty of the world. Whatever happens in the world or is verified in its own domain, the globality of the world's uncertainty, is without appeal.

Taken in its totality, the sphere of the economy—the sphere of exchange par excellence—cannot be exchanged against anything else; it is unexchangeable. There is no "meta-economical" or cosmic equivalence of the economy. Therefore, in the last analysis, the sphere of the economy is also part of definitive uncertainty. It would rather ignore it, but this fatal indetermination that echoes inside of this economical sphere, affecting the way it works by its unpredictability (variables, equations, postulates) and ultimately by its exponential drift into speculation, into the unregulated interaction of its criteria and its elements.

Any sphere whether, political, aesthetic, and so on, is affected by this same equivalence, this same incompatibility, this same eccentricity. Taken in their totality, these spheres cannot be exchanged. They literally have no meaning outside of themselves. The political is the space of all tactics and exchanges; it is rotten with signs and significations, which makes no sense when seen from the outside. Nothing can justify it. The political is like a black hole: it absorbs everything that comes near it, converting it into its own substance. The political could not convert itself or think about itself in the name of a superior reality that would give it a meaning. Therefore the political is also part of definitive incertitude, which translates into the growing indecisiveness of its categories, strategies, and stakes. The exponentiality of mass politics, its mise-en-scène, and its discourse, are the endless expansion of the political sphere at the level of this uncertainty, this fundamental illusion. Uncertainty, indecisiveness, exponentiality.

The sphere of the real is no longer exchangeable against that of the sign. It becomes unstable and undecidable, exponential: everything becomes real, everything is unconditionally realized, but no longer signifies anything. All metalanguages of reality (human sciences, social sciences, etc.) develop as well in an order eccentric to the image of their centrifugal object. Metalanguages become speculative. A parallel universe grows, a virtual universe, but it has no relationship to it.

This universe is its screen, its total reverberation; and yet the screen doesn't reflect the universe, it develops for itself. The virtual is no longer bound to become the real. Without ballast or referent, it falls under the sway of uncertainty. The virtual produces indecisiveness and itself falls prey to indecisiveness.

We could continue as such into infinity. In the sphere of the biological, not only does the mass of the living expand exponentially, but the schemes of explanation, of genetic command—which commands death—divide into infinity, translating the fact that the phenomena of life and the living cannot be exchanged, neither against any ultimate and definitive causalities, nor against any ends or telenomy. It can only be exchanged against itself or rather against nothing. This uncertainty of life contaminates the science of life, the biological, making it more and more indecisive from discovery to discovery—this has nothing to do with the temporary incapacity of science, but with its increasing proximity to the definitive incertitude that is its absolute horizon.

To summarize: The world itself is under the sign of an impossible exchange because it is free from value and equivalence. It cannot be exchanged against anything else—it can only change into itself at any moment. Ultimately it exchanges itself against nothing. After insane speculations for which the virtual economy is both the apex and the symbol, the entire edifice of value is exchangeable for nothing.

Behind the exchange value, and providing it in some way with a background, a bail, an invisible counterpart, with the antimatter of matter—behind each exchange of the same thing always looms the exchange of nothing. Could symbolic economy of the nothing exist? A sign of the nothing? Obviously potlatch, death, illness, the negative can be exchanged—even the debt of the Social Security is traded on the stock market.

The illusion of the economic order is precisely to have tried to ground a principle of economic reality on the total disregard of this fundamental uncertainty: the exchange of the nothing that lies behind all the exchanges (we should clearly distinguish from nihilism: nothing is not nothingness; it corresponds rather to Mr. Cassé's void, endowed with all possible potentialities). The principle of reality only works inside a circumscribed and artificial sphere whose global singularity has been purified, foreclosing the principle of nothing and of evil.

We must pay the price of this foreclosure, this forgetting in terms of the illusion of political economy, the political, and the backlash of singularity in exile, especially in terms of the strong return of indecisiveness: the forgetting of the nothing and radical uncertainty make all value, judgment, and meaning in this world indecisive (including thought and consciousness).

This parallel, eccentric, and singular universe of the nothing no longer comes to us through signs, only through traces. Our alleged "real" universe is perpetually colliding with the universe of the nothing, just as the material universe collides with the evasive antimatter universe; just as the economic collides with the anti-economy. Hence the impossibility for economy, as for any other structure or any other existence, of being identical to itself or coherent to itself. Economy is haunted by its double, and this pushes all systems toward exponentiality, overbidding, toward a level of extreme phenomena and critical mass—pushes them toward annihilation.

Besides this strong return of the nothing that undermines the system from the inside, are there any manifestations, any breakthroughs from this parallel universe into our own? I believe that there are events that are on the order of the shock-matter/antimatter, particle/antiparticle phenomenon. This happens when a power meets its antipower, and can result in an immediate dissolution into light. May 68: not just subversion, revolution but an annihilation that produced an exceptionally luminous intensity. The melting of Communism? Krach?

The question then becomes, Why is there something rather that nothing? Otherwise stated, has there ever been an economy or organization of value that had an intrinsic value, destination or meaning? In the absolute, the answer is no. But we must address the question from the inside of the economic system itself (or from any other system), at the point where, following its own exponential logic, it burns its own postulates and becomes brutally conscious of its own illusion.

Has the real ever existed? In this ocean of uncertainty, the real, value, and law are the exceptions; they are exceptional phenomena. Illusion is the fundamental rule. The real is the mystery; economy and value are the mystery.

There's no way of rebalancing this radical uncertainty, no possible polarity of the nothing or of something; no dialectics. It's the same with antimatter: either invisibility or total illumination. On the other hand, a principle of equilibrium, exchange, and value is being reinvented in every restricted domain—causality, rationality, finality. These restricted systems rely on regulated oppositions. It's the domain of values, as value never goes by itself: good and evil, true and false, riches and money, real and its representation, subject and object, effect and cause, masculine and feminine—the entire realm of difference and regulation through difference. The principle of reality relies on two poles, on a bipolar relation which, as long as it exists, guarantees the stability and the dialectical movement of the whole.

So far, so good. One enters the critical zone only when this system breaks down—the critical zone of the critical mass, the depolarized zone where polar opposition and dialectics don't operate anymore, where confusion and short circuit, the collision of every pole, open up on an exponential drift.

Every time this short circuit, this confusion of poles happens, it creates a mass. Value, ultimate meaning become aleatory and the process exponential. When there's no more system of equivalence between the real and the sign, everything tends toward the infinite: the real comes on its own all for itself; it hyperrealizes itself and the sign becomes total simulation, both being confused in the virtual. The same is true for good and evil: when their polarity fades away, we are led toward a total positivity or toward an unconditional negation quite different from traditional negativity and the labor of the negative. No more ethics are possible; no more ethics in general of extreme phenomena.

In order to exorcize this exponentiality, this aleatory capable of reducing this definitive uncertainty, the virtual remains—positioning a perfect double, virtual, and technological that allows for the exchange of the world against its artificial double. Finally the world can be exchanged for something, for its double—and therefore the radical uncertainty ends, although this obviously ends the world as well in some way. Thus I exist in a parallel universe, the cyberspace. At least on 250 sites I am being sighted. The Internet thinks about me. Internet sites irresistibly make me think of prehistoric or archeological sites—my fossilized double wanders along the net, or my electronic superego, the one I will never meet. This other universe has no relation with this one—it is exactly parallel to it, but they never join together. For the first time maybe since the first effraction of geometry, the universe is not unique. But is it still a world, this world, for which by definition there is no double?

Does this double really think that way? In any case he doesn't reflect it. It presents rather its total screen and total reverberation, so that this initial world, our own, stops having any reflection, becomes like an opaque body or a dead star. The virtual then would be the final solution capable of providing a total equivalence of the world in virtual reality. Hence the absolute security of the Net as a niche where it is so easy and so fascinating to disappear. But what if this parallel universe that feeds on the disappearance of the other is meant in turn to disappear?

In other words, is the virtual universe really another world? (In this case the world is not one anymore.) Or is it, at bottom, only a fraction of this world artificially de-doubling itself? In which case this world continues to exist as it is, and all we do is give ourselves the comedy of the virtual.

Every mass is potentially exponential, and everything exponential is "critical," opposite to critical judgment or critical thought, which precisely presumes the tension between two poles. Whenever it turns into a mass, critical mass presumes the abolition of this distance.

In the same way, uncertainty is not relative to cultural differences considered from the point of view of critical thought—restricted relativity, true on this side of the Atlantic, false on the other—always truth's point of view, even if it is differential. What we have here instead is generalized incertitude—a sidereal point of view that relativizes the system through its escalation to the extremities, through its passage to its outer limits.

There is no longer a critical point of view, nor a moral, political, or philosophical one. Going back to our initial scheme: thought can't be exchanged with either truth or reality. Thought becomes unexchangeable with anything. Having already surpassed a critical point of view by radically delocalizing thought toward the inhuman, going so far as to say that it is the world that thinks us, that is by totally inverting the game, what is thought at this point? Is it part, as well, of critical mass? What is thought once it has become inhuman, nonsubjective, eccentric, a thought-event, a thought-catastrophe? Does not the irruption of such a thought change the course of the world? What's at stake is not an ideological transformation through ideas, but whether the irruption of consciousness actually interrupts the course of the world. Is consciousness a reflection or an acceleration of the world? Is it thought that creates the uncertainty of the world, or is it just its reflection? (Does not the thought of thought change the course of thought?)

"Human consciousness gave bad consciousness to the universe," says Jean Rostand.

What about thought beyond this critical moment? (*Critical* in every sense since it puts an end to critical thought, to judgment, and inaugurates a thought of matter—thought that is simultaneously subjective and objective. He who thinks matter and who is taken by matter, a thought that reverses or inverts the course of the real (and of time?), simultaneously dismissing subject, object, or mass—the masses are neither object or subject—is consequently an indecisive phenomena and a strange attractor.

What we must aim for is a reciprocal alteration of matter and thought. Whether it is it matter that destabilizes consciousness or consciousness that destabilizes matter and gives it in a way bad consciousness, as Rostand has suggested—we can't decide on that. On the one hand there is a metaphysical alteration of the world by consciousness; on the other, there is a physical alteration of consciousness by the world, in the sense that consciousness thinks of itself as the mirror of the world, a critical mirror participating in its material destiny, a destiny of matter from which consciousness doesn't detach itself absolutely and therefore misses the radical uncertainty of the world, its fundamental illusion. The universe does not know the mirror stage; or could thought be this mirror stage for the universe? One must go beyond this stage, get beyond identity (and psychology as well), this ultra-comfortable stage of the subject facing its object, in order to reach the ultimate stage of the object that thinks us, the world that thinks us. (But what is this subject who thinks this world that thinks us?) Matter's thought is not reflexive, it is reversible. It becomes the concatenation and the reversibility of appearances. Matter's thought is now only but one particular example in this concatenation of the world—maybe the smallest link? Both factual and phenomenal, it is part of the world. From the point of view of singularity, of the incomparable event in the world, it no longer has the privilege of the universal. In the world's disorder, thought is irreducible to the subject's consciousness. Thought must be no longer be considered metaphysically as outside of time, but physically in the cycle of the evolution of the cosmos, as a specific attribute and destiny of the species.

We must return to the irruption of consciousness in the world as the original crime. But it is not the first crime. We are dealing with a double, original crime, even though there is a distant correlation between the two. The first one is what Michel Cassé spoke of, the inaugural event: at some point, light separates from matter and the universe becomes in some way transparent to its own light, observable. From now on everything becomes visible and observable (but there is no one to see it), with the exception of antimatter, which is rejected into darkness, rejected into definitive nonexistence, such as Lucifer in Christian theology. This irruption of light corresponds to the true murder of antimatter, whose trace is found in blood-red cosmic rays that come to us from the bottom of time. But this murdered antimatter is yet hiding, or at least that is what some believe. It is on this murder (not quite perfect, we hope) that the material universe is founded. This is the first great fracture of symmetry.

The second great fracture of symmetry, this one metaphysical, happens in the mass of the living, when consciousness in some way separates from it and inaugurates another form of transparency, not only the physical one of pure light, but also the metaphysical one of thought: reflexivity—lucidity and transparency—makes it possible to analyze and know the world. By the same token it leads everything as in the first fracture of symmetry. Thought disposes of the black mass into darkness, the black matter of the living and of thought. This second great cleavage one can assimilate to a murder (not perfect either).

In this double peripetia we can see the decisive moments of the cosmos' ascendance toward total transparency, like a rising process of rationalization, negentropy, and redemption. Against this we can see a process of loss—dilution, entropy, and the loss of differential energy through this foreclosure—beginning first with antimatter, then proceeding with the dark continent of thought and the living. Moving toward a state of hyperlucidity and hypertransparency, we distance ourselves further and further from the initial conditions, probably bringing us closer to the final conditions.

In the last stage of microphysics, "particles are what they are and at the same time are not what they are." It is marvelous to see theoretical intuition confirmed by "science" on the most elementary and objective level. At the same time, this is all quite problematic. What does it mean that this intuition could finally be "verified" (looks as if it were verified) in whatever reality, in any physical referential? Was theory made for this, was it meant for this, to coincide with fact, or was it more likely aimed at the unverifiable, at the de-realization and destabilization of the objective world? Or else, in a kind of cosmology or reversed ontology, is it not theory that ultimately destabilizes particles?

See Ceronetti and his astrological reverse: "The personal horoscope is only worth the pleasure it gives us, however insignificant we are, of being inextricably connected . . . to huge phenomena, to the passage of planets in the sun and perceiving ourselves as subjects and fragments of a history beyond the famelic limit of a legal identity."

And what if it were human acts and thoughts that provoked the fall of meteorites, the dissolution of planets, black holes, comets? What if it was the French Revolution that had forced Neptune from his hiding? Does not man, in his innate ambiguity, infuse his reversible symbolic order, and end up by altering the universe, affecting or infecting it with this uncertainty that is his own? In short, do uncertainty and aleatory belong to that order, objective, of the universe or to that of the subjective, of man? Consciousness would not only have projected itself onto the world (furthermore it is perfectly identical to itself, and both man and his consciousness are a part of it as well) but would be contaminated by its nonbeing, having contaminated the world through its own way of not being in the world?

This begs multiple questions with regard to the objectivity of knowledge (not only that of classical knowledge, but also for quantum and stochastic knowledge). It is not only man, the subject of knowledge, who corrupts objects through his own intervention, but man who has dealings with a universe that he himself has corrupted and destabilized. Assuming that there are objective laws of the universe, it is man who made these laws impossible to be formulated or implemented. Man wouldn't be the one embodying reason in a chaotic universe; to the contrary, man would embody disorder through a contagious mental static capable of demoralizing particles themselves. His act of knowledge and consciousness constitutes an unprecedented coup: identifying a point (even simulated) outside of the universe from which to look at and think about the universe. If the universe has no double, nothing existing beyond it, the mere attempt to assign a point outside of itself expresses a will to put an end to the universe. Or at least to make the universe go through the mirror stage, just like any human being, and therefore to confuse it definitively with its identity.

According to Dirac, "We must revise our ideas on causality." Causality only applies to a system that remains undisturbed. Once disturbed, a measured system is no longer causal. The chain of causality is broken by measure because measure brings about an uncontrollable disturbance, as in all forms of interaction with the fragile, quantum landscape. Measure shatters determinism in order to introduce a fundamental, stochastic element. Before measure, the system had a variety of states at its disposal. Measure only realized one of those. Measure is the act by which the range of the possible to the real is being reduced. Every state of the system disappears except for one, the state that is "realized."

Dirac's sentence, though, hints that were it not disturbed the universe would be causal without measure. The universe would be real without the presence of man. This seems to be a rather beautiful and fantastic hypothesis (mildly disturbed by the fact that it is precisely man who created measure, instituting the only real world); a bit of contradiction amongst scientists. This still begs the same question: Is not this man who carries disturbance through his intervention, through a measure (that he believes is objective), himself being a probabilist, and doesn't he render the world probabilist in his own likeness? (Until now we were imagining the contrary: man bringing and imposing meaning and causality to a disordered universe.) In any case, whether the principle of incertitude is objective, cosmic, or bound to mankind, it remains total.

Translated by Alison Gingeras

Sketching an Intellectual Itinerary

GÉRARD GENETTE

If I attempt to reflect a bit, as I have been asked to do, on the intellectual itinerary that at once separates me from and brings me back to the first text, published in 1959 and subsequently incorporated into my first book, without going back to the motives and the circumstances that had led me to this apparent starting point, it seems to me that this exercise, let us say, of self-articulation (autodiction) can take two rather distinct forms, which I will try to assume before you as well. The first consists of measuring and defining the possible theoretical coherence of this body of work synchronically: I am not certain of being able to do this with the utmost rigor, but I can always make the effort without yielding too much to the rationalizing illusion that pushes us often to impose an artificial unity on all things assembled by chance, which governs us. The second consists of diachronically reconstituting, as faithfully as possible, the actual progress that led me, from one subject to the next in this itinerary: I do not know if this reconstruction will be accessible to the interested outside observer, but it seems to me capable of bringing some information on this point. Useful or not, it has been, at least—as they say in the United States—gotten from the horse's mouth.

A first very apparent fact shows that, starting from literary "criticism," as we have understood it for more than a century, I proceeded very quickly to what has been known, for a much shorter period of time—though by a term revived from the ancients—as "poetics." These two terms, whose current transparency may be deceptive, actually call for a few clarifications. What I call *criticism* is the internal analysis, formal or interpretive, of singular texts or a singular corpus or the entire opus of a writer considered in its singularity. Academic studies, at least in France, have barely started, and still only slightly dedicated themselves to this type of research, centered as they have since Lanson on an essentially historical and philological approach, done plainly in the spirit of positivism and, as has already been noted by Péguy, with an attention that remains voluntarily peripheral to the works themselves. When I began to work in this field, the split between these two approaches, which would soon erupt during the debate known as the "new quarrel of the ancients and the moderns," was still latent. The first approach was still rather reserved, as it had already been from the time of Péguy, Proust, Charles du Bos, Albert Thibaudet, or Jean Prévost, to that of those authors outside of academia or at the fringes of the university, like Roland Barthes, or teaching at foreign universities, like Georges Poulet, Jean Starobinski, Jean Rousset, or, at that time, Jean-Pierre Richard. I myself taught at that time in a preparatory class in a high school, outside of the university in the strict sense of the word—that is to say, outside of higher education—and I did not feel at all attracted to the latter, of which I had had, as a student, a rather deterring experience, and for which I have never truly felt a great affinity. Of the four rather bleak years that I spent as an assistant at the Sorbonne, from 1963 to 1967, I do not have any recollection of an intellectual order, having been much more inspired by the seminars given in the École des Hautes Études, and particularly by Roland Barthes, to whom I furthermore owe my definitive departure from the university for the école, a typically peripheral place, at least in the domain of literary studies, and which, for this very reason, was a place of true research and inventiveness for some.

My first essays then, collected in 1966 in *Figures 1*, concerned French baroque poetry, then Proust, Robbe-Grillet, and Flaubert, followed among others by Barthes himself as a semiologist, and Valéry and Borges as critics. The last three were obviously of the metacritical type, and were a sort of step toward literary theory; all the more since I did not hesitate to translate these works according to my own theoretical tendencies; but one cannot deny Valéry, at least, the role of modern refounder of poetics, nor Borges a panoptical vision of the universal library. But let us not get ahead of ourselves. I mentioned just a moment ago of the "new quarrel of the ancients and the moderns." During the nineteen fifties and nineteen sixties, the expression seemed self-explanatory: this criticism was "new" in that it opposed itself, as I pointed out, to this discipline held in contrast to be "old," even though it went back only to the end of the nineteenth century, known as literary history. From a distance, it does not appear to me today that the "nouvelle critique" was as innovative in its method as it was thought to be. In many respects, it only extended the critical activity of the nineteen thirties, whose manifesto, though published posthumously in 1954 was, in short, Proust's *Contre Saint-Beuve*. This work by Proust signifies largely "against" a historicizing and above all biographizing approach, which seeks an external explanation for texts in life and in what Hyppolite Taine called "the race," the "environment," and the "moment" of their authors, and "in favor of" a more immanent reading—that is to say a reading that is more engaged in the internal relations of their text. Thus the nouvelle critique, as before it and in a different context, the American new criticism, wanted essentially to be an immanent criticism, deliberately, if provisionally perhaps, enclosed in what some (but not I) then willingly called the "closure of the text." The French new criticism did not take long to split itself, not without interactions between the two branches, into criticism known as "thematic"—of a psychological, even psychoanalytical bent, even though it meant for Sartre and his circle a heterodoxical "existential psycho-analysis"—and a criticism designated as "structural," which concerned itself more with the formal configurations of texts. My first essays were slightly a product of the first type of criticism, but fundamentally I felt more attracted by the second, never having had too much taste for individual psychology. I therefore wrote, for an issue of *L'Arc* dedicated to Claude Lévi-Strauss in 1965, a highly symbolic pa-tronage, an article somewhat naively programmatic in its appearance and inten-tion, titled "Structuralism and Literary Criticism." I tried, like a good neophyte, to cover the whole field evoked by the title, by envisioning a sort of equitable di-vision between the two branches of "new criticism," but it became quickly appar-ent to me that the most relevant involvement for the "structural method" with lit-erary studies was not so much in the formal criticism of singular works, as in the general theory of the "literary field" considered in itself as a larger structure, just as structural anthropology studies each society through the entirety of its practices and institutions, and just as structural linguistics studies the entirety of internal re-lations constitutive of the language system. From that moment, the objective was no longer to keep to the immanence of works, but rather to leave it for a more far-reaching exploration, for which the term *criticism* was no longer suitable at all, and for which several of us proposed, some time afterwards, the synonymous terms of *literary theory* or of *poetics*. The first term came to us from the celebrated manual of Wellek and Warren and from various texts by the Russian formalists, and the second, of course, via Valéry, from the founding text by Aristotle. This double or triple reference forced us rather clearly to leave the French tradition, strictly speak-ing, and open out onto a more stimulating, apparently universal movement of thought. That made, in summary, for quite a lot of immanence to overcome, but I would not, until later, formulate in these terms a conceptual opposition (imma-nence and transcendence) that would, little by little and in different ways, domi-nate the entirety of my theoretical work.

I reiterated the first application of this overly ambitious program in Septem-ber 1966 during a talk at the famous ten-day colloquium at Cérisy-la-Salle cas-tle in Normandy about *The Current Paths of Criticism* with the provocative title "Reasons for Pure Criticism" ("pure criticism," in my mind, precisely was poet-ics). The first application, then, probably was a revisitation, if I dare to use this neologism, or, even further, a reinterpretation of classical rhetoric. Many essays from this period bear witness to this, one of which would lend its title to my first three books. My idea was to research the field of classical rhetoric, and in fact, more specifically the theory of figures, for a sort of ancestor of semiology (a science that was at that time rapidly expanding, and which has not yet fulfilled all of its promises), or at least of modern semiotics. I had to subsequently realize that rhetoric is not limited to this one aspect, and that such a restriction was evidence of a rather restricted view, and most likely prevaricated by an overly partial comparison. I do not regret however, having brought back to light, thanks to this semi-misunderstanding, texts as significant as those of Dumarsais and Fontanier, and having contributed, after and with others, to the reintroduction of this method of analysis (because it is one) into our conception of language.

The second involvement was with the analysis of narrative, which before long was baptized, by Tzvetan Todorov, as "narratology." I have to specify that this subject was suggested to me by Roland Barthes, who had, for a reason that is still unknown to me, initiated and undertaken the direction of a special issue of the review *Communications* dedicated to this topic. I went with hesitation into this field, not finding it very attractive, having always understood narrative, the novel included, as the least enticing function of literature, as demonstrated in my 1966 essay "Silences of Flaubert," which is an apology for non-narratives, even of antinarratives, in the work of this writer who was a novelist despite himself, for whom narrative was "a very tedious thing."[1] When I objected on the basis of this distaste, Barthes more or less said to me, "Here is your topic, deal with it the way you want." And that was the article titled "The Frontiers of Narrative," in which I tried to limit as much as it was possible, by making it relative, the territory of this cumbersome practice. Afterward, I got a bit more caught up in the game, trying my hand, in 1968, on the narrative aspects in a baroque epic and in the novel by Stendhal. It was in 1969, at the time of my first stay on the American continent, that I undertook the analysis of the entire *Remembrance of Things Past,* which served as my touchstone, or rather as my first fieldwork, as ethnologists are wont to say, for an essay about the general theory of narrative structures. After various partial and experimental presentations, this essay finally saw the light of day in 1972, in *Figures 3,* with the title "Narrative Discourse." I said "narrative structures," but I should add that I was speaking here more of formal structures, those that have a bearing upon the *modes of narration* (the handling of time, the management of points of view, the role of the narrator), and not the "deep" structures, logical or thematic, explored by authors like A. J. Greimas or Claude Bremond. Narratology, being a strictly literary discipline, is above all linked to the study of the former, so much so that the term today is spontaneously understood to have this meaning, but this restriction is not a priori more justified than the restriction of rhetoric to the study of literary figures, nor that which has until now focused the attention of narratologists on fictional narrative, leaving historical narrative and other types of nonfiction narratives for others, generally philosophers like Arthur Danto and Paul Ricoeur. I do not insist on these points, to which I had the opportunity to return later in *New Narrative Discourse* (1983) and in *Fiction and Diction* (1991).

During the same stay at Yale, I had started another project, that concerned another major aspect of poetics, that which was readily called "poetic language": my intention therefore was apparently, in all modesty, to cover the two principal continents (fiction and diction) of the literary universe. The notion of "poetic language" itself, whose detailed history remains to be written in all our cultural traditions, had come to us, in France, essentially from Mallarmé, then from Valéry; the analyses of Roman Jakobson had, in their own way, put it back in the saddle. The idea, at its postromantic and "symbolist" foundation, accompanied a rejection, or at least a weakening of the classical conception—a "formalist" conception in its own way—according to which the essential criterion of poetic discourse relies on the presence of versification. Once abandoned or relativized by the poets themselves, this criterion, and at the same time the thematic criteria that sometimes complemented it (some subjects would be more poetic than others), remained nothing but a specific semantic treatment of language, whose principal aspect would be, according to Mallarmé's expression, to "remunerate the defect of natural languages," namely their conventional character, or according to the controversial adjective used by Saussure, their "arbitrariness." Poetry, by diverse means, would confer, or at least would give the illusion of conferring, on language a mimetic motivation that it lacks ordinarily and, it appears, cruelly, in its common usage. This hypothesis unavoidably raised a question, one not of a literary, but of a linguistic nature, or even from the domain of the philosophy of language: What exactly is—or more modestly, what can we know exactly about—the motivated or unmotivated nature of, or the degree of arbitrariness and of motivation in, human language? This question itself led to an investigation of the diverse theories on this subject, starting with antiquity. It was on this investigation, preliminary in principle, that, in 1969, I embarked more or less without interruption, and to which I devoted myself exclusively after finishing *Figures 3*. I noticed very quickly however, that the debate—because there has been a debate at least since Plato's *Cratylus*—between the supporters of mimetic motivation and the supporters of convention was in a way of unequal aesthetic interest, the supporters of convention, like Hermogenes in *Cratylus,* not having anything to oppose their adversaries with other than refutation or at least laconic skepticism, whereas the supporters of motivation, like Cratylus himself, supported and illustrated their thesis with a speculative arsenal indicative of great imaginative power. The story of this controversy thus became essentially one of "Cratylian" or "Cratylist" speculation, as Roland Barthes baptized it. That is how a project for a theory of "poetic language" transformed itself little by little into a (cavalier) story and into a theory, or at least an attempt at typological classification, of the diverse variants, in our literary, linguistic, and philosophical Western tradition, of the Cratylian or "mimologistic" fantasy—hence the dual title of the book published in 1976: *Mimologics: Voyage in Cratylusland*.[2] At the same time, the theoretical project came with a study of genre, as it is rather clear that mimological speculation, through the centuries, from Plato to Francis Ponge and beyond, constitutes a misunderstood literary genre, that one can study in its diverse stages and through the historical evolution that led it from one stage to the next, not without bifurcation, omissions, and resurgence, as this tradition most often does not know itself and reinvents itself constantly at new expense without being aware of repetitions or contradictions.

I had thus entered the field of poetics by the study of a mode—narrative— that is not really a genre because it encompasses many: the epic, the story, the novel, the tale, the novella, the fable, and so on, and by the study of a subliminal and quasi-clandestine genre, mimologism. This situation called for a vaster reflection on the status of these sorts of generic, parageneric, and meta-generic categories, which distribute the field of literature in every possible way. Narrative is rather clearly a more formal category, because it can be defined by the act of relating an event or an action, whatever the content of this event or action might be. Mimologism is just as clearly a thematic category, because it is the content of its position in the metalinguistic debate that defines a reflection or a speculation on the nature of language as mimological. Thus there was room for me to wonder about the relationship between the general categories, some of which are a product of a more formal definition, others from a thematic definition, and most, maybe, from the meeting of these two sorts of criteria: thus, one knows, *tragedy* can be defined as a noble action represented dramatically, the epic as a noble action in the narrative mode, and *comedy* as a familiar action represented in the dramatic mode, which leaves the space open for a familiar action in a narrative mode; it is this empty space that Aristotle fills with a more ghostly genre, whose antique manifestations did not survive until our time, and which he baptizes "parody" in his *Poetics*, but which one tends, today, to find illustrated by the novel—at least according to the English definition of *novel*, a "comic epic in prose" according to fielding, the *romance* being in our eyes closer to a sort of epic in serious prose, heroic or sentimental. In this picture implicitly proposed by Aristotle, a picture that is certainly rudimentary and incomplete but fundamental and adaptable to the subsequent evolution of literature as the beginning of a general system of past, present, and future literary genres, there is a system that fascinated and excited the theoretical libido of all the ages, and that had led some to attempt to therefore complete it, namely by adding, on the dramatic and narrative sides, a third, rather undefined, mode in order to include and federate all that escaped them but which, it seems, does not entirely correspond with the other two: the "lyrical" form. It is to this complex, even muddled, or at least shaky, situation, that I consecrated a long article in 1976, "Genres, Types and Modes," published in *Poétique* in 1977 and which became, in 1979, the *Introduction to the Architext*. This small book did not pretend to be an exhaustive theory of literary genres, like the *Anatomy of Criticism* of Northrop Frye, but rather a historical and critical examination of the types of problems and difficulties that such a subject raises. The problem, thus left in suspense, would come back a little later in *Fiction and Diction*, where it would be looked at again from a new perspective: that of an examination of the modes and regimes of literariness.

The table of the four fundamental genres discussed or evoked by Aristotle had thus put me unexpectedly face to face with the "minor" genre of parody, which Aristotle defines in the terms that I mentioned above, yet the rare examples that he cites make one think rather of "parodical" literary practices according to the modern definition of the term: among others the heroicomical poem of which the *Lutrin* of Boileau-Despreáux is a classical accomplishment (a farcical action treated in a heroic style), or a travesty of the type done by Scarron (*Enéide travestie*), which inversely treats a heroic action from a famous earlier text in a farcical style. With respect to the Aristotelian categories, it was no longer a question of searching, like Fielding, for a modern genre that could occupy the place that Aristotle assigned to parody, but rather of asking onself how to define and classify the totality of the genres that we still commonly call, sometimes confusedly, "parodical." This is the work that I undertook in 1979, and that culminated in 1982 in *Palimpsestes*, subtitled *Literature in the Second Degree*. It is indeed secondarity that characterizes all of these different works, which go from the pseudo-Homeric *Battle of the Frogs and Mice* to Giraudoux's *Electra* or to Tournier's *Friday*, and which all have the common trait of sort of grafting themselves onto several anterior texts, from which they borrow the topic, in order to subject it to this or that type of *transformation*, or the manner (the "style"), in order to apply it to another subject. These two fundamental practices of transformation and imitation combined with the three cardinal functions, the ludic, satirical, and serious schemes, furnished me once again with the framework of a double entry table, where the innumerable manifestations of what I then chose to call *hypertextuality* divided up and regrouped themselves. It is a somewhat unfortunate name, because, among other reasons, the term *hypertextuality* would soon, if it had not already, acquire a rather different meaning (though not completely unrelated) that would get the upper hand and open the door for various misunderstandings. I would also add, as an autocriticism, that my overall definition of the hypertext, "a text grafted on an anterior text in a manner that is not that of commentary," was not very satisfying because it entailed a purely negative criticism that risked not being a sufficient condition for its application if one were to discover one or several sorts of derived texts, neither of them commentaries nor hypertexts. The positive criterion that was thus glaringly missing from my definition, but fortunately, not from my description, was that contrary to commentary, the hypertext does not *refer to* but is *based on* its hypotext, resulting always in a modification, direct or indirect, of the latter: a modification through a change in style, as in travesties, through a change in subject, as in the pastiche, or by means of a minimal transformation, as in parodies in the strict sense of the term, for example when Giraudoux makes one of his characters say, "One sole being is missing from you and everything is repopulated." I should have said therefore, more positively, "a hypertext is a text that derives from another by a modification process, formal or thematic." It is true that, at the same time, this amended definition is applicable to translations, which I did not then have in mind, but which I would go back to later: indeed, translations are truly in their own way hypertexts, whose principle of transformation is simply, or tries to be, of a purely linguistic nature.

The exploration of the hypertextual continent had alerted me to the existence of a larger object, that is the totality of ways in which a text can transcend its "closure," or immanence, and enter into a relationship with other texts. It is the text's transcendence that I then called "transtextuality": explicit and massive hypertextuality is one of the ways; punctual citation and allusion, generally implicit, qualified at that time as "intertextuality," are another; commentary, already mentioned, and renamed *metatext*, is a third; the "architextual" relations between the texts and the genres to which one assigns them are a fourth; and I just found a fifth by studying the first. Indeed, hypertexts almost always establish a sort of "contract of hypertextuality" with their readers that permits them to recognize the hypertextual project, and thereby gives it its full efficacy: if you write a parody of the *Iliad* or a pastiche of Honoré de Balzac, it is in your interest to *declare* your intention, which otherwise risks not being seen, and thus not having its effect, just as, in the Austinian theory of language acts, a question has to first let its illocutionary status as a question be known if it wants to reach its perlocutionary status, which is to obtain a response: a literary work is also a language act, and we know, at least since the studies of Philippe Lejeune on autobiography, the importance of these types of "pacts" for the understanding of their status as a genre, and thus for the pertinence of their reception. Thus, hypertextual works always announce their hypertextuality by means of a more or less developed self-commentary. For example, a title expresses with more brevity and efficiency what a preface, a dedication, an epigraph, a note, an insert, a letter or a statement to the press can also indicate. Consequently hypertextual works, as others, but maybe more than others, necessarily have recourse to the resources of these practices known as *paratextual* practices, to which I would dedicate, in 1987, a book titled *Seuils*, which knew itself to be doubly paratextual. A perceptive journalist (they all are) asked me on that occasion if by chance I was aware of having given my book, as a title, the name of my editor; I replied obviously that I wasn't, and that he had just revealed this stupefying coincidence to me; we then spoke a while of Freud, of repressed acts and revealing lapses.

Thus it is a detail of a book that gave me the general subject of the following book, and this genetic, somewhat oblique process seems to me to be a constant in my work—as it is perhaps for everyone—but to each, in these matters, their own experience. Nevertheless, once again, this same genre of collateral filiation would lead me from the study of the paratext to the last stage of my present theoretical course.

In order to present things according to their most tangible relationships, the sequence of events seems to me to be more or less the following. I had essentially written in *Seuils* that the paratext—which includes, I must point out, all editorial practices, or at least their legible traces—is in short *what makes a text become a book*. I do not at all deny this expeditious formula, and I would rather say that I did not see its theoretical implications until afterward, or, to use a more specific term which I here strip of all metaphysical connotations (as I did for *transcendence* elsewhere), the *ontological* implications, that is to say those relating to the existence of works. The question that this formula raises implicitly (from text to book) is, in fact, a question that is very easily worded and very difficult to resolve: What is the difference between a text and a book? In an article published by the *Magazine littéraire* in February 1983—that is, between *Palimpsestes* and *Seuils* (though I was already involved in the preparation of the latter)—I said, and I will have to cite myself a bit extensively, that the paratext is

the place where the essential nature of the literary work is put into question: its *idealness*. By this I mean (I added) the manner of being that is specific to it among the objects of the world, and more precisely among the products of art. The ontological status of a literary work is neither the same as the status of a painting, nor of a piece of music, nor of a cathedral, nor of a film, nor of choreography, nor of a happening, nor of a wrapped landscape [in the way of course, Christo wraps monuments, or at least encloses landscapes]. The type of ideality, that is to say, I think, the relationship between "the work itself" and the occurrences of its manifestation, is without a doubt, in each of these cases, specific and *sui generis*. The manner of being of *Remembrance of Things Past*, for example, is not the same as the *View of Delft*, for the reason among others that the *View of Delft* "is found" in a gallery of a museum in the Hague, while the *Remembrance of Things Past* is at once everywhere (in all the good libraries) and nowhere: no owner of a copy of the *Remembrance of Things Past* "owns" the work like the Mauritshuis owns the *View of Delft*. It could be said that the work of Vermeer transcends the painted rectangle of canvas preserved by the Hague in its own way, but certainly not *in the way that the Remembrance of Things Past* transcends the innumerable copies of its various editions . . . , without counting the translations. Copies, versions, editions, translation: here we are in the thick of paratextuality, and this is what I was thinking of when I said above that the idealness of the text is put into question in this space: this idealness appears as such and is compromised in the paratext. It appears by being compromised—let us say in one word that it is *exposed* and leave the details, which I am unaware of still, for the rest of the work. Nevertheless it will have been understood, of course, that the idealness . . . of the literary text is a new form of transcendence: that of the work in relation to its various manifestations, or graphic, editorial, even readers' "presentations": in short, the whole circuit from one brain to another.

I hope that one will pardon this autocitation, not much more narcissistic in the end than the discourse that preceded it, and let me sum up by observing that this page from 1983 contains a kernel of the predominant theme of a book that would not appear until 1994: the first volume of *The Work of Art*, whose specific subtitle is, as one could expect, *Immanence and Transcendence*. In this article I do not find anything to correct today apart from, on one hand, the idea of an idealness specific to the literary text, having realized since then that the literary work shares its status at least with the musical score or choreography, and on the other hand—I will come back to it in a moment—the created confusion between the idealness of the text and the transcendence of the work. In short, the preparation of *Seuils* had put a nagging idea into my head that would not bear fruit until ten years later—if ever a nagging idea does bear fruit—and not without a few intermediary stages. The first of these stages was the writing of the *New Narrative Discourse* (November 1983), which is, as the title indicates, an at once defensive and self-critical postscript to *Narrative Discourse*. The second was the actual writing of *Seuils*. The third was a small collection of four essays, *Fiction and Diction* (January 1991), which appears to me today as a transitional work—that is to say: a transition from poetics, or the theory of literature, to aesthetics, in the sense, moreover disputable and thus provisional, of the theory of art in general.

When I ask myself after the fact about the motivation behind this new extension (after the one that had led me from criticism to poetics), I find two, which are no doubt complementary: the first is the one that I just spoke of—the need to clarify the relationship between the idealness of a text and the materiality of the book, or more generally between its written and oral expressions. The second, no doubt simpler to state, is that if one considers literature as an art, or the literary work as a work of art, a commonly held view, and if one draws out the consequences of treating it as such, which are a little less known and which was my idea from the beginning, there must come a moment in which one experiences the desire to confront the larger question in itself and for itself, even if it comes after many others: "What is a work of art?" or, in the equivalent words of Jakobson, "What makes a verbal message into a work of art?" This intermediary question was the topic of the first chapter, for this reason transitional, of *Fiction and Diction*, the chapter that gave the work its title. My response, fortunately (I hope) more pertinent than original, was that the literary work was a "verbal object with an aesthetic function," and thus that literature was the art of producing verbal objects with an aesthetic function. This is evidently the specified version of what will become a more general definition given in *The Work of Art*: "A work of art is an artifact with an aesthetic function."

The other chapters of *Fiction and Diction* have a more strictly literary topic, but all of them, and particularly the last, "Style and Signification," hint at a late discovery, that of Nelson Goodman's theory of art. I say *a late discovery* because the *Languages of Art* is from 1968, but it is known that one of the constants of French intellectual life is the discovery, long after the fact, of certain foreign contributions, of which we make an even larger case and profit because it took us a longer time to discover them: that is called the "staircase mind-set," and it is perhaps better than having no mind at all. If memory serves me it was then, in 1986 after having finished *Seuils,* that I immersed myself and my poor students in the study of this fundamental work, which brought a few gratifying confirmations to my hypotheses about the status of works of art, and some decisive clarifications. The branch of aesthetics known as "analytical," to which I discovered other contributions around the same time, thanks to two or three suggestions of Thomas Pavel, was from then on the support, sometimes positive, sometimes negative, of my own thoughts, and *The Work of Art* registers its influence.

The proposal of this first volume is thus to clarify the question of the modes of existence of the works of art, which I divide, in the words of Goodman, into two fundamental categories: the *autographic*, which is for me that of works made from material objects, like painting, sculpture, and artisan architecture; and the *allographic*, which is that of works made from ideal objects, like literature, music, and architectural layouts. I must point out that the term *regime*, and above all the notion of a "material object" and "ideal object," are foreign to Goodman's thought, and are an association that I made (already hinted at in 1975 by James Edie[3]) with Husserlian analyses that do not at all agree with his philosophical tendencies, even though I do not think that they are incompatible. Nevertheless this disagreement is not the only one. In fact, it became apparent to me along the way that the ontological status does not suffice to account for the existence of these works, because the works in many ways transcend the object, material or ideal, of which they seem to be made: thus, certain paintings, as is often the case with Chardin, are made up of not one but many paintings, which are replicas of the first, such that the real place of the work is *between,* or *beyond* its multiple versions, and this fact of plurality can be found obviously in all the arts, in literature for example (*The Temptation of Saint Anthony* or *The Satin Slipper*) or in music (*Boris Godounov* or *Petrouchka*). Or furthermore, certain works—here again, to whatever art they may belong—came to us, by accident or abandonment, in an incomplete or unfinished state, and this incompleteness does not stop us from having a relationship with these works that in a way extends beyond the partial object that bears witness to it, like the *Venus of Milo* without her arms, or *Lucien Leuwen* without its third part. It even happens that we often have a relationship *in absentia* with a work that has entirely disappeared, like the *Athena Parthenos* of Phidias or the lighthouse of Alexandria, and that we know because we have heard about it, or even more frequently, with a painting that we "see" only in reproduction, or a novel that we "read" only in translation. So many partial or indirect presences that do not entirely annul our aesthetic relationship with these works, without having even undergone the slightest modification in the object that they manifest, constantly change their signification, and thus their aesthetic function, as history changes their public. That is what gives all the meaning to a famous fable by Borges, "Pierre Ménard, author of *Don Quixote*": the same text produces a different effect according to whether one reads it as the work by a Spanish author from the beginning of the seventeenth century, or by a French author from the beginning of the twentieth—which signifies among other things that the same text does not have the same effect on contemporary readers and their distant descendants in three centuries, a fact that is valid, of course, for all the arts.

Thus in these different ways, works transcend rather than embody the object in which they reside, which I call, in order to take into account this restriction, their "object of immanence": thus the literary work transcends its text, as the pictorial work transcends the painting, and as the musical work transcends its score and its performances. This idea is evidently completely outside of the work of Goodman, for whom, for example, the literary work is identified entirely and without remainder with its text, which inevitably entails that the slightest modification in the text, particularly its translation into another language, determines a new work, as each replica of Chardin's *Bénédicité* becomes a work of its own, and not a new version of the same work, or like a simple transposition or transcription of a musical work constitutes a new piece of music. I willingly admit that this is a simple disagreement in definitions, which are free, and that

Goodman's definition is the only one appropriate to his nominalist philosophy, but it seems to me that convention demands more general or flexible definitions, which take into account the discrepancy between the work and its "object of immanence." This gap accompanies, or rather makes up, the entire life of works, that is to say our relationship to them, a mobile relationship that is always being modified by history—the history that Goodman's theory of art dismisses in a way that seems costly and indefensible to me. Art, as production and reception, in my view is an historical practice through and through, and a theory of the work of art has to take it into account from the beginning, that is from the definition of its object, at the risk of not addressing how it functions. This necessity, in my view, calls for the notion of "transcendence," which is not a superfluous appendage but opens the work up to its function, that is, its reception. I observe in passing that it is a necessity of the same order that had pushed me thirty years earlier to leave the "closure of the text" dear to certain supporters of the first structuralism, or rather the first supporters of the fundamental structuralist principle, that we ultimately owe to Georges Braque,[4] according to whom the relation between terms is more pertinent than the terms themselves: this principle of relation cannot, without contradicting itself, restrain itself to an object separated from its context, that is to say from its field of action. As Umberto Eco has so acutely perceived and expressed since 1962, the work of art is only a *work*, that is, an act, in as much as it is open, opening onto other works, onto its own becoming, onto the world where its action is carried out. In this sense, the principle of transcendence is synonymous with the principle of relation, and it is evidently not by chance that the second volume of *The Work of Art* is entitled *The Aesthetic Relation*, risking a sort of pleonasm, since in my opinion the aesthetic fact can only be, by definition, relational. Nevertheless, redundancy is often better than a misunderstanding.

I had defined the work of art, provisionally and at the beginning of the first volume, as an "artifact, or human product, with an aesthetic function"—an object produced with the intention of producing an aesthetic relation. This definition called urgently for another: the definition of the aesthetic relation itself. This is the specific subject of the second volume, which develops in three stages.

The first, "Esthetic Attention," concerns the preliminary condition of all aesthetic relations, which is, as Kant demonstrated in the *Critique of Judgment*, to consider the object for its appearance rather than for its practical function. This type of attention can be bestowed on all sorts of objects and events, natural or man-made. It has been partially described by Nelson Goodman under the objectivizing heading "symptoms of the aesthetic," which I propose to interpret in a more subjective manner as all of the indices of an attitude that one has when faced with an object rather than all properties of the object, because it is not these kinds of objects that make attention aesthetic, but the privileged attention to its appearance that makes any object aesthetic. I say *aesthetic* and not *beautiful* because it is self-evident that a negative appreciation is as aesthetic as a positive appreciation.

Nevertheless, the attention given to appearance—which can be of use in other types of approaches (for example, in purely cognitive research, on the origin of the object, artistic or not)—does not become strictly aesthetic unless it orients itself toward a question of an affective nature, indicative of pleasure or displeasure, and often expressing desire or repugnance, as in: "Considered for its appearance, *does this object please me, or does it displease me?*" That question is the focus of the second chapter, entitled "Aesthetic Appreciation." Kant, once again, thoroughly analyzed the essentially subjective character of what he called the "judgment of taste," but he shrunk from the relativizing consequence that results from it, namely that appreciation, even if it is shared by a large number of individuals, always remains relative to the aesthetic dispositions common to this group, and that nothing authorizes the consideration of these dispositions as universal. The famous "legitimate pretension to universality" depends on nothing else other than the spontaneous, largely illusory movement of *objectification*, inherent in all appreciation, and consists in the belief that it is uniquely founded on the properties of the object, whose "value" would then impose itself on everyone. I analyze this movement, while discussing the objectivist propositions that had been upheld by certain contemporary aestheticians and that make up the "indigenous theory" of this aesthetic illusion.

Finally, the third chapter, "The Artistic Function," considers the specific features of the relation to works of art only. This relation is fundamentally characterized by the perception, at the origin of an object, of a productive intention that some called the "pretension" to or the "candidacy" for an aesthetic reception. This perception is of a hypothetical order: faced with an object, for more or less solid reasons and with more or less certainty, I can suppose that it was produced by a human being with the intention to receive a positive aesthetic appreciation. When justified, this hypothesis constitutes the recognition of the artistic nature of the object, even if the appreciation that I have of the object is negative or neutral: that which one calls "aesthetic value" does not in any way define the work of art, nor the artistic relation, which depends entirely on the recognition of the intention, whether or not this intention can be considered "fulfilled." I do not need to appreciate a work positively in order to recognize it as a work: if I appreciate it negatively, I consider it to be simply failed—or, let us say more subjectively and more truthfully, to be displeasing to me—which does not in any way prevent me from accepting it as a work, or rather which assumes logically such acceptance: For it to be a bad work, it necessarily must be a work. On the

other hand, the recognition of artistic intention brings about significant consequences, which stem from the historical nature of the act of production, and from
the consideration of this historicity and thus from the act of reception itself: our
relation to the work of art can scarcely be as "innocent" or *primary* as our aesthetic relation to a natural object like a landscape, which, moreover, is not always as innocent as one might think. The natural relativity of the aesthetic relation is therefore not limited, but on the contrary is accentuated by the cultural,
and thus historical, relativity of the artistic relation, which is at once the foundation of its liberty and its responsibility.

These two volumes were intended as a comprehensive theory of the work of
art, in accordance with their overall title, and aimed to account for, at the same
time and as much as possible, the work of art as an *object* and as *action*. It is evidently not up to me to say if this intent was accomplished. What is clear to me
is that it constitutes the logical conclusion, even if provisional, of the progres-
sively expanding work, that I had undertaken thirty years earlier, looking in art
for the raison d'être of literature, and in the aesthetic relation, which transcends
all that by far, for the raison d'être of art. The most consistent feature of this
work seems to me to be, once again, the principal of its method, or more simply, a mind-set attracted more by the relations between objects than by the objects that they unite—and, by way of consequence, by the relations between the
relations themselves. This mind-set, if I were to have to qualify it (which I do
not at all feel obliged to do), would be indifferently, and without much regard
for the decrees of the trend and the countertrend, *structuralist* or *relativist*—a
structuralism that has nothing poststructuralist about it and is even less post-modern and a relativism that is not at all, in my view, skeptical (or eclectic), and still
less retrograde, because it simply endeavors to account for, as clearly as possible,
the relations that it observes—or that it establishes.

To say this probably amounts to recognizing that in forty years I have scarcely
changed my opinion—which, if I subscribe to the proverb, is the privilege of im-
beciles. To this mitigated observation, I will keep myself from adding any prognosis for an eventual continuation, because the hour is more ripe for assessments
than for predictions. I will rather note, to conclude, that this itinerary will have
consisted, in its own way, of a constant questioning of what I called in the beginning its "apparent point of departure": the study of literary works. Because
this initial choice, if it is one, was not, for me, self-evident: by the way, "Why
literature?" To this question, which was not at all incongruous, my answer, I have
said, was: "Because art." But this answer would obviously lead to another question: "Why art?" I attempted to say it, but the answer, probably calls in its turn,
for another question, and so on. As Figaro says, "Why these things and not oth-

ers?" Now, thinking, as is well known, is not in the answers, but rather in the questions. Let us then leave these open.

Translated by Joanna Augustyn

Notes

1. "I have created a narrative. Yet, for me, narration is a very tedious thing," Flaubert wrote in a letter to Louis Colet, May 2, 1852.
2. The title for *Mimologiques, Voyage en Cratylie* chosen by Thaïs E. Morgan in her translation of the book (Lincoln: University of Nebraska Press, 1995), p. 21.
3. James M. Edie, "The Current Relevance of the Husserlian Conception of Language," in *Sense and Existence: In Honor of Paul Ricoeur* (Paris: Edition du Seuil, 1975).
4. "I do not believe in things, but in the relation between things." Cited by Roman Jakobson, *Selected Writings* I, p. 632.

Jacques Lacan, or the Erasure of History

ÉLISABETH ROUDINESCO

When Tom Bishop suggested to me last July that I come and speak about Jacques Lacan at Columbia University as part of a series of conferences devoted to French thought, I told him that I would gladly accept, but that rather than present an overview of the material covered in my book—a long treatment of the system of Lacanian thought that had just been translated into English—I would prefer to discuss this thought in terms of the method I had used to assemble this rather unusual book, a work that is in many ways unprecedented. As I point out in the preface and in the original title, which was not used for the American edition (*Outline of a Life: History of a System of Thought*),[1] my book is ultimately not a biography, even though it has been read as one in the most classical sense of the term. What I welcomed, actually, was the opportunity to speak about Lacan, about his work and about his thought "in the first person," as both a historian and a historiographer at the same time.

It seems to me that in telling other people's stories, a historian tells her own story through the other, through the things she says about others. A historical approach always involves not a mere method, but an "ego history," or, as Freud put it, a *Selbstdarstellung*.

Hence the following paradox: undertaking a history of psychoanalysis also means doing an analysis, means analyzing oneself through history. Writing a history the way historians do, producing a historiographic work, means taking an additional step, as a second phase of analysis, as what in Lacanian terminology would be called a "passe," as a way for the "I" to become an other.

Thus, there is a very strong link between the act of doing history and the clinical approach of psychoanalysis. Usually, history gets written when theory is in crisis, when the masters disappear and make way for their institutional legacy. There is also in the act of doing history a way of reviving theoretical questions as well as an "acting out." The recollection of the past is like a passage through hell. The historian passes through death and returns from the realm of the dead. Essentially, the historian works only on death, even when she writes the history of the living, since she projects the present and the living person into an eternity that resembles the silence of tombs and cemeteries. The historian converses with the gods and myths. Even when she objects to hagiography, she still produces gods.

By exhuming the dead, she allows the living to question the gods and to interrogate themselves concerning the present. Increasingly today, historians of Freudianism and, notably, the so-called revisionist American school no longer belong to the psychoanalytic community. They are isolated from the object of their study, and their works are often not read by psychoanalysts who are afraid of history and who show a resistance to their own history when it is written as ferocious as the hostility that ordinary people have toward psychoanalysis. As a result, they make historians out to be crazy, or violently anti-Freudian, as is the case today.

Lacan always had an ambivalent attitude toward history. On the one hand, in his desire to be the interpreter of a new orthodoxy based on a return to the texts of Freud, he rejected the historicization of Freudian thought in any shape or form. On the other hand, he was obsessed with a desire for history and with the will to leave posterity with the trace not only of his teachings, but of his person. Hence this dialectic of erasure and recognition that endlessly crosses through his work.[2]

Combining with the above dialectic were a passion for logic and a tendency toward fusion with the Freudian text to the point of thinking that everything to be found in Freud was already Lacanian. In every work, Lacan saw the mirror of his own thought. Hence his obsession with plagiarism and purloined ideas.

Underscoring in 1964 the extent to which Descartes's desire to distinguish the true from the false went hand in hand with a concern for biography, he affirmed nonetheless that biography was always secondary with respect to the meaning (importance) of a work. Some fifteen years later, he made a sensational declaration to the historian Lucile Ritvo during a conference at Yale University:

> Psychoanalysis has weight in history. If there are things that specifically belong to it, they are things of the order of psychoanalysis. . . . What one calls history is the history of epidemics. The Roman Empire, for example, is an epidemic . . . psychoanalysis is an epidemic. . . . Without the written document, you know that you are in a dream. What the historian demands is a text: a text or a scrap of paper; in any case, there must be something in an archive somewhere that certifies in writing, something which when absent makes history impossible. Whatever cannot be certified in writing cannot be considered history.

This is the way Lacan assailed the biographical model, although in his private life he was extremely fond of life stories and anecdotes. If he made the written archive into the very condition for history—to the point of giving it the weight of a commandment for the very future of history, much as Jacques Derrida would do later on[3]—his work, unlike that of Freud, was essentially oral in nature. Everything happened as if this paradoxical teacher were thinking against himself.

The direct heirs of Freud established the written archives. Ernest Jones wrote the first biography based on rigorous sources: correspondences, memories, testimonies, research. As for Anna Freud, as a devoted heiress she did not misplace a thing. In other words, in the case of Freud there are a number of considerable archives available to historians, notably an immense collection of letters: material for putting researchers of all tendencies to work, material for constituting a Freudian historiography, material for giving birth to disputes, to debates. Even if they are censored or inaccessible until a given date, one still knows that these traces, these archives, exist. They have not disappeared.

In the case of Lacan, the situation is entirely different. Lacan's work is oral. It was articulated over the course of twenty-six years by means of living speech, during his famous seminar, and it was only due to the energetic intervention of a great editor, François Wahl, that the collection of Lacan's articles, the *Écrits*, was able to be published. These writings were in fact often no more than transcribed conference papers that had subsequently been corrected. The remaining work had been left to the family of heirs—notably to Lacan's son-in-law—who are today assured considerable control over Lacan's work: not merely juridical but also interpretive control.

The manuscripts, notes, and correspondence have not been classified, nor have they been indexed or "copyrighted." They simply do not exist, and this absence of an archive is the symptom of an erased history, of an erasure of the trace that makes it possible for the Lacanian community to believe in just any old legend. Since there is no accessible trace, everything happens as if Lacan's work had no sources, no history, no origin, as if the subject Lacan did not exist except by hearsay, by means of the fragile and phantasmatic testimonials that one can gather about him: turns of phrase, pious stories, rumors, anecdotes.

This absence of an archive answers not only to the Lacanian ideology of legitimacy, but to the conception of history handed down by Lacan to his heirs, who monumentalized him while alive without managing to actually mourn the death of his person.

It was to somehow erase this erasure and to supply the missing archive that I decided in 1990 to dedicate a book to a historical study of the genesis of Lacan's system of thought. To this end, there was of course his oral and written work, in which one could find all kinds of references and other information to draw on. But as for the private intellectual itinerary, in the absence of any "real" correspondence (there exist only 250 letters) and without a single note from his work, I had nothing at my disposal but a few fragments from the scattered sources of those who knew Lacan, of those whose archives were available and whose oral testimonies were still possible to gather: his brother, Marc-François Lacan, the children from his first marriage, Thibaut and Sibylle—all those, in the end, who were willing to report on their treatment or to provide archives and whose transferential relationship to Lacan was not too hagiographic.

It is because this work of assembling archives had never been done, neither for Lacan's life nor for his work, that my book ended up functioning as a biography, even though it is not one. If it is a history of Lacan's thought, it is but a sketch of his life, which would never amount to much since the archive does not exist. Thus, I had to "reconstruct" Lacan, a Lacan unfettered by rumors and legends but nonetheless hypothetical in the absence of any guarantee of sufficient evidence.

I borrowed the notion of a "system of thought" from Henri Ellenberger on the one hand,[4] who establishes a link between the subjective consciousness of the scientist and the state of the sciences during the period in which he lives, and from Foucault, on the other hand, who, on the contrary, seeks to "destroy" this link by raising the history of systems of thought above all conscious subjectivity.

The real genius of Lacan's work was to have dared to introduce, during the period between the two wars, the very essence of German philosophy into the Freudian doctrine. Through Lacan, and against the dominant current of Germanophobia, an act of subversion was produced on French soil of which Freud would never have dreamed, since he constructed his theory on a biological model in a conscious refusal to take philosophical discourse into consideration, whether of his contemporaries or of those who came before his own discoveries. It was thus Lacan who first introduced Nietzschean thought, Hegelian philosophy, and Heideggerian reflection into the work of Freud.

Of course, he did not accomplish this feat alone. It was by following the teachings of Alexandre Kojève and by frequenting the circle of Alexandre Koyré that he was initiated into Hegelianism and was able to discover the importance of the work of Heidegger. At the same time, it was in his contact with the work of Georges Bataille and of the Collège de Sociologie that the Nietzscheanism of his youth found fertile ground.

At the heart of the second psychoanalytic generation in France (the third in the world, i.e., that did not know Freud personally), Lacan can be considered not only as the initiator of a system of thought but as the founder of a movement that would assume the name of Lacanianism, just as there had been Kleinianism corresponding to the overhaul of Melanie Klein, it being understood that Lacanianism and Kleinianism are themselves part of Freudianism.

Lacan occupied this position not due to the miracle of an alleged solitude of the "great thinker," but simply because following 1932, with the publication of his dissertation on the famous case of Aimée, and with several other texts that came later, he forged, without even being aware of it, a new synthesis between the two major directions of Freudianism, the medical and the intellectual. In other words, he carried out a synthesis between the advances in psychiatry at the time and the core questions being asked in French intellectual circles (from the surrealists to Kojève, to the Collège de Sociologie). As a consequence, he immediately occupied the position of master: the very position that had been left vacant by the pioneers of the first psychoanalytic generation in France (the second with respect to the rest of the world).

I called Lacan's return to the texts of Freud in the 1950s an orthodoxical sublation of Freudianism. I say *sublation* because it is a matter of a defiance, a reconquest, and a Hegelian *Aufhebung* all at the same time, "orthodoxical," because this sublation runs counter to all the other directions Freudianism had taken since the second generation. Whereas all of these directions aimed at surpassing or deepening Freud's doctrine and at adapting to new clinical imperatives, Lacan sought to restore or rediscover an original and subversive Freudianism in the straight line of an orthodoxy of which he would be the mouthpiece.

Two prewar pieces serve to situate the prehistory of this turn: the 1932 dissertation on paranoia and the major 1938 article on familial complexes.[5]

The novelty of the dissertation—which was praised by the intellectual community and by psychiatrists, but misunderstood by the first French psychoanalytic generation—lies in the fact that Lacan combines a philosophical interpretation of madness with a radical critique of academic psychiatry, keeping in mind all the while the writings of the patient.

This dissertation is above all a critique of the so-called doctrine of the constitutions that still dominated psychiatric knowledge in the 1930s in France, despite the fact that it had already come under devastating attack, notably by Henri Ey. According to this doctrine, born of hereditarism, madness was always *constitutional* in origin (today we would say *biological* or *genetic*) and not psychical. Now, Lacan demonstrates that its origin is "psychogenetic." To do so, he adopts the theses of modern dynamic psychiatry developed by Freud and Bleuler. He makes himself into the flag bearer of the dominant thought of the new psychiatric generation of the 1930s and it is for this reason that his description of the case of Aimée is received with such fervor—both by his generation and by the surrealists who were interested in the language of madness, and more specifically in that of female madness.

Lacan would later say, with respect to this dissertation, that he was not yet Freudian when he wrote it. I was able to show that this statement consisted in a kind of retrospective illusion that testifies to the way in which he himself re-constructed the history of his thought in 1966, at the time of the publication of his *Écrits*. In reality, Lacan was already Freudian in 1932. Yet he was not Freudian the way he would be later on, in 1953, with his return to the texts of Freud. In 1932, Lacan was still a classical Freudian. He had not read the work of Melanie Klein and employed a lexicon belonging to Anna Freud in close proximity to the school dedicated to the analysis of resistance. It was precisely because he was Freudian in this way that he would later not recognize himself as having been Freudian during that period.

In 1953, he effectively combatted the followers of Anna Freud (analysis of re-sistances and *Ego Psychology*) and thus he could not recognize himself as having been shaped by the movement: hence the erasure of history. From the point of view of his structuralist Freudianism of the 1950s, Lacan could not imagine that he might have been a Freudian in 1932. In order to carry out his structuralist turn of the 1950s, he first had to make his way through Hegelianism. Yet in 1932, it was the model of Spinozian parallelism (that of the *Ethics*) that he employed for describing the relationship between the normal and the pathological in the ques-tion of psychosis.

In order to understand the impact of Lacan's dissertation on the history of his work and its reception, it is also necessary to grasp the nature of the clinical and passionate bond that Lacan had with the real Aimée, Marguerite Anzieu. I was able to reconstruct the story thanks to the testimony provided by her son, Didier Anzieu.

The story of this major inaugural case brilliantly illustrates the extent to which the "sick"—no less than the doctors who care for them—are actors in an ad-venture that is always dramatic and in which the genealogical lines of uncon-scious nature are interwoven.

Marguerite Pantaine was born to a landed Catholic family from the central region of France. Raised by a mother who suffered from persecution anxiety, she dreamed early on—like an Emma Bovary—of escaping from her situation and becoming an intellectual. In 1910, she entered into the postal administration and seven years later she married René Anzieu, himself a functionary. In 1921, when she was pregnant with her son Didier, she began to exhibit behavior associated with persecution mania, states of depression. Following the birth of her child, she assumed a double life: on the one hand the quotidian universe of a postal worker, on the other an imaginary existence made up of delusions. In 1930, she wrote two novels back to back and wanted to have them published. She soon convinced herself that she was the victim of a persecution plot orchestrated by Huguette Duflos, the famous comedienne of the Parisian scene in the 1930s. In April 1931, she tried to kill Duflos with a knife, but the actress dodged her attack and Marguerite was committed to the Sainte-Anne hospital. There she was entrusted to Lacan, who subsequently turned her into a case of erotomania and paranoid self-punishment.

The rest of Marguerite Anzieu's story reads like a novel. In 1949 her son Didier, having completed his studies in philosophy, decided to become an analyst. He underwent his formative training on Lacan's couch while preparing his dissertation on Freud's self-analysis under the direction of Daniel Lagache—all the while having no idea that his mother was the famous case of Aimée. Lacan did not recognize him, and Anzieu first learned the truth from his mother when she, by an extraordinary twist of fate, was placed as a governess in the home of Alfred Lacan, Jacques's father. The conflicts between Didier Anzieu and his analyst were as violent as those between Marguerite and her psychiatrist. She had accused Lacan of treating her as a "case" and not as a human being, and above all she reproached him for never having returned the manuscripts—a section of which is reproduced in his dissertation—that she had entrusted to him during her stay at the Sainte-Anne hospital.

In retracing the events in Marguerite Anzieu's life, I realized that Lacan had simply followed in the footsteps of a Freud, a Breuer, of even a Janet. Actually, every case study is constructed as a fiction necessary for the validation of the thinker's hypotheses. The case has no truth value outside the fact that it is written as a fiction. In general, it is adapted to the nosography of the period in which it is written. In other words, Bertha Pappenheim—Anna O., the principal case of hysteria in fin-de-siècle Vienna—would not be considered a hysteric by our standards today, so much has the conception of hysteria changed with the emergence and development of Freudian knowledge.

Furthermore, each time that the real patient comments retrospectively on his own case under his true identity—as did, for example, Sergueï Constantinovitch Pankejeff (the "wolfman")—he tells a completely different story than that of the thinker. He wants nothing to do with his double and refuses to play along with the fiction. In short, he feels himself to be the victim of a discourse that is not his own. There is thus a perpetual division, as Michel Foucault pointed out, between a critical awareness of madness (that of the alienists) and the tragic awareness (that of madness itself) of the patient when he is in a position to break the silence.

In his other major prewar text, *Les complexes familiaux*, Lacan paints a dark picture of the Western family and its universe, a veritable melting pot of all forms of social depravity, subjective violence, and conformity. The thematics of the sacred and of antibourgeois nihilism that fuel his pen do not prevent him from being skeptical toward the October Revolution. At the same time, he considers communist attempts at abolishing the family to be damaging. Since they depend on the idea of a utopia, they threaten, in Lacan's view, to lead to more pernicious form of authoritarianism than the one imposed by familial legitimacy.

On the eve of the war, he thus defends the values of an enlightened conservatism, in the manner of de Tocqueville, all the while relying on the theses of Georges Bataille and Marcel Mauss, all the while advocating the cult of a subversive Freudianism as the only possible instrument for conceiving of the social bond, the imaginary, the sacred, or the subject. One can now chart the path taken by Lacan since the publication of his dissertation in 1932.

If Freudianism is able to serve as a shield against attempts to abolish the family, it is only because it is born in the social context that saw the beginnings of an inevitable decline in patriarchy, expressed by creators at the fin-de-siècle, from Richard Wagner to August Strindberg by way of countless Viennese.

Doubtless, Lacan takes his inspiration not from these creators, but from the works of Bachofen cited in his bibliography. In any case, I have always been struck by the analogy. We know that in his account of the case of "the ratman" Freud drew a link between the progress made in science and in rational thought and the formation of patriarchy, while at the same time pointing out that the identity of the father in the filiation was always dubious. In 1938, Lacan draws on this thesis in order to demonstrate that Freud attempts, in his theory of Oedipus, to revalorize the paternal imago.

Thus, following Freud, Lacan takes up the torch of the revalorization of the paternal function, as is apparent in the two major concepts he develops in the 1950s, that of the signifier and that of the name of the father.

It was in reading Claude Lévi-Strauss's *Elementary Structures of Kinship* (1949) that Lacan discovered the theoretical tool that would enable him to consider the paternal function in structural terms. Relying on the principles of Saussurian linguistics, he elaborated his new and definitive *topoi* once and for all (the symbolic, the imaginary, and the real) along with his theory of nomination. Thus the dispossessed, humiliated, haggard father that haunted the conscience of the fin-de-siècle—which materialized in France in, among other things, the legislation concerning paternal dispossession—reappears with Lacan as invested with the power of language. All that the father now possesses is a symbolic force tied to the power of the name.

Let us pause, for a moment, to consider one of Lacan's central concepts, his famous "name of the father," which he capitalized and held together with hyphens (Nom-du-Père). It was Marc François Lacan, with whom I met over the course of ten years, who was the first to draw my attention to the fact that the Lacanian doctrine of paternity (and its debasement) stemmed from an experience that Jacques himself had recalled by cursing the name of his paternal grandfather. This violence was inscribed into three generations: Émile (the grandfather), Alfred (the father), Jacques (the son). The son considered the "father of the father" to be responsible for a tyranny of which he himself ended being the victim. Jacques Lacan claimed to have suffered under the spectacle of the debasement of the paternal function caused by the fact that his own father never recognized him for what he was: an intellectual disconnected from his original environment and thus from any interest in the business of selling vinegars or mustards.

As a result, the concept of the name of the father does not have the same status in the Lacanian doctrine as the others. It was not borrowed from an already existing corpus and was not developed by means of theoretical elaboration. It has its primary source in Lacan's life, in his personal and painful experience of paternity.

As a son, he suffered under the breakdowns of his father, Alfred Lacan (1873–1960), who had himself been crushed by the tyranny of his own father, Émile Lacan (1839–1915). Later, when he became a father for the fourth time, in July 1941, during the darkest period of the German occupation, Lacan was unable to give his name to his daughter, who was registered under the surname Bataille, because her mother (Sylvia Bataille) was still officially married to Georges Bataille. Due to French legislation on filiation, Lacan was caught in this infernal turmoil surrounding the name-of-the-father until 1964. The fact that this experience filled Lacan with a terrible sense of guilt can be seen in the many ways it manifests itself in his life.

For further evidence one could look to his seminar on the subject of identification, held from 1961 to 1962, in which he violently attacks his paternal grandfather—"that horrible character to whom I owe my precocious arrival at the fundamental function of cursing God"—as well as to the 1975 conferences on James Joyce in which, evoking the writer's relationship to his schizophrenic daughter, he speaks in covert terms of his own paternal drama.

It is in 1951, in a discussion of the case of the "wolfman," that the syntagm "name of the father" first flows from his pen.[6] In 1953, it appears again in a discussion of the case of the "ratman" (Ernst Lanzer), written "nom du père" without hyphens. Relying on Lévi-Strauss, Lacan demonstrates that the Freudian Oedipus can be considered as a passage from nature to culture. From this perspective, the father exercises a function that is essentially symbolic: he names, he gives his name, and by this act he incarnates the law. As a result, Lacan underscores the idea that human society is dominated by the primacy of language, which is to say that the paternal function is nothing other than the exercise of nomination that permits the child to acquire its identity.

Lacan comes to define this function first as the "function of the father," then as the "function of the symbolic father," and finally as the "paternal metaphor," which leads him to no longer interpret the Oedipus complex with respect to a model of patriarchy or matriarchy, but as a function of the system of kinship. This is a first in the history of Freudianism, and as such it carries with it the necessity for a new concept.

In 1956, during his seminar on psychoses and his discussion of Daniel Paul Schreber's paranoia, Lacan conceptualizes the function itself in writing "Nom-du-Père." The concept is thus associated with that of foreclosure, which he had also forged for designating the idea of the rejection of a primordial signifier outside the symbolic universe of the subject (the inability to symbolize that characterizes psychosis). Evoking the nature of Paul Schreber's relationship to his father, Lacan turns the son's psychosis into a "foreclosure of the name-of-the-father." He then extends this prototype onto the very structure of psychosis.

By way of this completely new interpretation of the case, he is the first of Freud's commentators to theorize the link that exists between the educational system of a father and the madness of his son. One can make the argument that this idea came to Lacan through his memory of the relationship between his father (Alfred) and his grandfather (Émile), which he had experienced as a lived drama.

From this perspective, and in the framework of the Lacanian theory of the signifier, one can argue that the oedipal passage from nature to culture occurs in the following way: the father, being himself the incarnation of the signifier since he gives the child his name, intervenes in this way as the one who deprives the mother, giving birth to his ego ideal. In the case of psychosis, there is no place for this act of structuring. The signifier of the name of the father being thus foreclosed, it returns in the real in form of a delirium against God conceived as the incarnation of all the accursed figures of paternity.

In retracing the different stages by which Lacan brought about his two structural sublations within the Freudian doctrine—the first in 1953 with his reliance on Heidegger and Lévi-Strauss, the second in 1957 with his theory of the signifier inspired by Saussure and Roman Jakobson—I proposed to define Lacan as the inheritor of what one refers to as the "dark *Aufklärung*," an inheritor of the philosophy of the Enlightenment but at the same time skeptical of its illumination and marked by a rejection of the notion of progress; in other words, a "Faustian" scientist caught in the division between the cogito and madness, wandering from doubt of truth to error, espousing the most extravagant theories while remaining adept at reason, as in the final part of his work, what I have called his "logical sublation," in which he believes in a possible mathematicization of the unconscious and elaborates "Borromian knots" and "mathems."

On this last point, moreover, Lacan resembles Freud in his correspondence with Wilhelm fliess and Ferenczi: a Freud capable of adhering, in the name of science, to all of the "false sciences" of his era, even to telepathy. Thomas Mann was the first to paint the portrait of that particular Freud; in 1929 he wrote,

> Freud, explorer of the depths of the soul and psychologist of the unconscious, inscribes himself into the line of writers of the 19th and 20th centuries who—as historians, philosophers, critics, or archeologists—position themselves in opposition to rationalism, intellectualism, classicism, hence in the spirit of the 18th century, and yet perhaps a little of the 20th century. They underscore the nocturnal side of nature and the soul, they see in them the true determining and creative factor of life, they cultivate it, illuminate it with scientific daylight; they defend by revolutionary means the primacy of all that is chthonian, anterior to the spirit—"will," passion for the unknown, or, as Nietzsche says it, "emotion over reason."[7]

In order to write Lacan's story, in order to recount his genealogy and to exhume his effaced history, I adopted a narrative mode, which turned him into a character in a novel, a character as in Balzac but also like one in Mann. Lacan is French, and it is precisely because he is French that he was inhabited to such an extent by German philosophy, as if what was at stake for him in this endeavor concentrated all the conflicting relations between *Kultur* and *Civilisation*, between the France of Charles Maurras and André Breton and the Germany of Goethe and Heidegger. The fact that Lacan had dreamed so much of Germany clearly demonstrates that he was the mouthpiece for the history of French passions, for which the best model was the Balzacian novel. It is for this reason that I turned Lacan into the story of a Balzacian passion: the youth of Louis Lambert, the maturity of Horace Bianchon, the old age of Balthazar Claës.

Balzac knew just as well as Thomas Mann how to bring to light the servitude, ambitions and disorder of the bourgeois family. No one drew up the genealogical tree better than he did. As a vehement messenger of disenchantment with the revolution, he sought in religion the seeds of new hope, at the risk of uncovering an impasse for reason in the face of the irrational. Thus, as with Balzac, the revolution and its disenchantment were always at the heart of Lacanian inquiries, at the heart of the fascination Lacan experienced for a desire that he ultimately never supported, at the heart of his strange relationship with Jean-Paul Sartre during the events of May 1968, in the face of Maoism.

In order to bring this analysis to a close in the first person, I would say that the revolution and its illusions were also at the heart of my own generation of intellectuals, divided, as Foucault pointed out, between Sartre and Lacan, between the idea that the subject can liberate himself of all "superego" by means of his conscious will, and the opposing idea that he is determined by the weight of his history, by his archives, by his genealogy, and ultimately by his unconscious.

Translated by Robert Hardwick Weston

Notes

1. Élisabeth Roudinesco, *Jacques Lacan* (New York: Columbia University Press, 1997).
2. I introduced some of these arguments in *Généalogies* (Paris: Fayard, 1994).
3. See Jacques Derrida, *Archive Fever: A Freudian Impression* (Chicago: University of Chicago Press, 1996).
4. Henri Ellenberger, *Histoire de la découverte de l'inconscient* (Paris: Fayard, 1994 [1970]).
5. Jacques Lacan, *De la psychose paranoïaque dans ses rapports avec la personnalité* (Paris: Seuil, 1975 [1932]); *Les complexes familiaux* (Paris: Navarin, 1984 [1938]).
6. This seminar is unpublished; it is only known through notes taken by its participants. Thus it is not known how Lacan wrote the term. See Érik Porge, *Les noms du père chez Lacan* (Toulouse: Érès, 1997).
7. Thomas Mann, "Freud and Modern Thought," in *Essays of Three Decades* (New York: 1947).

What Is the Creative Act?

GILLES DELEUZE

I would like to ask some questions of myself. And ask some of you, as well as of myself. This would be of the type, What do you do, what do you make, particularly those of you who make cinema? And then, what do I do in particular, when I do, or hope to do, when I make philosophy? Of course, this is a difficult question; it's painful for you, as well as myself. I could reformulate the question in another way. What is it to have an idea in cinema? If one makes cinema, or if one wants to make cinema, what is it to have an idea in this medium, specifically at that moment when one articulates, "I have an idea"? For everyone knows that to have an idea is a rare event, it occurs infrequently. To have an idea is a sort of celebration; it does not happen every day. In another way to have an idea is not a general thing. One does not have "an idea in general." An idea is always consecrated; all as if he who has an idea has already consecrated it in such-or-such domain. What I would like to explain is that having an idea, such as in painting, or in the novel, or in philosophy, or in science, might not be the same thing.

Ideas should be treated as types of potentials, as consecrated potentials— potentials that are already engaged in one or another mode of expression and that are inseparable from that mode of expression. In conjunction with some techniques that I know, I can have an idea in a domain, an idea in cinema, or an idea in philosophy. What is it to have an idea "in" something? So, I speak again about the fact that I make philosophy and that you make cinema. It would then be too simple to state, "Yes, everyone knows that philosophy is made to reflect upon everything. So why then does it not think about cinema?" Philosophy is not for reflecting on everything; it is made to think about other things. In treating philosophy as a force that "reflects upon," we give it too much credit, and in fact we take everything away from it. Because in fact no one has need for philosophy in order to think or reflect. The only people capable of reflecting upon the cinema are filmmakers, or film critics, or those who love the cinema. They absolutely do not need philosophy in order to think about the cinema. The idea that mathematicians would need philosophy in order to think about mathematics is quite comic. If philosophy was made to think about something, it would have no reason to exist. If philosophy exists, it is because it has its own content. If we ask ourselves what the content of philosophy is it is very simple. Philosophy is a discipline equally as creative, equally as inventive as all other disciplines. Philosophy is a discipline that consists of creating or inventing concepts. Concepts do not just exist. Concepts do not just exist in the sky where they are waiting for philosophy to come up and seize them. Concepts must be fabricated. Of course they are not made just like that. One does not just say to oneself, "Okay, I am going to make a concept, I am going to invent a concept." Not any more than a painter says to himself one day, "Okay, I am going to create a painting just like that." *There has to be a necessity*, in philosophy as elsewhere. If there is not some necessity, there is nothing at all. This necessity, if it exists at all, is that which makes a philosopher. At least I know what the philosopher is not occupied with; he is not occupied with thinking. He proposes to invent or to create concepts. I say that I make philosophy, which is to say that I try to invent concepts. I do not try to reflect upon other things.

If I say to you who make cinema, What do you make? accord me this puerile definition, even if there are better ones: if I were to say that you invent, it is not concepts that you make, for that is not your task. That which you invent is something that we could call blocks of *movement-time* [*mouvement-durée*]. If one fabricates blocks of movement-time, perhaps one is making cinema. Notice that this is not a question of invoking a certain story, nor to challenge one. Everything has a story. Even philosophy tells stories. Philosophy tells stories and speaks of concepts. Cinema tells stories with blocks of "movement-time." I could say that painting invents another type of block, which is neither blocks of concepts, nor of movement-time, but, let us suppose, that they are blocks of lines and color. Music invents another type of particular block, a very, very particular one. But what I am saying in all of this is that science is not any less creative. I do not see so much opposition between the sciences, the arts, and all of that. If I ask a scholar what he makes, whether he invents—and he doesn't invent, or discover but what exists—it isn't there that one defines scientific activity as such. A scholar invents and creates as much as an artist. To keep for a moment to these summary definitions as I have been doing, a scholar is someone who is not complicated, it is someone who invents or who creates functions. He does not create concepts. In the end, the scholar has nothing to do with concepts; it is happily for this reason that philosophy exists. On the other hand, there is something that only a scholar knows how to do: to invent, to create functions. What is a function? One can define it quite simply as I will try to do, as we are coming upon the most rudimentary level. Not at all because you would not understand better, but because it would already pass me by. Let us be as simple as possible. What is a function? As soon as there is a putting in correspondence ruled by at least two ensembles. The basic notion of science (and not since yesterday, but for a very long time) is that of the ensemble. And an ensemble is completely different from a concept. It has nothing to do with a concept. And as soon as you have made a correlation between two ensembles, you obtain a function and you can say "I do science." If anyone can speak to anyone, if a filmmaker can speak to a man of science, if a man of science has something to say to a philosopher, it is in the measure where, and in function with, each of their own creative activities.

Creation (the creative act) is something that is very solitary. It is in the name of "creation" that I have something to say. If I string together all these disciplines that are defined by their creative activity, it is because there is a limit that is common to them—a common limit in this whole series of invention, invention of function, this sort of block of movement, invention of concepts, and so on. Common to all of these disciplines is "space-time" [*espace-temps*]. If all these disciplines communicate together, it is at the level of that which never disengages for itself, but that which is engaged in all creative disciplines, to know the constitution of space-time. It is well known that there are rarely entire spaces in Bresson's work. His are spaces that could be called *disconnected*, which is to say, for example, there is a corner of a cell, and then one will see another corner or another place of partition. It is as if Bressonian space presented itself as a series of little bits whose connection between them is not predetermined. To embed two little bits whose connection is not predetermined—there are some great filmmakers who employ contrary strategies. I suppose that Bresson was one of the first to make space with little disconnected bits and pieces. When I said that in any case, in all forms of creation, there is a space-time and there is nothing but that, it is there that Bresson's blocks of time-movement are going to tend toward this type of space. The answer is a given: these little bits of visual space of which the connection is not given in advance, why do we want them to be connected? Is it but by the hand? There is no theory; it is not philosophy. It is just deduced like that, but I am saying that Bresson's type of space is the cinematographic valuation of the hand in the image. It is obviously linked. The very fact that these little bits of Bressonian space, from the very fact that there are just bits, disconnected bits of space, can be nothing but a manual joining, a connection, or at least the exhaustion of the hand in Bresson's entire cinema. We could continue to speak about this at length, because it is here that the block of Bresson's area-movement [*étendue-mouvement*] received, like the character of its creator, the character of this very particular space—the hand's role. The hand can effectively make its connections from one part of this space to another. Bresson is without a doubt one of the greatest filmmakers for having reintroduced tactile values into cinema, simply because he knew how to take an image into his hands. The reason for this is that he needed his hands. A creator is not a being that works for pleasure; a creator does nothing but that which he has need to do.

Again, to have an idea in cinema is not the same as having an idea else-where. There are ideas in cinema that could have some worth in other disciplines. There are ideas in cinema that could be excellent ideas in the novel. But they would not at all have the same allure. There are ideas in cinema that can only be cinemagraphic. There are ideas in cinema that can only be cinematographic. These ideas are engaged in a cinemagraphic process and are consecrated to that process in advance. Yet, saying this leads me to another question that is very interesting: What happens when a filmmaker wants to adapt a novel? It seems evident to me that if a filmmaker wants to adapt a novel, it is because there are ideas in cinema that resound with the novel yet still present ideas particular to the novel. This is what often makes an extremely great meeting. I am not posing the problem of the filmmaker who adapts a notoriously mediocre novel; he may have need for the mediocre novel. He does have this need. It does not exclude the possibility that the film could be great. I am asking a slightly different question. It is because the novel is great when it awakens this sort of activity where someone has, in the cinema, an idea that corresponds to that idea in the novel. One of the most beautiful examples is the case of Akira Kurosawa.

Why is it that Kurosawa, a Japanese filmmaker, finds himself in a sort of familiarity with Shakespeare and Dostoyevsky? I can give you one possible response that is among a thousand other possibilities, and which also, I believe, touches upon philosophy. Under Dostoyevsky's characterizations, something very curious occurs quite often. Generally, his characters are very agitated. A character takes off, goes out toward the street; he tells a woman he loves her. "Tania calls me for help. I go. I am running. I run. Yes, Tania is going to die if I don't go, and so I go down the staircase and meet a friend, or see a run-over dog on the street." He forgets completely. He forgets completely that Tania is waiting for him as she is in the process of dying. He starts to talk, just like that, and he comes across another friend, and he goes to have some tea at this friend's house, and then all of a sudden he says, "Tania is waiting for me, I have to go!" What does this all mean? It is there, in Dostoyevsky, that the characters are perpetually taken by urgency. At the same time that they are taken by this urgency, questions of life and death, they still know that there is another question that is even more urgent, even if they are not exactly sure what it is. And that is what stops them. Everything happens as if in the worst kind of urgency—"There's fire, there's fire. . . . I've got to go!"—I say to myself, "No, no there is a much deeper problem, but what problem?" Something that is more urgent, and I will not move as much as I do not know what it is. It is the idiot. That is the idiot; "Ah, but you know, no, no, there is a much deeper problem—what problem? I can't see it very well. But leave me alone. Leave me. Everything could burn down to the ground but nothing happens, one must find out the most urgent problem." It is not Dostoyevsky that Kurosawa is learning; all of Kurosawa's characters are like that. I would say there is a meeting, a beautiful meeting. If Kurosawa can adapt Dostoyevsky, surely it is because he can say, "I have a common cause with him; we have a common problem; that exact problem." Kurosawa's characters are exactly in the same situation. They are taken by impossible situations. "Yes, there is a more urgent problem, but I have to know what problem is more urgent." Maybe *To Live* is one of Kurosawa's films that goes the furthest in this sense, but all of Kurosawa's films go in this direction. *The Seven Samurai* is very powerful for me. It is because all of Kurosawa's space is dependent on the necessity that it be a sort of overall space that is battered down by the rain: finally nothing would take too much time because, there too we will cross again the limits of space-time. The characters of *The Seven Samurai* are taken by urgent situations. They have agreed to defend a village yet they are taken by a more profound question. This question will be articulated by the head of the Samurai toward the end of the film—"What is a Samurai? What is a Samurai, not in general, but what is a Samurai during this epoch?" Someone who is no longer good at anything, noblemen that we no longer have use for, and peasants that will soon know how to defend themselves without any assistance—and throughout the film, despite the urgency of this question that is deserving of the Idiot—which is in fact the Idiot's question: We Samurai, what are we? Here it is—I would call it an idea *in* cinema, it is a question of this type. You would reply to me in saying, "No! Because it is in fact an idea proper to the novel"—but the idea in cinema becomes as such because it is simultaneously engaged in a cinematographic process.

You could say to me that you have an idea, but if you borrow from Dostoyevsky, an idea is not a concept, it is not philosophy, and concepts are something else. From that *idea*, one could maybe take a concept. Consider Vincente Minnelli, who had an extraordinary idea about dreams. It is very simple: one can engage this idea within the totality of the cinematographic process that is at work in Minnelli. It seems to me that Minnelli's idea about the dream concerns those who don't dream. Why? There is danger soon as there are dreams of the other. At the moment that people's dreams are devouring, it risks to engulf us; the other's dream is dangerous. Dreams have a terrible will to power and each one of us is a victim of others' dreams. Even when it is the most gracious of young girls, her dreams are terrible devourers, not of her soul but by her dreams. Beware of the other's dream, because if you are caught in the other's dream you are screwed.

I could mention another example, an idea that is rightly cinematographic. I will take the most common one, whether it can be attributed to Sylberberg, Straub, or

Marguerite Duras. What do they have in common and what among them is rightly cinematographic? To make a disjunction between the visual and sound is a rightly cinematographic idea. Why can't this be done in theater? Well, it can be done. But if it were done in theater, it would be a theater that is applying cinema to itself. To assure the disjunction of the visual and the audible ("the spoken") responds to the question of having a purely cinematographic idea. Simply stated, a voice speaks of one thing and we show something else. But in fact, there is more. That which one is speaking about is actually *underneath* that which one is showing. This is a very important point. It is in this last distinction that you can feel that this is not something one can do in the theater. To be able to speak simultaneously and to then put it *underneath* that which we see is necessary, or else this disjunctive operation holds no sense, would have no real interest. The great filmmakers had this idea. It is not about saying that it has to be done. Nothing *has* to be done. Whatever they may be, one must have ideas. That is a cinematographic idea.

It is a prodigious one because it assures in cinema a veritable transformation of its elements, a cycle of large elements that makes an impact. Cinema echoes with a sort of qualitative, physical set of elements. It makes a sort of transformation. Earth, air, water, and fire must be added.

We do not have time here to discover what role other elements play in cinema, but in saying all of this, I am not repressing the story. The story is always there, but what interests us is why the story is so very interesting with all of these things behind it or working with it. This question is what is so recognizable in most of Straub's films. There is a grand cycle of elements in Straub's work. All that we see in it is the deserted earth. But this desert is heavy with everything that is underneath it. What is underneath? It is that which the voice is speaking to us about. It is as if the earth was warping itself with what the voice tells us, and is coming to take its place underneath the earth, in its hour and its time. And if the voice speaks of cadavers, it is a whole lineage of cadavers that have just begun to take their place on the earth. Even if at that moment the littlest quivering of the shot of the deserted earth, of the empty space that you have beneath your eyes, on the deserted earth, and so on, takes on all of its meaning. The slightest hollow in this earth, et cetera.

But I could it say again—take note: to have an idea is not on the order of communication. Everything that we have been speaking about is irreducible to all communication. What does that mean? It means, in one sense, one could say that communication is transmission and propagation of information. What is information? That is not a complex question. Everyone knows that information is an ensemble of *order words*. When one informs you, one tells you that you are censored for having believed them. In other words, to inform is to circulate ordered words. Police declarations are said to be "communications" [*communiqués*].

One communicates information, which is to say that we are censored by being in a state, or censored from being able to believe, or that we are held from believing or not from believing, but to make believe that we are believing. Be careful: we are not being asked to believe. We are just being asked to *behave* as if we believe. This is information that is communication. And at the same time in these ordered words and their transmission there is in fact no communication. There is no information; this is exactly the system of control. It is true that it is a platitude, it is obvious. It is evident except in the fact that it is this that should concern us particularly today, because we are entering into a society that we could call a society of control.

A thinker such as Michel Foucault analyzed two types of society, which were quite close in their relationship to power. The first was called the *sovereign* society, and the other was called the *disciplinary* society. Those he called *disciplinary* were called as such because there are all of these transitions, such as with Napoleon, who typified the passage from a sovereign society to a disciplinary society. The disciplinary society defined itself by the constitution of the milieu of enclosure: the prison, the school, the studio, and the hospital. Disciplinary societies needed all of these things. This could engender some ambiguities within certain readings of Foucault because one could believe that this is Foucault's last word, but this is not the case. Foucault never believed that, and even clearly stated that these disciplinary societies were not eternal. He thought that we entered into a new type of society. Of course, there are all sorts of remnants of the disciplinary society, and they will remain for years and years, but we know already that we are in another type of society that we must call, as Burroughs did first (and Foucault had a great admiration for Burroughs), the "society of control."

The society of control moves in a different direction than the disciplinary society. We no longer have need for the space of enclosure. Prisons, schools, and hospitals are all still places for permanent discussion. What could be better for us to spill into than the domicile? Yes, of course, that is the future. Studios and factories are crackling around the edges. Is there not a better place to punish people aside from the prison? All of these old problems are reborn. In any case, the society of control will not come to be through spaces of enclosure. Nor through the schools. We must now observe the new capitalists. It will take forty or fifty years to explain this splendid phenomenon to us, and it will be at the same time in the schools and in the professions. It will be very interesting because the identity of the school in the profession and in its permanent formation is our future. It will inevitably imply the regrouping of schoolchildren in a space of enclosure. Yet it could be done in another way. It could be done by Minitel.

That which controls is not discipline. I would give the example of the freeway that encloses with the unique goal that people can turn into infinity without ever enclosing everything yet are completely controlled. This is our future. Why am I telling you all of this? Information is a controlled system of order words. Order words that are given in our society. What can art do with all of this? What is the work of art? In the very least, there is counterinformation. For example, there are countries where conditions are particularly cruel and harsh, countries where there are very, very extreme dictatorships, where still also exists counterinformation. In Hitler's time, the Jews who escaped from Germany were to tell us of the extermination camps—they were giving counterinformation. It seems to me that counterinformation never accomplishes anything. No form of counterinformation ever bothered Hitler. The only response would be when counterinformation effectively becomes efficient, when it becomes an act of resistance. And the act of resistance is not information nor counterinformation. Counterinformation is only effective when it becomes an act of resistance.

What is the relationship between the work of art and communication? The work of art is not communication. The work of art has nothing to do with counterinformation. On the other hand, there is a fundamental affinity with the work of art and the act of resistance. Then it is there that it has something to do with information and communication—in the same way as the act of resistance. What, then, is this mysterious relationship between the work of art and the act of resistance, when in fact those who resist often do not have the time or sometimes the necessary cultivation to have a relationship with art? I don't know. Malraux developed a beautiful philosophical concept about art. He said, "Art is the only thing that resists death." I'd like to come back to what I said in the beginning concerning, what is it that I do when I make philosophy or when I invent concepts? This is the basis of a rather beautiful philosophical concept; think about it: What is it that resists death? The statue from three thousand years ago can respond to Malraux, and it is a pretty good response. But we could say, "Art is that which resists."

All acts of resistance are not works of art. In a certain manner, all works of art are not acts of resistance, but in another way they are. But in what way is art mysterious? If you permit me to go back to the question, What is it to have an idea in cinema? What is a cinematographic idea?" I would say let's take the case of Jean-Marie Straub as he operates within this disjunction of voice and sound. In his work the voice rises up, rises up, rises up, and again that which it speaks of passes over the naked earth. The desert is the visual image that is simultaneously being shown, and it has no relationship to the sound image; there is no direct relationship with the sound image. What is the act of speech that is rising upward in the air as its object passes underneath the earth? *Resistance*—an act of resistance. And in all of Straub's work, the act of speech is an act of resistance. In the last Kafka, in passing I would cite "the unrecognized name," and would continue with Bach. Think about what the act of speech is in Bach. What is it? It is his music that is an act of resistance. Resistance against what? Not an abstract act of resistance. It is an active struggle against the profane and the sacred. And this music's act of resistance culminates in a scream, just as in the writing of Woyzeck. There is Bach's scream, "Outside, outside, get out of here! I don't want to see you!" That is the act of resistance. Or when Straub brings out this scream, this being Bach's scream. Or when Straub brings forth the scream of the old schizophrenic woman, the woman from the film *Not Reconciled*. Her trace makes me realize the two sides of the act of resistance: it is human, and it is all an act of art. This is the only kind of resistance that resists death and order words, control, either under the guise of the work of art, or in the form of man's struggles. What is the relationship between the struggles of man and the work of art? For me, this is the most mysterious thing, it is exactly what Paul Klee wanted to say when he said, "You know, people are missing. People are missing but they aren't." This fundamental affinity between the work of art and people who no longer exist is never clear, and it will never be clear.

Translated by Alison M. Gingeras

2

French Theory In America

Marshall McLuhan, Canadian Schizo-Jansenist and Pseudo-Joycean Precursor of and Preparer for the Dissemination of French Theory in North America

DONALD F. THEALL

Some cultural objects associated with commercial expositions and with France, the United States, and Canada haunt my discussion of the relationship between McLuhanism and the rise of French theory in North America: the Eiffel Tower; the Trilon and Perisphere (of the New York World's Fair, opening just before World War II); and the Fuller Dome and the theme pavilions of Man and His World (at Expo 67 in Montreal). As the Eiffel Tower fascinated everyone from Duchamp and Joyce to Roland Barthes, and the Trilon and Perisphere domesticized European modernism for the United States, so Expo 67 was the utopian mediazation of the postmodern moment.

Why begin by juxtaposing these objects of excess? Partly because McLuhan was fascinated by architecture and by popular culture, and his writings were heavily influenced by architectural historians Louis Mumford and Sigfried Giedion. Because of those interests Canada and Québec's Expo 67 became McLuhan's Fair, a fact openly acknowledged by the extent to which the postmodern theme pavilions of Man and His World—whose design blended Canadian history and culture—were based on McLuhan's writings, liberally quoted on plaques throughout the pavilions.

McLuhan's Fair marked a special moment in time: a year before Paris 68, on the threshold of the popular movements in Québec, and at the moment when French theory was coming into its own in North America. A little chronology: McLuhan wrote *The Gutenberg Galaxy* in 1962 and *Understanding Media* in 1964, taking off as international media guru by 1965. Johns Hopkins University held its conference on the structuralist controversy in 1966, the same year de Man met Derrida. Equally significant, the French translation of *The Gutenberg Galaxy* was launched at Expo 67—a translation that was to mark the opening of the major debates on *macluhanisme* in France. Ironically, in 1967 McLuhan had virtually no knowledge of contemporary French theory. In 1959, in conversations I had participated in with McLuhan and two structural linguists at the University of

Toronto, he flatly and summarily rejected structuralism and de Saussure as relevant to his project. It was not until 1974 that he finally read Saussure. Nevertheless, although he would not become personally familiar with poststructuralism, postmodernism, and other French theory until the mid-1970s he preconditioned a very broad North American audience to the issues that French theorists were going to raise.

Before continuing to explore further McLuhan's role in relation to French theory in North America, it is important to note how as a Canadian professor of English literature who founded the first graduate communication seminar at the University of Toronto he related to the officially recognized discipline of communication studies in the United States in the 1950s and 1960s. McLuhan's relationship with the major debates on communication in the United States from 1953—when his Ford-sponsored communication seminar started—until virtually the end of his career in the late 1970s was quite complex. From the outset, when under the urging of the anthropologist E. S. Carpenter and with support of the university's vice president, Claude Bissell, he established those Ford-sponsored seminars in culture and communication at the University of Toronto and was one of the associate editors of the seminal interdisciplinary journal *Explorations*, edited by Carpenter, McLuhan was aware of the major scholars in the newly emerging discipline of communication in the United States. However, he professed not to regard the work of the trailblazers as very significant in shaping the discipline of communication. His major reservations prompting his relative indifference to their work were related to the then dominant statistical, empiricist, and behaviorist emphases in mainline communication studies. In contradistinction, McLuhan's approach was historical and interpretative (i.e., hermeneutic, although he would not normally have used the term at that time). While after 1950 he had also been affected by the new cybernetic theories of communication being developed in the United States and England (Wiener, Bateson, and the figures involved in the Macy conferences), he also criticized them for being logico-mathematic rather than rhetoricogrammatical.

There was little contact between McLuhan and mainstream communication studies until late in his life, and his writings had relatively little impact on the academic study of communication in the United States until they were embraced by French theory in the late 1960s and early 1970s. However, from 1964, with the publication of *Understanding Media*, he began to have a wide impact in other areas inside and outside the academy, which partly paved the way shortly afterward for French theory's emergence as a major factor within American academia. Other aspects of the differences between U.S. approaches to communication and those in Canada should also be noted. These were a result of the then dominant affiliations of Canadian universities with England or France. Early in the 1950s McLuhan showed an interest in the work of Raymond Williams (with whom he shared a Cambridge undergraduate education, as well as also having a Cambridge doctorate). Even more than McLuhan, Williams had a considerable impact on the early development of communication studies in Canada in the 1960s. At the same time, the Francophone universities in Québec and Ontario were being influenced by the beginnings of communication theory in France, as represented in the work of Roland Barthes and the journal *Communications*.

Since McLuhan was consciously suppressed by large segments of official academia, it is not overtly recognized that McLuhan's writings first raised, poetically and hermeneutically, most of the very same issues that French theorists were later to raise more rigorously for a majority of North American scholars, particularly those in contemporary literature, communication and speech communication, sociological theory, film media studies, and cultural studies. Emerging as a significant figure during the final stages of the prominence of the "New Criticism," McLuhan, its last major exponent, was situated to mark those moments that epiphanized the rise of poststructuralism and postmodern theory.[1] His significance at the culmination of the New Criticism underlines why deconstructive criticism first arose at institutions where the New Criticism had been entrenched, such as Yale University, particularly among students who had encountered figures such as William Wimsatt Jr., Cleanth Brooks, and Robert Penn Warren.[2] Through the immense popularity of his books and through his comments as a personality pontificating about media and everyday culture, McLuhan contributed to establishing the groundwork in the late 1960s and 1970s that in the later stages of the introduction of French theory partially created the climate in which enthusiasm for Deleuze, Guattari, Virilio, and Baudrillard would exponentially increase.

It was not his initial affinities with Richards, Leavis, and the Southern critics of the *Sewanee Review* that enabled him to occupy this role, but what he identified in his correspondence as the key to his work: "Nobody could pretend serious interest in my work who is not completely familiar with all of the works of James Joyce and the French symbolists."[3] In another letter (also in 1974) he added,

> The reason that I am admired in Paris and some of the Latin countries is that my approach is rightly regarded as "structuralist." I have acquired the approach through Joyce and Eliot and the Symbolists, and used it in *The Mechanical Bride* [published in 1951]. Nobody except myself in the media field has ventured to use the structuralist or "existentialist" approach.[4]

For interested, informed audiences within and without the university, frequently without their full realization of what was happening (leaving aside momentarily the problematic equation of the structuralist with the existentialist), he popularized insights, strategies, and styles of the *symbolistes*, the Anglo-American high modernists, Wyndham Lewis, and Joyce, particularly his *Finnegans Wake*.

Think of North America in the 1950s and 1960s, with a rising postwar consciousness of media—the pervasiveness of advertising, the power of TV, the maturing of film, and of the recording industry, which made Elvis a mythical media demigod! It is in this context that McLuhan, first, intellectually and academically in 1962 with the *Galaxy*, then mass mediafied and popularized in 1964 with *Understanding Media*, and continuing into the 1970s, used an unholy modernist medley of symbolists, Joyce, Lewis, and European modernism in architecture and art, to build a vision—partly demonic and partly utopian—of the future impact of the "electric" revolution of the 1950s. Part of McLuhan's shock tactics was the sudden dissemination in practice and in explication of strategies and concepts derived from literature and art: Joycean ambivalence rather than symbolist ambiguity; protosemiotic signs rather than symbols; a use of analogy in which difference rather than similarity was the dominant factor; a transformation of the empiric and pragmatic *explication du texte* of the New Critics into an intuitively satiric, semioanalytic (protosemioclastic) reading of cultural phenomena; the Alexandrian-derived rhetoricogrammatical hermeneutics of the trivium, freed from logic through his use of a poetic dialectic, becoming instruments of cultural analysis; and his application of the concepts of landscape, the picturesque and Edmund Burke's analysis of the sublime to the technoinstrumental sublime of the interior landscape of modernism, *une peinture de pensée*.[5]

There are strong intimations in the 1950s in articles in *Explorations*, edited by McLuhan's collaborator, Carpenter, and from the 1960s in his books, of his already being paleo-Barthesian, paleo-Derridean, paleo-Lyotardian, and paleo-Baudrillardian. The 1960s were a time when the New Criticism, subsequent to Northrop Frye's pseudoscientific revision, underwent a still further, more profound revision by McLuhan—a reversal he later capsulated in the title of a book, *From Cliché to Archetype*, but which in a more profound way was akin to asserting the materialist and anarchistic nature of the poetic, somewhat in anticipation of Baudrillard's analysis of Saussure's anagrams and Freud's *Witz*.[6] If Frye, following Richards, insisted on the New Criticism becoming a "science of poetry," McLuhan rather emphasized its empiricism, in which the resources of the poetic become instruments of unmasking. The development of deconstruction in France was concurrent with McLuhan's moving beyond the New Criticism, transforming it into a historically grounded, poetic hermeneutic that would engage the everyday world of media as material processes. This project was coming to fruition as deconstruction was being imported from France first to Johns Hopkins and then more dramatically to the home base of the now ancient New Criticism, Yale.

As Jean Baudrillard has always insisted, McLuhan was not a theorist; his approach was empiric. In *The Medium Is the Rear View Mirror*, I argued that he was also a Menippean satiric poet, as well as a poet manqué, because he wished simultaneously to conceal his poetry behind an alleged instrumental purpose of assisting "the public to observe consciously the drama which is intended to operate upon it unconsciously" by satirically generating the "light" to offset the "heat" produced through manipulating, controlling, and exploiting minds by "the prolonged mental rutting" of media, ads, and entertainment.[7] His deliberate use of *crypsis* was directed at concealing that motive behind a complex, nearly unfathomable, subversive ambivalence, like that of the ritual jester and the carnivalesque in the Middle Ages and the Renaissance—pointed jokes, teasing deceptions, and devastating *Witz*. All were strategies he had first learned from his early research on Thomas Nashe, the history from which Nashe's writing emerged, and its persistence until the early eighteenth century, and later in McLuhan's fascination with Joyce's *Ulysses* and *Finnegans Wake*.

Within this McLuhanesque, empiric, satiric poetry manqué, designed for a social scientific era, the topoi generating the problems and paradoxes of French theories characteristic of postmodernism, poststructuralism, and beyond first began circulating through North America. McLuhan's primary source for this strategy was the ambivalence of Joyce's modernism.[8] The wave of *m(a)cluhanisme* that hit Paris after 1967, just when Joyce was being promoted by *Tel Quel*, Sollers, and Kristeva as a major object for cultural commentary, attests to the French theoretical interest in McLuhan with his affinity for Joyce. But his preconditioning the reception of French theory in North America is by no means as familiar, partly because of the massive negative reaction to McLuhan in academia in the 1970s, followed by his decline and suppression as a major figure by the 1980s. In spite of the reaction in the 1970s and after, McLuhan continued to haunt the North American cultural debates about communication, media, and technology as a primarily unspoken presence, for he had provided the language used in those debates by the media, by policy makers, among researchers in human interface technology, and, especially for present purposes, in the discussions and writings of the social sciences, cognitive sciences, and social theory in the academy. His reputation rose again in the 1990s with a new urgency resulting from the widespread interest generated by the emergence of hypermedia and cyberculture and the adoption of McLuhan as the patron saint of *Wired* magazine.

That there was in France in the early 1970s a major debate as to who deserved to be nominated the French McLuhan reveals the significance of McLuhan's continuing ghostly presence. In that debate Barthes and Baudrillard appeared as the leading contenders. The interests that McLuhan anticipated or shared with Barthes, as I pointed out in seminars at the University of Bordeaux in the fall of 1975, are numerous: their respective work on the high classical moment of English and French drama; an early concern with the history of classical rhetoric (McLuhan in his unpublished but widely cited thesis on the Harvey-Nashe controversy and Barthes in *Communications*); the striking similarities between their first major books (*The Mechanical Bride* and *Mythologies*); the later reflexive, ironic self-examinations of their careers (in *Culture Is Our Business* and *Barthes par Barthes*). These are complemented by many other areas they explored: photography, fashion, visual images, media, mass myth, and even the new orality. While McLuhan rejected the semiology characteristic of the early Barthes, he shared an interest in the "sign" that was to become the central concern of the later hermeneutic, poststructuralist Barthes. And while he overtly rejected Barthes's social critique, McLuhan's analyses were semioclastic.

Derrida has far less claim to being the French McLuhan than Barthes, and himself apparently wanted none of it, as he indicated in his single reference to McLuhan, in a paper delivered at a conference at the Université de Montréal in Québec:

> We are not witnessing an end of writing which, to follow McLuhan's ideological representation, would restore a transparency or immediacy of social relations; but indeed a more and more powerful historical unfolding of a general writing of which the system of speech, consciousness, meaning, presence, truth, et cetera., would only be an effect, to be analyzed as such. It is this questioned effect that I have elsewhere called *logocentrism*.[9]

Yet, as John Fekete has pointed out, "Derrida takes up again and again, without reference to McLuhan, the same themes McLuhan develops throughout the 1960s [and, I would add, throughout the 1950s]: logocentrism, phonocentrism, the eye, the ear, technic as [exemplified by] the impact of the phonetic alphabet, abstraction, writing, linearity as the repression of pluri-dimensional thought, simultaneity, synaesthesia, etc."[10] Although not often mentioned, it is significant that Derrida and McLuhan, the philosopher-theorist and the publicist poet-manqué, shared a fascination with Joyce, for Joyce had explored much earlier and more extensively the very same themes that Fekete says Derrida shared with McLuhan.

There is one aspect of Derrida's writing that apparently echoes a very specific genre, mode, or "tone" of writing that McLuhan had developed in the 1960s from Joyce's transformation of the work of practitioners of learned satire—from Lucian, Seneca, Petronius, and Apuleius to Rabelais, Swift, Sterne, Pope, and Carlyle.[11] It is this "tone" or genre with which Derrida associates *La Carte Postale* and with which, following an *envoi* of August 13, he also relates this work to Joyce's

Wake with its "Babelian implications" and their apocalyptic affiliations. Only two *envois* later (on August 18), Derrida speaks about his "anatomy" of the "post card" (Plato standing behind the seated Socrates) and identifies this "tone"[12]:

> If you want to understand what an "anatomy" of the post card might be, think of the *Anatomy of Melancholy* (this is a genre that is not unrelated to Menippean satire: Frye recalls the influence of the Last Supper and of the Symposium on this genre, interminable banquets, encylopedic farrago, the satiric critique of the *philosophus gloriosus*, etc.) Be Stoic, it will be our ex-pyrosus: the end of the world by fire.[13]

McLuhan in 1975 had also told his readers that his writings and his presentations were Mennipean satires (although rather a lesser version compared to Joyce). In his practice of this poetic satiric technique he predisposed audiences to a tolerance for the "anatomy" as well as other modes of Menippean discourse. It should also be noted that Joyce's *Wake* is affiliated through Shaun (a twin son of Anna Livia) who, as post, is delivering a note that Shem, the other twin (a perversely diabolic poet) had written for ALP, his mother. Derrida obviously relates his own use of the "post" to Joyce's—just as McLuhan does—when *The Post Card* plays on the postelectric technological role of the postal service, such as telegrams, in order to situate electric media as a central aspect of his exploration of technology. Thus McLuhan's project, influenced by Joyce, partly contributed to preconditioning and predisposing the reception of Derrida's complex anatomical play with post, telecommunications, and digital technologies.

While not exactly candidates for being "the French McLuhan," Gilles Deleuze and Félix Guattari spoke more positively than Derrida of McLuhan and shared a variety of perspectives with him or, through Joyce, with McLuhan's project. In *Anti-Oedipus*, they note McLuhan's significance in showing "what a language of decoded flows is, as opposed to a signifier that strangles and over-codes the flows."[14] In noting this connection of McLuhan's intuitions about a language—whether phonic, graphic, gestural, or audiovisual—in which no flow is privileged, they specifically recognize the significance of McLuhan's describing the electric light as "pure information," a medium without a message, for they note that "the electric flow can be considered a realization of such a flow"—indeterminate and amorphous, though a continuum. It is not surprising then that in *A Thousand Plateaus* Deleuze and Guattari associate McLuhan's perceptions in discussing nomadology with respect to counterpointing his description of a neoprimitivism, a new tribal society against the "worldwide ecumenical machines" as producing a society of "war machines."[15] It is not exclusively the direct citations of McLuhan, but the shared body of knowledge that French theory and McLuhan experienced in *symbolisme*, modernism, and particularly the work of James Joyce. For example, Deleuze's discussion in *The Logic of Sense* has McLuhanesque aspects. McLuhan spoke frequently of the significance of Lewis Carroll, whom he saw as a precursor of Joyce. Also, from his early research into the grammaticorhetorical traditions of exegesis and the trivium, he intuited the connections of Carroll and Joyce with Stoic logicians. The entire Joycean spectrum, which meant a great deal to Derrida and which Deleuze recognized in his earlier works—*Proust and Signs* (originally published in 1964), *Difference and Repetition* (originally published in 1968) and *The Logic of Sense* (originally published in 1970)—bore on motifs of fragmentation, transverse communication, disparation, dissemination, polysemy, polyvocity, writing, rhizomic structure, and so on. It was these motifs that McLuhan would emblazon and broadcast throughout North America in the late 1950s and particularly after 1965. And as exasperating and imprecise as that combined poetic and promotional public relations exercise may have been, it implanted in the artistic community and the avant-garde and radical elements of the academic community a predilection for the discourse of French theory.

Before probing more deeply the role of Joyce, who was neither French nor North American, although he lived a substantial portion of his life in France and he opens *Wake* by punningly referring in the fifth line to Tristan and Isolde's "North Armorica," verbal play that links France, North America and Ireland, let's briefly note that the third and perhaps prime candidate to be the French McLuhan was Baudrillard, the only figure who repeatedly cited McLuhan's work. Ultimately Baudrillard's nomination to be the French McLuhan, as Gary Genosko attests, proves to be the most revealing for understanding the role McLuhan played in North America, since it owes as much to the striking differences between them as it does their numerous similarities.[16] The sharp difference between Baudrillard's vision of contemporaneity in the *Transparency of Evil* and McLuhan's humanistic, somewhat quietistic but, more specifically, Jansenistic Catholicism is particularly revealing, for while the schizoid McLuhan shared a fascination and substantial involvement with the post-Nietzsche world, he was a fully committed, pietistic believer in a very conservative traditional Catholicism. Any explanation of McLuhan's role in preconditioning North America to French theory must ultimately take into account his neo-Catholic revisionist attempt to sanitize radical high modernist theory.

Joyce is at the crux of the story, since his writings, as a valuable resource to be exploited, fascinated the North American scholarly industry, while his avant-garde stance fascinated Parisian and Swiss intellectuals.[17] So an interest in Joyce provides a link between many French theoretical interests and McLuhan's empirical, pseudopoetic unmasking of the culture industry. Against McLuhan's schizo-Jansenism, Joyce's own poetic, closer to that of Bataille, is clearly a true poetic of excess dedicated, if I may borrow a phrase from Baudrillard, to "the extermination of the name of God." For in *Wake* Joyce's deity "is vrayedevraye Blankdeblank, god of all machineries and tomestone of Barnstaple" (253.33–6) and his poet is "a skipgod, expulled for looking at churches from behind" (488.22–3). Similar to Baudrillard's analysis of Saussure's anagram and of anathema, the *Wake* grounds the word, moving beyond the word through the interactive virtuality of his dream of the postelectric world. Finn's fatal fall initiates a symbolic exchange and death within a design in which Joyce plays games with political economy, contemporary science and math, and the ritualistic use of analysis.

In 1946, in a letter to a friend, the Jansenist McLuhan noted the darkness of Joyce's poetic, for as *Ulysses* had opened with the first words of the Catholic mass, *Wake* closed with a "rendering of the last part of the mass," making the *Wake* "an intellectual Black Mass." He noted that Joyce's recording "concludes with an imitation of the damnation of Faust. As he reads it . . . it is horrible. Casual, eerie," suggesting that it reflects the "hatred of language" in the philosophy of "Existenz."[18] On the other hand, the schizoid McLuhan disseminated a poetry of excess, for the presumed purpose (unless we take him to be one of the greatest cynics of this century) of undoing and exposing through empiric observation the workings of Joyce's rebellion—that carnivalesque resurrection, which is in reality a revolution—an insurrection, a phallic erection, and the resurrection of Nietzsche's superman. McLuhan correctly sensed the Nietzschean depth of Joyce's poetic, for what Nietzsche describes as 'poetic violence which replaces the order of all the atoms of the phrase" becomes in Joyce's *Wake*, "the abnihilisation of the etym." This is why McLuhan's most extensive use of Joyce's *Wake* occurs in *War and Peace in the Global Village* (1968)—the title ironically echoing that of a later essay in which Derrida analyzes two *Wake*an words, "he war."[19] Intuiting, then reproducing and exposing those Nietzschean depths as an empiric observer to defend the Catholic *logos* against the Joycean "letter as litter," while preparing a ground for radical French theory in North America, is oddly enough a paradoxical move worthy of the witty apologetics of McLuhan's early role model, the Edwardian Catholic, G. K. Chesterton. To perform these empiric, poetic acrobatics, McLuhan produced penetrating aphoristic insights for late radical modernity and poststructuralism, such as "The Medium is the message, the massage (tactility) and the mass age (the abyss of the crowd)," events whose importance Baudrillard identifies in unveiling the implications of "symbolic exchange"—the simulacra, ecstasy, transparency.

McLuhan, who felt there was too much communication in the modern world (perhaps in a manner similar to Joyce's treatment of silence), communicated about communication primarily to detour, delay, conceal, and eradicate it. From the outset McLuhan had intuited the cosmos to be the Joycean "chaosmos" (a term

Deleuze and Guattari apparently borrowed from *Wake*)—a chaosmos of a *deus absconditus*, a hidden god. In the 1940s McLuhan had used Edgar Allen Poe's "The Maelstrom" to explain symbolically the nature of the whodunit as the tension between a world moving toward chaos and the sleuth, who, while paralyzed with horror discovers the "power of detached observation," thus taking a "scientific" interest in the action of the storm. In 1951 in *The Mechanical Bride*, whose working title had originally been "The Guide to Chaos," McLuhan used the same image to explain his new empiric method.[20] In 1970, in *From Cliché to Archetype*, schizo McLuhan still declares that chaos is the devil's world—and that such chaos is produced by the very type of cyclical reversal that Baudrillard considers characteristic of the simulacra, resulting in the ecstasy of communication, and is also characteristic of Joyce's Viconianism.

While Joyce's chaosmos is the comic, carnivalesque domain of an earth goddess whose "redtangles are all abscissan for limitsing this tendency . . . to expense her selfs as sphere as possible, paradismic perimutter, . . . [while] the infinisissimalls of her facets [are] becoming manier and manier as . . . her umdescribables . . . shrinks from schurtiness" (298.25–30), McLuhan's naturalistic chaosmos, has affinities with his acoustic space, the return to the oral, tribalized society. Developing and adopting this notion from Carpenter's analysis of preliterate Inuit culture to the postelectric world, McLuhan explained, "Acoustic space has no center. It consists of boundless random resonations."[21] His description of this approximates the twelfth-century Augustinian theological poet, Alain of Lille's description of God, in which "God is an intelligible sphere, whose center is everywhere, and whose circumference is nowhere."[22] This situates McLuhan's hidden or absent God as a deity beyond nature, like that of Pascal's *deus absconditus*, for both say nature, not God, is an intelligible sphere. For Pascal, as Borges notes, absolute space becomes the abyss, for he "hated the universe. He was sorry the firmament could not speak; he compared our lives to those of shipwrecked men on a desert island . . . and he expressed his feelings [saying nature] is an infinite sphere, the center of which is everywhere, the circumference nowhere." Borges also notes that according to the manuscript version, Pascal first wrote *frightful* (*effroyable*) rather than *infinite*, reminding us that McLuhan, too, fears the postliterate death of the book and insists on the *logos* as a primal writing— for his God is absent from the media world. Consequently his vision disseminated a sense of panic to North American intellectual discourse as it assimilated French theorists—first Derrida, who had rejected McLuhan, and ultimately, Deleuze, Guattari, and particularly Baudrillard, who was the most appreciative of McLuhan's ambivalent awareness of the transparency of evil and of his awareness of "fatal strategies" and "cool memories." Even though personally committed to the Vatican and its defense through a pseudo-Thomism—yet actually a schizo-Jansenism—McLuhan chose to be of what Blake, describing Milton's Satan as Jehovah, called the devil's party; simultaneously becoming the prophet for the global, transnational electronic entrepreneurs, while intensifying and accelerating the hysteric broad reception of the insights of French theory.

If Virilio and Baudrillard—and to a lesser extent Deleuze and Guattari—appear to have a greater affinity with McLuhan than Barthes, Derrida, and Lyotard, McLuhanism has played a role in their rise to prominence in North America because the schizoid McLuhan's demonic side that was let loose in his empiric poetry provides familiarity with the issues that Baudrillard and Virilio, not being encumbered by McLuhan's hidden Jansenist agenda, reveal as the transformation of reality into virtuality. Through his immersion in the symbolists, and particularly Joyce, which released his demonic side, McLuhan's work has disseminated for more than four decades intimations of retribalization, becoming object, rhizomic nomadism, seduction, simulacra, ecstasy, exponentially accelerating speed, the aesthetics of disappearance, and the new "chaosmology" of the chaosmos, familiarizing an increasingly less naive North America with the Continental visions of excess, but always with the intent of inverting the reversal implied in that project by turning Joyce and French theory upside down and inside out. For that reason, remembering how in the eighteenth century the middlebrow popularism of Addison had essentially tried to stem the insurgence of the French thought of Montaigne, Fenélon, and Pascal embraced by Pope and Swift into England, Pope's aphoristic closing to his satire on Addison—which is the epigraph of my book *The Medium Is the Rear View Mirror: Understanding McLuhan*—seems more apt than ever when applied to the "pseudo-socio anarchist" man for all seasons, Marshall McLuhan and his project:

> Who would not laugh, if such a man there be
> Who would not weep, if McLuhan were he![23]

Notes

1. John Fekete argues McLuhan's central role as the culmination of New Criticism in *The Critical Twilight: Explorations of the Ideology of Anglo-American Literary Theory from Eliot to McLuhan.* (London: Routledge and Kegan Paul, 1976). Although in that work he is quite critical of McLuhan, he later revisits the subject in "Massage in the Mass Age: Remembering the McLuhan Matrix," *Canadian Journal of Political and Social Theory* 6, no. 3 (1982), pp. 50–67. Toward the conclusion of this more positive revaluation of McLuhan, there is an extended discussion of the way in

which McLuhan and Derrida, although by no means in agreement, raise a surprisingly large number of similar questions.

2. McLuhan's close relationship with Cleanth Brooks and W. K. Wimsatt Jr. (especially the latter) is clearly indicated by their extensive use of McLuhan's Cambridge doctoral thesis, *The Place of Thomas Nashe in the Learning of His Time*. It is noted with considerable approval in their preface to *Literary Criticism: A Short History*, p. 11, "A more or less pervasive debt in several chapters to a manuscript book by H. M. McLuhan concerning the ancient war between dialecticians and rhetoricians is here gratefully acknowledged and underscored by the quotation following chapter 4, of two substantial excerpts from published essays by Mr. McLuhan." See pp. 74–76.

3. McLuhan to Marshall Fishwick (July 31, 1974), *Letters*, p. 505.

4. McLuhan to Marshall Fishwick (August 1, 1974), *Letters*, p. 506.

5. See the forthcoming study of McLuhan by Donald Theall, *The Virtual McLuhan: Poetry, Prophecy, Piety and Technology*. For McLuhan on Burke and the sublime, see McLuhan, "Tennyson and Picturesque Poetry," in *The Interior Landscape: The Literary Criticism of . . .*, ed. Eugene McNamara, pp. 135–55, especially the discussions of Arthur Hallam's influence on Tennyson and note especially Edmund Burke's role in the discussion on pp. 245–51. See Jean-François Lyotard's discussion of modernism, postmodernism and the sublime in *The Postmodern Condition* (Minneapolis: University of Minnesota Press, 1984) trans. Geoff Bennington and Brian Massumi, pp. 77–81 and his remarks on Burke and Kant in *Lessons on the Analytic of the Sublime* (Stanford: Stanford University Press, 1994), trans. Elizabeth Rottenberg, pp. 60–66. While McLuhan's overt discussion of Burke and the sublime is brief, it permeates his discussion of landscape, interior landscape, the picturesque, and other aspects of late Romantic and modernist aesthetics. See, for example, McLuhan's introduction to *Alfred Lord Tennyson: Selected Poetry* (New York: Holt, Rinehart and Winston, 1956).

6. Jean Baudrillard, *Symbolic Exchange and Death*, trans. Iain Hamilton Grant (London: Sage, 1993), pp. 195–213, 229–33.

7. Marshall McLuhan, *The Mechanical Bride*. As Greg Wilmott points out in *McLuhan or Modernism in Reverse* (Toronto: University of Toronto Press, 1996), his ongoing commitment to this goal is attested by his reading this on the vinyl record that was produced by CBS in 1967, paralleling the book publication of *The Medium is the Message*.

8. For a discussion of Joyce's relationship with French thought, see Geert Lernout, *The French Joyce* (Ann Arbor: University of Michigan Press, 1990). *Post-Structuralist Joyce: Essays from the French*, ed. Derek Attridge and Daniel Ferrer, presents a selection of current discussions of Joyce, including essays by Jacques Derrida and Hélène Cixous.

9. Derrida, "Writing and Telecommunications," in *Margins of Philosophy*, p. 329.

10. Fekete, "Massage is the Mass Age."

11. The term *Mennippean satire* became more widely recognized and prevalent in literary criticism after the publication of Mikhail Bakhtin's *Rabelais and his World*, trans. Helen Iswolsky (Cambridge: MIT Press, 1968), originally published in Russia in 1965, and *Problems of Dostoevsky's Poetics*, ed. and trans. Caryl Emerson. (Minneapolis: University of Minnesota Press, 1984) [the entire 1963 text had been published in a "faulty" English translation in 1973]. See Julia Kristeva's *Desire in Language: A Semiotic Approach to Literature and Art* (New York: Columbia University Press,

1980), originally published in France in 1979. The term was familiar in North American criticism in the 1950s as evidenced by its appearance in Northrop Frye's *Anatomy of Criticism* (Princeton: Princeton University Press, 1957) to which Derrida refers in *La Carte Postale*. McLuhan's interest in and familiarity with Menippean satire in the early 1950s is discussed in the penultimate chapter of my forthcoming book, *The Virtual McLuhan: Poetry, Prophecy, Piety and Technology*. I first noted the relation of Joyce and McLuhan to Menippean satire in *The Medium Is the Rear View Mirror: Understanding McLuhan* (Montreal: McGill Queen's University Press, 1971).

12. Jacques Derrida, *The Postal Card: From Socrates to Freud and Beyond*, trans. Alan Bates (Chicago: University of Chicago Press, 1987), p. 240. Originally published in 1980.

13. Derrida, *The Postal Card*, p. 245.

14. Gilles Deleuze and Félix Guattari, *Anti-Oedipus*, trans. Robert Hurley et al. (New York: Viking, 1977), pp. 240–41; originally published in France in 1972.

15. Gilles Deleuze and Félix Guattari, *A Thousand Plateaus*, trans. Brian Massumi. (Minneapolis: University of Minnesota Press, 1987), p. 360; originally published in France in 1980.

16. Gary Genosko, "McLuhan, Baudrillard and Cultural Theory," a series of seminars posted on *Semiotica*'s website. www.chass.utoronto.ca/epc/srb/cyber/gent.html

17. Donald F. Theall and Joan Theall, "Marshall McLuhan and James Joyce: Beyond Media," *Canadian Journal of Communication* 14, nos. 4–5 (1989). There is a chapter on McLuhan in Donald F. Theall, *Beyond the Word: Reconstructing Sense in the Joyce Era of Technology, Culture and Communication* (Toronto: University of Toronto Press, 1995). In the forthcoming *The Virtual McLuhan* there are two chapters on Joyce's role and a third in which there is a discussion of Joyce's role in McLuhan's being a Menippean satirist.

18. McLuhan to Felix Giovanelli (May 10, 1946), *Letters*, p. 18.

19. Jacques Derrida, "Two Words for Joyce," in *Post-Structuralist Joyce: Essays from the French*, ed. Derek Attridge and Daniel Ferrer (London: Cambridge University Press, 1984), pp. 145–59.

20. Greg Wilmott, *McLuhan or Modernism in Reverse*, pp. 51, 159.

21. McLuhan and Bruce R. Powers, *The Global Village: Transformations in World Life and Media in the 21st Century*, (New York: Oxford University Press, 1992), p. 133.

22. Jorge Luis Borges, *Other Inquisitions: 1937–1952*, trans. Ruth R. Sims (NY: Simon and Schuster, 1968), 6–9.

23. This is the epigraph to my book *The Medium Is the Rear View Mirror*.

Doing Theory

SYLVÈRE LOTRINGER

> What is done with the art is what gives it meaning. The way my movie was used—that was the meaning of the movie.
>
> —*Jack Smith*

> There's no idea in general, it's always an idea in something. Ideas are some kind of potential already engaged in a domain.
>
> —*Gilles Deleuze*

I knew about French theory before arriving in America in the late 1960s. It wasn't called that, in fact didn't yet exist as a distinct phenomenon, but it really is through America that I discovered theory, or rather realized its full potential. I could as well say, of course, that I discovered America through French theory, the two being hardly separate in my mind. This may explain why my reaction to America wasn't to isolate "theory" and treat it as a separate entity, as happened later when it finally caught on, but rather to bring it out from what already existed here.

French theory is an American creation anyway. The French themselves never conceived it as such, although French philosophers obviously had something to do with it. In France, French theory was considered philosophy, or psychoanalysis, or semiotics, or anthropology, in short any manner of "thinking" *(pensée)* but never referred to as *theory*. The closest French thought ever got to be unified in France was much earlier on, in 1965, a few years after Claude Lévi-Strauss's major theoretical statement, *Savage Mind* (*La Pensée sauvage*), was published. Suddenly the French media started lumping together as part of the "structuralist school" a number of essays and books that had just come out and seemed to share some common features: Roland Barthes's "Introduction to the Structural Analysis of Narratives," Jacques Lacan's *Écrits*, Michel Foucault's *The Order of Things*. A well-known cartoon in *Le Nouvel Observateur* represented the four men sitting half-naked around a campfire, feathers stuck in their hair. This was, of course, a way of acknowledging the role structural anthropology had played in the new "philosophy," which now seemed poised to become a major intellectual movement, challenging existentialism. Lévi-Strauss, in effect, had done to contemporary culture what Ferdinand de Saussure did to general linguistics starting from his own specialty, the study of Indo-European languages: he applied a reduced model (dead languages, archaic societies) to order a far more complex phenomenon. It was not the first time that French thought projected itself onto the New World, long before America repaid it in its own coin, turning French thinking into an American phenomenon, another glamorous product: French theory (made) in the U.S.A. "No epoch worth its salt ever started from theory. first it was a game, a conflict, a voyage," Guy Debord wrote. This is the kind of voyage, or rather *spectacle*, that America gave itself under the name *French theory*.

Theory already existed in America, but in a more pragmatic form. Actually, the first book of French theory published in America, by *Semiotext(e)*, was a book by John Cage. French philosopher-musicologist Daniel Charles made with Cage a series of interviews in English which were published in France in 1976 with the humorous title *Pour les oiseaux (For the Birds)*. But Charles lost the original tapes and I had the book retranslated from the French. This strange hybrid, a stranger in its own language, perfectly embodied the paradox of theory in America: the first book of French theory, of the kind of French theory I liked, was American. Charles's questions, of course, were informed by French philosophy, but Cage's responses were already taking us to another dimension: they were to theory what noise is to music.

What John Cage once said of music would perfectly apply to theory. "In music," he wrote in *For the Birds*, "we should be content to keep our ears open. Everything can enter *musically* in an ear that is open to every possible sound. . . . But then, in some way, one has to give up on music for this to happen. Or at least give up *on what one calls music*. And the same goes for politics. I am quite willing to talk about 'non-politics,' the way people refer to my 'non-music.' It's the same problem. If we were ready to put aside what is known as 'music,' everything in life would become music."[1] A theorist's dream: giving up on "theory" so that the entire world would become theoretical. But then, of course, music or theory would have to be put aside, or return differently. Any noise becomes musical *once you focus on it with a musical mind*. This is what I tried to do in relation to "theory."

You can learn a lot from artists—all you have to do is keep your ears open. It didn't matter whether they had read French theory or not. Actually, those I first met in New York hadn't and probably wouldn't have been interested in knowing about it—that is, before French theory came in, of course. Artists are theorists in their own way, so we each had our own way of theorizing. I wanted to figure out how *they* went about it, understand what kind of relation existed between my concepts and their ideas about music or painting. I was convinced that one should be able to derive something *like* theory from "nontheoretical thinking" as long as one paid attention to the issues at hand. Artists used to refer to that simply as "getting the information," which mystified me at first. I was still thinking in terms of the *theory* of communication. Thinking theoretically, sometimes, makes you miss the simplest things.

Jack Smith got things right for me one night at his apartment in New York's Lower East Side. He was sniffling and whining as he used to do when he was making a major point: "Listen, you are a creature, artistic I can tell, that somehow got hung up on the issue of language. Forget it. It's *thinking*. . . . If you can think of something, the language will fall into place in the most fantastic way, but the thought is what's going to do it."[2] Whether one can think without words is a major controversy among semioticians. Some artists, at any rate, could do that. They didn't have to grope for words or stop being artists when they conceived things. They didn't conceive things the way theorists do. Even when they stopped doing art (viz. Duchamp), it was for "conceptual" reasons, not theoretical ones.

I liked to think that concepts could be directly read in movements, and as movement, the body presenting itself just for what it is, stripped of all meaning, becoming an "abstract machine," mobile parts occupying multiple positions in space; or a musical piece freed from harmony that would let sounds be heard for what they are, in their singularity. Theory was not just where people generally saw it. I never believed that theory existed for its own sake anyway, or had to elicit a special reverence. It was all right that people would tinker with theory— Levi-Strauss's *bricolage*—and adapt it for various purposes. I liked this kind of pragmatism. And yet, theory also has an integrity of its own and deserves to be read carefully and thoughtfully. One shouldn't meddle with concepts unless one makes them better than what they were before. As Deleuze said, you should make sure that authors you write about don't turn over in their grave. But then it was up to each reader to ruminate these concepts on their own, so they had a chance to quicken their mind, sharpen their sensibility, focus their activities. In a word, lovers of theory would serve only for what Nietzsche expected history to serve— for life and action, and not as a way to avoid both. For "to value its study beyond a certain point mutilates and degrades life." Theory doesn't always have to be answered in kind; it can be dealt with in a "nontheoretical" way as well, by perceiving everything as a theoretical problem. Theory then becomes an eye-opener and can be put to task everywhere. Everything can become an object of reflection. Everything can become political.

The point of a theory, anyway, isn't to be something (someone's intellectual property) or belong somewhere (France, Germany, America), *but to become everything it is capable of.* The kind of question that should be raised more often is whether America was capable of bringing out what was most powerful in French theory, and also whether French theory was capable of bringing out in return what was most vital in America, revealing aspects or prospects that Americans otherwise would have remained unaware of.

This is why it was so important to me that French theory would stop being singled out, "packaged" as French, even as theory, and become American. By *American* I don't mean what is generally understood by that term, something big and flashy that allows things to fulfill their destiny as a disposable commodity. To the contrary: becoming American in America, for French theory, could mean only one thing: *becoming imperceptible.*

T. S. Eliot tried something of the sort when he realized that poetry by now was too noticeable and estranged from everyday life to be effective, and the only way to make it permeate the culture, and restore a sense of order and tradition in a world that was sorely lacking in both, was to make it vernacular, fluid, invisible. This is, in a sense, what I tried to do with *Semiotext(e)*, but for a very different purpose, of course.

Semiotext(e) is a magazine I started with a group of friends from Columbia University in 1974. Just thinking about it now—some things you only understand much after the fact—I realize that each issue was a way of "doing theory" the way artists "do art," by establishing between found material, displaced documents, original essays, interviews, photographs, quotes, and so on, what Cage called a "nonrelationship" and Deleuze and Guattari a "nondisjunctive synthesis." Things can coexist together, each can remain what it is in its singularity, its own temporality, each preserving a life of its own while interpenetrating the other in a richer, more complex way. And this nonsynthesis wasn't restricted to the space inside; it also was meant to hang thought between worlds outside that remained separate— disparate milieus of artists, punks, young academics, activists, and others that existed apart—sliding each along the other without touching, like continental plates. Each issue of *Semiotext(e)*, in a sense, was like an aphorism, an amalgam of disparate forces waiting for something from without to give it meaning. Looking simultaneously for different readerships, and constantly switching readerships also made sure that you weren't caught in a single one. Later on, in 1983, the little "Foreign Agents" volumes of theory were added, and they were pretty much conceived along the same lines: black as leather and small in size—"Steal that theory!" They were a steal, too, in terms of price, being meant for a young readership. The idea was to make "theory" less formidable, something that could be read like "how-to" books, how to think with your own mind, philosophy for the boudoir, short in words but intensely focused; how to eroticize thinking, make it a pleasure of the senses. People would read them with one hand standing in the subway among all the din and disruption; or they would take them around in "downtown" clubs in New York just for their look, quickly leafing through for the hot passages. These books extended theory beyond itself as only theory could.

Although outwardly "academic," they were just for the having, deliberately stripped of academic credentials, introduction, footnotes, anything that would establish their credibility as a scholarly reference. (A friend told me recently that the only thing *Semiotext(e)* ever did was *not* do what everybody else does—"substracting, substracting . . ."). And it apparently worked: academics and art critics would read theory in the "Foreign Agents," but they would go out of their way *not* to quote these little books, going back rather to the original version. There was something suspect, *outlandish* about them. They remained somewhat illegitimate.

This is what I meant by *becoming imperceptible:* the "Foreign Agents" weren't invisible, but they didn't show on the screen. They couldn't be represented within existing institutions, not even at Columbia University, which hosted them for twenty-five years—a feat of "nonrelation"—and never subsidized them either, although everyone else believed it did and envied them for that. These books, like the magazine, were more like a "homing-head" looking for outlets in between the various constituencies. And there are no remaining in-between institutions if you share in their benefits. The only profit *Semiotext(e)* ever derived from this "nonrelation," actively cultivated, was this mirage of institutionalization. Steal this status, but don't pay for it (you always pay in other ways). Working with artists, it would have been easy, natural even, to publish art projects, and we were often asked to do so, but abstained. As soon as you consent to become a reflective medium for the art world—or for any world, for that matter—you're embraced and neutralized, deluged with proposals and manuscripts (for which you have to set up committees, bureaucracy) and enticed by conditional financial support. It's no use then criticizing "the system" and "powers-that-be": you're already part of it, one of them, one of us. And raising one's voice to a pitch won't change that.

Purity is a myth; you're always part of something. One of the things the American academic Left could have avoided is its identification with the institution, its lures and rewards. Camille Paglia was not far off the mark when she asserted that "most of America's academic leftists are no more radical than my Aunt Hattie. . . . These people have risen to the top not by challenging the system but by smoothly adapting themselves to it. They're company men."[3] But so is everybody else for that matter, and I don't see why one should hold a special grudge against them. It's more important to preserve one's energy intact than yielding to the dubious pleasure of criticizing—feeling right, righteous—and entering the circle of rhetorical negation and subversion, *the dialectics of resentment.* As Deleuze saw, the man of resentment needs to conceive of someone other than himself in order to position himself. "Strange syllogism of the slave who needs two negations in order to create the appearance of an affirmation," he termed it.[4] It is the same dialectic that threw women academics into the patriarchal hands of Jacques

Lacan, a worthy adversary to negate and deconstruct, giving one's critique the appearance of an affirmation. The negation of a negation, though, never becomes an affirmative action. You have to step aside and see the whole picture, with yourself in it. Patriarchy is among us all, not just among the patriarchs. And yet there's no way of opposing them in their own ground without replicating in some way the same strictures. *Americains, encore un effort. . .*

There's no glorious alternative to the pleasure of criticizing, just a long patience: keep on a separate course, deliberately choosing to *differ* from something else rather than oppose it. It may not be easy to *forget* what it is that you don't agree with, but being too aware of oppositions would limit your range of choice. It would turn your "differences" into yet another turf war, losing sight of what's really at stake. Better assume that one shares something—*anything*—with what one differs from, and go somewhere else. Political rhetoric in the other is no worse than a culture of resentment in oneself. But maybe this attitude is a luxury of the "beautiful soul." It may not survive the reality test. In the late 1970s embattled Italian "autonomists" like Toni Negri, Franco Piperno, and Oreste Scalzone, innovative Marxist or post-Marxist intellectuals, were being jailed for their alleged association with the Red Brigades.[5] *Semiotext(e)* directly appealed to other "radical" academic journals for political solidarity, and *Telos*, especially, expressed a genuine interest, although never followed up on it. Finally they showed up with a few others to a meeting we were supposed to have coorganized and quietly walked away from the issue. Who was it who said that the Left always betrays?

There's no gain in becoming cynical. Cynicism is a rampant disease in capitalist societies, and a bit of calculated naïveté sometimes helps: playing dumb, resisting the pleasure of asserting one's own truth at someone else's throat. *The best "critique" is no critique.* Create rather singular paths for every situation, experiment with the tools at hand, and eventually everything will fall into place around that. This is what Deleuze and Guattari did in *Anti-Oedipus*, outwardly an attack on psychoanalysis, but in fact a subtle subversion of Marxism. The book wasn't "anti-Marxist," it just looked somewhere else, not at Marx himself, but at the object he kept addressing: capital. Lyotard perfectly understood that "what the book subverts most profoundly is what it doesn't criticize."[6] Why would they have wasted energy criticizing Marx when they never stopped using elements of his analysis?

Instead of opposing Marx, Deleuze and Guattari looked anew at the nature of capital itself, updating Marxist analysis to the limitless movement of capital in its advanced form. They went beyond Marx, while holding him by the hand, becoming more Marxian than him, but on their own terms. Marx expected capital to reach its limit and trigger a general crisis that would open the way to socialism. What Deleuze and Guattari hypothesized instead is that capital is always beside itself, going beyond its own borders, its end being not the production of objects, but the production of itself through them. The first aim of capitalist production is to ensure its own circulation. And yet it can only persevere in its own thrust if it keeps creating artificial frontiers, folding back within itself in order to contain the irrepressible movement of its own flows. Capital, too, always betrays.

Hypothesizing is really what the *theory* in French theory is about, as opposed to philosophy, which mostly refers back, critically, to its own history. And this may account for the fact that French theory never got a foothold in academic departments of philosophy in America. For one, the place was already occupied. And then it had no academic ax to grind. Deleuze did that in his formative years, grinding at academic essays in order to get out of the tradition. The way he did it, though, was getting onto the back of an author, giving him a "monstrous child" made with his own text, "because the author actually had to say everything that I made him say."[7] American analytical philosophers never took French theory seriously, actually couldn't wait until it went away. These kinds of wild "speculations" were good enough for departments of comparative literature and English, which merely dabble with ideas and found in "deconstruction" a further incentive to return to what they had been doing all along: a close reading of texts. Derrida's brilliant textual strategies fed right into literary studies, and it is there that they remained for the most part: in the margins of the text, at the center of academe.

Rather than philosophy, the term *theory*, borrowed from American linguists,[8] actually conveys pretty accurately the tentative outlook and intellectual daring of systems that are, in a sense, joy rides for the mind, the freedom to push new paradigms as far as they could go, temporarily bracketing traditional ethical concerns or dominant ideologies regardless of consequences. A hypothesis, Webster says, is "a tentative assumption made in order to draw out and test its logical or empirical consequences," or simply a supposition made for the sake of argument. French theory obviously belongs to the *hypothetical* genre,[9] since it refuses to consider ready-made answers, rather problematizing them in a number of ways. Unlike a *law*, inferred from scientific data explaining a principle operating in nature, a *theory* "implies a greater range of evidence and greater likelihood of truth." These distinctions, of course, are kind of blurred, and it would be all the more difficult to assign the various "hypotheses" a place in relation to truth since the notion of truth itself has become problematic. Foucault's major concern precisely was to establish a history of truth, making clear that history was a tentative construction, something made in the present tense.

Overlapping and often contradicting themselves on major points, all these theories washed over such wide areas of knowledge and gave out such a sense of momentum and discovery that they were rightly grasped as a full-fledged theory of culture. And it is true that, whatever their differences, which they themselves often considerably magnified, what Deleuze and Guattari, along with Foucault (the Nietzscheans), and Baudrillard and Virilio (the extrapolationists) shared is a paradoxical hypothesis about the nature of reality in advanced capitalist societies. This reality could be expressed in terms of the radical exchangeability or "deterritorialization" elicited by capital: exchange, flows, simulation, speed. They differed about the way this exchangeability occurs, or where it eventually leads, if anywhere, but the overall picture they made of advanced technocapitalism is deeply at variance with everything that had come before them. The Frankfurt school was not hypothetical in the same way. It was more of a moral philosophy, looking at its own assumptions before taking one step in any direction. It never attempted to grasp the nature of contemporary society by *going to the limit*, as all French theorists, in some way or other, do.

French theory has something to do with science fiction. This may explain why it would exert such a strong fascination over American readers, often generating something like a cult. But isn't that what a theory should do: look ahead, in a world that's going full speed to an unknown destination, going nowhere really but spinning wildly, gears in neutral, in the void, engine shrieking, hysterically *marking* time as time itself is slipping away at a dizzying speed? Right after World War II, Jean-Paul Sartre described William Faulkner strapped to the back seat of a fast car *and looking backward*. Thirty years later, in a striking update, Paul Virilio put on the front cover of his *Speed and Politics* the picture of a test pilot dressed in full technological regalia with helmet and gas mask, strapped to his seat, body bent to one side, hands hanging loose, obviously unconscious. This may well be the state in which we are, or are going into, half-dazed, half disappeared, but still at the control desk; only virtually alive. We're still looking toward Marx or Freud for guidance when they may already be farther away than they appear, or are already out of sight. French theory was the first sustained attempt to see what was coming up in the mirror when these immense theoretical objects didn't block the entire view. This is the job French theory was there to do in America, and the struggles it eventually got embroiled in because it was French or difficult to read or prestigious to refer to are pitifully small compared to the magnitude of what is at stake. Coming out of half a century of Cold War, and anticipating its end in so many ways, these theories offered the possibility of looking around, of thinking the world anew without blinders, in real time, figuring out where things are. What America did to French thought, but also with French theory, isn't just an episode in an ongoing culture war but the measure of our capacity to face up to the situation of urgency we're in.

It was unavoidable that these theories would deeply antagonize those who had powerful stakes in a less fluid and destabilizing view of reality. Foucault was rapidly accepted throughout the American landscape as "a stern prophet of doom," something that he himself strongly objected to. His analyses happened to feed right into neo-Marxist analyses of late capitalism based on alienation and ideological control. Deleuze and Guattari's "psychotic" vision of contemporary society met with far more resistance. It may be that their analysis was too *radical* to be acceptable to the "radicals" themselves, too close in any case to the actual workings of American society, which keeps stripping everything to the bone, leaving only more desert behind. Who would want to be told in so many words that they're mere conduits of capital, self-important zombies confusing workaholism with freedom and entertainment with life? The closer one gets to embodying the perfect form of capital, coping with the flows, embracing corporate nomadism and the values of the global marketplace, carried away at "broadband" speed toward a gaping future, the more imperative it becomes to re-create everywhere islands of identity, of meaning, of neurosis, of security in an ocean of cynicism and meaninglessness. And this is why, paradoxically, the only French theories that were readily acknowledged, even avidly sought, in America were *not* those that could have helped people understand something about their own reality, but rather those that offered something to hold on to, the crutches of structures (Lacan's "symbolic"), the romance of meaning (Kristeva's "semiotic" process), or the repeatable protocol of their endless undoing (Derrida). It's always the same blackmail: first they instill fear in you, then comes the racket of protection. Gated intellectual communities, models of thought, a prison of one's own.

What Deleuze and Guattari were saying, drastically updating Freud, is that neurosis is incurable *because it is not an illness*. Neurosis is just the most widespread form of normality. The "neurotic" isn't sick or irreparably disfunctional, but merely trying to customize the madness of capital as best he can in order to remain operational. Sane from 9 to 5, "psycho" the rest of the time. The "neurotic" (me, you) is always on the verge of a terminal breakdown, and it is this threat that keeps people in line. The "reactive strength," the energy it takes to keep the lid on, makes us akin to the slave who refuses to go "to the limit of its potential," running instead to the master for protection.[10] The only alternative to neurosis, at once enforced by the system and desired by the subjects themselves, is a form of cultural psychosis. It is psychosis that Deleuze and Guattari, and not Lacan (as he claimed), have explored *in its own terms*, the schizoid, celestial, celibate machine of capital wildly oscillating between creative bursts of glory and the abject terror of paranoid delirium. No wonder Americans didn't especially go for it, rather rushed for cover, looking for more manageable models of subjectivity, those liable to keep anxiety at abeyance. *Who needs more psychosis in a psychotic universe?*

In America what everyone would prefer is to reinforce the artificial dams and fragile reterritorializations that make life possible in an impossible world; anything to turn away from reality. (The greatest paradox, of course, is that the "psychotic" is traditionally described by psychiatrists as "cut off from reality.") Baudrillard had a point: people prefer Disneyland, or rather they want a Disneyland outside of their home, the better to deny that it is everywhere. A Disneyland of the mind. People would rather believe that they have a body of their own, so it needs deconstructing; an identity of their own, so it needs endless fixing and probing; desires of their own, so they should be paid attention to and satisfied. They delude themselves into thinking that they still can oppose the flux of the market; fight censorship, this *trompe-l'oeil* that serves everyone; preserve a niche to the artistic avant-garde; secure an identity in the programmatic impersonality of the system. And everyone holds tight to this mirage of identity, *and to theories that seem to give them a handle on it.*

It takes an entire society to make a single individual. Hence the obsessive emphasis in America on the "free individual." No one is ever "free" in that sense, and even less "individual" (self-sufficient). All the more reason for what Deleuze calls "dividuals" to be made responsible for themselves. American pragmatics at its best: do it *to* yourself. The only way of *becoming human*—I don't mean "all-too-human"—is first to confront in its own terms the unhumanity of the system, becoming unhuman oneself, orphaned, genderless, a bachelor machine, as deterritorialized as capital itself when it actually goes "to the limit of its potential." Capital, of course, never goes all the way, but fakes out at the last moment. It plays at being its own slave in order to remain on top. Any other attempt to directly reinject humanity and meaning is bound to fail, or turn into a parody of what it allegedly is about—"New Age," cosmic cosmetics.

American radical academics, Frankfurt scholars who keep analyzing late capitalism in terms of social and psychic repression, waiting for fascism to return— it's already here in small ways—felt all the more challenged by post-Marxist and post-Freudian theories developed by French theorists because these thinkers claimed to be exceedingly faithful to the workings of capital and of the unconscious. All French theorists did, in fact, was remove two stumbling blocks, the production of surplus value in the economic sphere and the production of anxiety in the psychic realm. Early on, Jean Baudrillard had the idea of pushing the axiomatics of capital to its extreme logical consequences, turning the iron law of equivalence into a radical process exterminating all values. This nihilistic hypothesis, the destruction of every referential, of every human goal through the multiplication of simulacra, is what he called "simulation."

Baudrillard's project consisted far less in testing reality empirically through a set of suppositions than in developing a paradoxical line of thinking. Simulation wasn't a new theoretical object, it was just the approach he was adopting in order to reveal this unchallenged hypothesis for what it was: the realism of the real. "Simulation," replication without an original, was a radical extrapolation of this commutation of signs engineered by capital, which left reality in doubt. What happened to Baudrillard was in every way the reverse of Deleuze and Guattari's own reception in the United States. Examining them both side by side could help bring together a number of points I have raised along the way, connecting yet more closely the two major poles, the New York art world and academe, in which French theory has been most actively debated and used for a variety of purposes.

The first book by Baudrillard to be translated in the United States, *The Mirror of Production*, came out in France in 1973, just one year after *Anti-Oedipus*. It completed the demolition work Baudrillard had started in *For a Critique of the Political Economy of the Sign* (1972), a devastating escalation of Marx's theory of value that set him right on his own celestial course. Characteristically, this essay wasn't a *critique* of Marx's own critique. Every critique, in Baudrillard's words, is a "negativity subtly haunted by the very form that it negates,[11] and he made sure that he left no holy ghost behind. Challenging the distinction between "use value" and "exchange value" according to Marx's own logic, he effectively turned them both into *models of simulation* reemploying use value as an ideological alibi. This reading of Marx caught the attention of the German Critique group then flourishing in the United States, and identified him summarily with "critical theory." This may explain in part why Baudrillard's *Simulations* would have been so widely misread as a critique of consumer society when it was published in America.[12] It had been years, in fact, since Baudrillard left critique behind to freely oscillate between pataphysics (the science of imaginary solutions) and metaphysics (a meditation on the nature of the real). For the most part, he was on his own, bachelor of capital and exterminating angel. His implacable course and imperceptible humor was on its way to wreaking havoc on America.

Mostly grounded in "sociology,"[13] Baudrillard's work was never a magnet for the kind of literature-minded academics who enthusiastically adopted Derrida and Lacan. It wasn't a matter of ideology, but of "pragmatics." Academics mostly use theory in two respects: either they "apply" it to a given object (deconstructing texts according to Derrida's strategy; referring to Lacan's theories of subjectivity, desire, etc.) or they take as their object the theory itself (viz. the feminist critique of Lacan). But there's no "applying" Baudrillard to anything, especially to the field of literary studies.[14] Making a critique of his "metaphysical" assumptions would also land you right in his trap, reintroducing the principle of reality in a work that skillfully manages to preempt any such judgment.

Criticizing an *agent provocateur:* incredibly enough, this is the kind of earnest approach that was taken by prominent academic Marxists like Mark Poster and Douglas Kellner, who even managed to make a career out of it. Both of them, left over from Baudrillard's earlier "critical" stage, found themselves in the paradoxical situation of promoting writings that they didn't approve of. Introducing Baudrillard's *Selected Writings,* Poster uneasily praises the author's work as "important to the reconstitution of critical theory" while taking every opportunity to condemn the "pessimistic implications" of his ideas, his "pathetic conclusion," and his "bleak view of the world." Douglas Kellner, in his own *Baudrillard: A Critical Reader,* acknowledged Baudrillard's pataphysical side, but he didn't take it seriously, as he should have, distancing himself as well from a nihilism "without joy, without energy, without hope for a better future."[15] What could better satisfy a "flasher" opening his coat wide than an expression of revulsion on his victim's face? The point of this strange exercise wasn't to address the ironic strategy adopted by Baudrillard, whose existence neither Poster nor Kellner ever suspected or could really understand, but to simply reassert the classical Marxist doxa at his expense. The telling detail is the way Poster hastened to pay his respects to Fredric Jameson (in a footnote), once the hatchet job was done. A Bouvard and Pecuchet of postmodern theory, this unlikely pair happened to be by far the best possible hosts for the innoculation against Baudrillard's virus in America.

I had my own reservations regarding his "politics" and it took me some time before I got his number right. I hadn't realized yet that his politics was all in his strategy and that objecting to it was like asking a planet to change its course. All one could expect from his work is to use it for what it is. But then it didn't even work that way: Baudrillard's ideas could never be turned to any purpose other than his own.

Playing cat and mouse with his readers is part of Baudrillard's game; but it may not exactly be a game, but more a way of thinking and living—and besides, the mice may not even realize that they are caught in a trap. This is the beauty of the strategy, and its intrinsic limitations. Like a passing angel, Baudrillard works magic, revealing everything for what it is, but then he tiptoes away, leaving things exactly the way they were before his discreet visitation.

Releasing a "simulator" among "critical theorists" indeed had no perceptible effect, critical theory already being, at best, a simulation of Marxism, its convenient retreat within the academic institution. Baudrillard's hammer was far too subtle, anyway, for the unsuspecting victims to even realize that they were victims. Only those who see the light can lose face. Besides, they didn't hold a special grudge against Baudrillard. Unlike Deleuze and Guattari, he had not "infuriated" them by claiming to be a "post-Marxist revolutionary." He wasn't like this "terrible pair of snobs," as Jonathan Ree called them in the *New Left Review*, acting "like machines for wrong-footing their readers."[16] Baudrillard was mild and unprepossessing, like his strategy. Besides, he had disqualified himself politically. He wasn't a threat.

Deleuze and Guattari were another story altogether, and it took them a long time to get anywhere in America. Paradoxically, it was Fredric Jameson, the most important Marxist critic in America, and "the only one working in English who writes as the peer of the French poststructuralists,"[17] who first registered the impact of their work in purely *aesthetic* terms, using the distinction they made between two types of multiplicity, "molecular" (masses, packs) and "molar" (classes), to qualify two narrative levels whose contradictions were meant to account for the alienation and fragmentation of existence in late capitalism.[18] Unlike Jameson, Deleuze and Guattari never privileged literature over other domains, let alone attributed to its reading the exclusive power of unraveling the nature of social formations. Actually what they were expecting of literature was not to confirm a grand vision of society caught in a dialectic of contradictions, but to bring out instead whatever managed to escape from it. Although they all were looking for a relation to the "outside," Deleuze and Guattari's use of literature was rhizomatic (American, in their own terms), while Jameson's model of interpretation, rooted in the text and growing out of it through an intricate system of dynamic and antagonistic cultural levels, was arborescent (European). What Jameson ultimately proposed was an idea of the "cultural text" mirroring in itself the internal antagonisms and cultural heterogeneity present in society itself. It was a huge improvement over Lucien Goldmann's reliance on mediations to bridge, dialectically, the text to its outside: *with Jameson, there was no more need to step out of literature*; the "cultural text" itself had become the place where any "cultural revolution" would occur or could be detected. The concept of cultural revolution, then, was nothing but "the reconstruction of the material of cultural and literary history in the form of this new 'text' or object of study."[19] Despite Jameson's critique of "deconstruction," his own strategy turned out to be hardly different from Derrida's in relation to the academic institution. It made of literary criticism more than a legitimate activity: a political act. Putting the political interpretation of literary texts at the center of all social understanding, it turned literary critics into full-fledged revolutionaries. The last Marxist "revolutionary," it seems, will be an American literary critic.

It is not surprising that a Marxist philosopher like Jonathan Ree would have little patience for the "insults" of "post-Marxist revolutionaries" like Deleuze and Guattari, with their "raucous mockery of Hegelianism and Marxism," and would see them rather as "piteous relics of a bygone age." Ree went as far as celebrating their last collaboration *What Is Philosophy?* as a symptom of their demise, sickness and death, and read with obvious satisfaction the opening pages of the book as "a bid for sympathy, if not a cry for help." Jameson himself was less blunt in his appraisal of their legacy. And yet, although he kept reiterating his "boundless admiration" for their "immense book" and "extraordinary work" in a paper called "Les dualismes aujourd'hui" ("Dualisms Today"), delivered in French to an assembly of Deleuzians in Brazil in 1996, his critique was no less virulent, except that in order to put them down he kept bringing them up sky high. Historicizing their contribution to philosophy, he saw in it a remnant of nineteen sixties exoteric political ideology which, he added, "doesn't seem adequate anymore to new and un-chartered contemporary problems." The brunt of his argument bore on what he considered their inveterate dualism, "a quasi-metaphysical passion for dualisms and duality" that he saw "sublated and transformed" (*aufgehoben*) through "the grandiose and mythical conflict" of the nomad and of the state.[20] In short, what Jameson reproached in Deleuze and Guattari, paradoxically, was not their anti-Hegelianism—he considered them *far too Hegelian* for a staunch materialist like himself. Their vision of the world, he implied, was incapable of accounting for the "third stage" of capitalism, globalizing and cybernetical, because it was regressive, not oriented toward the future: it was quasi-metaphysical or religious. Even their passion to embrace the whole range of disciplines and present specialties in a "totalizing project" was not just dated, but "deeply suspect," their dualisms allegedly leading toward the constitution of a new myth at the border "between ideology and prophecy." Subjecting their text to the kind of textual analysis about which he theorized elsewhere, Jameson flatly concluded that these dualities expressed the primordial and empty form of ideology itself.

It is interesting that Jameson would have lifted his curious accusation of "binarism," but also the bold idea of pushing Deleuze and Guattari toward myth and religion, directly from an essay by Manfred Frank specially translated from the German by *Telos*.[21] Frank wrote, "Wish machines form binary machines depending on binary rules and associative arrangements. *But this is a binarism extending to infinity.*" The same sentence can be found in Jameson's own attack on Deleuze and Guattari's alleged strategy, which aims at "pushing the multiplication of dualism farther, and even to infinity." *Telos* was obviously trying its best to import in America the violent *Kulturkampf* that was raging at the time in the German university against so-called "French irrationalism."[22] It wasn't just the anti-Hegelianism of Foucault, Deleuze, and Guattari that brushed German academics the wrong way, but the "neo-vitalism" of Deleuze, "fascistically coloured," and the "arbitrariness" of their anarchism, which could, they asserted, go either way, "in the direction of the 'kingdom of ends' (Kant) or in those of a fascistic anarchism," being incapable of "differentiating between Stalin and Hitler, Bakounin and Gentile," in as much as it was devoid of ethical values. Jameson couldn't possibly have himself picked up this kind of argument among the Deleuzians he was addressing in his paper, but references to Spengler, Gentile, Morand, Drieu de la Rochelle, theorists or followers of fascism, all in Frank's own essay, insistently showed the way.

These references became strident in another article translated as well from the German two years later by *Telos*, this time targeting "Rhizome."[23] Once again the question of dualisms and "blatant dichotomies" was raised, joined by suggestions of "degeneration" redolent of Spengler, evocations of French fascist Drieu, and Carl Schmidt and Deleuze and Guattari's German disciple, Klaus Theweleit, stigmatized as well for his ambiguous analysis of fascism. Frequently invoking Adorno, Christa Burger repeatedly probed not only the "political ambivalence" of rhizomatic thinking, but the dangerous consequences of proclaiming with Nietzsche the identity of domination and reason: "The anarchistic gesture turns to authoritarianism," "absolute decoding" leading to the destruction of "Culture," any critique of fascism "ceasing to be possible" because there was no subject available "to judge from a conceptually established standpoint." Burger's conclusion was unequivocal: Deleuze and Guattari's "anticultural" book came just on time to counter the work of remembrance now taking hold in Germany, reinforcing the systematic "denial of historical experience."

This controversy, artificially transplanted from Germany to America via proponents of the Frankfurt school and obviously meant to counter French theory in America, hadn't come entirely unannounced. Actually, it had already been indirectly ignited in another crucial area, the New York art world, and among New York art critics, by the irruption of neoexpressionist art coming from Germany and Italy in 1980. Barely twenty years after New York stole modern art from the French through the skillful promotion of such homegrown pre-pop artists as Jaspers Johns, Robert Rauschenberg, and Andy Warhol, the supremacy of American art, apparently unshakeable, was being seriously threatened for the first time. Many of the arguments raised in New York as a shield against the European invaders, starting with the insistent accusation of protofascism, were actually in keeping with those developed in Germany against what they called "French irrationalism" by disciples of Adorno. And there was a good reason for that congruence: "critical theory" wasn't just dominant in Germany, it was also prevalent among American art critics, and more generally in American academe, in which many ex-student rebels and reconstructed radicals from the sixties, originally adepts of Herbert Marcuse, had taken position. Unlike French theory, the Frankfurt school wasn't "foreign" in America. Just before World War II, the Institute for Social Research had relocated in New York, where Adorno spent some fifteen years of his life. German critique, in short, was far more *heimlich* in America than its recent rival, French theory, actually far too serious and entrenched in traditional disciplines to even be called "theory." The Frankfurt school had permeated the entire American Left. Breaking away from the old Left compromised far too much with the Soviet Union, American-style Marxists had pruned Marxism of some of its major tenets, especially the primacy of class, and now emphasized reification and commodity independently of their conditions of production. Celebrating negativity and disenchantment may have been less a result of Adorno's own negative dialectics than a way of making thinking legitimate in a country otherwise brimming with shoddy optimism. In short, starting from the Frankfurt school, a toothless kind of Marxism had emerged, custom-made for the American academy, of which art critics and art historians were increasingly a part.

It wasn't exactly the first time that "French irrationalism" confronted the American radical constituency, and their first direct encounter hadn't been exactly auspicious. The main bulk of French theory, mostly that of Lévi-Strauss, Barthes, Lacan, and Derrida, had been introduced to American academe much earlier, in 1966, during the symposium on "The Languages of Criticism on the Human Sciences" held at Johns Hopkins University, and had subsequently established a solid foothold in the American university. But the "French Nietzscheans"—Deleuze, Guattari, Foucault, and Lyotard—only made their first public appearance in the United States some ten years later in a very different context, with the "Schizo-Culture" conference on Prison and Madness organized in New York in 1975 by *Semiotext(e)*. Although it happened at Columbia University and involved both lectures and panels, it wasn't exactly an academic meeting, rather "the last counterculture event of the 60s," in Michel Foucault's angry words (he had publicly been accused of being paid by the CIA), two thousand people flocking "uptown" for two days to argue about psychiatry and repression with Foucault and R. D. Laing. It didn't take long before Deleuze, Guattari, and Foucault clashed with the radical constituency, or all those who demanded a more orderly debate. Deleuze slowly explained in French his yet unpublished ideas about the "rhizome," drawing roots and crabgrass on the blackboard; Guattari gave a speech about "microfascism" at the university and elsewhere; Foucault bluntly dismissed the *antirepressive discourse* of "critical theorists," the kind that "circulates so obstinately between university auditorium and analytic couch," as the "enunciator's pay-off";[24] Lyotard invoked the Sophists to question further the status of the "master's discourse," meaning their own, effectively breaking off with his former French friends. Actually, things were breaking down all around, with provocateurs from Larouche's Labor Committee throwing accusations at the speakers, the audience splitting in disorder over questions of lecture or debate, workshops about "psychiatric repression" sprouting everywhere in the halls after Jean-Jacques Lebel, the inventor of French "happenings," called the population of New York to show up en masse at the conference. Guattari was booed off the podium by followers of extreme feminist Ti-Grace Atkinson, who happened to take him as a target in their fight against the male "political class."[25] This momentous event was still remembered five years later when "French irrationalism" happened to come back to America in the bandwagon of European neoexpressionism.

Except for the subcultural fringes in Berlin, the German academic institution had been staunchly opposed to "French irrationalism," and it was an ironic twist that the waves of German neoexpressionist art arriving on the American shores in 1980 would have been prefaced by an young outlaw curator from Berlin, Wolfgang Max Faust, whose political strategy, opposing capitalism from within, was directly inspired by Deleuze and Guattari's work.[26] And it is true that many of Faust's exalted pronouncements published in *Artforum*, his advocation of desire and productive anarchy, his celebration of "lines of escape" and "expressive intensity," the way he upheld "becoming revolutionary" over revolution, were all lifted from both *Anti-Oedipus* and Lyotard's *Libidinal Economy*. Italian curator Achille Bonito Oliva's manifesto for the new Italian Trans-avant-garde was less explicit, but claimed as well its allegiance to some vaguely defined "creative nomadism," loosely using a number of libidinal markers, pleasure and pulsions, eroticism, energy, instinct, direct expression, affirmative movement, to describe the new Italian painters.[27] Yet Faust's emphasis on spontaneity and self-expression, the aesthetics of symbol-making and personal style, like Oliva's celebration of the artist's "flash of genius" and "manual furor" owed much more to German romanticism rewritten by punk or New Wave than to Deleuze and Guattari's philosophy. Neither manifesto's glamorizing death wish or personal expression, with their yearning for a romantic death or disaster, for the "auto-suggestive proximity to those who expressed themselves out of deep, inescapable need, who suffered pain and ecstasy, found and destroyed themselves," would have especially appealed to them.

The reaction against this European invasion was massive and vitriolic. It wasn't just a matter of ideology or aesthetics; New York critics were ready to defend their turf and maintain the New York art world's supremacy over world art by all means possible. The foreigners, Donald Kuspit wrote, wouldn't be allowed to "take the scepter of advanced art back" from the New York artistic avant-garde.[28] The same critics had found nothing wrong with the fact that postwar Germany had been colonized by America, or that American artists had been lionized in European galleries for the past two decades at the expense of local production. American art had achieved, Hal Foster imperturbably declared, a superior stage of radicality in art, and *through* art. New York art had really rendered the entire world a service by producing what Faust called "universally meaningful statements in which the importance of individual and regional character was reduced." Europe had become a province of the empire, but what should it complain about? Europe had been handed out a piece of the cake. Benjamin Buchloh made a point of reminding Europeans that even in their attempt to "supplant the dominance of American art through the programmatic return to a national idiom" they had to acknowledge the dominant "foreign" style and assimilate its pictorial standards in order to have any chance of success on the art market. Translate it in multicultural terms and you have here a pretty damning statement.

Laconic, allusive, self-referential, impersonal, and intensely aware of its mission in art historical terms, New York art wasn't only dominant worldwide, but deserved to be. It was impossible to do anything without treating with due reverence what Lawson called the "severe respectability" of its recent production. Anything less universal, meaning American, would be merely indulgent. The "neoprimitivism" of the neoexpressionists, Lawson went on, was just an "exercise in bad faith." A "newly promoted art of local sentiments and archaic forms," as such devoid of "a suitable critical frame," Hal Foster added, it was just masquerading as historical consciousness, actually dismissing the particularities of history "in favor of a generalized mythology."[29] Buchloh in turn launched a heavy-artillery attack against the "morbid symptoms" exemplified by contemporary neoexpressionism. Like its predecessor German expressionism, he asserted, the new art resulted from an internalization of oppression, its "apolitical humanitarian stance," its devotion to spiritual regeneration, infantilizing melancholy and romantization of primal experience eventually leading to "the outright adulation of manifestations of reactionary power" (meaning: fascism). This belabored interpretation certainly was necessary to counter the obvious, the anarchistic and subversive radicalism of neoexpressionism, and to demonstrate, history and psychoanalysis in hand, that it was just the reverse, authoritarianism coming to the fore "in the guise of irrationality and the ideology of individual expression," its "proto-fascist libertarianism" preparing the way for "the seizure of state power by a reactionary autocratic elite."[30]

The accusation of fascism wasn't something new. Stalinists had used it to discredit their adversaries, and the tradition hadn't been lost. Fascism happened to be a failed remedy to the capitalist crisis but the horrors it generated in its crash course toward a "suicidal state" (Virilio) had by now turned it into an allegory, a moral entity in the West, something like evil incarnate. A good deal of Deleuze and Guattari's reflection on desire, precisely, was an attempt, after Wilhelm Reich, to account for this bewildering phenomenon in terms that wouldn't merely be moral or simplistic: how could a rational people come to desire their own repression, even rush to their own annihilation, not to mention, of course, the extermination of entire "races" decreed inferior? Lightly accused of irrationalism in Germany, Deleuze and Guattari were in fact trying to explore in specific terms the mechanisms that turned that highly civilized nation into a roving mass of murderers. It was easier, of course, to attribute the phenomenon to a bunch of political psychopaths and perverts and thus forget about the possibility of its recurrence not just among frustrated adolescents wearing swastikas on their back, but inside more mature and sanitized corporate minds. It has become accepted practice to throw around the accusation of fascism to discipline and punish people, instead of thinking it through. And this is true as well of outwardly sophisticated and responsible people, art critics, or social critics, whenever they feel threatened in their own careers and national interests—interests that they tend to present as universals in order to hide their own particular slants. That these irrational reactions would be greeted uncritically by otherwise so critically minded people, even celebrated as legitimate objections in the media at large, as happened with Camille Paglia, is deeply troubling. I wonder how much more irresistible the recourse to such easy slander and intolerance would become in times of real crisis and emergency.

The new European art didn't just stand accused of regression in aesthetic terms; for these New York critics, this was also indicative of a more damning kind of political regression. Both Italy and Germany, as it happened, had readily embraced fascism in the thirties and this made their present aesthetic threat even more ominous. Curiously, no one acknowledged any possible economic rivalry in this affair at a time of weakening American hegemony—not even Marxist critics, who were far more busy invoking Freud and psychic repression in general terms. Although the foreign painters were doing nothing worse than pushing their own wares on the American art market, backed by the strong economy of their respective countries, they were instead immediately made responsible for the entire history of their own countries. The very fact that they were often trying themselves to deal openly with the fascist past, instead of safely burying it in minimalist strictures along the American model as they could have, made them even more suspicious in the eyes of people who had not shared that experience, or realized what it takes to make art at all in spite of this heavy legacy. To say it bluntly: the fascist past made it easier for American critics to raise their own scepter like a cross against the specter of a Gothic Dracula. By invoking fascism, it became "us or them"—that simple.

These critics—including German-born Benjamin Buchloh—superbly ignored as well the fact that many of the young European painters they lightly accused of fascism had emerged from an intense political climate of exacerbated ideological terrorism and police repression. These artists had often been associated with the squatters' movement or the alternative/autonomous scenes still ruthlessly squeezed among state paranoia, the communist party's dialectics of power, and the last murderous outbursts of Stalinist vigilantes. "Politics" in these embattled countries wasn't just a matter of casting a vote, or being elected to Congress. Deleuze and Guattari happened to have been closely involved with these European movements.[31] In the early 1980s, both of them had taken part in a huge meeting in Berlin protesting the cycle of terrorism and repression, and Guattari, especially, actively supported the leaders of the Autonomia movement unjustly accused by the Italian Communist Party of having masterminded the Red Brigades. The idea of a fluid and nomadic response to the encroachments of capitalism found a strong echo among the disaffected youth ("no future") and the loose network of activists and artists extending from Berlin's Kreutzberg bohemia to neo-Dada "Radio Alice" in Bologna. It wasn't just coincidental then that some of Deleuze and Guattari's ideas would have worked their way into the manifestos that claimed to present in more theoretical terms the cultural values that had contributed to shape the new expressionist art and lifestyle.

Neoexpressionism wasn't just threatening the New York art establishment from the outside, but from the inside as well—a paler version of German neoexpressionism had sprouted "downtown" in the midst of Manhattan night life, at Max's Kansas City, the Mudd Club, and CBGB. Initiated by the Ramones, punk and safety-pins were being reimported from London, and New Wave/No Wave rock was thriving at new heights of sleazy glamour. Blood-stained terrorism was sported by leather-clad socialities, young "political" artists just out of art schools (the Co-Lab group) giving object lessons in capitalist ethos—the Money Show, the Real Estate Show—before the eighties real estate and money craze actually engulfed everything, including art. Graffiti weren't just sprawling on subways cars, they were making their way into the rundown storefronts and small-time galleries then multiplying in the East Village, challenging Soho's established art circuits, cartoonish art dripping into acrylic disasters. The disease had to be contained at the gate, and on the premises. Art critics and historians weren't going to take any chance.

Although Buchloh was careful enough to recognize in the "petit bourgeois anarchism" of Faust's discourse "a *pastiche* of Deleuze and Guattari, Stirner, and Spengler," but associating in turn the French theorists with these tainted German thinkers and condemning Oliva for his "proto-fascist language" didn't especially cast the French philosophers in a favorable light. Actually, this amalgamation merely confirmed the strong warnings of German academic circles obligingly relayed by *Telos* to the American academic Left. Already marginalized in academe and targeted by "critical theorists" both in Germany and in the United States, the French Nietzscheans were now being crudely identified in turn among New York critics as a foreign threat.

Looking at the larger picture, the return to painting heralded by the European neoexpressionists coupled with the embrace of pop culture and club life by

East Village artists irreversibly changed the face of the New York art world. From a small minimalist tribe inhabiting cavernous lofts in a former industrial neighborhood called Soho, it suddenly mutated into a more deterritorialized network of artists, critics, curators, galleries, collectors, and museums pumping money and fame into the international art community. The art market boom being directly indexed to the artificial frenzy of the eigthties stock market and Manhattan real estate speculation, soon it forced the cheap, mostly artist-run East Village galleries out of business. By 1984 neoexpressionism was losing steam and the new generation of neoconceptualist artists which had been waiting on the sidelines started coming out publicly. Paradoxically, neoconceptualism emerged among some of those more socially conscious young artists of the late seventies, like Jenny Holzer and Barbara Kruger, who had been preoccupied with money and the stock market. Like Richard Prince, Robert Longo, or Jeff Koons, who had worked as a stock broker for a few years, they were moving to the "real world" of consumerism, advertisement, and corporate productions, outwardly confronting the capitalist image, or mirage.

Unlike many young East Village artists, these neoconceptualists had been formally trained in art schools and were ready to tackle the media on its own terms, with posters, billboards, and photographs, reappropriating elements of the market in order to *turn it against itself.* Their strategy, in that sense, mirrored that of the neoexpressionists (and of Deleuze and Guattari) except that they seemed willing to abandon art altogether to directly manipulate social signs. This neoconceptual art was less art in the traditional sense—a tradition that the neoexpressionists, it is true, had once more made legitimate by returning to painting and producing art objects, objects for the art market—than what Gary Indiana called "a form of market criticism," a "smart art" capable of redeeming the commodity by merely pointing at it critically. It was Duchamp all over, the "found object," but post-pop, and politically corrected; American situationism, but with an undeniable gusto for the "spectacle" and little of Dada's anarchistic playfulness. Actually, it was often stern and self-righteous in its mimicry, giving counterorders in guise of subversion, or glamorizing glamour with a critical intent. Reintroducing "critical intelligence" in art through critical photography and reappropriation, it claimed to "demystify" consumer society by reusing its symbolic products, icons, logos, ads, and consumer items. Neoconceptualists were semioticians of sorts, but they made their own analysis of myths—of the archaic myth of what the media is in advanced capitalist societies—by lifting some of its elements. Literally, they fulfilled Lévi-Strauss's vision of the mythologist becoming a part of the myth under study, with the difference that they were unaware of the extent of this contagion. Taking on Roland Barthes's *Mythologies,* they meant to crack the "consumer code," exposing its theft through their own.

They already were, unknowingly, caught in the logic of simulation, and it isn't surprising that they would instantly have recognized in Baudrillard's "simulacrum" exactly what they had been looking for, or what had been looking for them. It is at this point that Baudrillard came in; his *Consumer Society* had been inspired by Barthes, but since then he had updated him with a vengeance, pushing his analysis beyond any critical or redeeming intent. Baudrillard was simply challenging the simulacrum to be the simulacrum of itself, and nothing else.

The new lines that were now being drawn within the New York art world affected the way French theory was being viewed, and the kind of readership it addressed. It happened to be exactly at that time, in 1983, as neoexpressionism was peaking and a new brand of conceptualism steeped in the great retentive American artistic tradition was beginning to assert itself, that *Semiotext(e)* published the first three volumes of its new "Foreign Agents" series: Deleuze and Guattari's *On the Line* (it included "Rhizome" and elements from Deleuze and Claire Parnet's *Dialogue*); Baudrillard's *Simulations* (it comprised a chapter from *Symbolic Exchange and Death*) and *Pure War*, a long dialogue on war and technology with Paul Virilio—then unknown—whose reflections on speed and disappearance, strangely parallel to those of Baudrillard's, had attracted my attention. The three books happened to be mapping out issues that would define the eighties and beyond. Tied down, for better or for worse, to neoexpressionist painting, now receding, and to "sixties thinking," Deleuze and Guattari's theories went on permeating the culture at a rhizomatic pace. Avidly read by young academics but at a safe distance from established academe, they kept working their way through the thriving subcultural and activist fringes all around the United States. Roaming through a formidable amount of material, *Pure War* was already exploring the self-destruction of civil society though war-inspired "new technologies." The interest these two books elicited at the time, though, could not compare with the overwhelming response instantly elicited by Baudrillard's *Simulations*.

I had an idea in mind when I decided to publish *Simulations*, using his radical nihilism to clear the air. I should have known better, of course, than to play the sorcerer's apprentice with Jean Baudrillard. Brushfires have a way of getting out of hand, spreading in unforeseen directions. The year the book came out, I had him invited by the French cultural services to tour a few East Coast universities—Columbia, Yale, Harvard—and no one (maybe two or three) showed up at his lectures. It was obvious that his audience wasn't there. I suggested that he should rather turn to the art world, a paradoxical idea, of course, considering that Baudrillard had retained his old situationist mistrust of "culture," of the aesthetic object. For him art had come to a close after Andy Warhol managed to turn banal images into pure fetishes. But what was there to lose? The art world, at least, would be receptive to his work. What follows remains one of the most bewildering episodes of French theory in America: the deadly embrace of Baudrillard by the art world—or maybe it was the art world by Baudrillard.

Part of the response to *Simulations* had to do with the quasi-fictional or science-fictional character of the book. Milazzo and Collins, curators of the first postconceptualist show in December 1984,[32] claimed that Baudrillard owed *them* his fame in the art world: his book, they said, was enthusiastically received because it was a relief from their own (turgid and confused) theoretical output. Collins and Milazzo weren't exactly known for their humor, but there was some truth in that. Anyone could read Baudrillard's essay, and yet it still felt like theory. It was an intensely American experience, the thrill of discovery in the safety of recognition. Baudrillard was apparently telling hundreds of young, career-minded artists—art was quickly becoming a legitimate "career"—everything they already knew, or thought they did, but with Gallic panache and the authority of "theory"—a theory that, furthermore, didn't read like one. It had the allure of a text, and "no one had to feel responsible for it as truth about the world," although quite a few actually did. This was, of course, Baudrillard's tour de force, giving the impression that there was something there to understand, while the kind of understanding it implied had to be paid for by a further realization that understanding wasn't really what it was all about. *Simulations* wasn't about explaining anything, let alone criticizing what it seemed to be bringing out as truth, the hyperreality of the world. What it actually did was catch you unaware in an endless hall of mirrors. It was this "strategy of deterrence" *encoded in his own text* (and not just described in it) that ended up provoking the near hysteria that engulfed the entire art world. Baudrillard's ideas, Milazzo flatly stated, "had nothing to do with understanding the market or the artworld. What was incredible is that the artworld had taken as its mechanism the idea of a man."

The mistake American artists made was *to recognize themselves* in an intellectual device that was far more real than they would ever be willing to accept as their own: a pure flux of images *without any possible reterritorialization*. Any effort they made to ground Baudrillard's theory into their work was bound to fail. Had they read carefully not just the title, but the very epigraph Baudrillard chose for his book they could have been warned about that: "The simulacrum is never that which conceals the truth—it is the truth that conceals that there is none." What provoked in its American readers a sense of illumination—the idea that simulation could actually reveal something else than itself—was in fact a black hole, and they hopelessly got sucked into it. *Simulations* was not *about* simulating, it was its own simulation as theory. Besides, this epigraph attributed to the Ecclesiastes, whose authenticity no one thought of questioning—"The simulacrum is true"—happened to be Baudrillard's own. He had just made it up himself, and yet it was truer than truth, being a simulation. It was true as a simulation of theory by theory itself, even.

"Within two years everyone had read *Simulations*," Bill Arning, director of the Soho gallery White Columns said. "People knew Baudrillard better than anybody else," concurred painter Nancy Spero. "His influence was so pervasive. Every artist was using him." The problem, of course, was how to do that. No one seemed to have wondered at the time, with burlesque consequences, whether it was possible to use Baudrillard at all, or even worth trying. "It was a giant misunderstanding," Richard Milazzo commented. "A lot of people were desperate to understand. But it was a bogus issue."

Collins and Milazzo were among the very few, it seems, who weren't outwardly fazed by Baudrillard. They had an agenda of their own that rivaled his, at least in one respect: they cynically—realistically—acknowledged that the power of theory wasn't so much in what it actually said than in the prestige it elicited among those who read it, or pretended to. And for a while it seemed as if these speculators in concepts would succeed in channeling the artist's desperation into their own self-serving project. Writing in deliberately cryptic terms and keeping their own theorizing close to the chest, they did manage in some way to up the ante both on Baudrillard's simulationist strategy and on the simulation of critique provided by the new conceptual artists, whose framing device ("framing the media") they decided to frame in turn. *Hyperframes: A Post-Appropriation Discourse*, the title of their collected essays, perfectly summarizes their intention: using discourse the way appropriationists themselves were using the media. Dismissing the appropriation mentality of picture theorists for their rigid ideological stand, they professed to succeed in *critiquing critique*. But they were even more opposed to ego-minded neoexpressionist painting, and endeavored as well to separate their expressionism from the *expressive* quality that could be found in the painting of, say, a Ross Bleckner.

All these metacritical declarations of intent wouldn't have been enough, though, to drive a wedge between the "self-righteous ideology of the picture theorists" and the "self-indulgent ideology of the neo-expressionists" had they not mobilized as well, more pragmatically, scores of young eager artists through a number of "hybrid" group shows ostensibly meant to act as "a critical form of the highest order." While neoconceptualists targeted the media world with their manipulation of social signs, Collins and Mizazzo targeted the art world itself with a discourse of art signs located between "Concept and the Spectacle," and they may well have succeeded to do to the art world what Baudrillard was doing to the world at large had Baudrillard himself been less uncompromising in his stand and eventually blown their cover by dismissing his own art world following. If the Marxist Bouvard and Pecuchet duet accused Baudrillard of promoting a bleak view of the world, what would they have found to say of this morose simulationist couple cunningly opposing neoexpressionism with "'meta-depression,' . . . failure and 'transcendental stasis,'" and neoconceptualism with "a morbid, internalized geometry of awkward ironies"? It was fitting that their "postdialectical terminal discourse" never mentioned Baudrillard once. What Collins and Milazzo were trying to do was to engage Baudrillard in a new spiral of simulation that would in turn leave him behind—*forget Baudrillard*. But the reverse happened: As soon as the Baudrillard tropism exterminated itself the art world forgot about the entropic couple. But extermination, of course, is never the end: the last word, maybe the most ironical considering Baudrillard's profound distrust of contemporary art, came from the heart of the art world. In 1984, abruptly dropping the flailing neoexpressionist aesthetics it had embraced for a few years, *Artforum* suddenly promoted an unsuspecting Baudrillard on their mast as contributing editor. At least *they* realized what simulation could be used for.

Not everyone could afford to do that with impunity. If someone got badly burned in this spiraling Baudrillard affair, it was abstract painter Peter Halley, whose "Neo-Geo" (New Geometry) group, masterminded by Collins and Milazzo, innocently jumped on the master's bandwagon, hoping to bask in his phenomenal fame. Peter Halley, originally involved with abstraction in nature, discovered French poststructuralism with Foucault and Baudrillard. An intellectual in his own right, Halley thought of using their theories to decode the tradition of geometric art, both in minimalism and postminimalism, as "the history of a real progression in the social." He also produced geometric art of his own, conceived as some kind of *social realism of abstraction*. In short, Halley historicized theory and art's relation to it, reading Foucault's panopticism and disciplinary continuum in terms of a critique of "the great orderings of industrial society" also present in the pictural space while Baudrillard's theory of the simulacrum, when he discovered it, became indicative in his eyes of the next stage of capitalist development involving "the soft geometry of interstate highways, computers, and electronic entertainment."[33] Heavily referencing Jameson, Halley's interpretation of theory ended up collapsing geometrical space into social space. "The history of abstract art," he flatly asserted, "is the history of a real progression in the social." No doubt, as Milazzo suggested, (and he knew what he was talking about), representing the theory was a way of participating in its power. But the power of simulation, in Baudrillard's terms, wasn't something that could ever be represented, it was more of a cerebral event, the dizzying realization of the destruction of any referenciality.

On March 31, 1987, the Whitney Museum of American Art invited Baudrillard to deliver a "Distinguished Lecture on American Art and Culture of the Twentieth Century" and the place was mobbed. The entire art world was so abuzz that an *Anti-Baudrillard Show* was quickly organized at White Columns with some forty artists exhibited, among them feminist artist Nancy Spero, political painter Leon Golub, and Tim Rollins and Group Material, with the explicit purpose of mocking the Baudrillard rage and the widespread use of his theory by New York artists. The idea was to raise the question of political action in the event, "that the real wasn't here any more," as director Bill Arning dryly put it. The Whitney lecture having been booked months in advance, I arranged for another lecture "uptown" at Columbia University. "Downtown" artists showed up by the hundreds. They were eager to ask Baudrillard what he thought of "simulationist art" and of "the Baudrillard School," Peter Halley's Neo-Geo group of artists, Jeff Koons,[34] Ross Bleckner, and Sherrie Levine, who claimed to be his disciples. Pressed to pronounce himself on this crucial matter, Baudrillard flatly replied that "there can't be a simulationist school because the simulacrum cannot be represented." It was, he added, a complete misunderstanding of his work. The public rejection of his "school" by the French master instantly made the headlines of art magazines throughout the country.

There was more: the debate went on afterward in galleries, artists wondering whether it mattered or not if Baudrillard didn't approve of them. Baudrillard had been clear: there wasn't such a thing as an art of simulation, and he added, characteristically reversing the proposition and sending his disciples howling, that, "simulation itself is the art." This pataphysical episode must have confirmed him in his life-long conviction that "in a world given to indifference, all art can do is add to this indifference . . . and add to our imaginary disillusion."[35] Confirmation isn't exactly what interests me here, but rather the disquieting light this handling of French theory throws on the American art world, or what was becoming of it as the influx of money and media was increasingly turning it into another glamorous, enviable, and intensely insecure community.

One can't expect artists to read theory as philosophers or academics do. There's nothing condescending about making this remark: artists have their own ways of thinking, and they are not inferior to the way philosophers think, just different. As Deleuze said, artists think with *percepts*, not with concepts. Their ideas are engaged as well in a material, which may also happen to be "conceptual" in the Duchampian stage. Whether their art is considered "correct" or not is of secondary importance as long as they are truly engaged in something: only engagement really matters. This applies as well to Baudrillard, who is, or has become over the years, more of a conceptual artist himself than a philosopher in his own right—a Jeff Koons of philosophy. It didn't bother me in the least then to hear Tim Rollins or Bill Arning assert that artists don't understand theory very well. As long as they understand it, or other things *in a way that gives more power to their art*, I consider them to be doing their job as artists. Artists are only responsible to their work, not to the integrity of the concepts. They don't have to subject themselves to the discipline of philosophy as philosophers do, but extend themselves to theory *as artists*, finding in philosophy the tools and ideas, or the intellectual gymnastics, that they might use for their own purpose without betraying their own integrity as artists. It is this integrity that counts, not the amount of theory one is exposed to, or actually understand. Artists can *lift* ideas from theory the way they lift them from any other domain—freely, *irresponsibly*.

That they would just be skimming the theory and dropping names is another story altogether, although it definitely is part and parcel of the "theory effect" that swept over the American art world and academic circles, the mixture of envy and anxiety, of nervous excitement and ravenous desire, the exhilarating sense of intellectual power it provided, the genuine passions it elicited; also the impatience, spite, rage, resentment that accompanied it or followed it, all compacted in this phenomenon, French theory. The obsession with theory, the intimidation by theory, the eagerness of appropriation and self-promotion feeding on the desire for credibility, prestige, authority—all these "surplus values" of the new code were present in this curious episode that suddenly moved hundreds of artists to behave the way Camille Paglia described academics, a "revolting sight" of "pampered American academics down on their knees kissing French bums." It wasn't the French bums that mattered, *it was the kissing*. More than anything else, it exemplified what the artword had become, all these young art people crowding to a Baudrillard concert like groupies. They had no respect for what they were doing. It wasn't just the neoexpressionist art that had allegedly "regressed," it was all those who were supposed to hold firm the scepter of New York's "radicality." Artists had stopped making a difference; they simply added to the world's indifference. The more they approved uncritically of Baudrillard, the more they confirmed his own distaste of contemporary art and the more they turned art into an indifferent activity. They were *looking for a quick pay-off* in the same way that critics discoursing on antirepressive themes were. And it was all the same. It was all "given to indifference." This is what capitalism was about, and it certainly was "useful" that someone like Baudrillard would be there to say it with a sense of integrity. "They wanted normalcy," Jack Smith summed up. Wanting normalcy was far worse than being normal. It went much beyond French theory reflecting on the competition, insecurity, and desperation that now beset the art world. And this is what Baudrillard was talking about *as an artist*, refusing to acknowledge his unwanted disciples. Paradoxically, it was *he* who was making a difference. He was making it by turning them down, refusing the scepter that they were offering him for their own benefit. Baudrillard was teaching them a lesson, *and they didn't get it*. And it wasn't just any lesson: it was a lesson *in theory*. They couldn't even recognize theory when they saw it live.

Baudrillard is often accused of being passive and cynical, and it certainly is true. It is passive nihilism, if you will, and yet very active in many ways, even *committed* to cynicism. Shouldn't one be cynical toward what *deserves cynicism* rather than embrace it as if it was, well, "normal"? Baudrillard was that kind of exterminating angel. Predictably, he was finished in the art world after that. But maybe it was the art world that was "finished," with its pretenses to be different. Paradoxically, it was Baudrillard who had been the "resistance." He had not accepted the world as it is. Baudrillard himself had been "anti-Baudrillard."

The "anti-Baudrillard" show hadn't exactly been directed against Baudrillard in any case; it had been a way, Tim Rollins said, of "engaging the psychological crisis" of those who were accepting hyperreality as real, by the same token legitimizing all the excess of the eighties ("always more celebrity," etc.). But it was Baudrillard himself who flatly refused to play that game, as he easily could have, and become, in Jack Smith's words, "a pasty celebrity," "a crust like Andy Warhol," "lobotomized, zombified," a normal individual in the conditions of advanced capitalism. "You can be entertained to death in this country," he added with a whine. "I can't take these exaggerated doses of pasty cheerfulness of capitalism in which you have to be happy all the time." Baudrillard wasn't as much of a zombie as people thought he was. He had done his job—and they hadn't.

Tim Rollins kept opposing Baudrillard's intellectual games, "his acceptance of the world as it is" to Deleuze, who had been "an enormous influence on politically active people." Deleuze had exerted "a major impact" on artists working in communities. The issues *Semiotext(e)* published on "Anti-Oedipus," he added, and the one reinventing Nietzsche in the United States, had been "enormously inspirational." That was great to know, of course. And it is true that there doesn't seem to be two theories apparently more at odds than those of Deleuze and Guattari versus Baudrillard. Deleuze and Guattari felt very strongly about it, too. They despised Baudrillard's ideas for "demobilizing" people, turning them away from political action. It is with Deleuze and Guattari in mind that I eventually paired Baudrillard's essay, *Forget Foucault* with an interview called *Forget Baudrillard*. They could never understand why I liked Baudrillard. "Lotringer publishes *anything*," Deleuze would say. You can't please everyone when "doing theory," even those you like, so I held fast. Later on I joked about the title with Baudrillard on the beach in California where I first met him. "Forget Foucault"? We should rather call it: "Remember Foucault." Foucault died six months later; French intellectuals never forgave Baudrillard for having attacked him.

Being very close to Guattari myself, I considered Baudrillard politically irresponsible as well, but I never reduced his thinking to a mere intellectual game. He was serious about it, even if the spirals of his thoughts kept taking him from left to right and right to left, dizzyingly. Then I realized that it wasn't something one could define spatially in traditional terms, it was more like a Moebius strip. Even when I disagreed with him, or when one of his spirals was taking him astray, I withheld my judgment. He was somewhere else, a special agent in the extraterrestial space that our world was fast becoming. He was a "mad scientist" trying out ideas just to see where they would take him, and us, regardless of immediate consequences. Often his ideas would cross other planets in their trajectories, impeccably registering their impact in the twisted way he has to think things through to their extremity, and then taking a step back he would let you fall in the "trap," like Ubu Roi. I couldn't help seeing him in Deleuzian terms, more Deleuzian than Deleuze himself would have ever wanted him to be, or acknowledged that he was. Deleuze and Guattari affectionately described this kind of itinerary as the schizo walk: "It's a better model than the neurotic lying down on the couch," they wrote in *Anti-Oedipus*. "A bit of fresh air, a relation with the outside. For instance, Lenz's walk recreated by Buchner. It's different at times when Lenz happens to be at his good pastor's, who forces him to figure out his position in relation to society. . . ."

When *Simulations* was published in 1983, the New York art world was desperately trying to regain the upper hand and the neoconceptualists were asserting their strategy of appropriation. Donald Kuspit had just turned around and was now opposing them, advocating neo-Expressionism. "Buchloh," Kuspit wrote, reversing the art historian's massive argument, "never considers the possibility that modernism might have become an empty stereotype of itself, and that its strategies of 'parody and appropriation' might have been overused and abused to the point of becoming mechanical reflexes."[36] Criticizing German painting, embracing "simulation" for its critical value, or for its "reality" as a reflection of advanced capitalism, Baudrillard's theory unwillingly contributed to reestablish the preeminence of sleek American art and even sleeker art market over the European assailants. And yet it never was quite the same after that. New York had to give some ground, let a few other places like Cologne or Milan, get a piece of the cake. The global economy was on its way, and would be dominated by America anyway. And French theory would have contributed to that, too.

Actually, when you think of it, the piggish, decisive, cynical decade that was the eighties, with its shoddy values and destruction of what still made the old art world a viable proposition, was powerfully dominated by French theory, whether it came as "deconstruction," giving some much needed energy to the failing social sciences in America, or at least to textual fetishism, a last-ditch academic specialty; or as "simulation," providing an unexpected boost to the antics of an avant-garde that had become undistinguishable from its alleged opponents. It is true that New York stole not just the *idea* of modern art, but the whole art show from the French Nouveaux Realistes in 1962. This wasn't the end of French art, but only its metamorphosis into French theory, which started exactly the same year as Lévi-Strauss's *Savage Mind*. Paradoxically, it is thanks to French theory that the American art world managed to regain the upper hand over the Continental threat. So theory hadn't all been for naught. The "new technologies" were on their way, and the neoconceptualists were onto something after all with their cute posters and billboards. Virilio was plenty ready for the war on perception that was still in the offing; actually, his theory was extraordinarily perceptive and *prospective* with its percepts/concepts communicated in telegraphic style, its powerful *vision* of speed and politics, of the dissipation of the world in real-time technologies. The real neoconceptualist of the world as it was being "consumed" under our very eyes, of this useless passion that life on this earth has become, of the massive invasion of the soul snatchers, of the total war waged by technology on humanity, was Virilio, who first conceived of it on the big screen of theory, and not in Hollywood.

Baudrillard was misinterpreted. But did people understand his Foucault any better? Americans used Foucault for a conspiracy theory. The thrill of prison and repression in bloodless lives. Better than the assassination of John F. Kennedy. What was anyone doing about the *one million* plus political prisoners rotting in the best real estate deal and growth industry in the "free world": prisons? At least "schizo-culture" was dealing with something real in 1975: prison and madness, the world as it is. *Semiotext(e),* a small, independent press, started with $200 in 1974, published *Still Black, Still Strong: Survivors of the War Against Black Revolutionaries,* texts by Mumia Abu-Jamal, Assata Shakur, and Dhoruba Bin Wahad, and this *in 1993.* What were committed Marxist presses doing in the meantime? *Selling* Marxism as an elegant product. Let's examine a book jacket at random, *Michel Foucault: Genealogy as Critique,* by Rudi Visker (London: Verso, 1995). "A lucid and elegant survey of Foucault's corpus. . . Visker shows him to be neither relativist nor positivist, neither activist nor detached observer. Instead, Foucault emerges as the inventor of a new analysis of our modern mechanisms of control and exclusion: precisely of 'genealogy as critique.'" Self-promotion, and promotion of what? Detached *neither/nors*. Foucault put on a leash. They wanted normalcy and they got it. At least Baudrillard is on the mark once in a while, not on the make at all times. Kissing Marx's bum. And what was Paul Piccone, the editor of *Telos*, doing while we were trying to help post-Marxist Italian intellectuals out of the jail? He was translating hate texts from the German and sending us hate letters calling us "charlatans."[37] This tells a lot more about the state of things in America than it does about the perversion of the French intellect.

So the "radicals" got entrenched in the university, learning the muffled corporate ways, talking loud on the podium and doing business as usual under the table—promotions, raises, careers, a piece of the academic cake—all in the name of Marxism and of the "cultural revolution," a paper tiger revolution that didn't need to happen anymore since it was all in the text. Negative dialectics: a disenchanted mask worn on top of the pasty cheerfulness of capitalism.

It took some twenty years for Deleuze and Guattari to start coming out of the woods, first through their concept of "minority," often confused with a new ghetto; then the shallow hipness of "nomadism." Now Guattari was dead and Deleuze dying. They didn't seem as dangerous anymore. Feminist theorists started softening their stand against the "terrible pair of snobs." For a long time they had remained suspicious of the outward masculine orientation of Deleuze and Guattari's philosophy, their disregard for the dialectics of sexes and women's attempt to achieve autonomy, identity and self-determination—for the desire to *be* women, instead of "becoming women." Their mutual estrangement, until the mid-90s, was inescapable. Actually a major revision of the feminist attitude toward them is on the way, with precise, thorough, critical but openminded analyses of their work finally coming out.[38]

But it may be too late. The vultures already have the scent. Over the last two or three years the academic industry has suddenly "discovered" Deleuze, and paraphrases, commentaries, and critical analyses are now coming out at an alarming rate. Whoever said, Better dead than read? They're dead and they're being read to death. Not that it changes anyone's life, or "the world as it is" in any way. It just makes sure that after *Genealogy as Critique*, something like "Critique on a Plateau" will be dumped on your plate. It came from Duke University Press in Spring 2000, a much needed "metacommentary" on Deleuze: "By explicating elemental concepts in Deleuze—desire, flow, the nomad—Buchanan finds that, despite Deleuze's self-declared moratorium on dialectics, he was in several important respects a dialectician. In essays that address the 'prehistory' of Deleuze's philosophy, his methodology, and the utopic dimensions of his thought, Buchanan extracts an apparatus of social critique that arises from the philosopher's utopian impulse." This, from the book jacket of Ian Buchanan, *Deleuzism: A Metacommentary*. Don't miss it. Everything Deleuze hated most and spent his life fighting—dialectics, utopia, social critique—is there. Like fugitives blowing up bridges behind them, Deleuze and Guattari made a great effort not to leave behind them any "model" that could be simply applied, even discouraging all too eager disciples to follow their paths instead of finding their own. "Applying theory": this kind of hands-on, hand-to-mouth attitude, of course, has little to do with what they themselves advocated as "pragmatic philosophy." What they meant by that wasn't a philosophy calling for a separate "praxis," or "use value," but on the contrary for a kind of experimentation directly engaged in reality and responding in the present, without any preconceived idea, to the singularity of the situation. This didn't prevent some recent critics from applying their "methodology" to the analysis of literature, or more generally to subject their "hermeneutics" to insistent reduction and paraphrasing. So was it all for naught? Twenty-five years of trying to get things right, and then this—what? This blank appraisal, blanket adulation, colorless rewriting of vibrant concepts. Jarry had one word for that: *merdre*. Critique or placebo—is there any other alternative? Baudrillard forgotten on his celestial flight, Deleuze and Guattari long brushed aside now, used and abused until nothing is left of the generous impulse, of their bid for life.

At least there was something crazily alive, and not just creepy, resentful, or crassly opportunistic in Camille Paglia rants, which managed to turn the tide against French theory in 1991. Time was ripe, hallucinated crowds of self-proclaimed disciples were already pointing their fangs toward fresher spoils. "Lacan, Derrida, and Foucault," Paglia kept repeating, lumping together these very unlikely bedfellows, "are the perfect prophets for the weak, anxious academic personality, trapped in verbal formulas and perennially defeated by circumstance."[39] She had a point, of course—the same as for the art world—but playing on people's insecurities isn't specific to French theory, or to academia for that matter. It is the essence of American society, and of capitalism in general. Neurosis isn't a matter of weak personalities; people have to be made weak and insecure in order to render them more pliable. So why not use theory for that purpose, too? Knowledge is never enough one way or another, and the only way many American readers of French theory found to integrate it into their lives, it seems, was to turn it into yet another excruciating test.

Paglia accused French theorists of having betrayed the "expanded vision" and emotions of sixties popular culture and replacing it with "high culture" and desiccated intelligence. It is the very seduction of theory that made it dangerous: "I now realize how lucky I was, in the total absence of role models, to have only men to rebel against. Today's women students are meeting their oppressors in dangerously seductive new form, as successful, congenial female professors who are themselves victims of a rigid foreign ideology." Theorists in their pods and podiums "pushing their shrink-wrapped products," cheap showmanship replacing the "authentic values" of scholarly research. This new academic order was just beginning to emerge when Paglia published her infamous essay, "Junk Bonds and Corporate Raiders," in 1991. In this huge mutation, the discrepancy was becoming even more glaring between the corporate cynicism of enterprising universities and the idealist values still being posted to keep foot soldiers in abeyance. Paglia's avocation was in fact playing right into the hands of this managerial "double bind" by sporting "true scholarship" at a time of virtual osmosis between university-sponsored research and the capitalist system.

Like the audience she courted and eventually got, Paglia needed to preserve the illusion that disinterested research existed somewhere, and that a distinction could still be made between the public and the private, between the civilian and the military—this at a time when all the sixties Rousseauist truths and ideals of "revolutionized consciousness" had played themselves out and turned, as she grudgingly admitted, "ugly." Actually, the real scandal was that there was no more difference between the two, or between anything. All the more reason to stamp out a corrupting product come from the outside to invade this world of scholarly innocence—and here she specifically addressed female academics— "in a dangerously seductive form." French theory in America as the mythical French lover and no less infamous disease. But, as Paglia recognized, the worm was already in the fruit. Freeing "academic slaves" from this "rigid foreign ideology" was all the more difficult since those whose innocence she wanted to reclaim were self-inflicted victims, "trash-talking foreign-junk-bond-dealers" in their own right.

The irony is that Paglia's rambling rage, which instantly rippled through the media,[40] was targeting an audience of nonacademics, media-drenched folks all too eager to dismiss difficult discourses that they would never fancy reading anyway—Paglia had hardly read them herself—and who basically shared the very same corporate mentality that she was stigmatizing in the university. If anything, the enthusiastic reception of her manifesto signaled how far French theory had traveled inside American culture, being frequently quoted in the *Village Voice*, referred to in the *New York Times*, and finally monumentalized anonymously— a full-screen on Jean Baudrillard's *Simulations*, like the tablets of the law—in the recent Hollywood movie, *The Matrix*.

What is most effective in Paglia's summary dismissal of "Gallic theory" is her vengeful giddiness, all the more contagious for collecting all the negativity lying around, solidifying along the way the slippery cultural identity of an "immigrant nation with overlapping and competing ethnicities." The format that readily offered itself was a public execution, and this is what her "Corporate Raiders" pamphleteering really was about. A measure of attraction and repulsion characterizes all sacred objects, but objects only become sacred when duly sanctified— French theory dumped in the gutter, like Champagne. "Let's dump the French in Boston Harbor and let them swim home," Paglia exclaimed. The same ritual sacrifice was enacted by Céline on behalf of the French themselves. Like Paglia, Céline launched himself headlong into an unbridled furor of abuse and derision, a delirium without remorse or repair from which he never managed to reappear. Céline claimed as well that he had to protect the French against the Jews, who were perverting Gallic values and pushing the country, unaware, to declare war on the daunting Germans. What right did the French have, Paglia protested in turn, to impose their "asinine" theories on their American saviors? "American GIs (including my uncles) got shot rescuing France when she was lying flat on her face under the Nazi boot. Hence it is revolting to see pampered American academics down on their knees kissing French bums."

Bagatelles pour un massacre was ferociously funny as well, and far more ambivalent toward the Jews, whose communal spirit Céline envied and held as an example to his own drunk and "degenerate" countrymen, than Paglia toward "the French" liberally accused of bringing into America "a foreign fascism," by promoting "fanatical, sterile mind-games," and embracing a "totalitarian world-view." And she went on stigmatizing Foucault, an "arrogant bastard," for his alleged lack of emotion, a typical modernist tirade used by Céline himself against the Jews. In turn Paglia stigmatized the French philosopher as being "rigidly schematic . . . cold, desiccated," divorced from humor and human compassion. "It is the same combination of maniacal abstraction with lust for personal power," she boldly concluded, "that led to the deranged orderliness of the concentration camps." Wouldn't you rather that French theory had remained imperceptible in this country?

As an adolescent in France, I often read *Focus* by Arthur Miller. The hero of the novel, Lawrence Newman, an average white American male, buys a new pair of glasses and his life is changed. The glasses make him look vaguely Jewish, and this throws him unaware into a destiny of oppression that he wasn't exactly cut out for. He suddenly becomes like an open wound, a poignant question raised in a society that only sells ready-made answers and sanitized situations. This "becoming Jewish" that arrives by accident, and that he gradually must adjust to, even accept as part of his own makeup, forces him to look at life differently. Everything he used to take for granted now takes on another dimension. By wearing these glasses, he hasn't just acquired another identity, he is made to question what identity itself is about. And one has to put aside everything that makes one identical and predictable for life to become something singular—"nonidentical," or "nonpolitical," in Cage's words. An insignificant action, an untimely event, is enough to trigger a change of such proportion that this man will never be the same again.

In Kafka's "Report to an Academy," the erstwhile ape captured during a hunting expedition quickly realizes that becoming human is the only alternative to spending his entire life in a cage. It is at this point that he decides to monkey his captors. Accidentally stumbling into human language, he manages to open the way of humanity. Becoming human, though, for him, isn't at all a promotion; to the contrary, he would rather remain an ape in the world of apes. He becomes an animal prodigy, a curiosity, a scientific anomaly in order to find a way out of captivity, and for no other reason. It is true that, at first, he finds the new knowledge he acquires exhilarating, "but I must confess: I didn't overestimate it; not even then, much less now." Knowledge isn't enough in itself; it only matters inasmuch as it opens up new possibilities. But possibilities themselves can't be known in advance—they have to be created in order to exist. And only an event can create the possibility of the possible, suddenly revealing how intolerable what had been considered acceptable, or even desirable until then, really was.[41]

I was very moved, when I heard Gilles Deleuze say that there was nothing he wanted more than to leave philosophy—but, he quickly added, *leaving it as a philosopher*. This is also what John Cage did his best to achieve: leaving music, but *as a musician*. Actually, many of Cage's own precepts or intuitions, derived from a variety of sources—from Thoreau's practical anarchism to Tchouang-Tseu's Taoism, from Marshall McLuhan or Buckminster Fuller's sense of the utilities to Zen's sense of multiplicity—anticipate or overlap many elements of Deleuze and Guattari's "theory." Theory, for Cage, wasn't a gilded cage, nor was it all "for the birds." It was a way out of the enforced silence that music had become.

"Theory" may even be a way out of "theory." This is what Deleuze did with the history of philosophy, rummaging everywhere for allies, only picking up whatever he needed to get out of the philosophical predicament. Cages are everywhere, and so is music. "All too often men are betrayed by the word freedom," the philosophical ape estimated. "And as freedom is counted among the most sublime feelings, so the corresponding disillusionment can also be sublime. . . . Freedom was not what I wanted. Only a way out; right or left, or in any direction . . ."

The "outside" doesn't exist unless you create it. Otherwise it remains an empty gesture, an enticing detour. It may not even be outside, but in the midst of things, the most unlikely things. But first *it* has to find *you*. Something goes wrong, goes right, an accident turns your life in an unpredictable direction. It ceases to be something personal and becomes a kind of experiment in which the world around you participates.

One only learns when forced to. What attracted me, like everyone else, to French theory at first was that it was an intellectual challenge, a new field of knowledge, an exciting entry into a world of thought that was as complex and many-faceted as the world we live in. But it would have remained just that, another piece of music, or a piece of knowledge, if it hadn't become by accident something vital, something that could be mobilized and put to task for a given purpose—a purpose that theory could also, precisely, help clarify.

This accident, which is enough to trigger a subjective transformation, is at the root of what Deleuze and Guattari called an *event*.

Notes

1. John Cage, *Pour les oiseaux* (Paris: Belfond, 1976). *For the Birds*. (London: Marion Boyars, 1980?

2. *Semiotext(e)*, 3, no. 2, 1978, p. 198. Special "Schizo-culture" issue.

3. Camille Paglia, "Junk Bonds and Corporate Raiders: Academe in the Hour of the Wolf," in *Sex, Art, and American Culture* (New York: Vintage Books, 1992), p. 210.

4. Gilles Deleuze, *Nietzsche et la Philosophie*. (Paris: PUF, 1977), p. 139.

5. *Semiotext(e)*, "Autonomia: Post-Political Politics" issue, 1982.

6. Jean-François Lyotard, "Energumen Capitalism," in *Semiotext(e)* 2, no. 3 (1977), 11. "Anti-Oedipus" issue.

7. Gilles Deleuze, "I Have Nothing to Admit: Letter to Michel Cressole," *Semiotext(e)* 2, no. 3, 1977, p. 112. See also Michael Hardt, *Gilles Deleuze: An Apprenticeship in Philosophy* (Minneapolis: University of Minnesota Press, 1993).

8. In his "Introduction to the Structural Analysis of Narratives," first published in *Communications* 8 (1996) and reprinted in *Image-Music-Text* (Glasgow: Fontana/Collins, 1979), Roland Barthes attributed the term *theory* to American transformational linguists.

9. Thanks to Johnny Philosophy for the conference on "the hypothetical," Maastricht, The Netherlands, 1999.

10. See the excellent exposé by Vincent Descombes, *Modern French Philosophy* (Cambridge: Cambridge University Press, 1980), p. 177.

11. Jean Baudrillard, *The Mirror of Production* (1973), trans. Mark Poster (St Louis, Telos Press, 1975), p. 51.

12. Jean Baudrillard, *Simulations*. New York: Semiotext(e), 1983, edited by Sylvère Lotringer. This short version of *Simulacres et simulation* (Paris: Galilee, 1981) includes as well a chapter from *L' Echange symbolique et la mort* (Paris: Gallimard, 1976).

13. Baudrillard denies having ever been a sociologist. "The only thing I ever did as a sociologist," he told me, "is putting an end to sociology."

14. After attending a lecture Baudrillard gave at Columbia University, one of my colleagues flatly said, "He's talking about nothing. But so did Mallarmé, of course, and Flaubert."

15. See Jean Baudrillard, *Selected Writings*, ed. Mark Poster (Stanford: Stanford University Press, 1988) and *Baudrillard: A Critical Reader,* ed. Douglas Kellner (Cambridge, Mass.: Blackwell, 1994).

16. Jonathan Ree, "Philosophy for Philosophy's Sake," in *New Left Review*, 211, May/June 1995.

17. William C. Dowling, *Jameson, Althusser, Marx* (Ithaca, N.Y.: Cornell University Press, 1984), p. 10.

18. Fredric Jameson, *Fables of Aggression* (Berkeley and Los Angeles: University of California Press, 1973).

19. Fredric Jameson, *The Political Unconscious: Narrative as a Socially Symbolic Act* (Ithaca, N.Y.: Cornell University Press, 1981), p. 96.

20. Fredric Jameson, "Les dualismes aujourd'hui," in *Gilles Deleuze. Une vie philosophique*, ed. Eric Alliez Rencontres Internationales Rio de Janeiro-Sao Paoló, 10–14 juin 1996. Le Plessis-Robinson: Institut Synthelabo, 1998.

21. Manfred Frank, "The World as Will and Representation: Deleuze and Guattari's Critique of Capitalism as Schizo-Analysis and Schizo-Discourse," *Telos* 57, (fall 1983), pp. 167–68.

22. *French Theory in Germany* was published by Heidi Paris and Peter Gente at the Merve Verlag in Berlin; they who coedited *Semiotext(e)*'s "German Issue" in 1982. The format for the "Foreign Agents" books was directly inspired by their own publications.

23. Christa Burger, "The Reality of 'Machines,' Notes on the Rhizome-Thinking of Deleuze and Guattari," *Telos* 64 (1985).

24. Cf. Michel Foucault, *Foucault Live*, ed. Sylvère Lotringer (New York: Semiotext(e) Double Agents series, 1996), pp. 154–80.

25. See Felix Guattari, *Soft Subversions*, ed. Sylvère Lotringer (New York: Semiotext(e) Foreign Agents series, 1996), pp. 7–23; and Ti-Grace Atkinson, *Amazon Odyssey* (1967–1972) (New York: Links Books, 1974). Atkinson had a point about "male supremacy" as well in terms of the sixties: as Chris Kraus has pointed out, women had been forcibly eliminated from all the leadership roles by the male antiwar movement as well as exiled from male-oriented pop culture. But none of this, of course, specifically addressed Guattari's talk.

26. Wolfgang Max Faust, "With It and Against It: Tendencies in Recent German Art," *Artforum*, September 1981. Unlike other art magazines at the time, *Artforum* sided early on with the neoexpressionist trend, both from Europe and at home.

27. Achille Bonito Oliva, *The Italian Trans-avantgarde* (Milano: Giancarlo Politi Editore, 1980.)

28. Donald B. Kuspit, "Flak from the 'Radicals': The American Case against Current German Painting." In *Expressions: New Art from Germany* (St. Louis: St. Louis Art Museum, 1983).

29. Hal Foster, *Recodings* (Seattle: Bay Press, 1985); Thomas Lawson, "Last Exit: Painting." *Artforum*, October 1981. The accusation of mythology is another point of contact between the rejection of the neoexpressionists and that of Deleuze.

30. Benjamin Buchloh, "Figures of Authority, Ciphers of Regression," *October* 16, Spring 1981. On all this, see my "Third Wave: Art and The Commodification of Theory," in *Flash Art,* May/June, 1991. Reprinted in *Theories of Contemporary Art*, 2d ed., ed. Richard Hertz (Englewood Cliffs, N.J.: Prentice-Hall, 1993).

31. Deleuze even broke publicly with Foucault over the question of German terrorism, which he himself opposed.

32. Milazzo and Collins's exhibit, *New Capital*, held at White Columns in New York, included Peter Halley, Jeff Koons, Peter Nagey, and Sarah Charlesworth. Cf. Collins and Milazzo, *Hyperframes: A Post-Appropriation Discourse*, vol. 1 (Paris: Editions Antoine Candeau, 1989), pp. 35ff.

33. Peter Halley, *Collected Essays, 1981–87* (Zurich: Brun Bischofberger Gallery, 1988), pp. 81, 95.

34. Peter Halley maintained that Jeff Koons's vacuum cleaners inhabiting a universe "strangely similar to the original," gave us "an intensified experience of the simulacrum." Halley, Essays, p. 101.

35. Jean Baudrillard, *Illusion, Desillusion esthetiques* (Paris: Sens and Tonka, 1997), pp. 16–17.

36. Kuspit, "Flak from the 'Radicals," p. 43.

37. My copublisher at *Semiotext(e)*, Jim fleming, reminded me recently of that letter, laughing in a restaurant as we were finally parting ways after twenty years of good service. I had *forgotten* about Paul Piccone. Thanks, Nietzsche.

38. See Elizabeth Groz, "A Thousand Tiny Sexes: Feminism and Rhizomatics" and Rosi Braidotti, "Toward a New Nomadism: Feminist Deleuzian Tracks; or, Metaphysics and Metabolism," in *Gilles Deleuze and the Theater of Philosophy*, ed. Constantin V. Boundas and Dorothea Olkowski (New York: Routledge, 1994).

39. Camille Paglia, *Sex, Art, and American Culture* (New York: Vintage Books, 1992), pp. 211, 213.

40. Paglia's "Junk Bonds and Corporate Raiders: Academe in the Hour of the Wolf" was eventually published *by The New York Book Review, Cosmopolitan* and the *San Francisco Examiner*.

41. See Deleuze/Guattari, "Mai 68 n'a pas eu lieu," *Les Nouvelles*, May 3–10, 1984. See also François Zourabichvili, "Deleuze et le possible (de l'involontarisme en poli-tique)," in *Gilles Deleuze. Une vie philosophique, op.cit.,* pp. 335–358.

Blackboxing in Theory: Deleuze versus Deleuze

ELIE DURING

> Blackboxing: an expression from the sociology of science that refers to the way scientific and technical work is made invisible by its own success. When a machine runs efficiently, when a matter of fact is settled, one need focus only on its inputs and outputs and not on its internal complexity. Thus, paradoxically, the more science and technology succeed, the more opaque and obscure they become.
>
> —*Bruno Latour,* Pandora's Hope

> Writing has a double function: to translate everything into assemblages and to dismantle assemblages.
>
> —*Gilles Deleuze and Félix Guattari,*
> Kafka: Toward a Minor Literature

The Mirage of French Theory

French theory, just like America, "exists only when our eyes are closed." Baudrillard writes about "a continent which, by its mass, deflects light rays and thus cannot be seen, deflects lines of force and thus cannot be encountered, deflects the radiation of conceptual influences and thus cannot be conceived." And he adds, "Such a mental object no doubt exists, but we shall never see it, except to spot the subtle distortion it engenders in reality."[1] French theory in America perfectly embodies this. It is a series of deflections and distortions of conceptual light rays, a phenomenon that only lives in our minds "like a synergic phantasm on the retina," but whose effects can be traced everywhere. From the academy to the art world, from *Social Text* to *Artforum*, a phantasm is relentlessly entertained: this thing dubbed "French theory" would account for a certain number of effects in theory *as well as outside it*. The question is not to decide the degree of reality attributed to a constellation of more or less heterogeneous texts or discursive practices. A priori, French theory exists no less than any other theoretical formation or historical category. The real problem with French theory is that it is not even clear how its unity (or "principle of dispersion," as Foucault would say) should be described. It is not a matter of metaphysics, but a very earthly matter of empirical definition.

The question of French theory's importation in the United States is not worth spending too much effort on; in fact it has never been imported and probably never been purposefully constructed. French theory was probably only inferred and fancied as that kind of indirect free discourse that Deleuze suggested as an alternative to the traditional gestures of criticality. When it comes to defining what is genuinely valuable in French theory, a set of theoretical attitudes or moves is generally invoked, rather than concepts or doctrines.[2] This hints at the fact that French theory may not be a theory after all, not even a set of overlapping and sometimes diverging theories. It forces us to revise our very concept of theory, or to redefine it in a way that is consonant with a certain French way of doing or undoing theory, of thinking about theory.

Deleuze in French Theory

Focusing on the optical workings of deflection and distortion themselves, instead of the problematic status of their cause, allows for a venture toward more operative hypotheses. The case of Deleuze is at once typical and rather odd in this respect. He shared many affinities with Foucault, but he never found it very comfortable to be associated with such figures as Baudrillard, whose work he truly despised, or Derrida, whom he almost never referred to (specially not when dealing with language and signs). Being highly skeptical about labels such as "postmodernism" or "poststructuralism," Deleuze felt above all part of a generation, "a strong one," as he would say, "with Foucault, Althusser, Derrida, Lyotard, Serres, Faye, Châtelet, and others."[3] Although it may be a fruitless task to spell out the common traits of the thinkers counted among the pantheon of French theory, its narrativization is fairly straightforward. If "poststructuralism" intends to provide a critique of "representational thinking"—the kind that has characterized the metaphysical tradition ever since Plato—it may seem that Deleuze provides the very philosophical foundation of this type of critique by defining the means and aims of a *philosophy of difference*. *Difference* here would stand for all that shatters the "logic of identity," in other words the harmonic chord of subject-concept-object, the hierarchical scheme of categories and its underlying doctrine of judgment. With *Difference and Repetition*[4] clearing the ground for a philosophy of divergence, decentring, exteriority, and so forth, Deleuze meets the expectations of a French theorist. Rather, he provides the philosophical credentials that the narrative of French theory needs. By the same token, poststructuralist social criticism, insofar as it draws upon French theory to define its strategy, finds in Deleuze (and Guattari) "the justificatory framework it needs in order to avoid collapsing into incoherence."[5] Despite the fact that Deleuze (and Guattari) always cautiously avoided direct engagement with poststructuralism or postmodernism, the typically Deleuzian notion of an immanent foundation is put to service as a counterweapon against accusations of lazy antifoundationalism. At the same time, his sophisticated version of perspectivism seems to provide a useful clarification of the relativist stance implied by poststructuralism. More clearly than Foucault (the genealogist) or Derrida (the trickster), Deleuze is *the philosopher of French theory*. Yet, it is unlikely that he would have welcomed this title.

In France, he has been recognized as one of the chief thinkers of his generation, and his *philosophical* reputation is certainly still more important there than that of many of his "postmodern" peers. Quite consistently he was explicitly cautious not to present himself as a provider of "theory"—he was too much of an empiricist (or a philosopher). In his view, tailoring concepts, not theories, is the specific job of the philosopher. This is one of the reasons why his reception in the United States has been much more delayed than that of other more famous figures of French theory: Deleuze did not appeal to scholars involved in Marxist, psychoanalytic, or linguistic theorizing. He was not interested one bit in the "signifier" (a "dreary" word), and from the outset his relation to psychoanalysis has been conflictual to say the least. Besides, he seemed to bear no relationship with the emerging paradigm offered by the proponents of textual deconstruction. It was only after the textual was extended to a general cultural field, and not just the literary sphere, that Deleuze's line of minor criticism (exemplified by his book on Kafka) became a cornerstone for the theoretical foundations of cultural studies.[6] Nevertheless, if his name may still be less widely quoted in the United States than that of Derrida, Foucault or Lyotard, as deconstructionism and postmodernism run out of steam, Deleuze continues to gain ground in the academy as well as in larger spheres.

Deleuze's Becoming Pop

Deleuze's audience indeed extends far beyond the scope of scholarly circles. Despite many *Derrida for Beginners* books that have found a niche in the publishing market, there are no children's books illustrating deconstruction to this date,[7] nor are there rock bands or electronic labels claiming a Derridean ascendency.[8] Much of Deleuze's appeal lies in the immediacy of a style that lends itself to all kinds of reappropriations. His readers are tempted and to a certain extent invited to cut through the academic rhetoric usually present in French philosophical or critical writings, in order to extract the conceptual soundbite, the "end product." Deleuze encouraged this practice by stressing the idea that philosophers should be judged according to the number and quality of concepts (not to be confused with theories, techniques, or strategies) they have been able to create. It is indeed difficult not to be in awe at the bewildering array of concepts displayed in his own works. Yet, such insistence on manufacturing concepts easily produces a form of heraldic fascination. Concepts become "brand names" made available for all kinds of ideological operations. They are emblems rather than devices, and their actual functioning is overshadowed by their discursive use value.[9] As a result, Deleuzian concepts are now on display everywhere in prepackaged slogans: "smooth space" and "rhizome" freely circulate in the jargon of web designers, music producers, architects, and art critics.[10] Books and conferences are devoted to exploring the direct applicability of certain Deleuzian ideas in the practice of architecture, film, or science studies, despite the master's own warning to his followers: "[My concept is] not another 'model.'"[11]

Deleuze sowed fertile pastures for the use (or abuse) of his own productions in yet another way. He actually called for a new, less stratified relationship to the book by opposing the war-machine book to the state-apparatus book.[12] His association with Félix Guattari was of course a catalyst for this new view of textual production. Through this collaborative work, hard academic rhetoric was purged from his writing. As he recalls, Guattari provided the "outside" and the political influx he just needed, while in return he provided the analytical power that Guattari's writing could never sustain.[13] What resulted was a new kind of book, that precipitated a new type of reader. As Brian Massumi writes,

> Deleuze recommends that you read *Capitalism and Schizophrenia* as you would listen to a record. You don't approach a record as a closed book that you have to take and leave. There are always cuts that leave you cold. So you skip them. Other cuts you may listen to over and over again. They follow you. You find yourself humming them under your breath as you go about your daily business.[14]

This emphasis on the pickup method (largely commented on in *Dialogues*) does not really ring with other concerns expressed by Deleuze (maybe as a result of some misreadings of his own philosophy). Yet, whether Deleuze liked it or not, many people have actually read him in this fashion, skipping through *A Thousand Plateaus* to end up having read only its introduction, "Rhizome," or perhaps the book's most appealing chapter, "Nomadology," leaving aside Deleuze's more directly "philosophical" writings. Such reading practices are not born of sheer laziness or dislike, but of the sincere belief that this is the way Deleuze should be used.[15]

It is rarely understood that Foucault's words about the century coming to be known as Deleuzian ("Mais un jour, peut-être, le siècle sera deleuzian"[16]) bear a double meaning in the common interpretation. *Siècle* is generally taken to mean "century" (by reference to Deleuze's place in the gallery of twentieth-century philosophers), yet in French it also hints, in a slightly derogatory way, at society and culture at large—the world of popular opinion. This interpretation is confirmed by an observation made by Foucault himself eight years later: "And I would say that this takes nothing away from Deleuze being an important philosopher."[17] In the same stroke, with the "diabolical sense of humor" admired by Deleuze, Foucault was heralding his colleague's inscription in the pantheon of great philosophers, and the massive diffusion of his thought in a more or less popularized version, its circulation beyond academic circles under the form of "cultural capital": buzzwords, formulae, models. Guattari probably had something quite different in mind when he said that

> in the long run, "Deleuze" has become a common noun . . . for a certain number of people who participate in "Deleuze-thought" [*la pensée Deleuze*], as we would have said years ago "Mao-thought." "Deleuze-thought" does exist; Michel Foucault insisted on that to some extent, in a rather humorous way, saying that this century would be Deleuzian, and I hope so. That doesn't mean that the century will be connected to the thought of Gilles Deleuze, but will comprise a certain reassemblage of theoretical activity vis-à-vis university institutions and power institutions of all kinds.[18]

It is doubtful whether Deleuze would have welcomed the leveling of his thought as a by-product of the kind of "pop philosophy" he advocated.[19] The emergence of Deleuzianism is probably the price he had to pay for becoming so inextricably linked with the "timeliness" of "le siècle."

Deleuze in America

Deleuze's reception in America, which Foucault prophesied in his discussion of *Logique du Sens* and *Différence et Répétition*, played an essential role in the construction of the mainstream Deleuzianism that now typifies the public image of the philosopher. Despite Deleuze's insistence on the affinity of his method (map-making, patchwork) with certain strands of American culture, as well as his repeated references to the pragmatic tradition,[20] it is pointless to try to trace any kind of preestablished harmony. At best, there are encounters and interplays between Deleuze and America. The truth is that the reception of Deleuze in America was prepared, and to a certain extent "arranged" (as in "arranged marriage"), by a very simple, yet very efficient machine. Its function is to sort out the available sources in order to produce the Deleuze that America is willing to use, a figure that is both user-friendly and sophisticated enough to retain its appeal. Its workings involve many actors (sometimes without their being conscious of it), institutions (academic or otherwise), and mediators (translations, reviews, publishing houses). Sylvère Lotringer recently commented on some of the strategies at work in the diffusion of Deleuze in the United States, when deconstruction à la Derrida and critical theory in the manner of the Frankfurt school were at the height of academic chic.[21] Despite these eye-witness accounts, nobody can claim to have intentionally assembled the black box "Deleuze in America," and it is instructive to pay particular attention to the importance of the very label "French theory" in the production of some of its most basic effects engineered by this sorting mechanism.

This blackboxing process is rather convoluted. It relies on a sorting mechanism inherent to the imposition of any category or label. On the one hand, *French theory* appears to be a very loose designation for a set of very concrete operations (distortions, displacements) that occur between French and American academia—a form of *a posteriori* reconstruction of their meaning. On the other hand, the nomination of French theory as a cohesive category plays an essential role from the outset in associating a heterogeneous set of doctrines whose common traits are not always apparent. By using the unifying term *French theory*, differences are overlooked, and common characteristics are emphasized such that the category retains some validity in retrospect. Hence, resorting to the French theory label is ironically and pragmatically justified to the extent that it succeeds in imposing a lens that filters and presents different philosophies as conforming to its own standards.

As Sylvère Lotringer explains, French theory never pretended to be "a mirror of Europe" or to reproduce "the divisions characteristic of French theoretical production."[22] French theory functions more like "an echo chamber," "a French seismograph" applied to the American reality. Its first aim, as a category, is political: "Given the political blockage that we inherited from the 60s, French Theory, as I conceived of it, was a way of provoking a real debate about society. . . ."[23] In this respect, it is not sufficient to say that the category *French theory* results from a process of appropriation or distortion whereby some French authors play a role within the American context. One must also acknowledge that "French theory" is directly instrumental in engineering these theoretical and political transformations. *It is both the name and the cause.* Thus Deleuze belongs to French theory and his presence in this category bestows some credibility to it because his philosophy has *first been reframed in its own terms.* This sleight of hand is far from innocent, for it produces very effective twists in the reception of Deleuze. One of them is that Deleuze seems to live a double life: along with the pop image of the nomad thinker, he simultaneously assumes the iconic position of the French philosopher, and thus contributes to the serenity of the academy's interpretative machine by lending himself to the twin distortions of being popularized and academicized all at once.

Presented in the larger setting of French theory, it is difficult to avoid comparing Deleuze with his peers: whether he is supposed as a better model (an alternative to deconstruction[24]), or considered as displaying certain typical patterns of French thought (a distrust of grand narratives, a taste for difference, discontinuity, instability, etc.), his work is generally understood as prolonging a lineage of issues and problems shared by other thinkers of his generation. Hence the presentation of Deleuze as a philosopher of *difference* (as opposed to identity, sameness, constancy), and his association with Derrida, Foucault, and poststructuralist theory in general.[25] As a result, in an uncanny reversal of the order of reception, it would seem that Deleuzianism precedes Deleuze himself in the guise of a stylized, partly self-fashioned, more or less academic version of his own thought corresponding to the inherent expectations of French theory's grand scheme.

Blackboxing the Master:
The Tricks of Deleuzian Scholarship

This stylized Deleuze is on display in every textbook. It is called "philosophy of difference," and it is not necessary to expand upon its main characteristics here. In his introduction to *A Thousand Plateaus* (reprinted in a slightly modified version in the opening pages of his *User's Guide to Capitalism and Schizophrenia*), Brian Massumi offers a sweeping summary of the (mostly negative) characterization found in *Difference and Repetition*: "Identity, resemblance, truth, justice, and negation" are the targets. Nomad thought, on the contrary, "does not repose on identity; it rides difference."[26] When one starts unpacking difference, things do not get much clearer. A brief glance at the titles of some recent studies devoted to Deleuze shows how the mainstream representation of Deleuzianism revolves around a few slogans or mottos that are relentlessly recombined in the flow of commentaries: *Multiplicity and Becoming, Pluralist Empiricism, Vitalism and Multiplicity*, and so on. On one level, such concepts are not very different from those Deleuze criticized for being "as big as hollow teeth."[27] They can in turn be spelled out into scores of erring signifiers that the commentator is invited to assemble at will according to the avant-garde method of cut-up borrowed from Burroughs, yielding a vertiginous refrain of buzzwords and gnomic formulae: "rhizomes," "lines of flight," "machinic assemblages," "smooth space," "flux," "heterogenesis," "singularities," "immanence," "minority," "deterritorialization" (Deleuze prided himself in having coined a truly unpronounceable concept). At worst, this produces barely readable accounts of Deleuze. In such instances, the authors do not mimic the philosopher's style, but rather its most apparent and less operative aspects, its lexical singularities, its vocabulary. These tasteless glossings over, interspersed with bursts of lyrical inspiration, are the very opposite of the dry prose and overall soberness that Clément Rosset was able to discern in the apparent luxuriance of Deleuze's concepts and fancy metaphors.[28] At best, the result is an uneasy mixture of philosophical recontextualization (in the purest academic vein) and direct application of Deleuzian notions to other domains (the famous "Deleuze and . . ." scheme, which the authors generally prefer to describe as a process of bringing "plateaus" into resonance).

The important point is that it is all too easy for commentators to rely on certain Deleuzian refrains—theory is a toolbox, concepts are bricks—in order to justify their own free treatment of Deleuze. The common wisdom states that Deleuze should be read as he himself used to read other philosophers: a practice of free indirect discourse, an experimentation. Deleuze then lends himself to a form of reading which, under the pretext of being faithful to the master's inspiration and recommendation, does not embarrass itself very much with the problem of understanding how his formidable machine actually functioned. The editors' introduction to *Gilles Deleuze and the Theater of Philosophy* displays a clear awareness of this risk, while trying to define a middle way between academic renderings and enthusiastic drifts: "We tried to trade off the search for hidden signifieds for a better understanding of how Deleuze's texts work. We wanted to trace the diagram of the series that make up his work, instead of 'representing' it or blurring its lines altogether, making it totally unrecognizable."[29]

Yet this remains wishful thinking, and the Deleuzian machine is never actually dismantled. Stepping out of the realm of representation is not as easy as one might think, and setting concepts on a new stage is not enough, for that stage can very well be that of representation itself. "I have tried to trace a diagram zigzagging from one concept to another,"[30] Constantin Boundas writes in the introduction to his *Deleuze Reader*. He adds, "Rhizomatic writing and reading are . . . preferable for turning a text into a problem and for tracing its active lines of transformation, stuttering, and flight, or for preventing its canonization." In fact, the very logic of representation from which Deleuzians think they are immune often brings them to seek a kind of writing in which the maneuvers of thought would stand out in full light, directly legible in the structure of a text, thus confusing *style* with *mannerism*. The truth is that mimicking the rhizomatic style of Deleuze (if there ever was one) can very well prepare the ground for his canonization. It may in fact be the best instrument to this end. Whatever their purpose, it is doubtful that such purely internal animations of Deleuze will help anyone get a grip on the gears and wheels of his mechanics.

At one level, it is hard to deny that there is a subversive potential in Deleuze that needs to be preserved. The temptation to "academicize" him, to freeze him in a canonical representation of his thought, should be resisted at all costs. As Ansell Pearson writes, "It is to be hoped that this century will *not,* as predicted, come to be known as 'Deleuzian,' in which his thought would acquire the status of a singular event. For at such a point Deleuze would become well and truly dead."[31] With a less tragic twist, Constantin Boundas and Olkowski make a similar point: "One, of course, does not pay Deleuze a tribute by canonizing his texts or by fencing them in with commentaries and annotations."[32] Yet those who would like to free Deleuze from the fixity of any closed system run another risk, that of freezing Deleuzian concepts into a series of order words. The exhortation to construct and connect, to trace further lines and move along, becomes itself a still thing: a mere rhetoric of pragmatism.

It is useful to bear in mind what Deleuze said about the epigones: "But that is not the worst of it: the worst is the way the texts of Kleist and Artaud themselves have ended up becoming monuments, inspiring models to be copied—a model far more insidious than the others—for the artificial stammerings and innumerable tracings that claim to be their equal."[33] Deleuze has a name for the kind of "mimetic procedures used to disseminate a unity that is retained in a different dimension"—"Technonarcissism."[34] There are indeed many technonarcissisms today, and their "lexical agility" only equals their laziness when it comes to actually producing the multiple. "In truth, it is not enough to say, 'Long live the multiple,' difficult as it is to raise that cry. No typographical, lexical, or even syntactical cleverness is enough to make it heard. The multiple *must be made.*"[35] No mannerism of the multiple will work as a substitute.

In the same vein, it is a clever but all too apparent rhetorical move that pushes many commentators to claim they are freeing Deleuze from the standard and canonical rules of the history of philosophy, when they are actually preparing the ground for the perpetuation of a monological version of his philosophy. Labeling and titling are an efficient tool in this process. Deleuze is presented as the antisystematic thinker of pure multiplicity, immanence, difference, heterogeneity, intensity—or in a more scientific tone, divergence, nonlinearity, nonequilibrium conditions. These valorized notions function like stamps or labels of quality. As entry points in Deleuze, they are interchangeable and do not require any clear definition, for they are said to communicate in a single rhizome, extending their branches in every direction.

As a result, it should not come as a surprise that the alleged aim of setting Deleuzian thought into motion, of dislocating it, of freeing it from its fixity and precipitating its own "becoming other," generally results in the most hackneyed and predictable pieces of Deleuzian scholarship. It is all very well to "resist the desire to fetishize" Deleuze,[36] to allow him "to reveal himself in his constitutive fragmentation and contradiction,"[37] but in the same turn one should be ready to actively dismantle Deleuze's own machine, instead of relying on the sleights of hand of criticism and on the kind of conventional play of concepts that can repeatedly be turned over (monological versus heterological, one versus multiple, transcendence versus immanence, etc.).

Whether one drifts along with Deleuze or sets out to "map" the tracings of his thought, whether one adopts the schizophrenic (experimental) or the paranoid (academic) stance, Deleuzian scholarship is never well served by a mere representation or staging of concepts that wraps itself in pragmatic clothes. What is the best way to follow in the footsteps of great philosophers? Deleuze and Guattari ask. "Is it to repeat what they said or *to do what they did,* that is, to create concepts for problems that necessarily change?"[38] In any case, playing Deleuze against Deleuze requires more than playful textual "*dérives.*" All the fuss about theory being like a toolbox is really a joke or a clause of style if one does not realize that a tool is something that must be used, and that something that is used sometimes *does not work.* It is time now to raise the question of what it means to truly experiment with Deleuze's philosophy.

Active Dismantling: Deleuze versus Deleuze

In the process of being filtered through the prism of French theory, Deleuze's own method of vampirizing philosophers (a method sometimes referred to as "buggering"[39]) has been turned against himself, producing a somewhat monstrous heir. It is productive to demonstrate what is left out of this picture by examining parallel accounts of Deleuze's reception that do not easily fit the framework of French theory. This maneuver may appear to restore a sense of "historical accuracy" by finding textual evidence in Deleuze's own work. But historical or textual accuracy (the quest for an allegedly "real" Deleuze) is not the point here. The issue is not to oppose a portable, edgy version of Deleuze on the one hand (the figure sketched in *On the Line,* a micro-manifesto assembled and published by *Semiotext(e)* out of *A Thousand Plateaus* and *Dialogues*), and more classically philosophical versions on the other (as found in *Difference and Repetition,* or the studies on Hume, Bergson, Nietzsche, Spinoza, Kant). Underlying the apparent concern for more seriousness in Deleuzian scholarship, what is at stake is the way Deleuze lends himself to sometimes radically divergent readings, and what this tells us about his own method.

Though not exactly false, it is not exaggerating to say that Deleuze's portrayal in many textbooks and secondary source studies is deliberately and consistently reticent when it comes to examining some of the most disturbing yet distinctive characteristics of his philosophical achievement. Again, the question is not merely one of textual accuracy. It is a pragmatic requirement to set the *whole* machine into motion, not the parts we have chosen to retain and hold up as fetishes. As he has noted,

> When you admire someone you don't pick up and choose; you may like this or that book better than some other one, but you nevertheless take them as a whole. . . . You have to take the work as a whole, to try and follow rather than judge it, see where it branches out in different directions, where it gets bogged down, moves forward, makes a breakthrough; you have to accept it, welcome it, as a whole.[40]

We are not looking for gaps or elisions in Deleuze; we do not wish to count ourselves among those "who can only feel intelligent by discovering 'contradictions' in a great thinker."[41] It is more a matter of pushing a theory to its limits, of accelerating and precipitating its own process. This forced movement continues until the theory comes to a deadlock and possibly breaks down. By experimenting with its points of resistance, blind spots, and blockages, it plays with what Deleuze himself called a "method of active dismantling."[42] Such a method "doesn't make use of criticism that is still part of representation,"[43] but it deals with contradictions insofar as discrepancies between interpretations force them to reveal the underlying procedures or moves.

What follows is a rather sketchy pinpointing of some diverging accounts of Deleuze on both sides of the Atlantic. Although it bears some affinities with the dialectical stratagem of *ad hominem* contradiction (outruling the statement of an author by pointing to another of his statements), the point here is not to track failures in Deleuze's discourse. It is a pragmatic strategy that implies the stretching of contrasting readings to their limits, playing interpretations off each other so as to bring out some typical Deleuzian gestures. It is an attempts at opening a number of Deleuze's own black boxes in order to put his tools to work, whether inside or outside French theory.

"Philosophy, Nothing but Philosophy"

The first black box to be opened, because it accounts for many aspects of Deleuze's reception as part of French theory, is that of philosophy itself, or rather, the use of this very notion, the effects it produces whenever Deleuze's thought is examined under its heading. When Deleuze returns to the question *What is philosophy?* at the end of his life, it is not enough to reassure oneself by observing that "philosophy has always been going beyond itself, becoming-monstrous, since it was 'first' invented."[44] Deleuze's reaffirmation of philosophy points at a much simpler fact: all along, Deleuze had never ceased to consider that he was doing philosophy in the most rigorous and traditional sense of the term—the sense where the notion of philosophical tradition can still retain its validity.[45] This consideration is strangely absent from most commentaries. Whether taken up by Rorty (as an example of the kind of philosopher-poet who would herald the coming of a "postphilosophical" era), or by postmodernists (as a protean provider of conceptual tools), the general tendency is to describe Deleuze as having broken ties with an accepted, dominant, orthodox way of approaching philosophy. This view, however, runs against repeated statements to the contrary, as well as many (mostly "Continental") readings that emphasize the classicism of Deleuze's conception of philosophy. Much of the misunderstanding here seems to stem from the fact that philosophy is not carefully distinguished from the history of philosophy, or on the contrary is too strongly contrasted with it. This swing from one extreme to another is a consequence of Deleuze's own ambiguous relation to the history of philosophy. Deleuze wrote, "I've never been worried about going beyond metaphysics or any death of philosophy. The function of philosophy, still thoroughly relevant, is to create concepts."[46] This simple statement refutes all attempts at forcing Deleuze into some narrative of the overthrowing of philosophy. It is no wonder that Rorty has so little to say about him. Philosophy in his view is all but shut off in texts or offered as a playground for the infinite interplay of language games. It operates on its own level, that of concepts, even when it is dealing with an outside. Yet philosophy, as it is commonly understood, implies more than just creating concepts.

"Philosophy, nothing but philosophy, in the traditional sense of the word,"[47] said Deleuze when describing *A Thousand Plateaus*. There should be no doubt about what "traditional" means here. It refers to two things: on the one hand, a way of doing philosophy with respect to its own history, the history of its problems; on the other hand, a belief in "philosophy as system." Deleuze's relation to the history of philosophy can neither be reduced to the techniques of "buggery,"[48] and "collage,"[49] nor to the discovery of an orphan lineage of "nomad" thinkers. At any rate, it was certainly not a "flirtation," as Massumi rather casually writes in his introduction to *A Thousand Plateaus*.[50] "I belong to a generation, one of the last generations, that was more or less bludgeoned to death with the history of philosophy,"[51] says Deleuze. This statement is not wholly negative, despite what comes next ("The history of philosophy plays a patently repressive role in philosophy"). One of the merits of Michael Hardt's presentation of Deleuze is to place particular emphasis on the notion of philosophical apprenticeship.[52] Deleuze was an expert and a craftsman. He was an impeccable teacher, one of the great masters in an age-old tradition of teaching and learning the history of philosophy, a tradition that can best be described as academic (this notion, by the way, does not necessarily imply scholastic erudition, although Deleuze had read a lot). Anyone who has attended his lessons on Liebniz, Spinoza, or Kant at Vincennes, or read their transcripts on the Internet,[53] will know what this means. These lessons, it should be noted, were not given in the early years of Deleuze's assistantship at the Sorbonne, but at the time of his full maturity, and until his retirement from the French academy in the late eighties.

Even when he seems to be speaking in a more personal tone, the degree to which Deleuze is still fed by the history of philosophy, its stock of conceptual moves and rhetorical techniques, should not be underestimated. For all his claims about overturning state philosophy and its categories, Deleuze remains a classicist. If he challenges the image of thought inherent in a certain rationalist tradition, and decides to take sides with a "minor" strand in the history of philosophy, he does not do away with metaphysics altogether. On the contrary, Deleuze draws heavily on much of the classical metaphysical tradition. He constructs a philosophy of immanence whose origins can be traced back to his readings of Duns Scotus and Spinoza, and which informs all of his work (consider the witty remark about the first volume of *Capitalism and Schizophrenia:* "*Anti-Oedipus* was about the univocity of the real. . . ."[54]). At the same time, his book on Leibniz, and above all his little study on Kant, are enough proof of the persistence of a very strong neo-Kantian concern for the genesis of thought and experience—a concern generally expressed by the more fashionable terms of *process* and multiplicity. Vincent Descombes is one of the first commentators to have brought out how much the very project of a "philosophy of difference" owes to Kant: "Deleuze is above all a neo-Kantian"[55]. Even his criticism of the dominant interpretation of the aims of philosophy is organically linked to the image he seeks to undermine. The perspective of the concluding chapter of *Difference and Repetition* is entirely guided by philosophical concerns about the self-definition of philosophy that date back to Aristotle. Finally, it has been argued that most of what seems to be original creations of Deleuze actually rely on schemes elaborated before him by Bergson. Guy Lardreau does not have to stretch things too far in order to make his point: "I defy anyone to find a concept in Deleuze—images notwithstanding, where his taste for rotten flowers and harmful insects may have yielded invention, although this too may be doubted—which does not have its adequate model in Bergson. . . . Deleuze is badly written Bergson."[56]

These remarks point in the same direction. Much of what struck people as a revolutionary way of approaching philosophy was indeed the result of running together a certain line of "nomad" philosophers (Hume, Spinoza, Nietzsche, Bergson) with contemporary theory. But this was made possible only by Deleuze's precise knowledge of the traditional themes and problems that make up the history of philosophy.

The question of whether Deleuze is *really* a philosopher or not, whether his practice of concepts falls under this general category, would be of little importance if it did not directly affect the way we picture the relation of conceptual constructivism to other kinds of constructive practices. There lies the root of a possible misunderstanding. Brian Massumi claims: "One of the points of the book is that nomad thought is not confined to philosophy. Or that the kind of philosophy it is comes in many forms."[57] He adds that "the reader is invited to lift a dynamism out of the book entirely, and incarnate it in a foreign medium, whether it be painting or politics."[58] This may be true of "nomad thought" in general, but then it is important to understand precisely what is meant by "philosophy." It may well be that Deleuze pushes philosophy out of itself in order to find philosophy everywhere at work (bringing out the philosophy folded into cinema, for example). Yet in another sense this movement entirely takes place within philosophy itself, so that one may argue that if nomad thought cannot be confined to philosophy, it is not because philosophy is too narrow, but on the contrary because it encompasses much more. Hence Deleuze can say, in the series of interviews with Claire Parnet entitled *Abécédaire,* that one only gets beyond philosophy through philosophy, by means of philosophy: "Mais sortir de la philosophie, ça veut pas dire faire autre chose. . . . Il faut sortir en restant dedans. . . . Moi je veux sortir de la philosophie par la philosophie, c'est ça qui m'intéresse." Using philosophy for something else (paintings or politics) reveals a poor conception of philosophy's relation to its outside. If one wants to say that nomad thought in general *is* philosophy (a philosophy that comes in many forms), it is all very well, it is only a matter of words. What is important is to retain the right differences so as to avoid conflating everything. Creating concepts is the specific task of philosophers, although many would like to pretend to be doing the same. As vital as the outside is, it is essential that artists, writers, and filmmakers, as long as they paint, write, and make films, *should not* be doing philosophy, even though their works unleash the powers of creation to which philosophy strives to equal by its concepts. If we want to grant that artists, writers, and filmmakers create concepts, too (or do philosophy, too), then we will have to find another name for the kind of thing a philosopher creates, and another name for philosophy itself.

When this idea is taken seriously and situated in relation to the importance of the history of philosophy in Deleuze's apprenticeship, another conclusion emerges. Deleuze cannot be reduced to a universal toolmaker, a schizophrenic yet prolific producer of concepts, or a talented inventor of new idioms. He must be seen as producing and adjusting concepts to particular problematic situations in a *systematic* fashion—even if this yields a system of the multiple, even if concepts are arranged according to "circumstances rather than essences."[59] Philosophy according to Deleuze aims at building systems, not at shooting concepts in every direction, or hurling them like bricks.[60] "I believe in philosophy as system," Deleuze writes. "Thus I have never been concerned with questions regarding the 'overturn of philosophy,' or 'the end of philosophy.' I feel like a very classical philosopher."[61] Or elsewhere: "It's become a commonplace these days to talk about the breakdown of systems, the impossibility of constructing a system now that knowledge has become fragmented. . . . Systems have in fact lost absolutely none of their power."[62] Of course, Deleuze does not have in mind the kind of architectonic structure wherein a finite set of propositions can be derived from the right combination of axioms and principles. His is an open-ended system, yet nonetheless a system. A system emerges whenever a certain number of interactions can be specified among things or concepts ("A system's a set of concepts"[63]) while allowing for further generalizations. It is the systematic nature of philosophical practice that gives concepts their *necessity*: "Philosophy's job has always been to create new concepts, with their own necessity"; "It's precisely their power as a system that brings out what's good or bad, what is or isn't new, what is or isn't alive in a group of concepts. Nothing's good in itself, it all depends on careful systematic use."[64] Far from partaking in the fashionable distrust of systems harbored by the postmodernist creed, Deleuze can ironically be said to offer the most vibrant defense of systematic philosophy.

Yet there is an additional turn of the screw: "I feel like a pure metaphysician,"[65] Deleuze confessed. As Alain Badiou puts it in his recent essay on Deleuze, "Constructing a metaphysics remains the aim of the philosopher, and the question is not: 'Is this still possible?' but rather 'Are we capable of it?'"[66] Metaphysics may be out of fashion, but this is what Deleuze thought he was doing. This task goes beyond a mere reflection on the history of metaphysical systems: Deleuze wanted to build his own metaphysics, a peculiar kind of metaphysics, yet surprisingly not very much in line with the common view of his thought as a philosophy of difference. Going back to the roots of the accepted view of Deleuze as "a joyous thinker of the universal *confusion* of things,"[67] "the liberator of the anarchical multiplicity of desires and errings,"[68] Badiou shows that Deleuze's work does not provide the kind of philosophy of difference that might be expected. In fact, "the fundamental problem of Deleuze is certainly not to set the multiple free, it is rather to fold thought unto a renewed concept of the One,"[69] so that it becomes necessary to "carefully identify, in Deleuze's work, a metaphysics of the One."[70] Badiou supports this rather unorthodox claim by referring Deleuze's ontology to its original source of inspiration: the doctrine of *the univocity of being*. The philosophical project developed in *Difference and Repetition* and *The Logic of Sense* stems from this intuition: "There has only ever been one ontological proposition: Being is univocal";[71] "Philosophy merges with ontology, but ontology merges with the univocity of being."[72] The notion of univocity is itself inter-changeable with that of immanence, whose rigorous definition is entirely com-manded by a metaphysical decision in favor of the destitution of all fixed cate-gorical division of being. The subsequent characterization of immanence in terms of "virtualization," and the choice of the Nietzschean vocable "life" as the ade-quate name for being, cannot be properly understood when considered apart from this metaphysical backdrop. In particular, the justification of immanence in opposition to transcendence, or its vindication on merely ethical grounds, are not sufficient to assign a rigorous content to its concept.

In terms of theoretical practice, the implication of the metaphysical stance is quite obvious: it shows itself in a sober and even ascetic kind of abstract philos-ophy, which very well accommodates itself with a renewed concern for matters of foundation.[73] To quote once again from Badiou, "'abstraction' does not mean that philosophy deals with what it radically dismisses, namely, the generality that applies to concrete cases"; rather, it means that "philosophy's only standard of measurement is the quasi-organic consistency of conceptual connections, and the constant setting into motion of these connections by the greater number of cases."[74] When dealing with cinema, for instance, Deleuze is not interested in cinema as such, or with concrete cases provided ("given") by cinema: he is al-ways looking for other *concepts* ("film theory is not 'about' films, but about the concepts elicited by films"[75]). Thus, despite the often dizzying richness of its sub-ject matter Deleuze's practice of philosophy remains systematic and abstract—a form of asceticism. For this reason it is also profoundly *aristocratic,* as is appar-ent from his contempt for the very principle of debates and discussions.

There is a general tendency to take a little too literally the idea of a "mon-strous" becoming of philosophy in Deleuze's thought machine. Undeniably, Deleuze lent himself to this kind of rhetoric, but it was in order to make a point about the rationalist image of thought, not about philosophy itself. In order to dismantle the packaged generalities about Deleuze's relation to "traditional" phi-losophy (whatever this means), it is useful to state the obvious: Deleuze was a first-class historian of philosophy doubled with a metaphysician of the purest vein. In all regards, and despite all his edginess, he remained classic.

This reading, of course, may be contested on many grounds. The point is that it can and has been supported—not only by (mostly French) commentators, but also by Deleuze himself. It is enough to cast a retrospective shadow of suspicion on the ready-made accounts of Deleuzian "monstrous" treatment of philosophy, and to give license to call for more attention to the actual operations that Deleuze puts into play when he comes to terms with the very notion of philosophy. Here again, the consensual image that is all too naturally attached with the name of Deleuze appears to be largely a matter of fabrication. Some would like to fancy him as a freelance conceptual expert, a universal provider of tool kits (a weakened, pragmatic version of the romantic thinker), but Deleuze is more complex. As a bricoleur philosopher, he is at once trendy and academic, accessible and remote, so very French and so American. He is neither a foreign agent, nor a double agent; he is a mole. His philosophical legacy, equivocally reengineered by his disciples, is bound to yield many misunderstandings.

Immanence and the Phantom of Spiritualism

What kind of philosophy, what kind of system are we talking about? Deleuze sometimes refers to his philosophy as a system of immanence.[76] This very notion of immanence is inseparable from a few others that actually give it its pragmatic meaning: process, multiplicity (Deleuze described philosophy as "a logic of multiplicities"), constructionism, expressionism. On this level, immanence is merely referring to the set of typical operations and procedures at play in Deleuzian philosophy. It is founded upon a metaphysical decision in favor of the univocity of being. However, it is also inseparable from its spontaneous interpretation as a *materialist* claim. Deleuze's materialism has been underscored in many studies of his work.[77] It is distinct from the question of empiricism (the exteriority of relations to their terms) and is not conceptually tied to it in any way. In order to pass from Deleuze's transcendental empiricism to his alleged transcendental materialism, it is necessary to consider his decision to refer to being (immanent and univocal) as "life." In other words, what is at stake is Deleuze's vitalism, a rather odd kind of "machinic" vitalism,[78] supported by a "materialist metaphysics" according to which "everything is a machine."[79] But this materialism itself is very peculiar too, for it does not match with any of the philosophical decisions that have so far recognized themselves in this category. His "new 'naturalism,'" in the line of Spinoza and Nietzsche more than Hobbes and D'Holbach, has been described as "an extraordinary challenge to orthodox materialist philosophy."[80] As Goodchild rightly emphasizes, it is "a strange materialism,"[81] something quite extraordinary, just like the marriage of "pure spiritualism and radical materialism" that Deleuze found in Bergson.[82]

On closer inspection, it appears that the move from vitalism to materialism, being entirely determined by the vitalist position (and its metaphysical backing in a conception of the univocity of being), cannot in any sense be considered as a materialist *decision*. A decision involves more than a gesture or a pose: a consistent practice and its theorization. Deleuze's pragmatism, his "superior empiricism," or "empiricism of concepts," does not provide this. At best, one finds in Deleuze a materialist interpretation, certainly not materialist operations. This unusual situation accounts for two unexpected effects: the insidious reintroduction of transcendence, and the inversion of materialism into spiritualism.

In this respect, Goodchild's *Gilles Deleuze and the Question of Philosophy,* "a highly interesting, but quirky and idiosyncratic version of Deleuze,"[83] is one of the few attempts at precipitating the Deleuzian movement of thought in a truly operative fashion. The project of experimenting with the Deleuzian machine is clearly stated from the outset:

> I shall attempt to repeat the movements and techniques of Deleuze's thought. At every stage, what I say is also what I attempt to do. I shall adopt a rhetorical strategy of utilizing some naive and vague concepts, such as 'life,' 'thought,' 'difference,' 'time,' 'desire,' 'outside,' 'immanence' and 'transcendence,' so as to draw attention to the movement of thought at work in the text rather than the meaning of its conceptual content. . . . The result is a return to metaphysics and transcendence through a complete inversion of Deleuze's thought.[84]

Hence the author's long and serpentine line of argument can be boiled down to a basic strategy, which consists of showing that the materialist assumptions or interpretations of Deleuze do not in fact proceed by immanent concepts, and are likely to engender "illusions of transcendence from an immanent philosophical perspective."[85]

In their description of philosophy, Deleuze and Guattari refer to an absolute plane of immanence, a plane that *de facto* transcends all the constructions that dwell on it, as well as all the particular views that try to represent it. The plane is nothing we can conceive, no concept can stand for it. And yet, thought cannot stop itself from interpreting immanence as immanent to something, the great object of contemplation, the subject of reflection, or the other subject of communication: then transcendence is inevitably reintroduced. And if this cannot be avoided, it is because it seems that each plane of immanence can only claim to be unique, to be *the* plane.[86]

Although no concept is ever adequate to *the* plane of immanence, and although *the* plane always transcends the particular assemblages that draw a particular plane, it seems that pointing to an unthinkable or unconstructible plane beyond every particular construction of immanence is the only safeguard against the tendency to transform the plane of immanence into just another figure of transcendence. For whenever this distinction is forgotten, immanence stands alone and occupies the whole ground, passing itself off as *the* plane: "all we need to do is to sink the floating plane of immanence, bury it in the depths of Nature instead of allowing it to play freely on the surface, for it to pass to the other side and assume the role of a ground."[87] The ground is transcendent: it conflates the plane with one of the concepts (matter, nature, spirit) whose construction it was supposed to make possible. The absolute plane, on the contrary, is what prevents immanence from collapsing into a trivial figure of transcendence. Deleuze and Guattari, consistent with their own line of thought, conclude,

> *The* plane of immanence is, at the same time, that which must be thought and that which cannot be thought. It is the nonthought within thought. It is the base of all planes, immanent to every thinkable plane that does not succeed in thinking it. . . . Perhaps this is the supreme act of philosophy: not so much to think *THE* plane of immanence as to show that it is there, unthought in every plane, and to think it in this way as the outside and inside of thought, as the non-external outside and the non-internal inside—that which cannot be thought and yet must be thought.[88]

It is difficult to avoid the conclusion that the absolute notion of immanence (absolute immanence) actually functions as a transcendence with respect to the conceptual assemblages and finite movements of thought. In other words, it seems necessary to posit a particular kind of transcendence (a transcendence of an even higher level than that of any principle, a truly unthinkable kind of transcendence) in order to maintain and preserve immanence at another level. This minimal form of transcendence, this slight excess, is the reason why Deleuze was prevented from falling back on a gross form of materialism, just as Bergson could not be entirely folded onto base spiritualism. Guy Lardreau develops this point in his remarkable and most critical essay on Deleuze, saying, "They had both posited—as a moment of their doctrine only, but too firmly to be forgotten and not to insist until the end—a dualism that obliterated the project of an integral immanentism: they always had to count with the slight gap which, in accordance with tradition, is commonly called transcendence."[89]

The problem is that Deleuze wants to stick to integral or absolute immanence. In trying to think, not so much *the* plane itself, which remains unthinkable, but its relation to its various constructions, he faces a dilemma. Either he fully acknowledges the transcendence of the plane, but then absolute immanence is not thinkable, or he emphasizes its interpretation in terms of immanence, at the risk of conjuring up a new transcendence whenever immanence is translated in the materialist idiom. Overshadowing the operative transcendence of the plane, a more common transcendence emerges from the elevation of an empirical determination (life understood in a materialist way, as the machinic fabric of the whole). Immanence becomes a principle that equals itself with the plane, a concept that does not function anymore, that does not come into play on the plane in order to connect with other concepts. Badiou makes a similar point when he shows that the notion of the "virtual" actually plays the role of an inverted transcendence, "a sort of displaced transcendence, 'beneath' the simulacra of the world, yet symmetrical with the classical transcendence of the 'beyond'."[90]

Deleuze knew he was running this risk; these considerations only precipitate the movement of his thought in the direction pointed at by his materialist stance. There are of course other directions in Deleuze. It is not a matter of exegesis, but of pragmatics. In every system there are "apparent movements," like dead machines that "don't function, or no longer function,"[91] that "never succeed in concretely plugging into anything."[92] Materialism is such a dead interpretative machine in Deleuze. It must be traced back to the actual movements that support it.

> Superficial movement doesn't mean a mask underneath which something else would be hidden. The superficial movement indicates points of undoing [*points de dévissage*], of dismantling [*démontage*], that must guide the experimentation to show the molecular movements and the machinic assemblages of which the superficial movement is the global result.[93]

Such experimentation is precisely what Goodchild has in mind: "One can radicalize and extend Deleuze's thought, however, by rejecting his materialist presupposition of the simplicity of the plane, and by experimentally thinking through pure immanence to the limit at which it transforms itself into something else."[94] Goodchild, no doubt with a certain agenda in mind, chooses to fold immanence onto itself and to dub it "spirit."[95] The question is not whether this operation, which it is not worth retracing here, is legitimate or not with regard to the "correct" interpretation of Deleuze. Never mind the interpretations; the point is that the operation can be executed. Deleuze himself acknowledged this philosophical *tour de force*, while consistently reasserting his materialist stance in a letter to his commentator:

> Of course, I don't think that one can reintroduce transcendence as you have done and *in the sense* in which you have done. You have a general tendency to relativize notions like immanence or chaos which only come to life when absolute. . . . I regard myself as 'materialist' as much as you regard yourself as "spiritualist.[96]

The use of such notions as immanence or chaos as *absolutes* is of course precisely the problem, and the reaffirmation of the materialist stance falls a bit short. Lardreau demonstrates that a materialist stance can very well be compatible with, and even supported by, an unavowed form of spiritualism. His first point is about the very notion of "pure immanence," which he opposes to "radical immanence," a notion Deleuze never deals with:

The idea of *pure* (or integral) immanence is devoid of any content, or is rather self-contradictory, for nothing can contradict it. *Radical* immanence, however, rightly names a decision, provided that some other term can contradict it. From Plato to Hegel, this concern bears the name of 'dialectics.' So much so that I am not embarrassed to speak of the radical immanentism of Plato, or if you prefer, of his materialism, whereas pure immanentism necessarily boils down to simple spiritualism. This is clear in Spinoza, in Bergson—dare I say: in Deleuze?[97]

Thus, absolute immanence, with the subsequent materialist pledge, is turned inside out like a glove, and falls back toward what might have seemed to be its opposite: pure spiritualism. In order to make his point, Lardreau takes sides with a tradition of transcendental philosophy that embraces negation, transcendence, and dialectics as opposed to a tradition of empiricist philosophy that holds up affirmation, immanence and life. His argument, however, is unreproachable; it relies on the purest definition of what real materialism should *do*. Deleuze, as it appears, is only disguised as a materialist, for he shares none of the materialist moves common to the materialist (dialectical) tradition. The apparent movement of materialism, in his work, relies in fact on a set of procedures that are all but materialist. "Deleuzianism, just like any 'monism' (whether its principles be life, flux, duration, matter, or anything else), and hence like any immanentism (not radical but absolute), presents itself as a spiritualism."[98]

Pure immanence, in other words, is not pure enough: it is too absolute to be pure. It is bound to restore the most vulgar forms of transcendence within the depth of nature—matter, spirit, or whatever name is preferred. Deleuze is still haunted by the image of a vibrant "Great Animal" or *Anima mundi*. He would probably argue that dwelling on the plane of immanence is not fundamentally different from efforts to keep transcendence at bay. In this regard, immanence all too often functions like a black box, obscuring the actual workings of the "Deleuze machine" by projecting on them a ready-made materialist interpretation. Deleuze has set up this black box himself. It runs smoothly as long as we take Deleuze's pledge of materialism for granted, but it cannot dispel the uneasy feeling that it is impossible to be a rigorous partisan of immanence without recourse to procedures that can be integrally assumed only by the kind of philosophy Deleuze could not endorse: a negative or dialectical philosophy (following the lineage of Plato, Kant, and Lenin).

The point is not to say that Deleuze is really a spiritualist, no more than he is a materialist. These contrasting interpretations play off each other, but it is precisely because at the level of absoluteness where pure or integral immanence stands, *there are no differences that can still make a difference*. In operational terms, materialism is equivalent with spiritualism. The real difference only emerges in the diverging reading strategies these two stances suggest.

What Next?

In Ansell Pearson's assessment, "Deleuze was a monster. His work is marked by a subversive, perilous attempt to map out a new becoming of thought beyond good sense and common sense, in which thought becomes monstrous because it forsakes the desire for an image of thought."[99]

Unfortunately, the rhetoric of monstrosity (directly inherited from Deleuze's appreciation of his own achievements in the history of philosophy) all too often masks a very conventional view about Deleuze's overturn of the metaphysical categories valued by a certain philosophical tradition (conveniently referred to as "Platonism"—Deleuze's favorite black box[100]). This is much ado about nothing. The so-called monstrosity does not reside so much in Deleuze's taste for striking apocalyptic poses, or dealing with such topics as hybridation, schizophrenia, and delirium—it is rather to be found in the unstable posture whereby an undercover spiritualist crafts a metaphysical system of "the One" while playfully adopting the rhetoric of a Nietzschean apostle of multiplicity.

Once the mannerism of monstrosity is put aside, many knots in Deleuze's philosophical assemblage remain to be disentangled, many black boxes to be unriveted and opened, both inside and beyond French theory. Sometimes a black box itself contains other black boxes within the cogs of its machinery, and the process of opening them can be further and further pursued. This seemingly endless task is an instance of the pragmatic critique Deleuze favored and applied, despite all of his reluctance to adopt any critical stance. It is actually a false problem that forces us to chose between hagiography and traditional critical practice, between continuation and succession.[101] As for the easy paradox of having to abandon Deleuze to be truly Deleuzian, it is of no great consequence, given that Deleuze himself was not a Deleuzian, and that dismantling his thought machine does not imply abandoning either his system or his philosophical praxis.

Notes

1. Jean Baudrillard, *Cool Memories II* (Cambridge: Polity Press, 1996), p. 1.
2. See the introduction to this volume.
3. Gilles Deleuze, *Negotiations* (New York: Columbia, 1995), p. 27.
4. See, in particular, chapter I ("Difference in itself") and conclusion ("Difference and Repetition").

5. Iain MacKenzie, "Creativity as Criticism: The Philosophical Constructivism of Deleuze and Guattari," *Radical Philosophy* 86 (November–December, 1997), p. 11.

6. On Deleuze's reception in the U.S., see Sylvère Lotringer and Elie During, "French Thought from Abroad," *Art Press*, May, 1999; Charles Stivale, *The Two-Fold Thought of Deleuze and Guattari* (New York: Guilford, 1998), pp. 7ff.; Constantin Boundas, *The Deleuze Reader* (New York: Columbia, 1993), pp. 21–23; Dana Polan, "Etats-Unis," *Le Magazine Litteraire*, 287 (September, 1988), pp. 62–63. The choice of *Sacher-Masoch* (translated in English under the sexier title *Masochism*) as the first work of Deleuze to be published in English (in 1971) is fairly symptomatic of the editorial and intellectual context that surrounded the penetration of French theory in the early seventies. As the author of *Proust*, Deleuze was tolerated in some departments of literature, but it took another fifteen years before he came to be accepted as a major academic reference. While *Anti-Oedipus* was translated in 1977, and *A Thousand Plateaus* in 1987, *The Logic of Sense* and *Difference and Repetition* were not translated in the United States before 1990 and 1994, respectively. Deleuze was in fact first admitted to the canon of French theory under the name "Deleuze-Guattari."

7. For a nice illustration of some Deleuzian concepts intended for children, see Jacquelines Duhême, *Duhême dessine Deleuze, L'oiseau philosophe* (Paris, Le Seuil, 1997).

8. See, among others, the German electronic label *Mille Plateaux*, and the compositions of D. J. Spooky or Heldon. Robin Mackay penned a ranting essay on the relation of Deleuze to new sound-making technologies in hip-hop, house, techno, and jungle. See Ansell Pearson, ed., *Deleuze and Philosophy: The Difference Engineer* (London: Routledge, 1997), pp. 247–269.

9. Jacques Rancière has recently examined the nature of Deleuze's reference to literature in *La Chair des Mots* (Paris: Galilee, 1997), pp. 179–204). He argues that Deleuze's constant emphasis on characters (singular individuals), as opposed to drama, is organically linked with the romantic or Schopenhauerian metaphysics he assigns to the regime of textual production known as "literature." Characters are the living allegories of literature. Obviously, Rancière has put his finger on a structural issue in Deleuze that keeps coming back in many forms. For just as characters stand for the very operation of literature, conceptual personae (the operators of concepts) tend to overshadow the actual procedures or formulas (connections) by conferring an emblematic function upon the concepts they set into motion. This maneuver itself is instrumental in preparing the ground for an allegorical reappropriation of Deleuze's philosophy. See Elie During, "Deleuze et apres?" *Critique* 623 (April, 1999), pp. 303–306.

10. See, in this volume, Alison Gingeras, "Disappearing Acts: The French Theory Effect in The Art World."

11. Gilles Deleuze and Claire Parnet, *Dialogues* (New York: Columbia University Press, 1987), pp. 1–24.

12. Ibid., 9.

13. Felix Guattari, *Les Années d'Hiver, 1980–85* (Paris: Barrault, 1986), p. 86: ". . . working in the long run with Deleuze imported a new sense of efficiency to my first attempts at theorizing. If you like, it's all the difference between J.-J. Rousseau writing the merry melodies of the *Devin de Village* and J. S. Bach composing *The Well Tempered Clavier* out of a few refrains!"

14. Brian Massumi, *A User's Guide to Capitalism and Schizophrenia* (Cambridge: Swerve Editions/MIT, 1992), p. 7.

15. Another aspect of the English-language reception of Deleuze and Guattari's work is that it has systematically "stressed the harsh tone of the more polemical parts of *Anti-Oedipus*," and privileged the "war machine" concept in *A Thousand Plateaus*. The "hard," apocalyptic approach apparent in many cyberpunk readings of these books, advocating a politics of deterritorialization without limits, does not elicit general agreement among the more pragmatically minded deleuzians. As Meaghan Morris writes, "A relentlessly monogeneric rendering of 'Deleuze and Guattari' as the theoretical equivalent of a Nick Cave murder ballad does a great disservice to a body of work that is immensely varied in its humors and tones and most formidable gaiety with which it launches into adventures of reading, writing, thinking" (quoted in Stivale, *The Two-Fold Thought*, p. 99). Charles Stivale cleverly comments on an alleged "American versus Warwickian 'split'" (Ibid., p. 91). by reference to the University of Warwick, a bulwark of british Deleuzian studies (see the reference to Pearson, in note 6).

16. Michel Foucault, *Dits et Ecrits,* 4 vols. (Paris: Gallimard, 1994), vol. 2, p. 75.

17. Ibid., vol. 3, p. 589.

18. Quoted in Stivale, *The Two-Fold Thought*, p. 193.

19. See the equation of "rhizomatics" with "pop analysis" in Deleuze and Guattari, *A Thousand Plateaus*, pp. 1–24.

20. See "Rhizome" in *A Thousand Plateaus*; "On the Superiority of Anglo-American Literature" in *Dialogues*. Deleuze explicitly claims to be taking up the project of "radical empiricism" (a Jamesian endeavor) in *What is Philosophy?*

21. Lotringer and During, "French Thought," pp. 57–59.

22. Ibid., p. 56.

23. Ibid., p. 57.

24. On the perception of Deleuze's pragmatic method as opposed to the strategies of deconstruction, see Andre Colombat, *Deleuze et la Littérature* (New York: Peter Lang, 1990), pp. 257ff; Philippe Mengue, *Gilles Deleuze ou le Système du Multiple* (Paris: Kimé, 1994), p. 60; John Marks, *Gilles Deleuze: Vitalism and Multiplicity* (London: Pluto, 1998), pp. 16, 24; Ian Buchanan, ed., "A Deleuzian Century?" In *South Atlantic Quarterly*, 96, no. 3 (1997), p. 389; Boundas, *The Deleuze Reader,* p. 23 (". . . to distinguish the minor deconstructive practice of Deleuze from the dominant 'restrained' deconstruction of Derrida . . .").

25. In a chapter entitled "Which Deleuze?" ("Quel Deleuze?"), Alain Badiou sketches and challenges Deleuze's commonly accepted portrait as a philosopher of "world democracy," advocating the values of difference, multiplicity, crossings, etc. (Alain Badiou, *Deleuze: "La Clameur de l'Etre"* (Paris: Hachette, 1997), pp. 17–19, 139–41). The mechanics of French theory is not entirely responsible for this public image of Deleuze, which prevails even in his homeland. However, for the purpose of this essay, it is more interesting to focus on the consequences of this common perception in the English-speaking world. On the actual function of "difference" in the philosophy of Deleuze, see the insightful analysis of Todd May in C. Boundas and D. Olkowski, *Deleuze and the Theater of Philosophy* (London: Routledge, 1994), pp. 33–50.

26. Brian Massumi, foreword to *A Thousand Plateaus*, pp. i–xii; Massumi, *User's Guide*, pp. 4–5.

27. Deleuze, *Dialogues*, p. 144.

28. Clement Rosset, "Sécheresse de Deleuze," in *L'Arc*, 49, 2d ed. 1980, pp. 89–91.

29. Boundas and Olkowski, *Deleuze and the Theater of Philosophy*, p. 2.

30. Boundas, *The Deleuze Reader*, p. 22.

31. Pearson, *Deleuze and Philosophy*, p. 13.

32. Boundas and Olkowski, *Deleuze and the Theater of Philosophy*, p. 2.

33. Deleuze and Guattari, *A Thousand Plateaus*, p. 378.

34. Ibid., p. 22.

35. Deleuze and Guattari, *A Thousand Plateaus*, p. 6.

36. See Pearson, *Deleuze and Philosophy*, p. 89.

37. Ibid., p. 88.

38. Gilles Deleuze and Félix Guattari, *What is Philosophy?* (New York: Columbia University Press, 1994), p. 28.

39. Deleuze, *Negotiations*, p. 3.

40. Deleuze, *Negotiations*, p. 85.

41. Ibid., p. 90.

42. Deleuze and Guattari, *Kafka*, p. 48.

43. Ibid.

44. Pearson, *Deleuze and Philosophy*, p. 13.

45. John Marks rightly insists on this point in the opening pages of his study; see note 24.

46. Deleuze, *Negotiations*, p. 136.

47. Interview with Catherine Clément, *L'Arc*, 49, 2nd ed., 1980.

48. Deleuze, *Negotiations*, p. 6.

49. Deleuze and Guattari, *What is Philosophy?*, p. xxi.

50. Deleuze and Guattari, *A Thousand Plateaus*, p. x.

51. Deleuze, *Negotiations*, p. 5.

52. Michael Hardt, *Gilles Deleuze: An Apprenticeship in Philosophy* (Minneapolis: University of Minnesota Press, 1993). On the value of work in Deleuze, see Stivale, *The Two-Fold Thought*, p. 231.

53. See www.imaginet.fr/deleuze.

54. Deleuze, *Negotiations*, p. 144.

55. Vincent Descombes, *Modern French Philosophy* (Cambridge: Cambridge University Press, 1980), p. 152; see, in the same vein, Paul Patton, *Deleuze: A Critical Reader* (London: Blackwell, 1996), pp. 7–11.

56. Guy Lardreau, *L'Exercise Differe de la Philosophie: A l'Occasion de Deleuze* (Lagrasse: Verdier, 1998), pp. 61–62. On Deleuze's Bergsonism, see also Badiou, "La Clameur de l'Etre," pp. 62–63, 79, 145; Eric Alliez, *Gilles Deleuze: Une Vie Philosophique* (Le Plessis-Robinson: Institut Synthélabo, 1998), pp. 243–64 and Eric Alliez, et al., "Gilles Deleuze: Immanence et Vie," *Rue Descartes*, May 1998 (Paris: P.U.F.), pp. 49–57. See also Hardt, *An Apprenticeship*, pp. 1–25, and Ansell Pearson's admirable *Germinal* Life: The Difference and Repetition of Deleuze (New York: Routledge, 1999).

57. Massumi, Foreword to Deleuze and Guattari, *A Thousand Plateaus*, pp. i–xiii.

58. Ibid., p. xv.

59. Deleuze, *Negotiations*, p. 31.

60. See Mengue, *Gilles Deleuze ou le Systèm e du Multiple*, pp. 11–13, 66, for a reconstruction of Deleuze's philosophy as system.

61. Quoted in Jean-Clet Martin, *Variations: La Philosophie de Gilles Deleuze* (Paris: Payot, 1993), p. 7.
62. Deleuze, *Negotiations*, p. 31.
63. Ibid., p. 31.
64. Ibid., p. 32.
65. Alliez, *Gilles Deleuze: Une Vie Philosophique*, p. 43.
66. Badiou, *Deleuze: "La Clameur de l'Etre,"* p. 148. See also Hardt, *An Apprenticeship*, xii: "Deleuze does not announce the end of metaphysics, but on the contrary seeks to rediscover the most coherent and lucid plane of metaphysical thought."
67. Ibid., p. 18.
68. Ibid., p. 19.
69. Ibid., p. 20.
70. Ibid., p. 20.
71. Gilles Deleuze, *Difference and Repetition* (New York: Columbia, 1994), p. 35.
72. Gilles Deleuze, *The Logic of Sense* (New York: Columbia, 1990), p. 179.
73. On the Virtual in its relation to the task of foundation, see Badiou, *"La Clameur de l'Etre,"* pp. 68–72.
74. Ibid., p. 29.
75. Quoted by Badiou, ibid., p. 29.
76. See for example, *Negotiations*, pp. 145–147.
77. See, among others, the texts cited herein by Alliez (pp. 49–57); Goodchild; Lardreau; Marks (especially pp. 47–50); and Buchanan (pp. 499–514, 439–63). See also, Pearson, *Deleuze and Philosophy*, p. 48.
78. Marks, *Vitalism and Philosophy*, p. 48.
79. Ibid., 49. This machinic theme has been widely put to work in relation to cyberculture. See John Mullarkey's essay in Buchanan, *A Deleuzian Century?*, pp. 439–63; and Stivale, *The Two-Fold Thought of Deleuze and Guattari*, pp. 124–42.
80. Buchanan, *A Deleuzian Century?*, p. 440.
81. Philip Goodchild, *Deleuze and the Question of Philosophy* (Cranbury, N.J.: Associated University Press, 1996), p. 154.
82. Deleuze, *Negotiations*, p. 48.
83. Jean-Jacques Lecercle, "Quirky," in *Radical Philosophy* 83 (May-June, 1997), 52.
84. Goodchild, *Deleuze and the Question of Philosophy*, pp. 20–21.
85. Ibid., 155.
86. Deleuze and Guattari, *What is Philosophy?*, p. 51.
87. Deleuze and Guattari, *A Thousand Plateaus*, p. 269.
88. Ibid., pp. 59–60.
89. Lardreau, *L'Exercice Differe de la Philosophie*, p. 72.
90. Badiou, *"La Clameur de l'Etre,"* pp. 70, 77. Badiou links this residual form of transcendence to Deleuze's interpretation of "the One" in terms of the whole. Badiou's book, recently translated and published in English, naturally raised quite a controversy in France. See the articles by José Gil and Arnaud Villani in *Futur Ant érieur* 43 ("Dossier Badiou / Deleuze," 1998), and more recently Badiou's response, "Un, Multiple, Multiplicité(s)," *Multitudes* 1 (March 2000). See also Alberto Toscano, "To Have Done with the End of Philosophy," *Pli* 9 (2000), and Ray Brassier, "Stellar Void or Cosmic Animal? Badiou and Deleuze on the Dice-Throw," *Pli* 10 (2000).

91. G. Deleuze and F. Guattari, *Kafka*, (University of Minnesota Press, 1986) p. 47.

92. Ibid., 48.

93. Ibid., 45.

94. Goodchild, *Deleuze and the Question of Philosophy*, p. 157.

95. For another spiritualist reading of Deleuze, see the interesting article by Peter Hallward, "Gilles Deleuze and the Redemption from Interest," *Radical Philosophy* 81 (January–February, 1997).

96. Goodchild, *Deleuze and the Question of Philosophy*, p. 185.

97. Lardreau, *L'Exercice Differe de la Philosophie*, p. 53.

98. Ibid., 82.

99. Pearson, *Deleuze and Philosophy*, p. 3.

100. On the fallacious construction of "platonism" and its function in philosophical modernity, see Badiou, "*La Clameur de l'Etre*," pp. 148–49.

101. Buchanan, *A Deleuzian Century?* p. 382.

Critical Inquiry, October, and Historicizing French Theory

SANDE COHEN

Introduction: Between Language and History

There are many dimensions to both French theory and "French theory in America," but in this chapter, I treat its historiographic writings: what conceptions of history indicate about representations of politics, philosophy, and culture. After some extensive remarks about French theory and historiography, I proceed to analyze the journals *Critical Inquiry* and *October* from the perspective of what their *historicization* of French theory can suggest about American intellectual life. Both journals made a "contract" of sorts with American intellectuals to explore alternatives to the state of criticism in the early 1970s. *Critical Inquiry* offered a model of pluralism in opposition to New Criticism and formalism, whereas *October,* clear from its very name, has been insistent upon historical reflection. Both journals will be treated as "didactic and magisterial," in that both have "redistributed the space of symbolic references . . . impressing a 'lesson.'"[1] *October* has claimed to give its readers an alternative history of critical art, stitching itself to the idea of "revolutionary energy" articulated by Walter Benjamin and the surrealists, while *Critical Inquiry* has organized its mission around enlarging the number of perspectives available to criticism. To make this analysis, I must first explain that peculiar concept, *to historicize,* which frequently works as an automaton of language and representation, often appearing in the strangest of places.

By "French theory in America" and historiography are meant those ideas that enabled Nietzsche's writings on historiography to come alive in France, exported to the United States as concepts for a critical theory of history. Nietzsche's writings on history did not submit to the idea of a dialectic or any other notion (e.g., class, natural selection) as "key" to historical understanding. Such ideas reduce social conflicts to ideal categories and norms, rather than creating games of thought that add something to intellectual conflict. In the conjunction of Nietzsche/French theory, the *intellectual jurisdiction* of the existing players is challenged along the axis of how they "use or abuse" history. Critical theory of history tries to change the rules of writing history or even to ask whether any game of writing about history is *worth it*. That is a harsh thing to say, but the French theorists discussed below were in agreement that after 2,500 years of *misrepresentation* by historians, by the sheer hit and miss of historical representation, by the transformation of *after the factness* into a *resource* for control on the future, that it was time to consider not playing that game. Not historical, that's the path to barbarism, isn't it? In this sense, French theory and Nietzsche took the writings of historians more seriously than the historians did.

Nietzsche, genealogist and student of mixture, of ascent/descent, of aesthetic sleight of hand, of persistent epistemologies, of strange moralities and power trips of all sorts, was filtered through French theorists who agreed that an active life was not "historical" but existential—making connections, objects, interpretations, relations, and so on was more important than representing what one thinks history "is like." Deleuze's phrase, "just an idea, not a just idea" condenses this relation *to make* in conflict with *to historicize,* because *to make* disappears into the innumerable events of other doings, untying ourselves from our own and others' historical projections. But once people project "history" into their actions as the genetic pattern tying "origin" to "goal," then *to historicize* serves as a self-protective/aggressive dimension of *having a future*. Hence, as Lévi-Strauss intimated in his *Tristes Tropiques*, an all-purpose source for French theory and historiography, nothing is more destructive, culturally speaking, than members of society "acting in the name of history," demanding a legacy which, in turn, becomes institutionalized as a drag on present cultural production. The institutionalization of modernism, its experiments with language and medium turned into constraints on criticism—like the Left's nostalgia for Adorno, or liberalism's use of enlightenment or affirmative action as a practice that makes "progress" a competed-for commodity—is an outstanding instance of historicization. Historical knowledge legitimizes nearly senseless wars over representing legacy, because such knowledge has no goal other than adding "the new luster of capital" to going routines of all sorts. The present is then overdetermined by layers of past actions that are not past yet used to assign many different values to events and processes that are a challenge to representation.

French theory's use of Nietzsche on history did not come out of a vacuum; French theorists made explicit dissident tendencies in twentieth-century critical historiography, adding to these tendencies an extended intellectual critique of scholarship's very own "political correctness," its relentless cleansing of dissidence, its relentless adherence to the master/slave pattern, its relentless aggressions in the name of prestige. Because historiography was so old, so monumentalized, and so institutionalized by scholar-historians, French theory added the problem sets of institutional analysis and intellectual credibility to a critical theory of history. Connecting with certain German counterparts—Hannah Arendt, Karl Lowith, Reinhart Koselleck, and Karl Heinz-Bohrer come to mind—French theory doubted scholarship's very own historicity. It doubted those histories of scholarship that always transformed the scholar into a hero of enlightenment, making a critique of scholarship's system of appropriations and inclusions, its idealizations and temper tantrums, its raising of ego to monumental status. French theory solidifies at the moment a *campusification* of the world occurs; this at once material/linguistic/institutional process was built into French theory, a kind of retrofitting of the intellectual as "on strike" at the very place that allowed the intellectual a "community." Denis Hollier writes about the college of sociology in France during the 1930s in terms that are applicable to French theorists from the 1960s.[2] In a sense, French theory applied to historians the latter's notions of progressive/regressive (something has a future, something else does not), and asked about the future of society after the effects of so much "historical knowledge." Paul Valery's writings form one of the important literary and critical sources in this overall process where knowledge is analyzed as production, recording, and consumption.

So French theory doubted the academic connoisseur by doubting aesthetic unity—the big synthetic book, the historian's "last word," finalities of knowledge. French theory's suspicion toward conceptual formulae like "Oedipus" was a way of keeping epistemological issues open in the humanities, instead of proceeding to a further closing down (political correctness again) based on exceedingly bizarre, and private, academic bureaucratic procedures of declaring issues important and consigning other questions to the refuse bin. Finally, French theory affirmed anarchist-type politics: criticism of state formations, of subject positions, of discourse, including academic relays to these relations. That is some of what is being summoned by the tag "French theory." Again, French theory let Nietzsche be reread in the United States, not through the filters of Marxism or psychoanalysis, but through contestation with everything linguistic, or better, by contesting language, power, and the myth of social bonds in a capitalizing system.[3]

For the purposes of this essay, then, French theory involves language and the lures of representation, history, and claims to mastery, criticized in the frame of a capitalism that exceeds both language and "ordinary historical consciousness." In the United States, the marketing, within academia, of everything that could claim to be *outside, different,* or *oppositional* indexes just how far capitalism has already gone. By calling into question every theory of history that turned capitalism into a "had-to-be" instead of focusing on the mechanisms by which capital "is/is becoming," French theory initiated resistance(s) to capitalism, focusing instead on capital's ability to integrate differences as well as its antisocial effects.

To make this critique, French theory also resisted *ordinary criticism*, not treating cultural or intellectual problems as reducible to "context" and narrative, and rejecting any sense of "loss" in considering Western history as such. Readers who are being introduced to French theory in relation to the competing models devised over the last thirty years or so should note that such resistance doubted everything that goes by the name *humanistic knowledge*. For if language, history, and capitalism are joined in ways irreducible to subjectivity, mastery, and representation, then French theory doubts humanism's contemporary liberal, conservative, and Marxist versions of knowledge about "history," about what "history is for." In this sense (developed below), because capitalism is "superhistorical," thus allowing no rivals, "historical consciousness" could no longer register the new twists of reality; the historians were "out of business" but didn't know it.

French Theory and Nietzschean Critique

What mattered to Nietzsche in relation to historiography was to figure out if the questions put to the past were questions that called into question the questioner: questions that opened the present to skepticism about *our* uses and abuses of the past. At what point are the heartfelt questions to the past—"coming to terms with the past"—self-deceptions, and worse, political instruments? Examples of which abound today. One historian has it that "modernist" rejection of "ancestor-worship" has created, in its own ways, the desert of the present, where "without ancestor-worship, meaning is in short supply." Modernism here means discontinuity with the supposed wisdom of past achievements of meaning; this "tear" and "break" from the past inhabits the present, giving the present its melancholic flavor, the short supply of meaning.[4] Is it really a "historical" question to imply the present lacks something the past (supposedly) once had? For Nietzsche, history is first of all about the things we do to language and existing social relations through our "use and abuse" of history. Nietzsche would have asked how the historian has concocted an intellectual schema so that the present is read as a continuation of the process of disenchantment; are we talking about the past or the continuity between past and present? How could something we had be taken away and affect social systems with very little in common with that past? And which experience of "ancestor-worship" that guaranteed meaning in said past does the historian have in mind?

As soon as one seriously considers history as representation, as word pictures, cutting across levels of language—naming things, classifying named things into lists of existents and occurrences, putting stories to these names, dissolving other stories in ceaseless rivalries over the "right picture" and on and on—then one has to become curious about history as representation. First of all, the *writing of history* testifies to contemporaries at war with one another over the use of representations in present disputes. Standard conflict takes the form of using concepts that are privileged in joining narration and coherence, such as class, power, and desire. Two well-known examples are Darwin's concept of natural selection and Hegel's notion of absolute knowledge, categorical relations that enable time to cohere with a sense of origin and outcome, genetic patterns that tie disparities together—history as truth. Historiography turns on *fictional* devices, so we can find natural selection or absolute knowledge or class conflict or racial dilemmas at work everywhere "in history" precisely because these concepts are removed from complex historicity. These concepts are linguistic anthropomorphisms idealized and integrated into the "unconsciousness of intellectuals."

If you radically *historicize* a phenomenon, you can both kill it—by reducing it to context—and monumentalize it, making it durative or a persistent example. In capitalism, one recodes to consume again. In either case, the polarity indicates no center to "historicity" at all. The main concepts used to think historically quickly give rise to all sorts of linguistic puzzles and enigmas. Nietzsche, drawing upon the critical science of his day, including philology, argued that what we claim to "find" in the "historical record" arises in the most variegated manner possible, added to which the historian has a genealogy in sacerdotalism, court politics, word spells, and more. In Western history the degree to which claimants to authority and legitimacy, on every level of representation, *use some concept of history that cannot be accounted for "historically"* is simply astonishing. Contingency of variations and factors of chance and stranger categories of social relations are always squeezed out by historical representation: narrative gives us a past that *we in the present can master.* Critical theory of history, if it can even survive in social systems that have convinced themselves that they "know" what history "means," has to do all it can to work against representation as ordinarily conceived (language), which is what concepts like "eternal return" try to signify—affirming an excess of sense and meaning instead of comfort with our all-too-certain representations.

The more we believe in our historical representations the more we actually sink into the alternations of cynicism and piety toward the future: how many past "truths" turned out to be manipulations of authority, of one kind or another? Cynicism tells us we already "know" tomorrow will not be not very different from today, and piety tells us that we have to have good Apollonian systems of representation to absorb the cynicism created by the disasters left in the wake of those who believed they were acting in the name of history. The most macabre venalities can be couched in the most reasonable language of history imaginable, as the case of Hitler attests.[5] Through such little words as *now, since,* and *tomorrow,* loaded in practice with accretions of all sorts, the disaster of historiography means that *training for cynicism and piety* becomes normalized as social failures increase, as negotiations and networking increase over the most minute aspects of life. At any given moment in Western society as a whole, we shake our heads over what we have "become" as we claim as little responsibility as we can. In this sense, French theory allowed itself to think intellectually about revolutionizing the means of criticism. If Vincent Descombes is right in saying that the dominant tradition of theorizing history in the West is a "terrorist conception of history" inherited from Kant, Marx, Hegel, and others—Deleuze said terrorism installs "history" from Platonism on out—then French theory attempted to think its way out of that "terror," shredding concepts, in particular the attraction of history figured forth as totality, coherence, necessity, or notions of determinism grafted to notions of obligations. A "fight against history"—the phrase comes from Nietzsche—stamps this aspect of French theory (in France) as *criticism* of all the "uses and abuses of history" to which populations are subjected, *raising the ante* on *representation,* where language and history connect.[6]

This *ordinary terrorism* of historiography took shape in the face of Enlightenment-generated "history in general." On the one hand, "history in general" is inclusive of senses pertaining to inheritance, legacy, heirs, and a panoply of related experiences of duration. But each successive "shattering" of reality (Lyotard) both dissolves historicity and reconstitutes it as expectations for the future, eliminating intellectual dissidence in each reconstitution.[7] Yet historical consciousness can't soothe these shatterings as it itself is shattered by further modernizations, nowhere better expressed than by Lyotard when he describes narratives dissolving and liquifying into "clouds" of description, the significance of which *drift* in relation to the most varied audiences. But, at the same time, capitalized experience is *overcoded* from the "inside" of the system, past experiences structured to encode a future no one is responsible for and to. This is not very far from Hannah Arendt's concern that it was "good society" itself that empowered the historians to integrate the negative as such, so "traits of humanity which had become extinct in society," like the productive isolation of the artist, gave way to an even more intense "functional" good society in which functionality determines what lasts.[8] Karl Lowith, living in some danger in Fascist Japan, escaped from Nazi Germany, wrote that the line from Hegel to Nietzsche could be imaged as sheer perplexity: "Is the essence and 'meaning' of history determined absolutely from within history itself; and, if not, then how?"[9] Terror and perplexity are concepts not popular with most historians.

Historical representation can be defined as that kind of representation that *tells someone* what is "living" and what is "dead" *for someone else,* where *to tell* and *for us* can be narrow (the audience who wants to know all about Andy Warhol's sex life) and wide (the American people); such representation must be so constantly rewritten that it never actually itself appears—a phantom discourse with institutional "clout." As *writing*, historical representation has been subject to the most varied analyses by French theory, and none of them accepted a psychological basis for narration as a *sui generis* mode of relation to the world.[10] This has nothing to do with contesting or calling for an "end" to history, and it definitely does not call for dismissal of how historical significance is a tactic in the political correctness factor.

On the plane of historical representation, French theory argued that no definitive "so that's what it was!" is possible. In one sense, it pursued the historian's very own claim that every narrative is incomplete, which requires more narratives: French theory tried to show that every narrative, any narrative, can only *simulate* distance from language, can only *say* its distance from things, as well as enunciate words that incorporate things. No one went further than Gérard Genette, in his aporias about description, when he argued that the simplest act of narration, such as "It was a beautiful day," is embedded in narrative problems of voice and author functions, unless it was Deleuze and Guattari, who, in *Anti-Oedipus,* insisted that writing never presents the historical when it is active writing.[11] Because language is as close, at the "highest" levels, to rumor, hearsay, ridicule, gossip, hysteria, and delirium as anything else, it had to be that "French theory" would contest historical representation along the lines of exploring language's incessant concoction of hierarchy, incorporation, linearization, and subjectification, or linguisticopsychological "elements" making up "ordinary historical consciousness." According to these readings of Nietzsche joined to linguistic theories and proposals about the structures and functions of language, *to historicize* was thoroughly deautonomized, where no *sui generis* mode of language or subjectivity could be found in which the past returns or the present enjoys continuity with the past.

Still speaking generally, for thirty-five years since the publication of Deleuze's *Nietzsche and Philosophy,* the historical profession has mostly shut its doors to French theory.[12] Many of the most interesting works in French theory—from extensive analysis of the fictions of realism that treated description as abruption, imposition, set against historiography's love of *enargheia,* or vivid writing, to analysis of other narrative forms, to critiques of "the violence of language"—are simply unread by historians since they cannot extract any use value or prestige value from them. One thinks here of Carlo Ginzburg's installation of the connoisseur as a historiographic model and his denunciation of Barthes's statement that "facts have only a linguistic existence," a denunciation that maintains the *hegemon* of the historian "over" facts, facts then said to be prior to language.[13] Or, in another context, one thinks of the typical historian's "need" to retain a discourse that destroys irony (irony negated because too close to amoralism), relativism, skepticism—"vices" regularly denounced by historians. This hatred of irony was exemplified in the denunciation of Lyotard's historiography, shunned for comparing the West to a psychotic break (prepared by Barthes's analysis of historical discourse as resembling psychotic discourse), who dared to suggest that the West had always used "history" for political ends.[14] One can say that today no national research department of history is contaminated by "French theory." The University of California system, for example, teaches historiography after reducing it to an intruder on the "real" work of historical "research," offering one in a hundred history positions to the teaching of historiography as a discipline in its own right. Those who would render "possession of history" seem to have a genealogical commitment to resisting critique of historical language.

According to arguments made in Deleuze's *Nietzsche and Philosophy,* the very idea of a *subject of history* is a political and cultural imposition, not a "historical idea." Join my continuum—*or else!* is the refrain of overhistoricized people. In a "fight against history," *Anti-Oedipus*'s arguments should not be lost. It is the liveliest discussion I know of any alternative to the historian's argument that normal people have a craving for narrative synthesis, to live life as a story. It is also the most resolutely nonpsychological model I know of in treating intersubjectivity and time. In that text's mixture of fabulation/criticism, "history" supposes, whenever it enters a culture, overcoming a proper paranoia of groups and people(s) who have not been completely assimilated to identity functions, groups, and people(s) that maximize inclusive conjunctions, where representation is not yet "signs that refer to concepts [but] diagrams and paths for the hand."[15] Liberals, conservatives, and Marxists get impatient with this. Be that as it may, "history" brings a "miraculating" writing and thought, a despotic thinking that conjoins absorption of anything excessive with bureaucratic functions, where language is twisted to purposes of incorporation, employing mental deliriums, a triumph of neurosis over psychosis, formed by "recording the process of production" and turning recording into a "true consciousness of a false movement"—for example, Marxism's idea of a dissolution of capitalism from within. "True consciousness/false movement" comes into word existence every time someone believes "movement" is correctly named. In other words, identification is the key to historical consciousness, but since identity always falsifies in the name of inclusions that are inevitably self-serving, the little openings in identity breakdown indicate the persistence of a nonhistorical inter-subjective world of experiences. *Nocturnal intensities* are driven by historical representation below the line of recognition in favor of direct filiations between a subject and transcendence.[16] Deleuze's *Nietzsche and Philosophy* conceived of "history" as the repression of active, productive, cultural life, even if the latter was sometimes embedded in cruelty, because the "historical subject" is always obsessed with genetic patterns, with the idea that origin and intention connect with purpose and end.[17] A "career" is an effect of historicist structures, and all such structures carry a high degree of *relay*, capable of connecting with other historicist structures—whatever perpetuates *being memorialized*. The demand that historical knowledge show what we can identity with is also then a terrorism of subjectivity, what the earlier reference to Descombes suggested: existence driven by the scramble for identity in time, smoothed by terms such as one's "life work," one's "project."[18] French theory reminds us, even at its most abstract and diagrammatical, not that the works of "high" culture are tainted by violence (Benjamin), but that they are violent in and of themselves, as representation. The inaugurative Western historical narratives, like the ones we continue to make, are "miracles" of continuity between language and things and between things and things, "spirit" and psyche wars, conflicts that are metaphysical and not "historical in themselves."

Finally, a word on this "miraculation" of historical writing. According to arguments made in *Anti-Oedipus*, the "writing of history" involves the removal from language of the virtual, or intellectual turbulence brought under the smoothness of syntax and semantic determination; only by such controls as reducing meaning to two terms, *referent* and *expression*, or restricting inventories of "existents" and "occurrences," can narrative furnish "or realize surplus value," writings that secure the "recording rights" necessary for state/subjectivity coordinations. Every act of collective violence involves telling a story, making a history. Narrative sometimes intensifies a conflict, sometimes ameliorates one; in both, readers are "gripped" by the vivid recounting, involving a certain "blindness" about this "enchanted recording or inscribing surface that arrogates to itself all the productive forces and all the organs of production, and that acts as a quasi cause by communicating the apparent movement (the fetish)." *Anti-Oedipus* argued that the decisive cultural/literary moment in the emergence of historiography as an overt bureaucratic function was extractive and reactive: "Legislation, bureaucracy, accounting, the collection of taxes, the State monopoly, imperial justice, the functionaries' activity, historiography: everything is written in the despot's procession."[19]

Whether in the texts of Deleuze and Guattari, Genette, Barthes, or Paul de Man and others, what has been conceptualized about historiography is that the act that posits "history" must also posit identities and differences, breaks and continuities, an act of language/thought that gives to historiography suspicious *dramatisms*, pseudocomparisons (e.g., the use of temporal distances, social resemblances), senses of descent and ascent in which temporal structure and aesthetic satisfaction reinforce the other. Historiography is a form of imposing ideologies, projections, and wishes that are regularly made objects of "public debate," and reinforce existing relations; ordinary institutional historiography always goes back to *some* good or common sense, at war with *parabasis* or interruptions that can strike at any point in a narrative. Perhaps historiography was once a place that subjects could come to language and dream of alternatives to intractable realities; today institutional historiography loathes uncontrolled irony and is more suspicious than ever of the claims of rhetorical or critical linguistic analysis.

Critical Inquiry and Historicization

Critical Inquiry began in September 1974 under the sign of providing "a reasoned inquiry into the significant creations of the human spirit." Its editorials have consistently made the claim that it provides a forum for "situating" the present, offering the best in contemporary criticism.[20] In relation to French theory in America, between 1974 and 1980 it devoted attention to the Yale school, publishing two essays by Paul de Man and two by J. Hillis Miller, along with Derrida's piece on the "laws of genre." From 1980 to 1983, the French theorists printed were Derrida and Foucault, the latter contributing one short piece that was folded into a special issue in September 1982 on the politics of interpretation, an issue that included a contribution by Kristeva. From 1983, beginning with an essay by Gerald Graff on "totalization and the politics of theory," French theory, never dominant, receded, and was displaced by questions of the canon, race, and multiculturalism, with the important exception that Derrida's essays came to stand in for anything readers could collate as "French theory and *Critical Inquiry*." The journal's special issue on "Race, Writing and Difference," 1985, deployed Derrida's essay as commentary on the issue as a whole, his work deemed magisterial and meta-critical.

A special issue the following year made clear the editorial policy of affirming a "dialectical pluralism" explicitly directed against what was called pan-textualism. "Dialectical pluralism" is almost an oxymoron, but it manages to avoid the accusation leveled against "pan-textualism," the incessant complaint that French theory stood for "nothing outside the text." Evoking a "sense of history" against "constructionism," *Critical Inquiry* granted to historical thinking the right to provide "reports" on new methodological and interdisciplinary "arrangements," encouraging conjunctions between disciplines so long as such a sense of history dominated. After 1986, short pieces by Bourdieu, Todorov, Genette, Deleuze, Kristeva, Marin, Lacoue-Labarthe, Nancy, Serres, Cixous, and tributes to Foucault by Marin and Canguilhem were printed; more exceptional was a spring 1988 "special feature" publishing Derrida's essay "de Man's War," and a 1989 symposium on Heidegger, with pieces by Derrida, Levinas, and Blanchot, along with responses to Derrida (later included in the volume *Responses* on Paul de Man's wartime writings). From 1990 to 1997, Levinas, Serres, Hadot, and Jankelevitch, were published, as well as chapters 2 and 18 of Althusser's *The Future Lasts For-*

ever; these were the two most sensational chapters, concerning manslaughter and special pleading, a selection that precluded understanding of the rest of his book, which was lyrical and gave a remarkable psychological genealogy, including a coming to terms with Lacan's ideas. The terror and lyricism of Althusser's work and life were turned into a humanist subject, contrary to his main writings. The executive editor of *Critical Inquiry* introduced a piece by Hadot in 1990 highlighting the latter's contribution to Foucault's notion of "spiritual discipline," and prefaced another piece by Levinas in 1990 in which Levinas's conception of "human spirit" was emphasized—that only responsibility for the other warrants any glimpse of self-transcendence, the "impossible" named the form of being more than oneself. Clearly, the editorial presentation of French theory has refused to disavow humanism; indeed, *Critical Inquiry* has stressed French theory only when it serves a more rigorous humanism.

This becomes apparent by the editorial introduction of an essay by Robert Musil from 1933 on Hitlerism and one from 1934 by Emanuel Levinas on the same topic. What do Musil and Levinas have to say to intellectuals today through the filter of historical representations of Nazism? Musil's lesson from 1934 requires us to think today, How much intellectual adaptability and assimilation is compatible with intellectual identity?—a fuzzy, but necessary question. The editor affirms, with Musil, that intellect has no "identity card"; that is, it is autonomous or should be in relation to the day's politics, whatever the day.[21] Musil offered that intellect and spirit are "global," and as Nazism had no intellectual support in any of Germany's philosophical or literary traditions, it showed "intellect being compelled to renounce itself."[22] Musil's struggle to achieve "insight and integrity" shows that they are hard to come by anytime. Nazism and philosophy are then led to this question: How can we know when thought has given up and when it has maintained itself? It is a more than defensible question. However, as if in horror at his own question, the editor invokes the writings of Jean Amery, inspiration for Primo Levi, who spells out the moral plateau of "intellect" and settles the matter: "Whoever repudiates the Enlightenment is renouncing the education of the human race." That judgment lays down an ultimatum—Enlightenment or not. The editor seems blind that the rhetorical force of the statement and use of Amery might itself be suspect insofar as it does not allow for any disagreement.

French theory is thoroughly stripped of *criticism* when the editor turns to Levinas's 1934 essay on Nazism. Levinas, unlike Musil, argued that Hitlerism was a philosophy, striving for a "universal," but committed "to the body" and self-reduced to racism.[23] In such a scene, the question How is the universality of truth to be understood?—another of those trenchant or attractive questions—is posed. The answer: by achieving a sense of *spirit*, defined here by "liberalism's free and autonomous reason," by transcendence of "matter," by a sense of "spirit's commitments," which leads both to Sartrean existentialism and, more important, to Levinas's break with existentialism, which is to say, to *ethical consciousness's* challenge to subjective sovereignty and autonomy, by embrace of "my subjection to responsibility-for-the-Other," and which is "nothing less than 'the original site of the Revelation."[24] Insofar as French theory places ethics/theology at the center of its writings, the writings are embraced. The emphasis upon the texts of Levinas, Hadot, and Derrida fully indicates that *Critical Inquiry*'s very own "cut" out of French theory pursued an intellectual program: intellectuals such as Musil and Levinas "write out of a concrete historical situation in which their *descriptions* produce *conviction* quite apart from questions of justification," this conviction based on spirit, and said intellectuals must never cancel their subscription to enlightenment, for without the latter, intellectuals end up serving "philosophy from below" and which harms others. In other words, intellectuals are enjoined to conditions of existence in which they are to be "humane" as they affirm "spirit"; Musil's "morality of the humane" defines the "local conditions" absent in Nazi Germany and meets Levinas's transcendence *for the other* in the only place they can meet: in the language of European idealism.

What *Critical Inquiry* provides, then, is the division of French theory into two components. On the one hand, the Nietzsche line is all but refused. In an acute and highly charged reading of *Critical Inquiry*, William Spanos has pointed out the editorial disavowal of any Heideggerian (here, read: Nietzschean) project of "posthumanism." In evaluating and judging the West from premises and grounds that protect the autonomy of philosophy led by "reason," *Critical Inquiry* has to resort to an archaic, if classical, instrument of humanism, the autonomy of "human voice."[25] There is always a living exemplification of this voice, and even if somewhat pluralized, such voice is still the voice of reason instead of introducing differences into reason and thereby changing it. In this sense, *Critical Inquiry* has tried to make *recuperation* of the West's humanist tradition necessary. Perforce, it has downplayed any "outside" or more analytic basis than the language of a certain *responsible subject*, who is thus rendered precisely "outside" conflict by idealist rhetoric. In this game of inside/outside, recuperation and responsibility, one could say that a selection is made "on" French theory. This second selection adheres to the "subject in responsibility" as ideal, and eliminates those notions that would contest it.

Critical Inquiry sponsors a progressive historicist agenda that is symmetrical with this "responsible subject." Complementary with defending "humanist responsibility," this second dimension is deemed *historical*, or Hegelian. A clear example of this, coming fifteen years after the first of the debates on multiculturalism, is a piece by the historian Michael Geyer that appeared in 1993. Geyer's essay is representative of *Critical Inquiry*'s overall treatment of French theory in the dissuasive mode. Geyer has it that multiculturalism is required by the times, for multiculturalism is a way of "reconstituting cultural capital," which is, institutionally considered, a "capital" necessary for the political economy of university-based education. Drawing upon two (re)sources, one attending to civil rights and democratic egalitarianism, the other a theorizing and intellectualizing associated with "French thought" (read: deconstruction), which is "much more limited and precarious" for present knowledge production, multiculturalism is offered as a "capital" infusion giving the academy "a recovery of submerged knowledge, a working through of the repressed."[26] A progressive model of history leads to a progressive model of pedagogy. It presupposes there is nothing repressive or otherwise problematical about multiculturalism.

Geyer's narrative model is a sophisticated defense of Ranke against Hegel, where singularities matter, but it is Hegel who surmounts Ranke: "It is the memory of the bondsmen rather than the monuments of the masters that assures the survival of humanity." This is a straight coding of progressive Hegelianism, or neoliberalism. It is neither reactionary nor avant-garde. It supposes that the truth of the master is "in" the bondsmen's empirical reality, and has very frequently come to mean that cultural analysis must never obliterate the perspective of one who has suffered life under the master. There are vast literatures on this subject. But since deconstruction or French thought is not of the bondsmen sociological type, or because it has come from masters, the insertion of multiculturalism in the context of the bondsmen gives it a claim of historicizing the present. The analytic/critical implications of French thought could only be secondary to the political impact of democracy and its tribulations. The "limited and precarious" aspects of "French thought" provide egalitarian multiculturalism with only a few devices for its passage to the future. The strategy of integrating multiculturalism is lifted from what Barthes called "inoculation": multiculturalism is rejected only when it descends into rigid insistence upon identity, but since multiculturalism belongs to democratization, it is "French theory" that is warned of as excessively critical and probably "mandarin."

In an astonishing passage, Hegelianism is said to provide an effective transition from a discredited universal history to that of "provisional histories," the present (but not presentistic) then "empowered" in semantic identifications figured by Geyer as "modes of inquiry . . . strategies of coping with the fear of otherness while honoring difference. Such strategies are familiar from a variety of therapeutic activities such as antirape or antiracist education."[27]

An older tradition of the Left would notice that antirape/antiracism has replaced labor and class as foundational categories. While rape and racism are never less than terroristic, they are returned here as the basis for "inquiry" and thus generalized to problematics between university and society and within knowledge production.

How far do antirape and antiracism really extend as models of academic politics and the politics of delivering a "serviceable" education? The first sentence of the above quote marks out "fear" and "honor" as the polarity of the social as such. We suffer from too many fears of the other (race, homophobia, identity) but this can be offset by inclusive politics of the victims, making their claims ours. What "French thought" might say about Geyer's instantaneous fusion of historicism, psychoanalysis, and theory is effaced by the signifier "coping," which affirms there are no critical strategies but those already *within* the transition. This is an extremely powerful *settling of accounts,* since "coping" operates as an order-timing: the text has already assumed as fact that "coping" is beyond analysis, or "to cope," infinitive mode, forms the substance of contemporary history. The primary "move" of this neohistoricism aims at providing an objectivist referent (we live "in" this New World) with forms of our recognizing it; the new realities of world history have generated problematics, the solutions of which are also here, now.

In short, *as edited,* which is to say *politicized,* by *Critical Inquiry,* "French theory" is tolerated only inasmuch as such theory does not interfere with the language and sense of history deemed necessary for transition to the future, nothing other than the classical subject of liberalism, the good people of enlightenment. It takes a lot of editorial energy to preserve this.

October and French Theory

October's working of French theory in America is of a different sort. The journal has explicitly historicized in the name of a commitment to "classical" leftist notions of critique and resistance; it is impossible not to notice the consistent transcendental aura given to the writings of Walter Benjamin and the surrealists. It is also more schizo: *October* is today, in de Certeau's terms, an institution in its own right; or, in Bruno Latour's designation, it functions as a network replete with branchings, alignments, connections, "tracers," what he calls cultural subscriptions, synthesized in practices, instruments, documents, and translations.[28] *October* is also heir to practices associated with academic despotism, replete with "public executions" of intellectual work it deems outside its own party line.[29]

What dominates as *October's* trajectory is the concern with writing a history of Western subjectivity, drawing on Lacanian psychoanalysis as narrative and periodized as the switch from modernism to postmodernism. The first issue put the subject in an "aesthetics of narcissism," latter called a "grid" by the main editor, who further insisted that modernism could be understood as arising in the "split" between sacred and secular, visual artists creating "a refuge for religious *emotion.*" It's astonishingly *unhistorical* to assume continuity between religious passion and art. Be that as it may, modernists turned this split into grids, into inadmissible evidence of the twentieth century's suppression of this very split between sacred and secular. Notice the amount of labor devoted to the binary. The figure of the grid presides as structural fact and as its own representation, over the shame of its materiality and its sheer figurability, able to inculcate belief in the autonomy of art. Art history is given a hinge connecting art to both life and politics. In short, the grid as found in art raised and repressed binarism, a synecdochic representation disclosing the historical process of subject formation—splitting. The history made available by the grid is smoothly folded with psychoanalysis, as "behind every 20th c. grid there lies—like a trauma that must be repressed—a symbolist window," repetition of the originary splitting of sacred and secular, of the division between art and history, art and society, self and other.[30] At once certain objects *display the history of* splitting better than others. Art history must write the significance of the "inadmissible evidence," which has turned out to be the canon, which, linked to history is thus reencoded to show us the suffering due to binarism. All of these connections coagulate as—to historicize. One can get dizzy with all this history.

A 1980 essay by another editor, "The Allegorical Impulse," borrowed in a sympathetic way from de Man, Barthes, and Derrida so as to articulate post-modernism as allegorical, but this French theory (deconstruction) was nonetheless said to be "complicit" in "participating in the very activity that is being denounced *precisely in order to denounce it.*"[31] The "self-criticism" of modern art and its "self-reliant" objects were transformed into symptom, frustration, and deferral, or escape from "history."

A special issue on film in 1981 cemented psychoanalytic discourse as unquestioned theory, and the fall issue that same year announced that modernism, avant-garde, and fictions of originality could only be grasped by historicism/psychoanalysis. An essay there had it that museums, historians, and artists share in modernism's exhaustion, but through the work of artists such as Sherrie Levine, modernist originality could now be deconstructed. Championing "smart art" (historicist insiderism), this was not the deconstruction Paul de Man had in mind. Levine's work was touted as having a better sense of historical reflexivity, rather than making all such genetic/historicist models more questionable and problematic: "her effort cannot be seen as an *extension* of modernism. It is, like the discourse of the copy, postmodernist. Which means that it cannot be seen as avant-garde either. . . . The historical period that the avant-garde shared with modernism is over."[32] Again, such colossal metahistorical judgments were not subject to the very reflexivity *October*'s editors insisted was the purpose of the journal.

Since it was announced that modernism was over, nearly every issue has raised the topic of psychoanalysis, subjectivity, and their relation to art history. The publication in 1987 of Lacan's *Television* was presented as not only devoted to a critique of institutions, but, in the note by editor Joan Copjec, to a defense of institutions as "signifying practices." Lacan was invoked to diminish the rival critical notions Copjec set forth as student romanticism and class essentialism. *Television* and Lacan were drawn into a defense of institutions, to a more proper "historical" treatment of their functions, institutions understood here as exceeding "any intersubjective intention or effect," hence impervious to the demands of that "split subject" Lacan taught as riddled with a "desire not to know."[33] That puts students in their place—woe to the student who does not understand the underbrush of Lacanian *cultics* (no matter what you do/do not, symptoms are read). Institutions could not then be the subject of critique since institutions embodied the very truth, as place holders, of divided subjectivity, that one has to be divided in order to not go psychotic. In the face of such ideas, of an imperial discourse on the fate of subjectivity, *October* has never presented a critique of Lacanian theory, subjecting it to critico-linguistic analysis.

This strenghtening of psychoanalysis was further signaled with the appearance, beginning in 1986, of essays by Slavoj Žižek, an up-to-date Hegelian trickster/con artist. In a discussion of logic and desire, in the midst of theorizing paradoxes, Žižek says that that the endeavors of Sisyphus "prove" the truth that a "goal, once reached, always retreats anew." This is reposed to mean that "the goal is the final destination, while the aim is what we intend to do, i.e. the way itself. Lacan's point is that the real purpose of the drive is not its goal (full satisfaction) but its aim: the drive's ultimate aim is simply to reproduce itself as drive, to return to its circular path. . . . The real source of enjoyment is the repetitive movement of this closed circuit."[34] The aim is the true goal—to keep filling the void, the hole, the lack; if Žižek is right, desire's desire is simply desire's self-reproduction, the assertion confirming natural selection as its model type, since "to reproduce itself" is identical to survival (why do behaviorist codes keep turning up in psychoanalysis?); or could we say that the subject as gap/void/lack is conceived as an effect of nothingness, active nihilism in place of its passive, cultural, aspect? Paradox is stripped of any event status—moved to the "timeless"—and functions as a transcendental a priori of the subject. In this sense, the invocation of paradox is a political move, a way of asserting that psychoanalysis is up to date in ridding itself of the charge that it projects nature onto culture. The price is that culture is absorbed by the metaphysics of neopsychoanalytic theory. And as philosophy (read: critical linguistic analysis) is blind as to the real metaphysics of the subject, since philosophy must always have a nonparadoxical foundation, psychoanalysis alone has reached the plateau of "true" philosophy. The history of the subject is told by the truths of psychoanalysis, or historicism grafted to dogmatism, with all its politics of ensuring that "aware" people are running the world.

Through Žižek, *October* affirms the Hegelian notion of culture as negation now become the self-confession of lack, hence a theory of any subjectivity whatsoever.

Indeed, one has the definite sense that just as world-historical dimensions can be modeled as the proliferation of "lack"—extension of the law, proliferation of gaps to be filled, the Western professional classes run amok on all the "badness" of the West—so too the turn to popular culture is of a highly political order. This is radical critical theory in the service of reactionary ends: the popular will not get out of place. If one reads *October*'s publication of Žižek's writing as a statement of editorial/intellectual *desire*, this put-down of the popular may then stand as a political proposition: *October*'s encoding of the intellectual resembles anti-intellectual mandarinism in the very name of intellectual renewal.[35]

In essays published in 1990 and after, the tribulations of the subject are encoded as a "dispersed subject" well on the way to "the utterly fragmented subject of contemporary mass culture."[36] Now sometimes termed the "derealized subject," such figures of subjectivity—or antifigures, since the subject dissolves—are said to have resulted in the definite capture of the subject by "the hysterical sublime," after Jameson. This "hysterical sublime," taking over from the grid, is structured by the lack of strong affective intersubjective relations joined to the pursuit of euphoria by anyone and everyone. Sometimes called a "technologized subject," new episodes are offered where to historicize increasingly meant one must accept the loss and lack of modernist history and ask as to what is recoverable from that "history."

Indeed, after the ascension of Hal Foster to editorial operations,[37] a new tone appears, in alignment with the narrowing provided by writers such as Žižek. In one of Foster's essays, French theory is singled out for negation. Foster has it that the "epistemological exoticisms" that connect Kristeva, Barthes, Foucault, Derrida, Baudrillard, and Deleuze and Guattari are so many "neo-orientalist oases and neo-primitivist resorts." None of these theorists is *correct* because their "epistemological exoticism" makes them all little Gauguins, "lines of flight" that reject the socially necessary "demand for recognition" by the contemporary subject ("hysterical," etc.). French theory as such doesn't make for good identity, preventing re-egoizing the unconscious of postmodernism. French theory is white and kinky—is there any other way to interpret "orientalist" and "primitivist"?—a politically correct thing to say for those within the academy who are married to historical analogies of guilt and sin, aka trashing. Only the historicist awareness of "now" can provide the narrative line of a "correct distance," one that would serve political and cultural "reconciliation."[38] With Foster's text, *October* entered into what can be called its phase of rigid antiepistemology, for the reduction of "French theory," save for Lacan, to oases and primitives is simply a refusal to *read* such texts, enclosing *October* in an antiproduction of thought, reconstituting Adorno-like negative identity. Don't think of an oasis, get rid of your primitive thoughts! Certainly intellectuals must not write that the very idea of the subject, "hysterical," "fractured," and "dissolved," is a game the West has played for a very long time. When have intellectuals not *outfitted* the present for rationalization of the invisible and inert abstract subjectivity?

In another essay by Foster, which notes that time tags such as "neo-" and "post-" are irrepressible in recent art and criticism, the question is how to periodize— How are we to distinguish them in kind?—raised in consideration of the work of Michel Foucault, in particular his famous essay "What Is an Author?" Foucault's work is asserted as more "useful" than Barthes's "Death of an Author" because Foucault maintained an interest in the subject (Barthes went too far, keeping only the linguistic-based subject of writing). Apart from this ill-claimed trashing of Barthes, since no rational reason is proffered for the negation, Foucault is used to confirm that the most useful critical "return" (the subject at hand that of "saving" Marx and Freud for current use) is a reading of past texts that can "cut through the layers of paraphrase and pastiche that have obscured its theoretical core and blunted its political edge." *Return* means *return to what is still there*, critical use value. To "cut through" semanticizes the action of *to periodize*, securing a past so as to engage present interests, a very frequent gesture of criticism: argument by authority, or return of the author. We can still *historicize* Marx and Freud; their writings are not those of Saint Augustine or, say, Rousseau: *dated, out of use*. What is it about Marx's and Freud's writings that allowed, even demanded, such figurations as paraphrase and pastiche to take hold in the first place? Could it have been Marx's own historicist rhetoric, the tragedy-farce pairing, or Freud's nihilism, in that tragedy is your essence? No doubt accompanies the indubitability that "return to" can make good on its promise "to cut through," or that Marx's and Freud's writings actually prevent this return precisely because all that they wrote challenges us to outwrite them. This is a stunning distortion of what Foucault's text actually says. Foucault insisted that "present discontinuities" are not necessarily "returnable" and argued that terms such as *core* and *edge*, where one would "return" to substance and subject, is itself to repeat "in transcendental terms a critical belief in [writing's] creative nature."[39] Foucault did not argue for return-as-model, so in this sense, the appropriation of Foucault turns out to be under a spell: of "return" as possession, as satisfaction of the idea that one can historicize the present and thereby possess it.

Let me bring *October*'s invocation of historicism and psychologism to bear on a reading of a "parallelism" Rosalind Krauss finds between a catalog essay from a Museum of Modern Art "high and low" exhibition and an essay by Andrew Ross, a proponent of cultural studies. Both have committed the antihistorical "sin" of discrediting surrealism, the catalog essay by overemphasizing the currency of graffiti, Ross by urging hipness and camp as practices of a partial distancing from capitalism. Both have reduced surrealism "such that surrealism has nothing but a purely predictive relation to [graffiti, hipness/camp]. Surrealism has almost no relation to anything in the field they are mapping . . . [surrealism's] dismissal.[40] Surrealism has been captured by a false narrative logic, reduced to a precursor and deoriginated. The catalog essay's use of *nostalgie de la boue* dumps surrealism out of history, or totally historicizes it by restriction to precursor status, draining its productivity, making it obsolete, without resonance, dehistoricized; graffiti is overhistoricized or given a current plus value. Judging this "almost no relation" to the present to be intolerable, this "story of sorts" objects to the cut performed on surrealism, its being "cut out" from present valuations. Ross, on the other hand, dismisses the "historical avant-garde" on account of its "actual distance and detachment from the world of commercial taste." That is, for Ross, standing in for cultural studies, postwar hipness replaced surrealist *nostalgie de la boue*, hip signifying an "'advanced knowledge about popular or commercial taste and style.'"[41] To define hipness as an "advanced knowledge" is to endow it with the power of resolving the categorical separation between art and life, an overcoming which, for Krauss, takes place entirely within this questionable "semi-autonomy" of cultural studies. Both the Ross and catalog essays suffer from premature synthesis, an error of historical investigation, for graffiti and hipness/camp cannot provide us with access to "real" history as surrealism did. Cultural studies is placed under suspicion due to its lack of reflection, what Krauss calls the "mimicry" such studies have with the present. Their sin: "presentism."

And what else is it about cultural studies that this historicism finds unacceptable? The former is said not to be historically critical but an aspect of the very consumerism it would criticize. Cultural studies' reliance on a model of consumption separated from production (e.g., the celebration of camp) "mimics" cultural studies as ahistorical. Whereas surrealism, when joined to Marxian psychoanalysis, gave its adherents a sense of resistance—"active critical users of mass culture able to rewrite or recode the materials they are given into new, critical, and above all creative readings"—cultural studies is but a symptom of a rejection of contemporary politics. Subculture has moved into the slot vacated by surrealism/the historical avant-garde and is not "restricted to artistic practice." Here's the "dissolved subject." Acknowledging that the Frankfurt school's notion of the avant-garde is "bankrupt" and "discredited,"[42] Krauss holds that the alternative, theories of the popular—"pleasure, resistance and politics of consumption"—have failed to create a more genuine populism.

What is not "historical" is thus the "mimicry" of the present cultural studies, here deemed destructive to the very "historical consciousness" that surrealism has bequeathed. The authority for this judgment then arrives to make the decisive rejection:

> As [Walter] Benjamin allowed his own early contact with surrealism to give
> him access to an experience of the outmoded as a source of revolutionary

energy, and as a way of decoupling historical time from the concept of progress, the presence of the outmoded began to play an increasingly central role in his thinking about history. But patterning his own attitudes toward the outmoded on that of the surrealists, he conceived of it as a category of objects over which commodity logic no longer has any sway; having dropped out of the logic of capitalism, these objects become powerfully symbolic of the possibility of imagining an "outside" of the commodity system, an outside of exchange.[43]

Surrealism got "outside" and congealed with obsolete things, creating a privileged figure, "revolutionary energy." The assumption is that Benjamin's nostalgia for the outmoded is not a "cutting consumption free of production" à la the present rivals, but a belief that human desire found a way of saving itself ("imagining") from the economic (and obsolescence). Do you believe in Walter Benjamin? In the swamp of false history and consumerism, something like "progressive desire" is properly surrealist. But Krauss excludes any consideration that many surrealists declared themselves revolutionary as a way of furthering the cultural indigestibility of their works, such works not serving as interpretations of history.[44] That revolutionary energy might also be found attached to a "sudden power of systematic associations proper to paranoia" *(Dali, The Conquest of the Irrational),* among multiple connections, is also eliminated from consideration. *The only surrealism tolerated is the one purified of the very history invoked to eliminate rival histories.*

Meaghan Morris is brought in for a last word, a completing "refutation" of cultural studies, saying, "before completely relegating [economics] . . . to the realm of the deja vu, however, it may be as well as to consider that in the late 20th c, after a century of romanticism, modernism, the avant-garde and psychoanalysis, economics, in fact, may be considerably more enigmatic than sexuality."[45] Thus, a *warning from history*: it is not too late for criticism to return to history—in this case, the supreme exemplification provided by Benjamin and the surrealists. It is worth noting, in the face of such super historical or monumental pronouncements,[46] that Benjamin's explicit statements that reproduction overwhelms production, aptly put by Baudrillard as "simulacra surpass history," are repressed. In this sense, Krauss's *nostalgie de la boue* polices the "sublimation" models of "high and low" through another sublimation—the projection of "enigma" back onto economics. It is time to return to economics rather than pursue cultural analysis. Benjamin will not be surpassed: a severe, and debilitating judgment, since it results in saying that historical reflection *is* Benjaminian.

If anything, the trajectory or temporal schema of *October* has become even more insistent upon historicism and psychologism. Recent essays have called for salvaging the "autonomy" of subjectivity, today said to be a Borgesian "disorder [that] is our order, this post-Surrealist heterotopia is our topos." Because "the foundational act of our identity is an imaginary mimesis, an identification with an image," the critic is warned to defend the autonomy of any sphere threatened with subjection to fetishistic images. As the present is historicized ("disorder is our order"), *October* continues to emphasize Frankfurt-style warnings, for example the American "accession to a set of social conditions as they are *re*produced through a process of (unconscious) identification with preexisting sources of authority and legitimation." In the face of this universal "unconscious identification," *October* claims to be able to historicize how subjects subject themselves to subjection.[47] But to what end? The current editorial tone of *October* is worried: cultural studies has itself become a symptom of the very psychosis it denounces. In the winter 1996 issue, in an essay by Foster, "Death in America," the preferred terms of historical analysis are a negation of the autonomy of subcultures, to be set aside by a holistic and universal "traumatic realism." The present is to be understood as a "historical" traumatic breakdown, a "pathological public sphere," a "psychic nation" with a new mass subjectivity.[48] Only by recognizing "the demand of others"—echoing the plea by the editor of *Critical Inquiry*—can intellectuals/artists/institutions do anything progressive, by acknowledging our multiple "dysfunctions."[49] We must make identifications across the "split." That is the project *October* announces: historical consciousness is to resist all the "impurities" of insufficient reflection. Correct reflection is predicated on trauma.[50] In this way, by historicist psychologization, *October* crosses over to the same resistance to Nietzschean projects that have sustained the editorial policies of *Critical Inquiry*. For wasn't Nietzsche/French theory the conceptualization of nonpsychological becomings?

Conclusion

So what if the Nietzsche/French theory conjunctions on historiography are resisted by these journals! Nietzsche doesn't join "hard" research with narrative presentation, giving truth and access to "history," thus knowledge of what the present "needs." Both journals editorialize that they join new research with public concerns, but a close reading shows something else—tight controls on what count as the very terms that intellectuals deliver to the public. *Critical Inquiry* and *October* all too often display the self-satisfaction of two kinds of connoisseurship, which is to say, a politics of language. On the one hand, *Critical Inquiry* places itself in charge of French theory along a spiritualized/idealized axis, characterized by the ethical charge of responsibility for others, which maintains a liberal *hegemon* on the subject: we "know" who the subject is, what it needs and lacks. On the other hand, *October*'s more explicit political slice into French theory radically historicizes the present in order to make contemporary art history "monumental," by elevating historical consciousness as itself the stake of historical reflection. Both journals involve historiography to install obligations and needs—the conjunction of historicism and psychologism—and suggest that *secure audiences* come first. By this I simply mean that *Critical Inquiry* and *October* give their readers security of belief, that "spirit" is a meaningful concept and that, in the case of *October*, we can monumentalize opposition. Readers will not find in either journal any ideas that will rattle the cages of our new scholars, for once you declare yourself or your work "progressive," how can it be possible that you are merely couching political and institutional filiations in the language of history?

In terms proposed by Paul de Man, we might see *Critical Inquiry* and *October* as transdisciplinary journals that unwittingly raise an altogether strange question: Why so much *truth without irony*, or what is at stake in getting the "right distance" on the past, of "correcting" the past, of idealizing? To the question What is historicization? de Man offers that it invokes the famous couple of irony and innocence in matters of representation. In "The Concept of Irony," from his *Aesthetic Ideology*, de Man suggests that Western thought makes "irony . . . secondary to a historical system." De Man means by this that literariness, rhetoric, textuality, is always absorbed by narrative's establishing a distance between then and now. A modern historical narrative might be ironic toward another narrative, but not toward its own narration of things. History, in the same text, is treated not as a temporal notion, but as an "emergence of a language of power out of the language of cognition." Our most cherished concepts of emergence, expressed in concepts such as "to happen" and "to occur," are neither dialectical nor continuous, de Man explains, because such notions do not escape the tropological and figurative; hence history cannot happen outside language, cannot be separated from it. The Apollonian dream image of historiographical "thought," its ever-present idealism, is that one can grasp history without language getting in the way. Hence historiography is a model of resistance to language, since, de Man concludes, "the event, the occurrence, is resisted by reinscribing it in the cognition of tropes, and that is itself a tropological, cognitive, and not a historical move."[51] No historical model, in short, can remove its own imposition of sense and meaning and, like the jump between cognitive discourse and performative discourse, one "cannot account for it according to a tropological model."[52] Imposition and violence sustain historiographic discourse, or historiography always carries in its writing violence toward interpretation and the labor of language. A strange result, indeed, from this mode of writing; or not strange at all, since, after twenty-five hundred years of it, we seem unable to surpass it.

These journals have used only those aspects of French theory that added to their respective projects of *historicizing*—making the present continuous with things that must not be lost, the "not-lost" (the "responsible subject," surrealism) then turned into criteria of evaluating text and object, integrating the present. *To historicize* can sometimes mean *to consume the present.*

Notes

1. Michel de Certeau, "The Historiographical Operation," in *The Writing of History* (Minneapolis: University of Minnesota Press, 1988), pp. 87–88. Thanks to Tom Conley for reminding me of the importance of this essay.
2. Denis Hollier, ed., *The College of Sociology* (Minnesota: University of Minnesota Press, 1988).
3. Two good introductions are Vincent Descombes, *Modern French Philosophy* (New York: Columbia University Press, 1980), and David Allison, ed., *The New Nietzsche* (Cambridge: MIT Press, 1985).
4. T. J. Clark, *Farewell to an Idea: Episodes from a History of Modernism* (New Haven: Yale University Press, 1999).
5. In the first chapter of *Mein Kampf,* "In the House of My Parents," Hitler writes, "To 'learn' history means to seek and find the forces which are the causes leading to those effects which we subsequently perceive as historical events . . . enchantment . . . into living reality." Aren't there *elements* here connected to "ordinary historical consciousness," e.g. knowledge and the hunt, grasp of the invisible ("forces"), and narrative presentation, as "enchantment"?
6. Descombes, *Modern French Philosophy*, pp. 9–15.
7. See the remarks by Reinhart Koselleck, *Futures Past* (Cambridge: MIT Press, 1985), p. xxiv. The triumph of Hegelian/Marxism in the nineteenth century was a "victory" over the dissidents of the day—those, like Kierkegaard and Nietzsche, who "saw" that historical consciousness was a political move to eliminate other systems of representation.
8. Hannah Arendt, *Between Past and Future* (New York: Viking, 1961), p. 208.
9. Karl Lowith, *From Hegel to Nietzsche* (New York: Holt, 1964), p. vi. Lowith answers this question at the close of his foreword by saying that to the question "what lives after us" in the face of "technological civilization" is only the possibility of "resignation without profit" from such a civilization.
10. Roland Barthes likened historical discourse to "psychotic" discourse in his essay "Historical Discourse," in *Introduction to Structuralism,* ed. Michael Lane (New York: Basic Books, 1970), p. 151. The cultural reading of historiography as Apollonian "innocence" with an anti-intellectual effect is given in Sande Cohen, *Historical Culture* (Berkeley and Los Angeles: University of California Press, 1986) and *Passive Nihilism* (New York: St. Martins, 1998).
11. Gilles Deleuze and Félix Guattari, *Anti-Oedipus* (Minneapolis: University of Minnesota Press, 1977), p. 134.

12. This is a matter of interpretation. An historian who calls herself a "deconstruction-ist" is more than rare.

13. Carlo Ginzburg, "Just One Witness," in *Probing the Limits of Representation* (Cambridge: Harvard University Press, 1993), p. 90.

14. Joyce Appleby, Lynn Hunt, and Margaret Jacob, *Telling the Truth About History* (New York: Norton, 1994), p. 210. But *Telling the Truth . . .* is a great index of historians' paranoia in the face of critical theory. It doesn't even mention the writings of Michel de Certeau, a scandal in itself, since his work remained within the parameters of historical representation. On one page the authors applaud their own work in social and cultural history as having revealed the limits of previous theories of history, but when it comes to post-anything writers, they become defenders of a "unified self" able to value "cultural self-affirmation" of the multicultural type (pp. 200–205). Lyotard's arguments are spelled out in a number of places, but the general outline is clear: the West has never ceased, after Christianity, to promise a reconciliation with lack and absence (resolution, knowledge, fulfillment, etc.); Capitalism dissolves historicity by waging a "convulsive struggle against the *mancipium* of time," accomplished, among other ways, by the lifeworld "built to lack nothing, except lack." See Jean-François Lyotard, "The Grip," in *Political Writings* (Minneapolis: University of Minnesota Press, 1993), p. 153.

15. See Alphonso Lingis, "The Society of Dismembered Body Parts," in *Deleuze and the Transcendental Unconscious* (*PLI: Warwick Journal of Philosophy*, 1992), p. 10.

16. See Brian Massumi, *A User's Guide to Capitalism and Schizophrenia* (Cambridge: MIT Press, 1993), p. 44.

17. Gilles Deleuze, *Nietzsche et la philosophie* (Paris: Presses Universitaires de France, 1962), pp. 158–161. "History then appears as the act by which reactive forces take possession of culture or twist it to their advantage."

18. See the essay by Christoph Wulf, "The Temporality of World-Views and Self-Image," in *Looking Back on the End of the World*, ed. Dieter Kamper and Christoph Wulf (New York: Semiotext(e), 1989), p. 57ff.

19. Deleuze and Guattari, *Anti-Oedipus*, p. 202.

20. Indeed, *Critical Inquiry* has published a number of transdisciplinary articles that have genuinely opened new directions of criticism.

21. Arnold Davidson, "1933–1934: Thoughts on National Socialism. Introduction to Musil and Levinas," in *Critical Inquiry* 17 (autumn 1990), p. 38.

22. Davidson, "Thoughts," pp. 36–37.

23. Davidson, "Thoughts," p. 42.

24. Davidson, "Thoughts," p. 45.

25. See William Spanos, *Heidegger and Criticism* (Minneapolis: University of Minnesota Press, 1993), pp. 182–84.

26. Michael Geyer, "Multiculturalism and the Politics of General Education," *Critical Inquiry* (spring 1993), p. 512.

27. Geyer, "Multiculturalism," p. 531.

28. Bruno Latour, *We Have Never Been Modern* (Cambridge: , 1993), p. 117–20.

29. After the editor Douglas Crimp's resignation some years back, a protege of one of the editors published an essay demolishing Crimp's work; see Tim Dean, "The Psychoanalysis of Aids," *October* 64 (winter 1993). For an artist's response to treatment

by *October,* see Joseph Kosuth, "Vico's Appliance," in *More and Less* (Pasadena: Art Center, 1999), pp. 172–85.

30. Rosalind Krauss, "Grids," *October* 9 (winter 1979).

31. Craig Owens, "The Allegorical Impulse: Toward a Theory of Postmodernism," *October* 13 (summer 1980), p. 79.

32. R. Krauss, "The Originality of the Avant-Garde," *October* 18 (fall 1981), p. 66.

33. Jacques Lacan, "Television," ed. Joan Copjec, *October* 40 (spring 1987), pp. 53–54.

34. Slavoj, Žižek, *Looking Awry* (Cambridge: MIT Press, 1991).

35. According to Žižek, popular cultural texts show that we "always find ourselves in the same position from which we tried to escape, which is why, instead of running after the impossible, we must learn to consent to our common lot and to find pleasure in the trivia of our everyday life." *Looking Awry,* p. 8.

36. R. Krauss, "The Cultural Logic of the Late Capitalist Museum," *October* 54, (fall 1990), p. 12.

37. Promoted from "the ranks," as it were, since a former student of Krauss's.

38. Hal Foster, "Postmodernism in Parallax," *October* 63 (winter 1993), pp. 16, 19.

39. M. Foucault, Language, *Counter-Memory, Practice* (Ithaca, NY: Cornell University Press, 1997), pp. 119–20; Hal Foster, "What's Neo about the Neo-Avant Garde?," *October* 70 (fall, 1994).

40. Rosalind Krauss, "Nostalgie de la Boue," *October* 56 (spring 1991), p. 111.

41. Ibid., p. 112.

42. Ibid., p. 113.

43. Ibid., pp. 118–19.

44. J. Baudrillard, *Selected Writings,* ed. Mark Poster (Stanford: Stanford University Press, 1988), p. 138. E. Lunn, *Marxism and Modernism* (Berkeley and Los Angeles: University of California Press, 1982), p. 57.

45. Krauss, "Nostalgie," p. 119.

46. *October* is fixated on Walter Benjamin to the extent that it was insisted that "our tradition is Surrealist." Hal Foster, "The Archive without Museums," *October* 77 (summer 1996), p. 118.

47. Rosalind Krauss, "Welcome to the Cultural Revolution," *October* 77 (summer 1996), p. 85.

48. Foster, "Death in America," p. 55.

49. Foster, "Postmodernism in Parallax," p. 20.

50. Is this the place to suggest that "trauma" should be studied as an index of new academic money-making schemes coming out of many different disciplines, including psychology, media studies, history departments, etc.? That "trauma" is a good resource for scholarly "pitches" to all sorts of funding agencies?

51. Paul de Man, *Aesthetic Ideology* (Minneapolis: University of Minnesota Press, 1996), p. 134.

52. Ibid., 137.

How French Is It?

ANDREA LOSELLE

> The arrival of new theories from France every few years
> has posed problems of assimilation. Investing time and
> effort learning a new theory may seem to be a waste of
> time if it is shortly to become outmoded. . . . Traffic is
> virtually one-way: French theorists pay almost no heed
> to British and American ones.
>
> —*John A. Walker and Sarah Chaplin,* Visual Culture

My introduction to French theory was as an undergraduate in a small alternative college during the late 70s and early 80s. As fresh translations of Barthes, Derrida, Lacan, Foucault, Kristeva, Althusser, Deleuze and Guattari, and others bombarded the American academic scene, everyone, or so it seemed, was enthusiastically taking up the new vocabulary of *traces, supplements, nonclosure, deferral, différance, epistemes, alterity*—all in the sincere effort to ferret out suspicious ontologies and binary oppositions. I was a philosophy major interested in not only these new theories coming out of France but also Marcel Proust. What then were my career options? No serious philosophy department would accept me into its graduate program without a strong grounding in Anglo-American analytic philosophy. My best option was French literature.

If French theory found a home in literature departments, it was because it gave to literature a special status as the most transgressive of discourses, the one that annoyingly disrupts the neat line drawn between fictional and nonfictional statements. Even though institutional, disciplinary boundaries founded on this division continue to be debated in the context of interdisciplinary and cultural studies, waning enthusiasm for French theory and widespread hostility to its theories of undecidability and indeterminacy have altered how literary studies are regarded. They have been charged with paradoxically overessentializing their object of study, language itself. At the same time, this backlash against theories of language has led the way to the rethinking of literary studies as a Europeanized "high culture" that has traditionally excluded other popular, hybrid, colonial and postcolonial literatures, women and gay writers, and so on.

Deconstruction became "de-con," as though it were a brand of roach poison. Jacques Derrida, singled out as the one responsible for disseminating post-structuralism's most pernicious strain of obfuscatory prose, was familiarly referred to as Derridoodle or by those who really resented his work as Derridoodoo. The attempts to put this proper name in its place testify to a need to neutralize deconstruction by emulating the movement's penchant for wordplay in a mutual, anxiety-ridden chuckle over Derrida's logorrhea. And yet, it cannot be reasonably maintained that the interpretative frameworks and approaches generated by French theory have not been digested and recycled. Acknowledgments abound; the "classics" of French theory reside now in footnotes and lists of secondary sources. The consequences of its noisy exorcism versus its relatively quiet absorption in the United States today cannot be assessed without some consideration of the main disciplinary context in which it once thrived. A certain identity crisis occurred in literary studies, causing some reflection on the point of literary criticism. One could either revert to a more traditional model of scholarly research or find another approach such as gender studies, postcolonial studies, or the new historicism, offering a chance to look at seemingly more relevant realities of (mis)representation. It was perhaps inevitable that Derrida's stunning critiques of Western logocentrism would later come back to haunt him in attacks on his apparent Eurocentrism, attacks that have occasioned more recent reflections on poststructuralism, colonialism, and the "other" by this same philosopher.[1]

I often "do" French theory without saying so; I avoid its distinctive terminology in the context of a discipline that once welcomed French theory and still refers to it but without its distinctive "style," the very butt of those anti-Derrida puns. Certain terms have, of course, survived. Camille Paglia, a critic gone public with her vitriolic attacks on "French-infatuated ideologues," applies the verb "to deconstruct" to praise Allen Ginsberg's howls at institutional authority.[2] *Deconstruction* is a safe word as long as it conforms to one of two possible meanings: aesthetic subversion, which is generally the artist's job, or sound literary explication, the critic's job. But the stylistic and terminological subversions of an unreformed deconstruction—that is, a name that popularly designated a diversity of theories from France—are today anathema. The failure to make one's ideas comprehensible to the reader, a charge equated with a lack of accessibility in one's prose, is justification enough for a quick dismissal of one's work as academic elitism. The gradual suppression of not so much French theory itself but its style or poetics occurs in the name of a moral obligation to one's reader. This suppression leaves theory an unquoted secondary source, with literature remaining a primary source, a potential vehicle to the conceptual and cultural, rather than an important category of pure representation that given certain (alas!) French, theoretical interventions can problematize the demand for aesthetic satisfaction and epistemological truth in the literary text itself.

What stands out is French theory's (that is, certain of its representatives') underlying desire to make of its own critical interpretations a form of literature, a style inseparable from the concepts it employed. American adherents tended to delight in this feature of much French theoretical language from Derridian word-play to Baudrillardian hyperbole. Everyone involved in French theory and literary criticism learned to some extent its poetics by playing with words, "unpacking" and splicing them with dashes and slashes. Roger Shattuck has observed that there is one major distinction between French and English: "This is, on the one hand, the reliance of English on the passive voice, and, on the other hand, the reliance of French on reflexive forms."[3] Of course the reflexive forms in French did not necessarily become in English those dreaded passive structures we are taught to avoid, but strange active structures in which texts do things to themselves that as inanimate objects they cannot do. (One wonders if there is a connection between this and one of the favored figures of the theorists of rhetoric [Paul de Man, Hillis Miller]: prosopoeia.) It seemed that too many native English speakers writing on or applying French theories were sounding a lot like French philosophers in translation, endlessly "turning back on themselves."[4] Critics have condemned the style as not only unidiomatic but also profoundly unpleasurable.

Looking over many of the essays and books from the golden age of theory in Franco-American translation I am struck by how remote the word games feel today; how, say, Geoffrey Hartman's enthusiastic statements in *Criticism in the Wilderness* (1980) that "literary criticism is *now* crossing over into literature . . . literary commentary *today* is creating texts—a literature—of its own" amounts to a historic instance of a critic's famous last words.[5] The failure of French theory to become a literature (if only because we do not read it anymore as such, but as a dead idiom) also recalls the paradox that such attempts at stylistic innovation were almost always articulated against the lure of sensory pleasure in language. If the lesson drawn from this language that both sustained and crossed the line between the uncertainty of epistemological claims to truth (killjoy) and the lure of aesthetic satisfaction (play) has become internalized, it is also deemed a mere side issue, just another one of those textual paradoxes, in light of other critical commitments to assessing more concrete subject positions, identities, marginalized literatures, globalization, border crossings, alternative curricula involving other media, and so on. Critic and artist now seem more than ever separate entities insofar as each employs a different performative language.

Reflecting on the purging of this distinctive poetics would thus also require a look at how French theory has influenced other later theoretical approaches, departures, and resistances such as new historicism; postmodernism; and cultural, gender, and postcolonial studies. I have chosen new historicism, an American invention, as my primary example in the second half of this essay because its proponents do openly acknowledge their debt to French theorists and because the object of study is mainly literary. But first, I will look at how French theory has become a cultural, historical artifact in the United States through the language in which it has been most widely available, English.

French theory in translation presents from the start a complicated picture of cultural and linguistic difference and resistance at the same time that its concepts are separated from the language in which they were originally expressed. What it has been charged with lacking, both in translation and in the original (culture, politics, history), does not prevent it from referring constantly to what it lacks in translation. For it refers to not just its original language but more specifically its own language-specific poetics, a condition that heightens the reader's awareness of language(s) as difference. Thinking about this aspect of French theory now, as French and other language departments debate the advantages and disadvantages of teaching courses in translation with the aim of broadening their curricula in programs of multicultural and interdisciplinary studies, offers the possibility of assessing the charge of poststructuralism's presumed refusal to privilege aesthetic pleasure, history, politics, or culture as that which perhaps most needs real historical and cultural contextualization. But such a possibility seems from the outset foreclosed by the words *French theory* as though all the different theories and approaches emanating from France for a period of three decades form an unadulterated unitary object that did not mutate through contact with other disciplines, cultures, and the arts. One hardly need point out the edgy exclusionary function of *French*.

At the same time, the title of this collection of essays, "French Theory in America," if it recalls for some a luxury import, borders more on a personification of "Frenchness," a cultured traveler to that mythic, ahistorical, promised land of America (not the United States). It brings to mind those visiting French philosophers on American campuses—not necessarily the native professors and students who adapted theories to their own intellectual interests—as well as cultural and institutional practices. A certain ambiguous Frenchness comes before the American reception of French theory, a reception that originally had very little to do with the distinctive cultural aroma of the theories coming from this country. (What sense would it make to take on a theoretical approach because it is French?) The assertions in my epigraph, for example, want there to be cultural borders, for if traffic is one-way it is the fault of the French for being, well, *French*; that is, for apparently showing no interest in American or British theorists. And it is our responsibility to recognize that, in the absence of fair trade, "assimilation" of new French theories may have to be sacrificed for practicality's sake. This strange bitterness over French lack of interest calls for setting up our own borders to regulate the influx of exclusivity. Even worse, the French produce too many "new" theories too rapidly. It implies a lack of stability in which the more theories there are the less value any single one has. A "new" theory is just another theory, arbitrary when cut off from its sources and let loose to wander onto the American scene. Absent from this characterization of French theory is consideration of the conditions of assimilation (linguistic, institutional, cultural) that allowed it to take root in the first place and to such an extent that it lives on as a less celebrated and more contested feature of academic production.

Thus one reason why I look back on my "formation," as the French say, is to recall the specific connection between this continental philosophy and its original language—that is, my introduction to it was in translation but it (and Proust) led me to the more complete acquisition of French. This acquisition of a foreign language and literature can also be seen as one of the major contributions of French theory in the United States. It had much to do with how French theory was published in translation. For how many contemporary philosophers and theorists, like Derrida, can boast of bilingual editions of their texts? Back then, quotations appeared more frequently—in translation and in the original, both on the same page. Translated words or phrases were almost obsessively accompanied by their original renderings in brackets. Long footnotes were generated to explain the complexities of the meaning of a single word in a foreign language. The functions of critic and translator were more visibly intertwined. What accounted for this excessive bi-, tri-, multilingualism, the attention to the subtle shades of meaning a single word in a foreign language has but for which there is no equivalent in English and without which one was forever being warned of misconstruing a key concept? "[A]ll too often," writes Derrida, "[theories of translation] treat the passing from one language to another and do not sufficiently consider the possibility for languages to be implicated more *than two* in a text."[6] Or in the words of the late Eugenio Donato, "Language has too much reality of its own to be the speechless accomplice of the philosopher."[7] It was this single-minded concentration on language in a multilingual context that gave rise to a theoretical poetics and turned each act of translation into an automatic commentary on the impossibility of treating French theoretical texts (*any* text, for that matter) as mere cognitive assertions. What this extraordinary attention to exact, exegetical detail did not foresee, however, was the problematic status of the "original," and the power it had to make the translations—and by extension the American reception itself of French theory—seem to critics mere copies of the theories. Although the translations themselves set off intellectual currents independent of the originals and inspite of pretensions to linguistic nonassimilation, this originality with an origin could also turn its American counterpart into unoriginal thinkers on the ever-grateful receiving end. It accounts for why it is so easy to castigate American theorists as "French infatuated ideologues." From this perspective, America was colonized in the 70s and 80s by French theory. Such spatial thinking turns former productive border crossings into pretexts for reestablishing borders in which traffic can only be one-way—that is, subservient. It preempts other, less subservient ways of thinking about French theory here in the name of reproducing that idealized image of the credentialed liberal humanist whose American pragmatic sensibility would bestow upon the reader the gift of meaning.

Translation serves as a model that goes beyond more traditional theories of the practice. The presumed hierarchical relationship between original and translation, implications of cultural, political inferiority and superiority (which texts get translated in which languages, "one-way" transmissions or "Europe is the home of the canonical originals"),[8] complicity with canon formation ("great books" courses)—these issues all play a role in what has been called the "shameful history of translation.[9] It is not coincidental that translation studies have experienced in recent years a significant revival spurred by research in "transnational" literatures and postcolonialism as well as heated debates concerning the curricular value of teaching literary texts in translation.[10] While much research and discussion have been going on in these areas, French theory itself has been undergoing a number of more figurative translations.

Again, French theory's endless meditations on multiple meanings of words, whether in French, German, or English (for these were the dominant, albeit Eurocentric, institutional languages), tended to resist commentary on the quintessential cultural, aesthetic feel of words and themes in texts. It is noteworthy, however, that a number of older, important essays on translation (texts that were also key sources for structuralist and poststructuralist theories of translation) tend to use as examples names of those satisfying basic foods common to many cultures, such as bread in Walter Benjamin's "The Task of the Translator" or cheese in Roman Jakobson's "On Linguistic Aspects of Translation," to point out a fundamental, cultural untranslatability from one language to another, and a classic problem of meaning. If *bread* in English calls up certain connotations contained within that language and not in another, then the translation of the French word *pain* into that language will fail to do full justice to the flavor of French bread, from its delicate crustiness to its cultural meanings. Commenting on Benjamin's essay, Paul De Man has explained why one may find an absence of cultural, hermeneutic aroma in deconstructive criticism: there is a fundamental disjunction between the meaning of the word (intent) and how the word arrives at meaning (poetics). The two approaches, he argues, are not compatible in that to stress one leaves out the other—usually poetics. To have to explain the difference between *bread* and *pain* kills the poetics of the original, shows the latter to have been open from the very beginning to a certain instability that is in language itself. From a more pragmatic point of view, however, a translator interested in capturing the cultural flavor of French bread might opt for a word more descriptive of the Frenchness of the bread—say, *baguette*—sacrificing poetics for the edibly recognizable. It is a synecdoche not functioning as the failure to mean *pain* in English, but as the part's success in accessing a hermeneutic whole of Frenchness. Or, as Paul Valéry bluntly stated, translations are "anatomical specimens. . . . Their number multiplied by the teaching profession, which claims them as *food* for what is known as the 'Curriculum.'"[11] A specimen also functions as a synecdoche, a part that is representative of a whole or class in which we apprehend the original in the literal artifact, the example. A text can become, then, a nourishing cultural object.

Much rewording has also been going on since poststructuralism's decline, a drifting from the "original" poetics of poststructuralism itself that alters the terms in which we are allowed to refer to it and texts. French theory can become French or become history, and be disciplined in the (now more literalized) original. Culture sets up the obstacle of essence in which the focus on what is untranslatable initiates a series of ethical approximations that defer those indigestible remnants of rhetoric and grammar studied by deconstruction's hunger artists. It is the instructive example of another's "daily bread," pedagogical nourishment when instructors feed students bitesized "original" truths of the foreign. But translation studies also play another role when they expose the values underlying the target language—in this case, idiomatic English. Hyperfidelity to the original language in American deconstructive criticism and translations has fallen prey to what appears to be inherent in French theory's own faithfulness to language: it has been accused of endorsing rather than rendering visible hierarchical relationships between original and translation, instructor and student, Europe and the United States. It becomes academic elitism to those who consider that fidelity a sign of unidiomatic, un-American scholarly activity out of line with communicating the right values to the reader and the student, values that tend to support a more efficient communicability of difference. If deconstructive translation has given way to a false clarity of expression, a translation (not recognized as such, a rewording) adapted to an audience's expectations, it has also shown itself to be adaptable to what Roman Jakobson has labeled *inter-semiotic translation*: the transmutation of linguistic signs into systems of nonlinguistic signs as French theory migrates to other areas such as architecture and design. The irony is that those (mainly in cultural studies) who have criticized "high" theory in literary studies as elitist have also absorbed its lessons, and have treated everyday objects, architectural and geographical space, cultural practices, the popular, bodies, and other phenomena as "texts" that are equally subject to interpretation.

But as I mentioned before, a lot of us in literary studies continue to use French theory without always explicitly pointing to the fact. The question is how its current use functions under the regime of accessibility. For the exorcism of the style has also struck at the heart of literature itself as a traditional discipline concerning authors, periods, a set of genres and forms, and so on, for all interesting texts, whether canonical or minoritarian, literary or critical, harbor the germ of difficulty. Literary texts can, however, be innoculated by contextualizing them so that they will not exceed their cultural and historical conditions of production. More emphasis is placed now on content than on style, on situating the text in a context than on calling attention to its literariness. Literary studies have been "translated" too, so that they can, at least, coexist as narratives with a more visually, technologically based culture in the present. For literature and the private act of reading, a seemingly highbrow, stubborn reliance on the old fashioned book, cannot compete with contemporary, hip, visually based forms; its presumed elitism cannot be made to coincide with contemporary interest in popular culture (a tendency toward collective presentism) and the politics that grounds that critical interest. It would seem that literature's survival would depend on wedding itself to history, it being itself both history and material of history.[12] This is the new status of the original insofar as history is believed to be more original than representation, and which enables readers to articulate literature's relevance in relation to (that is, as a difference with) current critical and ideological practices. And it explains, in part, why advocacy for teaching literature in translation means more than the innocent wish to share a greater diversity of cultural perspectives with English speakers. The original is more weighed down by its chronological place in time and its pure foreignness, whereas its translation is not, for the existence of first, second, or third translations of works indicates the possibility of revision, which is addressed more to a present readership than to posterity.[13] Translation studies are anchored in their own contemporaneity when they ask that readers unveil in the language of the translation itself (not in that of the dated otherness of the original) hegemonic assumptions and values of this culture in old and new translations. Reading, language, and the book, when considered artifacts of a historical materialism, also manifest new partisan borders (and new technical horizons) that are being erected in the name of crossing cultural borders on American terrain (i.e., a translational *imaginaire*).[14]

Translation serves as a good metaphor for French theory's absorption and exclusion in the United States, in part because of this relationship with time. It is similar to what Foucault, in "What Is an Author?" has called *transdiscursivity*, the term itself having also been taken up by translation theorists to describe discursive migrations such as the adoption of English words and phrases in another language.[15] Foucault's notion of transdiscursivity differs fundamentally, however, in that a discursive movement is launched by a "founder" (that is, by a very rare kind of author; Freud and Marx are Foucault's examples). A discursive movement is then the afterlife of a founder's discourse, a proliferation of related discourses, transformations, and deviations. While it may be stretching it to give to any single French theorist the status of founder, it is interesting the extent to which French theory in general has spawned a certain interlinguistic and intersemiotic transdiscursivity by virtue of itself performing one of the tests of true discursivity: if one can return to a founder's discourse, as French theorists have done repeatedly in their readings, one can create new departures from it. "I believe," Foucault writes, "that in this way [by returning to the beginning] one can designate a movement which has its own specificity and which accurately characterizes the establishment of a discursivity. In order for there to be a return, in effect, it is first necessary for there to have been a departure, not an accidental loss, not a confusion through some kind of misunderstanding, but an essential omission. The art of establishing a discourse is such, in effect, that in its own essence even, it can be forgotten."[16] But if French theory—a "discourse" that has no single founder—it cannot make a claim to establishing a discursivity, it has gone beyond being merely influential. As part of a larger transdiscursivity, French theory cannot be ignored. Its lessons have been absorbed whereas its style, its commitment to language, and its vocabulary have been suppressed or reworded. The art of establishing a discourse comes about, then, through the simultaneous dating of French theory's historical moment (return) and an interpretation (an essential variation and violation). Such interpretation, like translation, domesticates in present terms the radical, provocative language (founding metaphors and instabilities) of a theoretical discourse.

A good example of such transdiscursivity is the new historicism, which got its start in the field of English Renaissance literature in the early 80s. The movement owes something to French theory, and, as it has been repeatedly observed, to Foucault's work in particular. The acknowledgment of this debt comes up in Stephen Greenblatt's essay on the new historicism, "Towards a Poetics of Culture."[17] I refer to this essay, which is the first in a collection of twenty essays by scholars writing in the new historicist vein, because it was Greenblatt who by his own admission accidentally launched the movement, and who in this essay wishes to explain how it happened, what the approach is (or perhaps rather is not), and his own position in relation to French theory as well as other theories. New historicism's sudden birth or departure, and the subsequent need to explain it is therefore also a retrospective response to theoretical influence—that is, a fundamental disengagement from it. Its difference with French theory is set up on the one hand as a reluctance "to enroll . . . in one or the other of the dominant theoretical camps" (Greenblatt 1) and, on the other, as a submission to the pressure of an implied demand for accessibility. When Veeser's introduction to the same volume of essays forthrightly concludes that "readers will be pleased to find that the contributors to this book have written in accessible language, clearly summarizing the issues raised by new historicism and explaining the debates within and around it" (xvi), the anticipated sigh of relief signals a final purging of the prolix prose of a Foucault or the microscopic word splitting of a Derrida. The reluctance to enroll in any of the dominant theoretical camps functions moreover to preempt closer examination of that which is presumed to have been ossified into a number of easily identifiable warring parties. The setting up of theoretical approaches in this manner submits them to the diplomatic mission of new historicism (one of the movement's by-laws is negotiation). The new historicism then plays a nonpartisan role that in effect summarizes them as extremist positions in need of some common-sense mediation. Greenblatt will carry out this mission in his essay when he selects the opposing interpretations of capitalism by Fredric Jameson and Jean-François Lyotard, deftly summarizing their theoretical positions, and reducing them to a working binary opposition: totalization (Jameson) versus differentiation (Lyotard).

Thus Greenblatt is careful to say that the new historicism, because of its accidental nature, is not a doctrine but a practice and as such cannot be defined. But it can be situated. One crucial situation responsible for how this new approach came into being was "the presence of Michel Foucault on the Berkeley campus for extended visits during the last five or six years of his life. . ." (1). Foucault's contribution to the shaping of Greenblatt's critical practice appears here as a physical presence at a particular historical moment brought to decisive closure by this person's literal death in 1984. His organic presence on an American campus, a situation, substitutes in a way for his actual work, his death thus a point of departure for a transdiscursive appropriation. Although one may argue whether or not Foucault has been comfortably incorporated into the circulatory system of the new historicism and its politics of power, it is not just his discourse that underlies in some forgotten way the new historicism. Other discourses are being repressively remembered. Derrida plays a small but significant role in Greenblatt's essay; his work may haunt the new historicism in a way that cannot be forgotten in that he occupies the singular position of an ambivalent secondary source. Whereas Foucault's presence is physically outside the text, this is significantly not the case for the presence of Derrida in this essay, to whom is granted another status not designated by time, place, or text when Greenblatt says "my use of the term circulation here is influenced by the work of Jacques Derrida, but sensitivity to the practical strategies of negotiation and exchange depends less upon poststructuralist theory than upon the circulatory rhythms of American politics" (8). Greenblatt's reference is not an essential omission but an open annulment. Fueling the sentence's logic is an internal judgment contained in the words *sensitivity* and *practical*. Derrida's "work" in general lacks a certain sensitivity to American political practicality, and cannot be incorporated because his work is not dependent on capitalist circulatory "rhythms." The author's use of the term *circulation* owes itself therefore to that which confirms the importance of borrowing, or acknowledging an influence in order to acknowledge in turn the "signs of the legal and economic system" (7) that paradoxically usurp and replace Derrida's authorship of a concept called circulation. That is perhaps why, despite his insistence on the importance of the notion that "the capitalist aesthetic demands acknowledgments—hence the various marks of property rights that are flashed on the screen or inscribed in a text" (7), Greenblatt has unconsciously singled out Derrida as the one reference undeserving of a footnote indicating where specifically or in what context he picked up the concept of circulation (he is quite conscientious in providing bibliographic data for his other references). There is a certain irony in this omission when we recall how much of Derrida's work has been devoted to the idea of the debt—for example his reading in *La carte postale* of Freud's symptomatic refusal to acknowledge his debt to Nietzsche, that phobic object-to-be-avoided. It is also true, however, that Derridian terminology has tended to circulate quite freely, that is, transdiscursively. One does not always need to cite a specific source when one uses the term *différance*. It belongs to public domain.

Greenblatt's avowed sensitivity to practical strategies finds its cogency in distinctly historical terms, supported by his background and other data in his essay that refer back to the English Renaissance and its historical links to American capitalism, such as a reference to proper names and tax law used earlier on in refutation of Lyotard's philosophy of proper names and the *différend*. In this latter instance, Greenblatt disagrees with Lyotard's statement that capitalism "wants a single language and a single network. . . ." For Greenblatt, proper names are not just the "products of property" (5). Names are forged "in the market place and in the state apparatus linked to the circulation and accumulation of capital" (5). They are at once the property we have in ourselves (individualism) and the means by which the state taxes our property and income. Lyotard's point of the *différend*, however, is that one's name could mean different things in different phrase regimes, with each assigned, instituted meaning the potential dispossession or exclusion of other meanings (such as those that might have been Marxist, or the notion that one's subjectivity does not count when the IRS demands that one declare all income in one's name). Proper names also become the property of scholars in other phrase regimes. Lyotard observed that "one striking feature of philosophical discourse in most of the forms it borrows . . . is that it avoids on principle, any use of proper names in its arguments. The names of authorities and adversaries that nevertheless remain persist only as the names of arguments."[18] Greenblatt's names are names of arguments by the adversaries Jameson and Lyotard. What makes them all the more tellingly adversarial is their very foreignness to American politics and to capitalist aesthetics because they do not, or they refuse to, consider capitalism a more "complex social and economic development in the West." Greenblatt replicates Lyotard's argument that "[p]roper names are indeed, if not passages, then at least points of contact between heterogeneous regimes."[19] If new historicism is to come into its own as a theoretical practice, if it is to be instituted, other heterogeneous arguments need to be pushed to the borders, such as those of Jameson and Lyotard. The meanings attached to these proper names can at the same time be cited as points of contact and dismissed since within the phrase regime of capitalist aesthetics no wrong will have been discerned as a wrong demonstrably suffered in other terms. Unlike the term *circulation*, the proper name remains untranslatable, a little point of resistance, a marker to be dealt with.[20] We recall that in Derrida's words the proper name is by definition "the reference of a pure signifier to a single being."[21] But such a rogue word poses problems beyond this classic definition. It has other uses in different contexts, such as that which dispenses with it in a way that Greenblatt forbids Lyotard's reading of names as an argument. The point here is that for Greenblatt, proper names must conform to a social system of indebtedness; if they do not conform, then they have violated a law that is essentially performative. They cannot be considered in other separate ways inasmuch as their use on a list for property taxation entails that they play the game of circulation, of negotiation and exchange, of speculating, and of assigning value. The theoretical economy of an argument that inflates proper names beyond their role in capitalist aesthetics is ill-suited to that which grounds names in the historical beginnings of capitalism.

The backlash against French theory does not therefore always find its impetus exclusively in the fact that it is French; it is un-American because it denies the meaning of, for example, the development of capitalism in the United States. And meaning is provided for, predictably, by reference to history and origins. For Camille Paglia, "Lacan was a psychoanalyst, untrained in history"; "Derrida is a Heideggerian philosopher who has convinced gullible academics that there is no meaning or order in history"; and "Foucault was a radical professor of modern intellectual history who was ignorant of anything before the Enlightenment and outside of France."[22] Greenblatt does not accuse Lyotard of ignorance but criticizes his presentation of historical revisionist Robert Faurisson's sophistic demand for witnesses of gas chambers "as a convenient anecdotal ornament upon a theoretical structure." Lyotard's argument, he contends, does not outline an epistemological dilemma but is a clear historical problem concerning the facts themselves.[23]

Although it is impossible to rehearse here the complexities of Lyotard's entire argument, some clarification is needed, first, because the immediate problem for Lyotard is not so much historical (a question once again of dating) as it is an ongoing question of proof or, as Lyotard puts it, the rules of cognition. Whereas Greenblatt cites the historical evidence of meticulous record keeping by the Nazis to question Lyotard's "theoretical satisfaction" with the difficult questions of witnessing and historical revisionism, Lyotard addresses an ongoing *current* minority interpretation. Greenblatt does not answer how despite the overwhelming and true evidence of the existence of gas chambers (a fact not in dispute either here or in Lyotard), a Faurisson is possible, how indeed, historical revisionism both there *and* here persists. He merely wishes to dismiss the phenomenon of historical revisionism as wrong, a perverted attempt on the part of one of its adherents to wish away evidence. Second, Faurisson is not Lyotard's principle exhibit of "this attempt by capital to institute a single language," a statement that appears several pages later in Lyotard's essay. The context here suggests that revisionists like Faurisson present themselves as victims of a wrong (one that Lyotard describes as "threatening") for which they cannot provide empirical proof, but not because the regime that does not recognize their idiom and under which they present their wrong happens to be capitalist; it could have been another one, one in which the wrong is presented by another group. "Taken to the extreme, this threat of a wrong promises to strike from history and from the map entire worlds of names: extermination of the Communards, extermination of counter-revolutionaries, extermination of the Armenians. The final solution."[24] Lyotard's reference to these heterogeneous historical exterminations is neither anecdotal nor ornamental. Nor does he conflate capitalism with fascism, as Greenblatt asserts. Lyotard differentiates them, citing capitalism as a prevailing phrase regime whose single language requires no translation: money. If Lyotard's respect for history has been placed into question, the name that he gave to capital's nondifferentiated, "indifferent" language—money—is not raised once by Greenblatt.

History perhaps supplements the indifference of money in the circulatory system of capitalist aesthetics because it gives it a narrative anchor. That is also perhaps why history is a key word especially where it concerns language and meaning and the limited areas of expertise to which Paglia relegates French theorists. Interestingly, Paglia views them as pure capitalists, entrepreneurial strip miners of nineteenth-century German scholarship and American humanist erudition. "Company men," she calls them. "[L]ily-livered, trash-talking foreign junk-bond dealers . . . plastic Ken dolls, beady-eyed, greedy, cutthroat," with "souls of accountants."[25] French theorists and their American disciples are depicted as so many rip-off artists who approach "art like a business deal" and are on the lookout to sell us a false bill of goods, or the biggest rip-off of them all, the signifier cut off from reference. If the evil capitalist is the "spinsterish," "timorous" American nerd boondoggled by history-ignorant French theorists, perhaps there is a good capitalist who understands the importance of history as capital, heritage, scholarly tradition, American erudition, as a high-minded discourse that stands at odds with Paglia's 60s revolutionary idealism of the body.

French theory is open to seemingly contradictory charges. Greenblatt can chide Lyotard for his monological, unrealistic view of American capitalism at the same time that Paglia can berate French theorists as covert supercapitalists who killed the 60s. What accounts for the difference is perhaps a confusion over temporal, cultural borders, French theorists hemmed in by their own cultural politics now or French imperialists transgressing our borders back when the movement started. It is important to recall that Greenblatt's essay begins by passing in review the new historicism's popular (circulating), postdeconstruction contemporaneity: "there are articles about it," he writes, "attacks on it, references to it in dissertations . . ." (1). Greenblatt's reading of Lyotard's reference to the revisionist Faurisson—a subject upon which one is called to make a stand concerning its conclusions by dating it with the facts but not with revisionism's continuing status in France, here, and elsewhere—may, however, also intersect with the tendentious link that was made between deconstruction as a whole and collaboration with Nazis at the time of the revelations of Paul de Man's wartime journalism; if, that is, one reads Lyotard's remarks as irresponsible consideration of a notorious quack or as a senseless pondering of historical facts. Although Greenblatt's article appeared in print during the heat of the debates on de Man's past, it was in fact written at least two years before the Occupation articles written for *Le Soir* (*volé*) came to light. Compounded by the slightly earlier debates surrounding Heidegger's fascist politics and Derrida's own debt to the philosopher's work, deconstruction and fascism were, however, conflated, and "French theory in America" never quite recovered from this charge. Attempts to get out from under the pall cast by the debates of 1988–89 lock one into endless justifications and corrections. The more one tries to disentangle deconstruction from the events and aftermath of World War II, the more one reinforces an imaginary context (such as that which I imagined for Greenblatt's article) in which French theory is no longer coherently contextualizable here in the United States. And the more it is thought to be bogged down by this history the more its consideration becomes an ethical question. It becomes tainted French stuff, or it is relegated to what some regard as the remnant heap of old-fashioned, European gentlemanly scholarship. Paglia's article, for all its outrageous misrepresentations and nostalgic idealism, strikes a refreshing note that pits the psychedelic 60s against the French 70s in the United States. By looking back on these two decades as particular idioms that seem opposed and yet bear some relation, it offers the possibility of other more productively cross-cultural ways to examine the dichotomy between undecidability and aesthetic pleasure endlessly played out in the post-70s reception and resistance to French theory.[26]

The scenario offered by the new historicism in the wake of the French theory movement tells another tale about literary studies today. A reactive return to separating the function of the critic (preventing his or her work from becoming a literature) from that of the artist is not what is in question. Functionalism itself blurs the difference between artist and critic in a way Hartman did not foresee in his essay of 1980. Artists negotiate with society and are extended "lines of credit": to achieve this, "artists need to create a currency that is valid for a meaningful, mutually profitable exchange" (Greenblatt, p. 12). Such profit is "pleasure and interest." Greenblatt tells us that we must understand this recent theoretical work of the new historicism as a search for new terms, that is, metaphors such as "currency," to understand the cultural phenomena associated with negotiation and exchange. The new terms are quite old mechanisms—metaphors themselves being complicitous as a form of verbal exchange—that buttress a reformist academic ethos. This recycling of the fetishes, myths, spectacles, phantasmagoria, and simulacra, as we attempt to discern the real and its collapse into fiction by looking for a new vocabulary, is not very new. As Derrida explains, "*L'emprunt* est la loi. . . . puisqu'une figure est toujours un langage d'emprunt, mais aussi d'un domaine discursif à l'autre. . . . L'emprunt rapporte, il produit la plus-value, il est le premier moteur de tout investissement. . . . Et toutes ces 'métaphores' confirment, à titre de métaphores, la nécessité de ce qu'elles disent."[27] Historical documentation, literature, and philosophy become secondary sources to a primary text/language called capitalist aesthetics. Greenblatt does not refute Lyotard; he confirms the argument that "capital accommodates them all *[différends]*, transforming them one by one into litigations that are judged according to the criteria of performativity."[28]

The operations of negotiation and exchange in the context of literary studies could alternatively be called narrative enactments. Something happens between the text and its historical, social context, that something being the thing to which the text not only owes its existence but which makes it indebted to its narrative context. Most telling is that crucial shift in terms made by Greenblatt in his conclusion: where he tells us what we must do to "chart the relationship between art and society," he shifts abruptly to telling us what the artist must achieve— create the currency so that there will be exchanges. In order for the new historicist to carry out his work, the artist must first perform her function of indebtedness to society, and in doing so also serve the critic equally indebted. Greenblatt's discourse embeds the author in a narrative context that is redemptive. "Narrative," writes Lyotard, "is perhaps the genre of discourse within which the heterogeneity of phrase regimens, and even the heterogeneity of genres of discourse, have the easiest time passing unnoticed."[29] Context, history, and conventions extend a line of credit inasmuch as these communicate with a public that assigns value in its pleasure or interest.

How then does the critic who translates this negotiation perceive her own negotiations, that is, labor? One must defer (economic) death or the end of negotiation and exchange by negating empty time (neg-otium), by making pleasure useful and instructive. Translational transdiscursivity may also occur within an accelerating system of exchanges. Greenblatt shows the symptoms of such acceleration when he characterizes modem capitalist aesthetics as a system that "oscillates so rapidly" (6) or as a "dizzying, seemingly inexhaustible circulation . . ." (8). Accessibility, an ethic that has reworded the interminability of poststructuralist poetics and its resistance to being put into translation as product, its value nothing but "currency," has a lot to do with time, with gaining time in the economic genre in which one's competency and productivity as a critic are determined by one's adeptness at discursive strategies of exchange.

To return to my epigraph, the "assimilation" of "new" French theories in the United States is also subjected to the economy of time by the terms *investing time*, *wasting time*, and *outmoded*. These telling terms do not demand of French theory that it submit to a policy of transnational assimilation as much as they place it in the temporally evanescent realm of fashion.[30] Our interest in their theories has been merely a passing trend. It seems easier to assign the globalizing rules of a capitalist aesthetics to French theory rather than to read it for its critique of those rules.

Notes

1. See, for example, *Le Monolinguisme de l'autre* (Paris: Galilee, 1996).
2. Camille Paglia, "Ninnies, Pedants, Tyrants and Other Academics," *New York Times Book Review*, May 5, 1991, pp. 1, 29, 33.
3. Roger Shattuck, "Artificial Horizon: Translator as Navigator," in *The Craft and Context of Translation*, ed. W. Arrowsmith and R. Shattuck (Austin: University of Texas Press, 1961), p. 146.
4. See, for example, Gerald Graff's comments on the "widely alleged mechanization of deconstructive readings this side of the Atlantic" that resulted in "a mode of reading that knows what texts are about before it reads them" in "Looking Past the de Man case," in *Responses: on Paul de Man's Wartime Journalism*, ed. W. Hamacher, N. Hertz, and T. Keenen (Lincoln: University of Nebraska Press, 1989), p. 253.
5. Geoffrey Hartman, *Criticism in the Wilderness* (New Haven: Yale University Press, 1980), p. 213; emphasis added.
6. Jacques Derrida, "Des tours de Babel," in *Difference in Translation*, ed. Joseph Graham (Ithaca, N.Y.: Cornell University Press, 1985), p. 222.
7. Eugenio Donato, "The Two Languages of Criticism," in *The Structuralist Controversy*, ed. R. Macksey and E. Donato (Baltimore: Johns Hopkins University Press, 1972), p. 91.
8. Charles Bernheimer, ed., *Comparative Literature in the Age of Multiculturalism* (Baltimore: Johns Hopkins University Press, 1995), p. 40.

9. Susan Bassnett and Harish Trivedi, eds., *Postcolonial Translation: Theory and Practice* (London: Routledge, 1999), p. 5.

10. See, for example, Lawrence Venuti, *The Scandals of Translation: Towards an Ethics of Difference* (1998); Susan Bassnett and Harish Trivedi, eds., *Post-Colonial Translation: Theory and Practice* (1999); Charles Bernheimer, ed., *Comparative Literature in the Age of Multiculturalism* (1995). The last reference consists of responses to the 1993 Bernheimer ACLA report on the state of comparative literature. While the report's statements supporting teaching more texts in translation tended to polarize respondents' positions on this issue, little was said about the report's assertion that translation studies and theory belong in the discipline of comparative literature: "In fact, translation can well be seen as a paradigm for larger problems of understanding and interpretation across different discursive traditions" (44); "Whenever they have knowledge of the original language, teachers in comparative literature courses should refer frequently to the original text of a work they assign in translation. Moreover, they should make discussion of the theory and practice of translation an integral part of these courses" (46–47). Similar assertions are made by Venuti in the context of English departments (1045). Giving translation theory a more central role in these two disciplines only makes foreign departments look more regressive than ever as they have tended to resist most the teaching of texts in translation. Comparative literature and English can, of course, more easily incorporate a mix of literatures in their programs. I am only questioning here the circular logic of an ethical stance that makes teaching in translation a virtue because the theories themselves show that the target language, English, does not do justice (ideologically, culturally, linguistically) to the original.

11. Paul Valery, "Variations on the Eclogues," in *Theories of Translation: An Anthology of Essays from Dryden to Derrida*, edited by R. Schulte and J. Biguenet (Chicago: University of Chicago Press, 1992), p. 116.

12. "After all, *No Respect* spans a history that included the last generation of American intellectuals to swear unswerving allegiance to the printed word and the dictates of European taste, and the first generations to use their involvement with popular culture as a site of contestation itself." See Andrew Ross, *No Respect: Intellectuals and Popular Culture* (New York: Routledge, 1989), p. 11. Ross's readings clearly historicize and render culturally foreign the printed word, today a "minority medium." Popular culture is active; it is a site of collective involvement that makes critical contestation more relevant. The printed word and "taste" as past intellectual values have become regressive, no longer involved with the real world insofar as they belong to the realm of private exclusivity, so exclusive that it is not even American.

13. As the following quotation suggests, translations are in need of periodic updating so that the language of both the translated and the original text will not fall "out of fashion," a situation that can also occur when the translator takes too literally the old idioms of the original: "Open the latest, 'modernized' reissue of *Les Miserables* and you will find, in every other paragraph, sentences such as this one about Napoleon: 'He had in his brains the cube of human faculties.' Undoubtedly, the routine discredit in which the novels of Victor Hugo now stand owes much to the bald transliteration of a rhetoric which could be out of fashion without seeming insane." See J. Barzun, "Food for the N.R.F. or 'My God, What Will You Have?'" *Partisan Review* November–December, 1953), p. 61.

14. "The material form that has constituted our object of study for centuries, the book, is in the process of being transformed through computer technology and the communications revolution. As a privileged locus for cross-cultural reflection, comparative literature should analyze the material possibilities of cultural expression, both phenomenal and discursive, in their different epistemological, economic, and political contexts. The wider focus involves studying not only the business of bookmaking but also the cultural place and function of reading and writing and the physical properties of newer communicative media" (Bernheimer *Comparative Literature*, p. 45).

15. See, for example, Clem Robyns's discussion of transdiscursive translation in "Translation and Discursive Identity," *Poetics Today* 15, no. 3 (fall 1994).

16. Michel Foucault, "What is an Author?" in *Language, Counter-Memory, Practice* (Ithaca, N.Y.: Cornell University Press, 1977), pp. 113–38.

17. Stephen Greenblatt, "Towards a Poetics of Culture," in *The New Historicism*, ed. A. Vesser (New York: Routledge, 1989). All page references to this essay will hereafter be given in the text.

18. Jean-François Lyotard, "Judiciousness in Dispute or Kant after Marx," in *The Lyotard Reader* (Oxford: Blackwell, 1989), p. 346.

19. Ibid., p. 356.

20. "The author's name plays a certain role in any discourse: it assumes a classificatory function; it allows us to group together a number of texts, to delimit them, to exclude others, and to contrast them with others."

21. Derrida, "Des Tours," p. 219.

22. Paglia, "Ninnies," p. 29.

23. "Faurisson complained that he had been lied to about the existence of gas chambers. To verify that a place is a gas chamber, he would only accept, he declared, 'a former prisoner capable of proving to me that he actually saw a gas chamber with his own eyes.' According to Faurisson, then, there can be no direct witness to a gas chamber other than its victim; and there can be no victim except a dead victim" (Lyotard, "Judiciousness," 352).

24. Ibid., p. 356.

25. Paglia, "Ninnies," pp. 29, 30.

26. Similarly, Lyotard asks, "what is the object of an Idea whose sign arose out of the 1968 movements to elicit the solidarity and enthusiasm of many people who had no stake in the events, and who were at a considerable remove from them? This object has not been elaborated reflexively. The movement has merely been explained; it has been placed, for judgment, under the regime of proof. The wrong to which it was perhaps trying to testify has not found its idiom" ("Judiciousness," p. 355).

27. Jacques Derrida, *La carte postale: de Socrate a Freud et au-dela* (Paris: flammarion, 1980), p. 410.

28. Lyotard, "Judiciousness," p. 356.

29. Jean-François Lyotard, *The Différend: Phrases in Dispute*, trans. G. van den Abbeele (Minneapolis: University of Minnesota Press, 1988), p. 151.

30. "Just as there are dress fashions, there are intellectual fashions. . . . It is not only academics who are conscious of intellectual trends. Some students are also fashion-

conscious: they demand an account of the latest theory and refuse to learn some-thing as fundamental as the Marxist critique of capitalism on the mistaken grounds that it is 'old-fashioned, out of date.'" John J. Walker and Sarah Chaplin, *Visual Culture:* An Introduction (Manchester: Manchester University Press, 1977), pp. 59–60.

Frenchifying Film Studies: Projecting Lacan onto the Feminist Scene

KRISS RAVETTO

> What are we going to do about Frenchspeak? Should we
> learn this new jargon-laden language, which is slowly in-
> filtrating the American scene through departments of
> French and comparative literature . . . ? The American
> Frenchspeak ghetto has complicated things by maintain-
> ing an elitist, separationist policy; initiation rites no longer
> are limited to a reading of Freud, Marx, and Saussure; now
> one must know Lacan, Althusser, and Derrida as well.
>
> —*Charles Altman,* "Psychoanalysis and Cinema"

> Form generally counts with us as a convention, as a vest-
> ment and disguise, and it is therefore, if not exactly hated,
> at any rate not loved; it would be even more correct to say
> that we have an extraordinary fear of the word "conven-
> tion" and, no doubt, also of the thing. It was this fear which
> led the German to desert the school of France: he wanted
> to become more natural and thereby more German. But
> this "thereby" seems to have been a miscalculation: es-
> caped from the school of convention, he then let himself
> go in whatever manner his fancy happened to suggest to
> him, and at bottom did no more than imitate in a slovenly
> and half-forgetful way what he had formerly imitated with
> scrupulous care and often with success. So it is that, com-
> pared with past ages, we dwell even today in a carelessly
> inaccurate copy of French convention.
>
> —*Friedrich Nietzsche,* "On the Uses and Disadvantages
> of History for Life"

It has not only been the French who proclaim to have invented the cinema (projecting the first films for mass audiences in 1895); shaped the practice of film crit-

icism and film history in the pages of *Positif, Cinémaction,* and *Cahiers du Cinéma*; created a language for film (*mise-en-scène, auteur, encouncé, jouissance, sujet, differance, appareils idéologiques d'Etat*); and provided its theoretical references (Jacques Lacan, Roland Barthes, Louis Althusser, Claude Lévi-Strauss, Ferdinand de Saussure, André Bazin, Christian Metz, and others). Many Anglo-American academics have also corroborated such actions by inscribing themselves within this "history" or legacy. That is, many Anglo-American film critics and historians reinforce the historicization of film and film theory by appropriating film language, applying theoretical assertions to their interpretations of film, rearticulating the difference between the *Actualités* of the Lumière brothers and Méliès's *féeries*, or trick films as the seminal point of departure for film history, and continually referencing discourses and debates centered on the *nouvelle vague* (French new wave cinema, criticism, and theory) of the 50s and 60s. Although such appropriations of and identifications with French filmmakers, critics, and theorists helped Anglophone film critics to establish film as an academic discipline in the early 70s, they have also served as scapegoats for the current "crisis" in film studies.

The backlash against French theory in America extends beyond the scope of cinema studies, but witch-hunts such as these threaten the very foundations of the field, since it was French theory, albeit secondhand (through the British interpretations thereof), that sanctioned the transformation of film into an academic discipline. Indeed, this "crisis" resonates in the current discussions and debates over the role of theory in academia. In the last few years scandals like "*l'affaire* Sokal" (or the Sokal hoax), public denunciations of theorists like Judith Butler and Homi Bhabha in the *New York Times* and the *Times Literary Supplement,* and the bestowing of "jargon awards" to literary, cultural, and film theorists, have generated not only public distrust for academics, but an academic panic over the role of theory within scholarly discourses. Last year alone various national conferences of the American Society for Cinema Studies, the Modern Language Association, and the College Arts Association allocated a good portion of time to this "crisis over the object of theory."

Many of those very same Anglo-American scholars who employed French theory as a means of justifying film as a legitimate field of study now disassociate themselves from it, holding it accountable for the failures, impasses, and dead ends facing Anglophone film theory. In part, D. N. Rodowick attributes this extensive disavowal of French theory to the inability of the British and Americans to recognize the complexity of French film culture. He writes, "The extraordinary work of translation and film theory accomplished in the 1970s by the British journal *Screen* has a continuing influence on film theory today, especially in the United States. However, it is not recognized often enough that *Screen*'s editorial perspective on French cultural theory of the sixties and seventies was very particular, and itself already thoroughly filtered by the editorial position of *Tel Quel*, with its specific triangulation of literary semiotics, Lacanian psychoanalysis, and Althusserian Marxism."[1]

The model the British film critics of *Screen* procured for the emerging Anglo-American discipline of film studies was not only one that combined semiotics (Saussure), psychoanalysis (almost exclusively Lacanian), and leftist political perspectives, but a model that applied these ways of seeing (reading) to specific topics: subjectivity, spectatorship, and film language. This unique nexus of theoretical models and political interests promulgated a series of discussions on spectatorship and its relationship to subjectivity, which in turn gave rise to debates over identification—who could identify with, and who was blocked from identifications with, positions of power (subjective agencies). This ultimately launched many other Anglo-American film theorists into their own articulations of identity politics—feminist, racial, and ethnic struggles for acknowledgment and self-determination within the field of cinema studies and the institution of higher learning. Furthermore, the focus on subjectivity and perception led to the extensive (psycho)analyses of film experience. Yet, embedded within the debate over film experience was the historicization of film theory itself. For example, Altman delineates the transformation in theories of perception as a progression of metaphors for the filmic screen: the more "simplistic" theories that treated cinema as a transparent medium (an expression of reality), a window through which we could perceive only a part of the action (Bazin), evolved into seeing the screen as a frame that organizes space and time, as well as aligning viewers with specific points of view or metacommentaries (Mitry), to a mirror in which we falsely see ourselves (Mulvey/Lacan), and finally to a veil that disguises its own ideological messages (Metz/Doane).

What was ignored in such debates over processes of identification and the coding of film language were problems later addressed by (1) Teresa de Lauretis, who argues that the positing of sexual difference as fundamental to identification (and therefore, spectatorship) disregards the difference between sex and gender, the latter a form of representation neither essential or primordial; (2) Geoffrey Nowell-Smith, who notes that film critics' correlation of the image to the filmic *énoncé*, and film narratives to the *grande syntagmatique*, assumes that meaning is linguistic, thereby isolating the image and subtracting it from movement; and (3) Bill Nichols, who points out that such semiotic readings of film mystify the image in order to reify analogical interpretations of film—here the image becomes more than a pure conventional icon replete with a variety of references.[2] Thus, preoccupations with subjectivity, sexual and racial difference, and semiotics, as well as the compulsion to justify film as an academic discipline, left many critics blind to the inherent problems of translating moving images or even fluid identities into fixed systems of signs—demarcating subjects from objects or "others." Such attempts to ground political and ideological issues overlook the fact that, as Stuart Hall explains, identity is a constant production that assumes political positions but also evades them, and, as Gilles Deleuze posits, subjectivity is a complex assemblage of images—of reception, perception, action, movement, response, and expression.

At the same time the select importing of French theory to Britain and then to America can be read as an oversimplification of complex cultural issues, it also reveals the political and ideological strategies on the part of the British and the Americans to circumscribe film studies in the discourses of sexual difference, subjectivity, and identity politics. Hence, this process of simplification is twofold. On the one hand, the Anglophone film critics appropriated only theories that could readily be connected to their own political practices. This appropriation is an extraction whereby discourses that compromise the integrity of such selected models are simply ignored or rejected. On the other hand, the application of these theoretical models tends to reduce complex political issues such as the women's movement, filmic practices, radical politics, and radical thinking to what are perceived as transparent (theoretical) oppositions between subjects and objects, men and women, the empowered and the disempowered. It is the simplification of these very issues that has caused such scrutiny of Anglo-American film theory in recent years. Yet rather than abandon these issues, as many film historians have done, I think it is necessary to examine their shortcomings, the translations, inconsistencies, contradictions, appropriations and misappropriations of French theory. My objective is to engage in critically thinking through the ways in which French theory has been handled.

Turn to History

Much like the initial constitution of film studies, which was predicated on a process of selecting (filtering, editing, disengaging) historical and theoretical references, the recent efforts to fortify film studies as an academic discipline aim to secure the discipline via a process of disengagement with or purging of theory. Rather than attempt to reinvigorate thinking about film, or challenge contemporary film theory to confront some of its own inertia—bottlenecks, blind spots, impasses—many American film critics have withdrawn from theoretical practices into the "fortress of history." The popularity of contemporary film scholars like Tom Gunning, Janet Stagier, Denise J. Youngblood, and David Bordwell attest to this movement toward historicism. The turn toward history veils its own attempts to secure film studies as an academic discipline, one that is seen as rooted in social science (facts, evidence) rather than the more "humanist" tradition of critical thinking (texts, criticality, politics). Ironically, this turn to history as a more scientific or factual model of legitimacy is also a return to France, to the Lumière brothers invention of the *Cinèmatographe*—a combined camera, printer, and projector—that allowed for the projecting of film to an audience. Only this time, it is the film critics who reclaim for themselves the discourse of transparency, claiming the ability to record all the relevant factors that contributed to the process of making a film, who represent the historical culture in which films were produced and recapture the excitement of seeing cinema for the first time.

This historical revision of film studies tells us almost nothing about the problems inherent in French theory and how it has been used or abused by Anglo-American film critics. What it does reveal is a shift in institutional politics, an administrative shift toward resource-centered management. This withdrawal into history coincides with departmental attempts to justify film studies to university administrations that want education to conform to the law of supply and demand (i.e., they want to downsize). Thus, the real question is not one of historicization, since cinema studies has always been historical; the very citation of French films, critics, and theorists, the narrativizing of French film culture, criticism, and theory alone attest to the central role of historicism in the founding of cinema studies. The problem now is that, not only are these theoretical models no longer critically or politically sustainable, but they are also no longer intellectually viable (many students cannot understand theory, nor are they willing to invest time to understand such theories), and therefore, they are no longer economically viable (departmental budgets are based on the number of students attending classes). Hence, the response has been overwhelmingly Darwinian, a brutal competition that directly translates into complying with the process of dumbing down, or, as Nietzsche calls it, "accommodating oneself to the facts," that is, "learning to bend one's back and bow one's head before the power of history, whether it be a government or public opinion or an numerical majority, and thus to move one's limbs to the precise rhythm at which any power whatever pulls the strings."[3]

Disciplining Film Studies

Neither the thinking about cinema nor cinematic thought can be said to begin in one place or time. Early cinema appropriated ready-made artistic techniques, representational strategies, ideologically coded narratives, character types from the stage, a fascination with movement, magic and the reproduction or reappearance of "reality." As Leo Charney and Vanessa R. Schwartz argue, "modern culture was 'cinematic' before the fact."[4] Cinema bridged a multiplicity of divergent discourses, connecting scientific studies like anthropology, ethnography, physiology, photography, and psychology to the artistic movements of the avant-

garde, modernism, and mass culture and to the politics of nationalism, socialism, anarcho-syndacalism, and fascism. But instead of producing consistent interpretations, artistic styles, and ways of seeing such convergences produced radically divergent cinematic and critical forms. In fact, the very fragmentation,
illusion, and ephemerality associated with cinema itself spilled over into film criticism. That is, cinema reflected as much as it augmented the radical inconsistencies, interstices, and intersections of modern culture and cultural thinking.

Cinema, therefore, challenged modern thinkers to master or discipline it, ig-
niting a series of attempts to classify, qualify, and quantify it, which in turn gave
rise to numerous debates. These debates have concerned:

1. The relationship of technology to the transmission of information. Is it transparent or a form of extreme manipulation (propaganda)? Marshall
   McLuhan, Guy Debord, Jean Baudrillard, Herbert Schiller, Ben Bagdikian,
   and, more recently, Pierre Bourdieu grapple with this question.
2. The classification of art as either high or low on account of its critical *effect*.
   This compartmentalization of art underlies the work of Bertol Brecht,
   Sergei Eisenstein, Walter Benjamin, Theodor Adorno, and Fredric Jameson.
3. How the moving image affects memory, the perceptions of time, and experience of presence: these aspects can be seen operating in the works of Henri
   Bergson, Georg Simmel, Martin Heidegger, and Gilles Deleuze.
4. The relationship of image to language, semiotic systems of signs, icons,
   myths, and symbols. Such meticulous systematization preoccupied thinkers
   like Charles Sanders Pierce, Ferdinand de Saussure, Claude Lévi-Strauss,
   Roland Barthes, and Umberto Eco.
5. The embedding of ideological and sexual identifications in cultural images: explaining these meanings was central to the work of Sigmund Freud, Jacques
   Lacan, Christian Metz, Laura Mulvey, Frantz Fanon and Louis Althusser.

However, all of these debates, enigmas, obsessions, and preoccupations intersect, overlap, disrupt, and conflict with other modes of interpretation only to
reveal others as well as their own inconsistencies. Nonetheless, all of these attempts to master (understand, read, classify) cinema have contributed to the disciplining of cinema/film studies.

Yet because the affects and effects of cinematic thought permeate multiple discourses—on technological reproduction, re-presentation, the perception of time,
modernity, the society of spectacle, collective unconscious, attractions/entertain-
ment, mobility, nationalism, urbanity, art/pop or mass culture—the disciplining
of cinema becomes a precarious task, one that necessitates artificial constructions
(alliances and maneuvers). This "precariousness" is not only reflected in the di-

verse influences of cinematic thought on fields of study, ranging from modern cultural to metaphysical, scientific, ideological, and political thinking, but the placement of cinema studies in academic institutions: in communication departments, in fine arts, production, English and foreign language departments, or in comparative literature, cultural studies, or even, in some cases, history departments. While cinema is now more than a hundred years old, the institutionalization of cinema/film studies is relatively recent. Many film critics and film historians argue that difficulty in legitimizing, and therefore, establishing film as a discipline rests on the fact that cinema has been territorialized by different disciplines and their subsequent theoretical apparatuses, or dismissed by theoretical practices that aligned film form with pop, mass, or low culture (i.e., deeming it unworthy of academic analysis). In fact, many anthologies of film studies, film theory, and film history affirm the interdisciplinary composition of cinema studies, as well as the struggle to establish cinema as a valid "object" of study—a struggle that has recently turned to scrutinize the "study" of film itself as an object.[5] This current "scrutiny" often slips into various forms of *ressentiment*, functioning less as an intellectual analysis than outright antitheoretical dogma. Because film critics in the early 1970s strove to prove that film, feminism, and film theory, like "high art," were worthy of elite scholarship—here's where Altman seems off the mark—they engaged the French theory they felt articulated their political and ideological concerns; but moreover, they used French theory to challenge existing institutional pedagogical, methodological, and ideological practices. However, this does not mean that they in turn should not be challenged on the grounds of their "selections" or "assertions"; nor should those critics be dismissed so that we can now return to more "traditional" forms of scholarship such as the archival, formal, or technical history of film.

Film studies has often been described as emerging from the conjuncture of French theory (semiotics, psychoanalysis, and neo-Marxism), feminism (that took its cue from the women's movements of the late 60s and early 70s), and the post-1968 obsession with radical politics and the political (practical) failure of the Left. Yet, the institutionalization of film studies suffers from many contradictions, hypocrisies, and discrepancies with its own political premises. A few contradictions come to mind. At the same time Roland Barthes and Michel Foucault pronounced the death of the author and questioned the notion of authorship—a gesture that dovetails with political questioning of authority as patriarchal, logocentric, Eurocentric, bourgeois, and fascist—film critics such as Andrew Sarris and Peter Wollen supported the *auteur* theory of the 50s, forwarded by the *nouvelle vague* (François Truffaut and Jean-Luc Godard in particular) as a means of "establishing priorities for the film student" (Sarris), and rescuing *certain* directors from obscurity (Wollen).[6]

Contrarily, "the death of the author" was met with much skepticism by feminists and self-identifying minority scholars; as Mary Ann Doane puts it, women and minorities "had to relinquish the idea of the author before [they had] had a chance to become one."[7] Ironically, like the *auteur* theorists, minority theorists denounced canonical practices and the ideologies that maintained them (elitism, classism, patriarchy, imperialism, racism, and bourgeois culture), but they did not deconstruct the ideological assumptions on which these systems of power were legitimized. For instance: while many feminist film critics have condemned patriarchal history, they often historicize their own subjective positions, establishing "alternative histories" or "herstories," thus overlooking the fact that history "stands in for unhistorical power" of right or legitimation (Nietzsche); at the same time that many critics who have followed the poststructuralist thinking of Derrida celebrate difference, they try to contain it through the systemization of opposition, thus ensuring the stability of their own histories and identities; while theorists have shown how rationality and facticity are forms of manipulation, they use "common sense" and statistics to demonstrate the inaccuracy of their opponents; finally, many progressive thinkers have challenged the notion of "humanity" as a ideological construct, one "that enables the ruling classes to ensure their domination" (Althusser), but they continue to demand basic *human rights*. Many progressive thinkers justify their own institutional and academic subjectivity on the same logic of dismissal that was once used to ensure the exclusion of those they profess to represent. This compliance with a predetermined binary model reverses orders, from one of humanism (the project of enlightenment, the civilizing, mission, the white man's burden) to what Jean Baudrillard calls the "new victim order."[8]

This new victim order has led to the deeply problematic migration of academic discourse from a barred identification with the subject to "inhabiting" the space of the other. My point is not to disavow the recognition of the various exclusions of canonized others (whether women, black, Chicano, Asian, Third World, or queer) from history or power, nor to dismiss the history of violence (oppression, repression, suppression), but to problematize what bell hooks calls "choosing the margin," since this gesture of "free choice" seems to be almost welcomed by the powers that be. That is, many feminists' and minority theorists' claims to authority, agency and subjectivity as minorities amounts to reinforcing the binary politics of established systems of power. The difference between choosing the margin and taking shotguns into the California state capitol in Sacramento (as the Black Panthers once did) clearly marks the great divide between an abstract act of choosing an image (a form of identification or representation) and a concrete act of refusing to be marginalized, represented, or identified. Identifying oneself as other (woman, black, Chicano, queer) may very well be a political gesture, but identifying oneself with a historical subject (the history of the oppressed, the victim, or even the Panthers) as a form of "representing" or "speaking for" seems to be mercenary at best. As Stuart Hall explains, identities are not transparent: "they are the names we give to the different ways we are positioned by, and position ourselves within, the narratives of the past."[9] Hence, this project of narrativization (positioning) that rejoins the past with the present under the banner of victimization undermines the very progressive politics many of these theorists claim to stand for, unless they really mean to stand only for revenge (the return of the repressed). Such identifications with the disempowered, dead, or downtrodden turn political "causes" into acts of commiseration whereby the critic/political activist cashes in on institutional recognition of his or her cause, thereby destroying the radical potential of critical or political movements. This is an exchange of potentially threatening criticality for moral righteousness and its institutional presence (job security). While at times this might squelch critical thinking, it has been a very effective political practice.

The division between theory and practice, as it has been articulated by academics, is also riddled with contradictions. This partitioning, paradoxically, draws on Marx's concept of *praxis*—a combination of theory and practice.[10] While Marx *philosophizes* that these two aspects are necessary complements of one another, recent debates over theory and practice have redrawn distinct territorial alliances between those who endorse theory and those who champion practice. For example, the women's movement of the 60s and 70s, which many feminists maintain was designed to raise women's consciousness, provide them with a sense of solidarity and function as a political force in undermining what they saw as "patriarchal hegemony," ended up splintering into numerous contending groups. As B. Ruby Rich points out, "the 1972–73 period marked a cultural watershed that has not since been equaled and . . . the unity, discovery, energy, and brave, we're-here-to-stay spirit of the early days underwent a definite shift in 1975." Rich attributes this shift in part to "specialization," which, for example, pulled "feminist film work away from its early political commitment . . . away from issues of life that go beyond form; away from the combative into the merely representational."[11] Here, Rich demarcates her own field of expertise. She draws her own lines between different forms of representation, between "[s]peaking in one's own name versus speaking in the name of history," which she accuses feminist film critics who wrote for *Camera Obscura* and *Women and Film* of doing.

Contrary to Mary Ann Doane, who argues that the division between those who supported (French) theory and those advocated (American) political practice was not as apparent in film studies as in literary studies,[12] Rich highlights this division within film studies. However, these lines are drawn not only within and between literary and film studies departments, but also on an institutional level, between the humanities and the social sciences. As opposed to film, literature, cultural studies, and art departments that argued about French theory, the majority of American women's studies departments still disapprove of the presence of French theory in their curriculum. Rather, they promote "practical" training in science, sociology, statistics, and politics. This self-identification with pragmatism allowed many feminists in women's studies departments to accuse feminist theorists of selling out. On the other hand, many feminist theorists see this reverence for practice and politics as at best a historic gesture (monumentalizing the women's movement). Indeed, such nostalgia for the age of bra burning and political activism is not only unproductive, but dismissive of the problems that the women's movement faced in determining a feminine subjectivity. In the good old days, as Audre Lorde points out, "white women ignored their built-in privilege of whiteness, and defined *woman* in terms of their own experience as women, women of Color became 'other,' the outsider whose experience and tradition was too 'alien' to comprehend."[13] The real irony is not that numerous political splits occurred along lines of difference—black from white, homosexual from heterosexual, African from Afro-American, Asian from Latino, and so on—but that all of these battles, including the battle among feminists, have been institutionalized. In other words, difference has been integrated within film: the very notions of exclusion and sexual difference that many of radical movements originally denounced as oppressive and unjustifiable have become the very foundations upon which fields of study are maintained. It is as if the women's movement and other such struggles for recognition/equality have been preserved via institutionalization. As Doane aptly puts it, feminism does not have to fear marginalization but, rather, "orthodoxy and institutionalization."[14]

This is not to say I support the popular backlash against feminism, since it grossly generalizes complex events. Furthermore, it maliciously dismisses important issues concerning the treatment and perception of women, as for instance issues arising from the "trial" of Clarence Thomas and Anita Hill, the media treatment of Nicole Brown Simpson, Bill Clinton's definition of sex, and the reduction of Monica Lewinsky, Paula Jones, and others to "bitches" and "bimbos" in television and press coverage. However, the fact that these media events were met with public backlash against women highlights the fact that feminists (film and media theorists, in particular) themselves are now largely incapable of speaking to such issues. Hence, unless we are willing to contest the *mediated* paranoia of "bad girls" who cry sexual harassment, take a simple side on a complex issue, or slip off into some hallucination of the heroic/mythic past, we need to address why such critical apparatuses have failed. Because the scope of such failures is so far reaching, I will now focus on these problems of feminist film criticism: (1) the avowal of sexual difference that engenders subjectivity as a masculine form of agency and, with it, the power of the gaze as a form of voyeurism, and ultimately, as sadism or fetishism (Is violence inherent in the act of looking? Should all films be considered pornographic and misogynist?; and (2) the pursuit of pleasure that turns into the seizure of the space of the other, via processes of rupture, invagination, and withdrawal from the site of phallic power (the law of the father, the rock of castration). The modeling of cinematic experience on the model of *Fort! Da!*—one of absence and presence, self and other, lack and desire that infinitely twists along Lacanian equations—ultimately collapses into no-thing-ness.

Only One Way of Looking, and It Is Masculine

At the same time that Laura Mulvey writes in her 1989 compilation of essays that her classic "Visual Pleasure and Narrative Cinema" (originally published in 1973, reprinted for *Screen* in 1975) was "not intended to last . . . [but] to articulate rather than originate, to catch something of interests and ideas . . . within the changing context of the Women's Movement and its aftermath," she instructs the reader to receive these essays as "documents that are separate and discrete but when placed in sequence [display] certain themes and strands . . . patterns or even story lines."[15] In other words, while she disclaims the monumentalization of what has come to be a seminal text of not only feminist film criticism, but of film studies itself, she reinstalls her work within what Nietzsche would call a *suprahistorical* narrative: one that re-presents itself as a historical "document" preserving the "spontaneous and tentative" as "stepping stones." This "disclaimer" may neutralize the project of theory by presenting it as a historical process (objective, documentary), but it cannot conceal the fact that the project was already grounded on suprahistorical assertions rather than critical practices: Mulvey's (1989) historical reenvisioning of her previous critical texts recalls not a *timely* (contextual) treatment of cinematic experience, but an *untimely* presentation of subjectivity, sexual difference and spectatorship.[16]

By reading subjectivity and spectatorship through the spectrum of Lacan, Mulvey and many film critics like her anchor their analyses of filmic experiences on predetermined (prehistorical, primordial), yet absolute (insurmountable) notions of sexual difference, which in turn give rise to subjectivity, ways of seeing, and systems of meaning even if they are based on an original *méconnaissance* (misrecognition). Although, like semiotic theory, Lacan posits that the relationship of the subject to reality is like that of the signifier to the signified—it constitutes an infinite slippage along a metonymic chain—unlike semiotic systems in which subjectivity is perceived as arbitrary, Lacanian psychoanalysis bridges the opposition of the signifier and the signified through the phallus, what Lacan calls the image of the "vital flow." That is, the phallus becomes the privileged signifier since it is the most tangible element in real sexual copulation; it is both visible and materially present in the literal (topographical) sense of the term. Thus, Lacanian theory, like Freudian theory, not only privileges male sexuality (heterosexual), but its material (object relations), visual (image of unification, uniting not only man and woman, but the thing-in-itself with no-thing) and symbolic (immaterial substitutions for the phallus such as the law of the father) manifestations/mystification.

Yet Lacan withdraws this *transparent* image of the penis as well as the "vital flow" from symbolic meaning and the process of signification, positing that meaning is defined not by presence but by absence or lack. Difference, however, is not so neatly organized into a binary division between man and woman, self and other, subject and object, activity and passivity, nor even an assemblage of multiple relationships or metaphors, as some critics would have us believe. Because signification is an effect of what Jacques Derrida will later call *différance*—a visible (sexual) difference and temporal deferral (postfactum or postcoitus)—it can identify (grasp) this "vital flow" that connects the process of signification to tangible reality only via metaphors (signs, symbols, and icons). In fact, for Lacan, the complication of establishing subjective identifications on differences and deferrals causes a series of reversals wherein the phallus itself "disappears" from the site of the "vital flow" (the erect penis or exchange of fluids), and reappears in the "place of the other." This other site of woman's unspeakable lack, the mystification of her bodily enjoyment *(jouissance)*, sensuality and materiality—as well as the symbolic—are metaphors for language itself covering up, veiling, and suturing its own irreconcilable foundations in trauma, the shock of nothingness. Therefore, Lacan, like Freud before him, establishes the phallus as a floating signifier that "stands for" everything not phallic so as to misrecognize difference as the same. Thus, everything will symbolically reify the existence of the phallus. However, at the same time symbolic language sutures or secures man within a system of meaning—giving him a narrative identity, a subjectivity—it radically disengages meaning from reality. In other words, the power of speech and subjectivity is contingent on man's forfeiting his shared immediacy with woman. Thus, as he hands over his desire in return for his self-image (subjectivity) he can only touch woman by bouncing his image and desires off of her. What is lost in this model of sexual difference is any sense of intimacy, pleasure, and intense criticality, other than a forced intimacy, an imposed intimacy.

It is therefore quite appropriate that feminist film theorists would reproach Lacan for metonymically linking anatomy to symbolic discourse, and inscribing all forms of signification in an economy of violent separation wherein the male subject can disengage from a bodily reality in order to identify/understand himself. But rather than point to Lacan's own inconsistencies—his reduction of the event (coitus) to a visible sign of sexual difference, which then withdraws into symbols, and finally slides into linguistic signification—many feminist film critics appropriate this pursuit of self-knowledge. That is, rather than questioning processes of identification that emerge from nothing, they choose to stand for feminine subjectivity, even if it means accepting mystical phallic signifiers. But in contrast to Lacan's affirmation or privileging of the phallus, their project is built on the disavowal of such symbolic and patriarchal authority. In fact, feminist film critics have applauded Lacan for providing a space from which women can speak: a space that is not a product of biological destiny but a sociocultural construct. For instance, Mulvey reads Lacan's shift from Freudian "biological imperatives" (object relations) to the symbolic intersubjective relationship of the father to the law as an indication that "anatomy is no longer destiny, [thus] women's oppression and exploitation can become contingent rather than necessary." Yet, she concludes, "Lacanian representation of sexual difference leaves woman in a negative relation, defined as 'not-man', and trapped within a theory that brilliantly describes the power relationships of patriarchy, but acknowledges no need for escape."[17] Indeed, Lacan shifts from a discussion of biological destiny to one of signification, yet this discussion also comes with its own forms of entrapment.

This site of difference (not-man) leaves woman in a double bind: she is both no-thing, and a defining negativity. Mulvey points to the double bind of phallocentricism when she writes that the masculine subject "depends on castrated women to give order and meaning to his world. . . [woman] can exist only in relation to castration and cannot transcend it."[18] However, all signification is also contingent on difference (the seemingly castrated), thus the site of difference, like the position of the slave in the Hegelian dialectic, emerges as the more powerful: the master not only needs the slave in order to define himself as master, but also knows only what it means to be a master, while the slave understands what it means to be both master and slave. Kaja Silverman illustrates this dialectical logic when she argues that "man may be on the 'right' side of the symbolic, but [he is] on the 'wrong' side of knowledge. The female subject, on the other hand, [may be] on the 'wrong' side of the symbolic, she is on the 'right' side of knowledge." Ironically, it is again anatomy that grounds women's intellectual advantage over man. According to Silverman, woman unlike man, has the "tangible 'proof' of her castration," which allows her to "turn away from what are in the final instance only illusory goals."[19] Nonetheless, such polemical positioning (enslavement to the dialectic) points to the fact that this knowledge, as Foucault argues, "is not made for understanding, it is made for cutting," endlessly disassociating its own subjective agency from its object of observation (even if that object is the self).[20]

Consequently, the project of criticism fosters a contagious dissembling (dissecting) of bodies, time zones, spaces, in order to reassemble knowledge as disembodied and, therefore, nonpartisan or universal. Yet once installed, this radical disembodiment (abstraction) of knowledge (which severs mind from body, self from other, original from copy, reason from passion) infects every level of discourse and thus, every level of knowledge. What is always already lost in this cognitive model is the present, the sentient experience of difference or becoming different. As Nietzsche comments, the effect of such dialectical reversals is intellectual *impotentia*, wherein everything remains as it was: the affixing of the project of criticism so that "the historical culture of our critics no longer permits any effect at all in the proper sense, that is an effect on life and action." Rather than reject the "historical culture" that produces such fixed libidinal economies (ways of seeing and reading), feminist film critics turn film criticism into an endless set of reversals, piling critique upon critique, yet endlessly returning to what Deleuze and Guattari call the "rock of castration." Hence, in order to be on the "right side of knowledge," woman must freely assume her own nonexistence. That is, she must give up her sense of presence (an effect on life and action) in order to hold on to those very metaphors that "prove" man's own nonexistence. As Guy Debord points out, this marks the end of cultural history, which "manifests itself on two opposite sides: the project of its procession in total history [an infinite slippage of metaphors], and the organization of its preservation as a dead object in spectacular contemplation." Finally he asks, "What is this if not the institutionalization of cultural critique?"[22]

Fetishizing the Negative

Interpretations of film derived from psychoanalytic models make cinema an eternal and universal formulaic equation of traumatic beginnings (witnessing primal scenes, discovering that the mother lacks a penis), and reactive or repressive means of forgetting such traumas—repressing desire for the mother by identifying with the law of the father, and submitting to his law of castration. In addition, these interpretations give latent symptomatic interruptions, latent effects of forgotten traumas that eternally return to haunt us, and mythic or imaginary narrativizations, the suturing of subjects to fictive narratives whose purpose is to both reaffirm narratives of continuity (give us a sense of coherence or security) and to maintain the structure of the whole symbolic law of repression. Within this paradigm even experiences of radical difference—interruption, effacement, otherness, loss, forgetting, and erasure—are subject to ordering principles, to repression, "working through," or interpretation that reencodes subjects/meaning within closed narratives, even if they are subject to misrecognition, latency and disruption.

What is often ignored by the fixation on male fantasies (whether their violent desire to control or their narcissistic desire to understand/love themselves) is the slippage of woman into the metaphors of lost time, a timeless sense of completeness. Although disguised, repressed, or effaced, a leap of faith exists underneath Lacanian discourse, a primal separation that allegedly is cut along clear lines—man from woman, past from present, subject from object. Thus by focusing on identification as well as signification as a form of disengagement, the project of criticism reinscribes itself in the very same act of violence that it accuses its male subjects of executing. For example, many film critics of the 1970s and '80s who concentrate their analyses on the intersubjective play between the spectator and the filmic subject privilege identification (recognized as male) as key to understanding the mechanics of cinematic experience. This identification, as Christian Metz suggests, is twofold: it primarily occurs as an identification with the cinematic apparatus itself (with the perspective of the camera), and secondarily takes place on the level of character identifications. Jean-Pierre Qudart elaborates this process of identification wherein the spectator occupies the empty space, what he calls the space of "the Absent one" created by the inability of the spectator to locate the subject (the one who looks) within the frame of the film. Hence, in order to identify (read or make sense of) the film, the spectator must repress this primary identification with the camera, since it reveals a radical disjunction of shot to reverse shot. That is, the camera takes on multiple points of view, thereby destabilizing the process of identification. The process of suturing therefore allows the spectator to identify with characters or images. However, it requires a constant act of erasure and effacement, a partial repression of the previous point of view, and thus, subject position. As Claire Johnston explains, "the suturing process addresses itself precisely to this process of fading by retroactively closing up the distance opened up between the subject and its mark, introducing 'stand-ins' to fill the gap opened up, establishing an imaginary unity."[22] While this process of standing in, creating an illusory possession of space, or misreading cinema as continuous is criticized as helping to secure the male agency of looking, it is not called into question. Johnston, like Mulvey and Doane, maintains the apparatus of identification as an apparatus of repression—repressing not only temporal and subjective discontinuities, but also sites of difference that challenge sexual difference itself.

Furthermore, Johnston, Mulvey, and even de Lauretis deploy Althusser's definition of ideology—that represents "not the system of the real relations which govern the existence of individuals, but the imaginary relation of those individuals to the real relations in which the live"—as analogous to gender-coded relations of power.[23] Yet, rather than follow Althusser to the conclusion that there is no outside of ideology or its dissemination of power, de Lauretis suggests that "there is an outside, a place from where ideology can be seen for what it is—mystification, imaginary relation, wool over one's eyes; and that place is the subject of feminism."[24] It is precisely this desire to construct a feminine subject that polarized many feminists: on the one hand theorists like Julia Kristeva return to the notion of femininity as a "privileged condition," as a site of affirmation where life bursts forth, which in turn perpetuated its own mysticism centered on the peace-loving, politically correct mother goddess; and, on the other hand, film critics like Silverman treat the feminine subject as a "point of resistance," a negative subject.

It is this second treatment of feminine subjectivity that allows Mulvey, Doane, and Silverman to critique film for reinforcing conventional (Freudian) understandings of sexual difference, psychoanalytic (Lacanian) explications of identification, comprising what they call the *masculine gaze*—whose visual pleasure hinged on seeing the female body as a sign of castration and sexual difference. Such thinking asserts that the system of representation ascribed to the cinematic apparatus determines visual pleasure (the look, the gaze) as predicted on either voyeurism (for Mulvey a sadistic way of seeing) or fetishism (according to Gaylan Studlar, a masochistic way of seeing). However, both ways of looking contribute to the cultural objectification ("figuration," according to Doane) of women's bodies, and establish the cinematic gaze as a process whereby the spectator disengages the visual object from its form of sensual imagery in order to consume and eradicate its seductive power (voyeurism), or as Freud argues, to block sexual difference with an imaginary (phallic) signifier so as to "make the image of woman acceptable as a sexual object"—as Luce Irigaray responds, to "desire oneself through the other."[25]

Although the position of resistance, negativity, or criticality permits feminist film critics to analyze how patriarchal power operates, it traps such critical discourses within a preestablished formal logic. For many feminist film theorists the appropriation of the place of "determining negativity" (not-man) poses fundamental problems: Where do we place feminine subjectivity? How do we define feminine pleasure (visual or otherwise)? How do we establish feminine desire (agency) from which we engender a feminine filmic *écriture*? Feminists, therefore, do not simply appropriate the theoretical assertions of Sigmund Freud and Jacques Lacan; rather, they critique them on the grounds that they succor patriarchal power structures, treat women as objects of exchange, desire, violence, and fetishization, thus promoting a misogynist visual culture while at the same time representing women as lacking agency (subjectivity, desire, a libido, access to the symbolic), even denying the existence of a feminine subject (as Lacan writes, *l'femme n'existe pas*). Yet, their critiques often focus on the content of these theoretical works rather than their formal logic.

In fact, Mulvey later admits that her work "has been deeply influenced by binary modes of thought"—opposing masculinity as an active subject of looking to femininity as a passive object of that look.[26] Even here she continues to extrapolate on this very logic. That is, at the same time she challenges Freud's and

Lacan's constructions of sexual difference as predicated on a series of mystifications about masculine and feminine sexuality, she maintains psychoanalysis, as does Mary Ann Doane, Judith Mayne, Kaja Silverman, and even Judith Butler, as a "a political weapon, demonstrating the way the unconscious of patriarchal society has structured film form."[27] These feminist theorists have disputed the political content of sexual difference—the privileging of the phallus as a symbol of power, the organization of systems of meaning on the law of castration, reading all desire as male, the normalization of a masculine subject, the barring of women's access to the symbolic, and the projection of male fantasies onto female images. But they have not discredited the systems of thought that advocate generalizations such as: all meaning is created on a "determining negativity"; all differences are read through the spectrum of lack; all identifications, subjective positions, and thus meaning is predicated on the obsessive fear of castration—woman has no "thing," someone must have chopped it off. In other words, while phallocentrism may be contested, these critics are unwilling to give up the metaphoric penis, since it also serves as an icon of oppression, sadism, and misrecognition of feminine sexuality, *écriture, jouissance*. Such sites of negation, oppression and "misrecognition" themselves avow the victim as a political subject, yet only within a political system of opposition, or what Gramsci would call a war of position.

Holding onto the Phallus

Mulvey, Doane, Silverman, and others have preserved not only "the traumatic effect" of castration, but also what Julia Kristeva calls "its powers of horror." Trauma is sustained in some feminist discourses as a threat to male agency (potential potency), and a revenge on what Mulvey calls woman's "being-looked-at-ness." Hence, feminists like Hélène Cixous reappropriate mythical metaphors, analogies, and images of castration, as for example Freud's infamous head of Medusa, so as to redeploy castration from an act of silencing difference (woman, the colonized, the other) to one of exposing castration as purely reactive—a form of projecting one's sexual anxieties onto "innocent" others. Thus, images of castration become strategic weapons designed to subvert not only the patriarchal authority (by forcing it to see its own violence), male subjectivity (disavowing the signification), but also the male gaze (the agency of possession). Mulvey, like Kristeva before her, believes that the "uncovering" of such images will cause visual displeasure—forcing man to witness castration, to see the other as victimized by the self, and to experience difference, a destabilization of self, thus barring the subject from pleasure. Mulvey posits "destruction of pleasure as a radical weapon." Her aim is to destroy visual pleasures that promote conventional notions of beauty as predicated on man-power. But, as a result, she leaves *woman* in the place of a "determining negativity," since from the site of absence she can "wreck the infinite," subvert, undermine, collapse, or rupture man's identification with the powers that be. D. N. Rodowick points out the paradox behind such theoretical maneuvers is that "the figuration of woman as castration from the point of view of the masculine subject becomes the ground for a utopian formulation in Mulvey's essay. It anticipates a force already inscribed within the forms of patriarchal pleasure and representation, that returns to dismantle or overturn those forms."[28]

Subversive gestures inscribed in the very forms of power produce what Jean Baudrillard calls "the scandal effect." This effect simulates artificial oppositions—it repeats conventional binary oppositions—which "always pay homage to the law, by concealing that there is no difference between the facts and their denunciation."[29] Within this system opposition is purely theatrical. In fact, feminist film criticism operates much like what Metz describes as the filmic system's essential method of displacement—"a movement of negation, of destruction and construction"—that undermines points of reference, relations of difference, the constitution of identity which also determines desire. Thus, by repeating the tragic cycle of repression (castration) and resentment (the return of the repressed, i.e., the revenge of castration), such critical models ultimately inscribe man and woman in a narrative of failure, failed unions, failed identifications, and failed desires. This adherence to the logic of failure is not just exclusive to Lacanian film theorists, nor to feminists who have inhabited the site of "determining negativity," though they may well have incited a massive migration from phallic models to that of a negativity; it also extends to Derrida's concept of invagination, Homi Bhabha's championing of the mimic man, and other such occupations with otherness.

The real scandal is not this inhabiting the space of the other (the victim) as a means of disengaging with a politically incorrect or tarnished subjective position, but that such academic projects of enlightenment and demystification hide the violence of the critic, who reduces the sensuality of the cinematic experience to a set of predetermined theoretical effects in order to secure for him/herself the affirmative position of academic subjectivity. Only then can the subject (man) as well as the nonsubject (woman) become suprahistorical (eternally fixed), metacritical. In this sense, the Anglophone use of Lacan only promoted what Luce Irigaray criticizes as the "imperialism of Lacan's deterministic cultural and historic codes."[30] Thus, rather than serve the promotion of critical discourse the appropriation of Lacanian theory amounted to anchoring film studies a "stable"/fixed cultural and historical model. With this in mind it seems odd to accuse film studies of anything but participating in institutional politics, those that will guarantee the future of the discipline. The backlash against theory then becomes almost something so simple as the (ironic) unwillingness on the part of academics and their students to learn a new critical language.

Notes

1. D. N. Rodowick, *Gilles Deleuze's Time Machine* (Durham, N.C.: Duke University Press, 1997), p. xii.
2. Teresa de Lauretis, *Technologies of Gender*, (Bloomington: Indiana University Press, 1987). See her introduction to Geoffrey Nowell-Smith's "A Note on Story/Discourse," from *Edinburgh Film Festival Magazine* (1976) reprinted in *Movies and Methods*, vol. 2, ed. Bill Nichols, (Berkeley and Los Angeles: University of California Press, 1985, pp. 549–56. Bill Nichols, from the conclusion of *Movies and Methods* vol. 1, ed. Bill Nichols, (Berkeley and Los Angeles: University of California Press, 1976), p. 661.
3. Friedrich Nietzsche, "On the Uses and Disadvantages of History for Life," in *The Untimely Meditations*, trans. R. J. Hollingdale, (Cambridge: Cambridge University Press), p. 105. For Nietzsche scholarship has become commensurate with historical culture, and it is this type of reverence to the past which leads him to write that "history has ruined us."
4. Leo Charney and Vanessa R. Schwartz, the introduction to *Cinema and the Invention of Modern Life*, ed. Leo Charney and Vanessa R. Schwartz (Berkeley and Los Angeles: University of California Press, 1995), p. 1.
5. In *Femme Fatales*, Mary Ann Doane remarks, "While structuralism and post-structuralism were stressing an attention to theoretical frameworks and methods, the emerging discipline of film studies was constantly impelled to justify the status of its own object, the value of analyzing the cinema. Struggling to establish its own legitimacy, film studies was confronted with relentless oppositions between high art and mass culture, single-authored works and collective industrial productions, art and mechanical reproduction" (p. 4).
6. See Roland Barthes' 1968 essay entitled "The Death of the Author" (in *Le bruissement de la langue* (Paris: Editions du Seuil, 1984), where he argues that the author is an image, a monumental construct that has been inscribed in the discourse of French rationalism, English empiricism, individualism of faith emerging from the Reformation, positivism, and capitalist ideology. He reminds us that the "empire of the author" has also been enjoyed by the critic, who deciphers and disentangles the meaning of the text (the intent of the author).

   Michel Foucault, "What is an Author?" *Bulletin de la Société française de Philosophie* 63, no. 3, 1969. Here he argues that it is not enough to simply denounce the author, or the death of God and man as Nietzsche declared in *The Gay Science*, but as Nietzsche suggested to genealogically trace the raise and demise of authorship—how it functioned, what kind of power is articulated via naming, or territorializing ideas, texts and concepts. Foucault rejects Derrida's notion of *écriture*—having a double reference to the act of writing and the metaphysical nature of writing—since, rather than uproot the hidden power of authorship, it "transposes the empirical characteristics of an author to a transcendental anonymity." It is this critique of *écriture* that problematizes Peter Wollen's redefinition of auteur theory from the study of authorship to one of "core meanings" and "thematic motifs."

See also Andrew Sarris, *The American Cinema: Directors and Directors*, Peter Wollen, *Signs and Meaning in the Cinema* (Bloomington: Indiana University Press, 1969), *Cahiers du Cinéma*, 31, 1954 (in which Truffaut's "A Certain Tendency" appears), and Godard, *Godard on Godard*, trans. Tom Milne (New York: Viking, 1972).

7. Mary Ann Doane, *The Desire to Desire*, (Bloomington: Indiana University Press, 1987), p. 9.

8. Jean Baudrillard, *The Perfect Crime*, trans. Chris Turner, (London: Verso, 1995). Baudrillard writes, "The assumption of human suffering into the media is accompanied by its irruption into political and sociological metadiscourse. This is because politics and sociology are themselves faced with their own destitution. . . . Sociologists speak wretchedly, and the wretched speak about expressing themselves sociologically. So we move into a situation of the celebration of one's deficit, one's misfortune, one's personal insignificance—with the intellectual and media discourse, by its simultaneously sadistic and sentimental takeover of these matters sanctioning people's right to their own suffering, their consecration as victims and the loss to their natural defenses" (p. 138).

9. Stuart Hall, "Identity and Representation, in *Exiles: Essays on Caribbean Cinema*, Ed. Mary E. Chame, African Press, New Jersey, 1992, p. 223.

10. In his "Theses on Feuerbach" Marx writes that "for centuries, philosophers have interpreted the world, the point, however is to change it." And in his *Contribution to Critique of Hegel's Philosophy of Law*, he writes that "it is not enough for thought to strive for realization, reality must itself strive towards thought" (*Collected Works* vol. 3, published in *Allgemeine Zeitung* no. 3 (Ausburg), April 20, 1844, p. 183).

11. Rich, B. Ruby, "In the Name of Feminist film Criticism," in Nichols, ed., *Movies and Methods* vol. 2, p. 343.

12. Mary Ann Doane, *Femme Fatales: Feminism, Film Theory, Psychoanalysis* (New York: Routledge, 1991), p. 7. Doane writes, "Feminist literary criticism has been haunted for over a decade by the opposition between French feminist approaches and Anglo-American feminism. This polarization generally indicates the seemingly unbridgeable gap between continental theories of signification and sexuality inflected by a long speculative philosophical tradition and the pragmatism and empiricism which are said to characterize American intellectual history. Feminist film theory felt the impact of this polarization, but its issues and concerns were also somewhat peripheral to the reigning arguments between French and American feminism. This was due in large measure to the greater influence in film studies of the British assimilation of continental theory, filtered through the journal *Screen* after its 1971 editorial rupture. . . . The major reference points to this approach were Louis Althusser and Jacques Lacan."

13. Audre Lorde, "Age, Race, Class, and Sex: Women Redefining Difference," in *Out There*, ed. Russell Ferguson, Matha Gever, Trihn T. Minh-ha, and Cornel West, (Cambridge: MIT Press, 1990), p. 283.

14. Doane, *Femme Fatales*, p. 6.

15. Laura Mulvey, *Visual and Other Pleasures* (Bloomington: Indiana University Press, 1989), p. vii.

16. Here I refer to Michel Foucault's return to Nietzsche's concept of the "suprahistorical" in "*Hommage à Jean Hyppolite*" (Paris: Presses Universitaries d France, 1971), in

which he points out that this placing oneself outside of history reveals its own de-
pendence on metaphysics, a belief in eternal truths, the immortality of the soul or
natural consciousness which is identical to itself.

17. Laura Mulvey, "Myth, Narrative and Historical Experience," in *Visual and Other
    Pleasures*, p. 165.
18. Mulvey, *Other Pleasures*, 14.
19. Kaja Silverman, "Historical Trauma and Male Subjectivity," in *Psychoanalysis and
    Cinema*, ed. E. Ann Kaplan, Afi Series, (New York: Routledge, 1990), p. III.
20. Michel Foucault, *Language, Counter-memory, Practice*, trans. Donald F. Bouchard
    and Sherry Simon, (Ithaca, N.Y.: Cornell University Press, 1977), p. 154. In his
    analysis of Nietzsche's theory of effective history, Foucault points out that the object
    of knowledge always "precedes the fall." It comes before "the body, before the world
    and time; it is associated with the gods, and its story is always sung as a theogony."
    Hence the site of origin directly contradicts the project of enlightenment thinking,
    which is grounded on the purification of scientific method. The cruelty of historical
    knowledge (the knowledge of origins) is in effect the abyss of impossibility and lack.
21. Guy Debord, *La société du spectacle*, first published by Editions Buchet-Chastel,
    Paris 1967, trans. and reprinted by Black and Red Press, Detroit, 1970, viii.
22. Claire Johnston, "Towards a Feminist film Practice: Some Theses," in Nichols, ed.,
    Movies and Methods vol. 2, p. 319.
23. Louis Althusser, "Ideology and Ideological State Apparatuses," in *Lenin and Philoso-
    phy*, (New York: Monthly Review Press, 1971), p. 165.
24. Teresa de Lauretis, *Technologies of Gender*, (Bloomington: Indiana University Press,
    1987), p. II.
25. Sigmund Freud, *Sexuality and the Psychology of Love* (New York: Macmillan, 1963), p.
    217. Here Freud argues that the fetish is a substitute for the "woman's (mother's) phal-
    lus, which the little boy once believed in and does not wish to forgo." This fantastic
    phallus conceals "horror of female genitals," which causes the traumatized fetishist to
    construct a phallus for the mother to disavow the law of castration. Luce Irigaray, *This
    Sex which is Not One*, trans. Catherine Porter (Ithaca, N.Y.: Cornell University Press,
    1985). Irigaray explains the dynamism of the patriarchy, who through its representa-
    tions and desiring of the other ultimately desires itself: "Phallicism compensates for
    this discursive crisis, sustaining itself upon the Other, nourishing itself with the Other,
    desiring itself though the Other, even without ever relating to it as such."
26. Mulvey, "Myth, Narrative and Historical Experiences," p. 161.
27. Laura Mulvey, *Visual and Other Pleasures,* p. 14.
28. D. N. Rodowick, *The Crisis of Political Modernism: Criticism and Ideology in Contem-
    porary Film Theory* (Berkeley and Los Angeles: University of California Press, 1988),
    p. 230.
29. Jean Baudrillard, *Simulations*, trans. Paul Foss, Paul Patton, and Philip Beitchman, p. 26.
30. Irigaray, Luce, "The Poverty of Psychoanalysis," in *This Sex which is Not One*, p. 87.

Disappearing Acts:
The French Theory Effect
in the Art World

ALISON M. GINGERAS

When approaching the topic of French theory and its dissemination in America, what better point of departure than Hollywood? In the sprawling terrain of Los Angeles County, concepts that originate in academia become simple plot devices. The great entertainment machine strips down complex discourse to the essentials; traces of theory are made digestible by transforming them into snappy sound bites, personifying them through visually seductive images. *The Matrix*—Hollywood's recent science fiction offering—provides an artful example of this process of reduction so dear to the American Way.

Weaving together literary references from the Bible to Lewis Carroll, *The Matrix* is a sexy update of the classical sci-fi trope of man versus computer. Its messianic hero, Neo (played by Keanu Reeves) is violently awakened from his "real life"—software engineer by day, hacker by night—to learn that he exists in a computer-generated *simulacrum* controlled by malevolent machines. During the opening two-thirds of the film, Neo struggles to understand the workings of this intricate web of illusion—a matrix of binary computer code—in order to fulfill his mission as the hacker-savior who will eventually lead the struggle to win back human freedom from digital slavery. Yet the astute filmgoer does not have to watch more than half an hour of the film before catching the bibliographic reference that lays the groundwork for this spectacular plot. *Simulacra and Simulations* is the title of a hollowed-out book that hides an illicit computer disk on Neo's shelf; he turns to the chapter entitled "Nihilism" to retrieve the disk in one of the first scenes. Without giving the author's credit line, these few fleeting frames at the beginning of the film signal the arrival of Jean Baudrillard on the silver screen.

There is another passing reference that confirms Baudrillard's importance to the founding premise of the film. In the course of an explicative monologue on the disarming verisimilitude of the Matrix, Morpheus (Laurence Fishburne's John the Baptist figure to Keanu Reeves's Christ) quips, "Welcome to the desert of the real."

Though certainly keeping with the Biblical imagery frequently submerged in *The Matrix* thread, this reference is probably culled from the pages of *Simulations,* in a passage where Baudrillard uses Jorge Luis Borges's image of a paradoxical map to speak of the porosity between the real and the simulated. Borges's map exactly covers the territory of an empire. As the empire fades, so does the map; "it became frayed and finally ruined, a few shreds still discernible in the deserts." For the initiated, this textual allusion might give pseudoacademic credentials to this otherwise typical Hollywood narrative where so-called postmodern theories become popular cultural "truths": representations have replaced that which they represent; the resulting simulacra replace reality; we live in a world of (im)pure simulation.

These footnote-less allusions to Baudrillard signal more than the fact that the directors of *The Matrix* (Andy and Larry Wachowski) did their French theory homework. Without a doubt, many French theorists (Baudrillard could be joined by Lacan, Derrida, Kristeva, or even Deleuze) have broken out of the exclusive domain of academia. The fact that one of these usual suspects should turn up in Hollywood is ultimately symptomatic of a larger phenomenon related to the dissemination (and Americanization) of certain examples of contemporary French philosophy, psychoanalysis, and sociology. Baudrillard's presence here is certainly no accident, not only because *The Matrix* is a film "about" simulation; but more important, in the context of French theory's reception in the United States, "theory" as such is absorbed into *The Matrix's* own "reality." It is no longer necessary to footnote or elaborate "simulation theory" (by Baudrillard or anyone else) in the film because it has been constructed in the discursive sphere and has become a *received idea* in popular culture.

Baudrillard himself has confronted and even encouraged this sleight of hand, the apparent "disappearance" of theory. In an interview with Sylvère Lotringer entitled *Forget Baudrillard,* he muses,

> Where is theory situated today? Is it wandering in realms which no longer have anything to do with real facts? . . . In my opinion theory can have no status other than that of challenging the real. At that point, theory is no longer theory; it is the event itself. There is no "reality" with respect to which theory could become dissident or heretical, pursuing its fate other than in the objectivity of things.[1]

Far from pitting theory against the real as a means of challenging or protesting it, Baudrillard sees theory becoming part of the real itself. No wonder one might be lost in the narrative exposition of *The Matrix.* By troubling the supposed borders separating ideas and reality, the sleight of hand or disappearing act becomes a necessary part of the dissemination process. There is "a kind of skidding endemic to theory. When theory manages to complete itself, following its internal logic, that's when it disappears. Its accomplishment is its abolition."[2] Baudrillard must not be upset that he was "forgotten" in the creative credits for *The Matrix,* but should revel in this paradox: at the same moment that theory is represented in terms of disappearance, it is more present than ever.

This paradox is not unique to Hollywood. As many recent critics might agree, the contemporary art world and the great entertainment machine are not that far apart—at least not in terms of spectacle production. In a recent publication entitled *Art at the Turn of the Millennium,* "the first publication to offer an authoritative overview of the art and artists of the 1980s and 1990s," the authors provide a glossary of "key words, concepts, and technical terms" to allow the broadest possible public a familiarity with the material at hand. Presented as tools for understanding the current state of contemporary art practices, the definitions offered in *Art at the Turn of the Millennium* give a different glimpse of this discursive machinery.

Again purged of the proper name, certain key definitions confirm the infiltration of certain strands of French theory into the *lingua franca* of the art world. A small selection of examples:

> **Postmodernism:** Unlike modernism, Postmodernism *starts from* the assumption that grand utopias are impossible. It *accepts that* reality is fragmented and that personal identity is an unstable quantity transmitted by a variety of cultural factors. Postmodernism *advocates* an irreverent, playful treatment of one's own identity, and a liberal society.
>
> **Simulacrum:** An illusionary image which is so seductive that it can supplant reality.
>
> **Structuralism:** Structuralism systematically examines the meaning of signs. The purpose of structuralism is to explore the rules of different sign systems. Languages and even cultural connections are seen and interpreted by structuralism as sign systems.
>
> **Poststructuralism:** Whereas structuralism considers sign systems to be closed, poststructuralism *assumes* that sign systems are always dynamic and open to change.[3]

Like the example taken from Hollywood, these extremely reductive definitions serve as grotesque instances of how French theory moves from the status of fact to a ready-made set of labels or categories. Postmodernism "starts from," "accepts," and "advocates"—all of these verb choices hide that theory is itself constructed so as to make theory ready-made concepts for a classification system. Not to be mistaken with accusations of misuse or abuse of theory, this example highlights a pervasive sense of pragmatism in the art world. Once theory has "disappeared" into a "given," it can reappear later in a watered-down if not more legible "category" or "label" that has immediate use value. This transformation process resembles a classical process of absorption, reduction, or disappearance that allows the critical function to be maximized. In the sphere of art, French theory can provide convenient labels such as "postmodern" or "simulacra art" in order to allow a huge range of practices, from Jeff Koons to Damien Hirst, to be neatly classified, ordered, and judged.

Yet theory does not simply beget classification systems—this is only one part of a double movement of a general *French theory effect* at play in the art world. In order for the first aspect of this effect to manifest itself, theory must be naturalized. As the origins of French theory are external to the sphere of art (imported from the university), the constructed nature of theory is forgotten. Concepts are engineered as much as the categories that the users of theory create in their transferal to the art world. The conjectural and artificial status of theory falls away. Theory—or rather what results from the transformation of a discursive strategy or conceptual construct into a series of statements about the world—appears to be like apples ready to be picked from the tree of knowledge. This process could be called *naturalization*, though it should not be considered as a term in opposition to historicization. In this specific instance, naturalization is understood in opposition to constructed nature of a theory or a concept; historical categories or historical narrativizing are part of this naturalization effect. In the writing of art history, the best example of this effect would be the assumed validity of trying to locate the shift from modernism and postmodernism in a series of specific artworks or in the advent of certain art practices in the twentieth century. Such a historiographic move is not illegitimate in itself, though it easily approaches a form of positivism that nominates this shift as if it was a historical "fact."

The naturalization effect—a common strategy that is often employed in art writing or curatorial argumentation—can be described as functioning like hypertext where a "boldfaced" proper noun stands in for the concept. *Abject Art: Repulsion and Desire in American Art*, one of the most overtly theory-driven and polemic exhibitions of the 1990s, clearly announces its foundation in the first sentence of its catalog:

> The concept of abjection, encompassing investigations of discursive excess and degraded elements as they relate to the body and society, has emerged as a central theoretical impulse of 1990s art. As described by the French theoretician Julia Kristeva, abjection is "what disturbs identity, system, order. What does not respect borders, positions, rules. The in-between, the ambiguous, the composite."[4]

The curators begin with this cursory definition of "abjection," then several sentences into the first paragraph they connect abjection with psychoanalytical concerns having to do with the unconscious and bodily ego. What is obscured is how Kristeva constructs her notion of abjection—in order to understand the fabrication of her theory the reader must jump to source texts, following a hyperlink signaled by the proper name, chasing down a bibliographic trail of bread crumbs. Yet this rarely occurs, because the point of invoking theory is its curatorial application. As a result, the reader is left with the impression that Kristeva is describing a natural phenomenon. Abjection exists *as such* in nature, reality, art. The simple presence of a present-tense verb—"abjection *is*"—in these opening sentences signals the disappearance of theory's construction.

This naturalism effect is even more evident when the "abject" is *applied* wholesale to art. The curators write in their introduction, "This term does not connote an art movement so much as it describes a body of work which incorporates or suggests abject materials such as dirt, excrement, dead animals, menstrual blood, and rotting food in order to confront taboo issues of gender and sexuality."[5]

To follow this line of curatorial logic, a viewer enters the exhibition gallery and perceives that the shit in the performance photographs by Mike Kelly or the pubic hairs on a Kiki Smith sculpture, or the stains on the diapers in Mary Kelly's *Post-Partum Document* themselves constitute the abject. As one walks through the show, it is as if one could point to the abject itself; it is the art object. In this tricky process of conflation, object, theory, and text seem to disappear. They are not gone, but the links are so tightly compacted that they become almost invisible. By placing shit in the museum, the curators inject abjection into the sphere high culture in the most literal and material way. In the compressed formula—shit equals abjection—the curators can make a leap in their argumentation: after nominating abjection as a series of existing material forms and practices, abjection as such can also be extended directly into a strategy of political subversion when applied to the field of the social. Readers of *Abject Art* are told that this curatorial project "was deemed urgent partly because of a disturbing trajectory of politics in America." Forms of domination in American culture—from the right-wing insistence on puritanical values to canon formation in art history—are "confronted" by the abject "in unexpected, transgressive ways."[6] Abjection equals shit equals a (left-wing) political panacea. With this domino effect, abjection becomes a magical tonic to cure (or better said, pervert) the normative social body.

This extension of a theoretical use touches upon the second part of this French theory effect in the art world, when the specificity of a given theory—in this case Kristeva's development of abjection—not only disappears into "fact" and becomes a huge sign itself. Abjection simultaneously loses the specificity of its own theoretical construction, becomes a model (hence an ironically normative force) and at the same time takes on a sign value that announces itself as "theory." Insisting on the "ism" (postmodernism, poststructuralism) or the proper name of a French theorist (Kristeva) connotes theory in general in addition to its first-degree meaning of a particular set of ideas. This is not an innocent connotation. The large, flashing lights of THEORY in a piece of art writing or in the wall text of an exhibition functions as a means of adding value. On the most superficial level, theory as such suggests seriousness or intellectual weight, and in more tricky instances, it serves as a tactic of intimidation. French theory is a form of capital like any other.

The tenth Documenta, a quintennial exhibition, held in 1997 in Kassel, Germany, delivered perhaps the paroxysm of the "theory as such" element of the French theory effect. Organized by the (appropriately) French curator Catherine David, this long-awaited event broke the traditional mold of large-scale international exhibitions. The actual display of artwork seemed to be an alibi for a much more ambitious exhibition of discourse and theory: the artists' presence was dwarfed by the publication of an 830-page compendium of primarily theoretical essays, literary extracts, and politically oriented discussions about aesthetic practices; a one hundred-day marathon of lectures by philosophers, writers, and artists; as well as a series of film, television, and Internet projects. David herself gave a simple explanation for this overwhelming emphasis on discursive practices in her editorial preface to the Calvinistic-titled exhibition catalog, *Documenta X: The Book*. Risking accusations of having enacted "cultural fascism,"[7] or "a massive conditioning . . . of an invisible, unknown public,"[8] David's choice to lean exclusively on theory as such is justified as a means to "indicate a political context for the interpretation of artistic activities at the close of the twentieth century."[9]

As one of the international exhibitions that art critics love to hate, David's ambitious project has, predictably, garnered many scathing reproaches. Yet the various commentaries on Documenta X indicate a surprising consensus. The dog and pony show of big-name artists was replaced by a barrage of theorist name-dropping: Adorno, Barthes, Blanchot, Foucault, Deleuze, Habermas, Ranciere, Said—while not all French thinkers, these proper names ordered and framed both David's book and show. As a result, critics and journalists were outraged because David didn't play the game properly. When asked by *Artforum* to identify the most interesting part of Documenta X, Richard flood (chief curator of the Walker Art Center) put his finger on the French theory effect:

> What I found interesting was the prelude to the exhibition: how increasingly
> at odds the curator became with the press. Catherine David's determination
> to keep the theoretical construct of the event front and center precluded the

naming of artist's names. It was as if the commissioner was being called as a hostile witness who chose persistently to take the fifth Amendment. As a result, the exhibition became a sociological phenomenon. *Theory was the point; it just wasn't the news.*[10]

Catherine David carried the *French theory effect* to an extreme. Blinded by the rays of theory's sign value, Documenta X became nothing but an orchestration of "heavy ideas suspended in tenuous equilibrium."[11] In fact, not only was the intended political or intellectual content eclipsed by the oversaturation of the theory effect, but "art" itself disappeared from the radar screen. If Catherine David has contributed anything to the practice of exhibition making, it would be the fashioning of a new curatorial art—a last-ditch attempt to resuscitate artistic activity from its own disappearance. Who needs the artists anyway? They only supply product. Curators ride the fluxes of supply and demand by creating a mise-en-scène of (empty) theory signs; this process produces capital—it strips down the art event to reveal the value-generating machine that animates the art world. Indulging in theoretical excess, David delivered more disappearing acts than the art world could handle.

Two short years later, the art world pendulum swung in the opposite direction. Another international art extravaganza, the 1999 Venice Biennale was apparently devoid of theory signs and even curatorial art. It might be said that the Biennale's curator Harald Szeemann took his cues from David's negative reception. Writing in the pages of *Artforum,* Daniel Birnbaum laments the supposed lack of theory in the Biennale's offerings:

> The Venice Biennale is by tradition less intellectual than Documenta, but this year's version was quite exceptional in its lack of theoretical framework. What really are the issues that this gigantic exhibition meant to tackle? . . . There was a time when every exhibition required a commentary by one French philosopher or another, and we all got sick of that. Now that we've reached the other extreme, I kind of miss Jacques Derrida.

This nostalgia for Derrida or any other proper name might have dissipated had the Biennale visitor turned his attention away from the curator's official (non)discourse (exhibition catalog, press releases) to examine more closely the actual work by certain artists in the exhibition.

Thomas Hirschhorn, a Swiss-born artist, was invited to create one of the spectacular installations that made up the Biennale's group show in the abandoned spaces of the old military site L'Arsenale. *Welt Flugplatz / World Airport* is the name of Hirschhorn's sculptural commentary on the phenomenon of globalization—

a giant model of a generic airport fabricated out of a series of humble materials such as cardboard, wood, plastic, tinfoil, and paper. On the central table that runs the length of the 25-meter-long gallery and serves as a "runway," about two dozen models of planes fashioned out of cardboard bear the names of national airlines, from Air Kosovo and Aeroflot to Air France and British Airways. Surrounding this runway, a host of other sculptural objects fill the room to overflowing. Everything in this space is linked together by tinfoil conductors. Trendy athletic shoe brands are networked to a host of nation-states—identified *Welt Flugplatz / World Airport* airplanes wired to informative panels, which are flooded with newspaper and magazine clippings recounting current events. In a swirl of overinformation, the banal bleeds into the insignificant while simultaneously conflating itself with the latest global trauma. Aluminum threads literally connect the war in Kosovo *and* Adidas tennis shoes *and* news articles about teenage bulimia *and* effigies of Spinoza, Gramsci, Bataille, and Deleuze.

By creating a messy mise-en-scène of all these proper names, trademarks, and nationalistic symbols, Hirschhorn simultaneously provides the signs of theory that Birnbaum claims are missing from the Biennale while also playing with the mechanisms of the French theory effect. The wildly differing discourses of Bataille and Deleuze are leveled out by reducing each of them to an image: a few lines photocopied from their texts are highlighted on the informational panels that line the installation's walls. This is not a parodic move, nor a derision of their theoretical content. Once part of Hirschhorn's globalization machine, Deleuze is rendered a sign like any other; theory disappears in the fluxes of capital along with the other corporate identities represented in the *Welt Flugplatz / World Airport*. On another level, Hirschhorn plays on the secondary signified of THEORY as such. Any name that connotes theory could inhabit Hirschhorn's work—he purposefully interchanges the names of theorists from artwork to artwork in order to make a stinging comment about the art world's fascination with French theory, or any discursive category in fashion. Beyond this illustrative function, there is another operative gesture at work in Hirschhorn's citation of theory. Using materials that are overcoded as cheap, disposable, and fragile to sculpturally render effigies or altars for these theorists produces an effect of weakness. Instead of using name-dropping as a tactic of intellectual intimidation, Hirschhorn causes Deleuze and his friends to instantly become harmless, as if to display the fragility of theory itself. In Hirschhorn's world, theory doesn't bite.

Using a bricolage strategy and handmade look for his renderings of these theory signs, Hirschhorn further counters the naturalization inherent in the French theory effect in the art world. He pushes to the limits the art world's disappearing acts by inscribing the signifiers of theory in the physical materials he consistently uses in his work. This is quite unlike the dubbing of certain works as "ab-

Thomas Hirschhorn, *"Welt Flug platz / World Airport,"* installation view at the 1999 Venice Biennale. *Photo courtesy of Galerie Chantal Crousel.*

ject art," a maneuver that relied upon a material embodiment of Kristeva's concept, which kept theory partially exterior to the objects in question. Hirschhorn actually plays on the signifiers of theory—if he were invited to create a work for the *Abject Art* show, it is easy to speculate that he would not present abject materials but rather build an abject rendering of the very signifier "Kristeva." No signifier, just Kristeva's name written in pubic hair.[12] Two effects follow: the logic of naturalization is paradoxically broken by using the trump card of literalness while at the same time his bricolage techniques are used to underscore the constructed, fabricated, handmade nature of theory. Theory itself is never given. In exclusively latching on to the theory sign, Hirschhorn strives to be stupid.[13]

Hirschhorn's installation provides but one example from the sphere of cultural production. Coming from an entirely different angle, M/M, a graphic design team (Michel Amzalag and Mathais Augustyniak) whose practice blurs the line between providing a traditional design service and creating autonomous art objects, have generated a number of cryptic images that harness the power of the theory sign. An image entitled *Deleuze avec bébé* shows an adorably chubby, diaper-clad child who clutches an alien toy in one hand while reaching for a copy of Gilles Deleuze's *Pourparlers* (1990), which is posed on a ledge at the top of the image. At a time when everyone from graphic designers to architects to music producers freely "use Deleuze" (or Deleuzianisms) to justify their practices,[14] M/M are one step behind their colleagues. In this image, as well as in any text or interview where they describe their work, theoretical language is almost absent. Without stringing together

M/M (Michel Amzalag and Mathais Augustyniak), *Untitled (Deleuze avec Bébé)* (1998). *Photo courtesy of Alison Gingeras.*

Deleuzian buzzwords, formulae, or models, the theory sign here is not invoked as a form of cultural capital. The proper name (or the cover of a book) is overshadowed by the codes of "cute" that saturate the image. M/M try to produce the antithesis of the serious, heavy, intellectual signs normally desired when the French theory effect is employed. The "cute-ification" of the theory sign—injection of chubby baby, grassy setting, cartoon figurine toy—renders Deleuze not only friendly, but as innocuous as a Hallmark greeting card.

Whether using strategies that veer toward the cheap or the cute, Hirschhorn and M/M both demonstrate an acute understanding of the mechanics of the French theory effect in the art world. While they come from different poles and announce diverging investments (Hirschhorn declares an overtly political intent, M/M adhere to a more ludic tradition), both play with a classic dichotomy in art. In each case, the "form" of the theory sign is valorized over its "content." Deleuze appears as a character (or formal element—image, sculpture) in both examples without adding any overt critical substance to the work. As a result, criticality is located elsewhere; it is displaced from the presence of the sign itself into the actual artist's strategy that manipulates the sign (rendering it "cute," "cheap," "harmless," or "handmade"). This should not be mistaken for a retreat from theory to practice, but an assertion of understanding by artists whose work pinpoints and dismantles the value-generating machines that surround them.

The task of identifying this double movement of the French theory effect in the art world—naturalization on the one hand, and the manipulation of the sign value of theory on the other—is not an exercise of nominating an imposture. It is all too easy to claim that the art world consistently misuses theory that it does not try to understand. Nor does it consist of revealing the "reality" of power games behind the sign value of theory that clearly circulates in almost every exhibition narrative or art review. Demystification is a dreary chore that drowns in a raging river of reactive forces. Academics might content themselves with the project of tracing back through three decades of art historical literature, exhibition catalogs, and magazines reviews to write a complete historiography of the reception and integration of various strains of French theory in the art world. Instead, a close reading of artists' work often reveals that they are far less intimidated by theory than other art professionals and that they are able to play with the effects of theory and its sign value in their own work. Artists do not need curators, critics, or historians to demystify, disseminate, or inject theory into their work. The art world is a strange sphere in which theory can simultaneously be reified, fixed, or crystallized in blocks or procedures, as well as a space where theory can become fluid; it can seem to disappear through sleight of hand, or reappear through tricky gestures. The disappearing act is nothing but this double, paradoxical movement: at the moment theory disappears, it is the most visible. Just like Hollywood.

Notes

1. Jean Baudrillard and Sylvère Lotringer, *Forget Baudrillard* (New York: Semiotext(e) Foreign Agents Series, 1987), pp. 123–25.
2. Ibid., p. 127.
3. Burkhard Riemschneider and Uta Grosenick, eds., *Art at the Turn of the Millennium* (Koln: Benedikt Taschen Verlag, 1999), p. 6; emphasis added.
4. Craig Houser, Leslie C. Jones, and Simon Taylor, eds., *Abject Art: Repulsion and Desire in American Art* (New York: Whitney Museum of American Art, 1993), p. 7.
5. Ibid., p. 7.

6. Ibid., p. 8.

7. This refers to an oft-cited review by a critic in the *London Times* who also described Documenta X as "a tragedy being enacted in the small German town of Kassel." Daniel Birnbaum, "Little d, Big X. Documenta X: The *Artforum* Questionnaire," *Artforum* 36 (September 1997), p. 106.

8. Sound bite offered by Ulrick Loock, director of the Kunsthalle Bern; ibid., p. 108.

9. Catherine David. *Documenta X: The Book.* Cantz, 1997.

10. Richard Flood, cited in "Little d, Big X. Documenta X," p. 110.

11. Nancy Princenthal. "Documenta X," *Art / Text* 59 (September 1997), p. 32.

12. In 1998, Hirschhorn constructed an "altar" on the streets of Zurich to venerate the Austrian writer Ingeborg Bachmann, who died tragically by burning to death in her bed. She was known for her chain-smoking—a smoldering cigarette caused the fatal fire. Hirschhorn fashioned the central element of his piece—Ingeborg Bachmann's name—entirely of boxes of Malboro cigarettes glued together. This sort of literality is noted here to give a dose of credibility to this speculation about Hirschhorn's hypothetical engagement with abjection.

13. For further discussion of this strategy see Alison Gingeras, "Striving to be Stupid: A Conversation with Thomas Hirschhorn," *Art Press* 239 (October 1998), p. 20.

14. See Elie During, "Blackboxing in Theory: Deleuze versus Deleuze," in this volume.

From Difference to Blackboxing: French Theory versus Science Studies' Metaphysics of Presence

MARIO BIAGIOLI

Few academics or academic disciplines in the United States have displayed a neutral stance toward French theory.[1] A few have taken it up with excitement, but more frequently it has been rejected without much detailed criticism, often citing its alleged pervasive and multiform dangers. In this respect, the position of science studies is interestingly atypical. Here we have a field that has adopted various blends of relativism in its methodological assumptions, is openly concerned with theoretical issues, and yet has only skirted French theory, using it as a tool for "special" problems but without allowing it to affect the canonical questions and assumptions at the roots of the field. This essay addresses this peculiar ambivalence.

The Peculiarity of Science Studies

Science studies is a loosely structured field that looks at science and technology from different perspectives (history, sociology, anthropology, as well as gender and literary studies).[2] Its active engagement with theoretical and methodological issues has been mostly the result of necessity, not virtue. In an attempt to take over the traditional epistemological questions of philosophy of science (while answering them differently), science studies practitioners have had to develop theoretical skills and sometimes reinvent themselves as analysts of the sociocultural and gendered production of scientific knowledge. Because many of the practitioners' original disciplines did not provide those skills as part of their standard graduate training, the range of interpretive positions that science studies has come to adopt is quite broad and has a certain self-taught, opportunistic quality to it. The absence of a theoretical canon has made the field hard to map, but it has also given it a good deal of unself-conscious freedom to experiment. Its adventurous theoretical bricolages may have raised a few philosophers' eyebrows, but have gained science studies an interested audience among more eclectic and cross-disciplinary fields in the humanities and social sciences.

Given such a genealogy, one would expect science studies to be a prime candidate for a productive engagement with French theory. Instead, the conversation has been either spotty or limited to those science-related topics addressed by French theorists themselves. Foucault's analyses of medicine, madness, sexuality, taxonomical systems, and biopower have provided the busiest area of conversation between science studies and French theory because of the topical overlap between the two fields.[3] But, with a few exceptions, Foucault's discussion of the power-knowledge nexus has been the source of ubiquitous citation, not sustained or detailed elaboration.[4] Semiotics makes cameo appearances in science studies, while some of Michel Serres's ideas (e.g., the "natural contract") have come into the field through the work of Bruno Latour but have not spread much beyond that.[5] Deleuze and Guattari are a background presence in the work of a handful of particularly theory-oriented authors, while Derrida's work (mostly his notion of "writing") has been taken up in, and limited to, a few specialized analyses of scientific inscriptions (with the exception of Rheinberger's notion of "experimental systems").[6] French feminism has had little direct influence on gender studies of science, and references to Lacan can be counted on one hand.[7] Similarly, Baudrillard's work or Lyotard's discussion of science in his *Postmodern Condition* have had almost no detectable effect on the field.

Such an ambivalence toward French theory, I argue, cannot be understood by framing it as a purely intellectual problem, something reducible to its pros and cons or to the possible relevance of its questions to science studies. This approach would risk reifying "pros," "cons," and "relevance" rather than consider these notions as products of the academic systems in which they are used. In place of an analysis of the philosophical rewards and problems of French theory considered as a body of texts, I take a more mundane look at the conditions of possibility of exchange between French theory and science studies as they develop when a body of texts produced in a specific intellectual and institutional context comes into contact with a field that has constituted itself in a different disciplinary economy—an economy that frames notions of reward, style, cross-disciplinary kinship, audience, and forms of academic reproduction.

For instance, what are the conditions under which certain fields can borrow freely and extensively from others (e.g., history from anthropology, film studies from psychoanalysis, literature from gender studies) and yet maintain or even expand their traditional niches in academia? And under what conditions, instead, are seemingly comparable borrowings (like the kinds of notions and approaches science studies could import from French theory) resisted as possible threats to a field's "identity"? What is it about the academic system of disciplines that frames what counts as a useful or relevant import and what, instead, as trivial or even dangerous? What can the relationship between science studies and French theory tell us about what "discipline" means in France and the United States and the role that notion plays in the economy of those two academic systems?

I begin by focusing on science studies' genealogy, its relationship to its subject matter, its borrowings from and relationship to neighboring disciplines, and the metaphysics of presence it has developed during its formation as a discipline. (By metaphysics of presence—a notion I will describe more extensively—I mean a set of assumptions about the socially constructed robustness of scientific knowledge). I will then try to show how such a metaphysics (with roots that are simultaneously philosophical and economic/institutional) has framed its interaction with French theory. I conclude by discussing the different academic ecologies of Anglophone science studies and French theory, as well as considering examples of the shapes that science studies has taken and could take outside of the U.S. academic system and its disciplinary economy.

Conservative Radicals and Their Metaphysics

Predictably, part of science studies' genealogy derives from research questions and models and the methodological canons that have sustained them. Much of the field's agenda has been framed by (or in response to) the issues and categories laid down decades ago by Fleck, Kuhn, and Feyerabend.[8] This heritage has placed an almost exclusive emphasis on the belief systems of groups (paradigms, thought collectives, research schools, etc.) and related issues. How is the production of knowledge and consensus tied to the social structure, hierarchies, forms of communication, and boundaries of these groups? How could the knowledge and practices of these groups be made to travel outside of them and become "universal"? How do controversies across groups reach closure and claims become "blackboxed"? Even gender issues (quite alien to the original agendas of the "founding fathers" of the field) have often been analyzed in terms of the beliefs and gender assumptions of groups, and how these framed their claims about nature, as well as the inclusion or exclusion of women from these communities.[9]

Traditionally the focus has been on the various group-based processes through which scientific claims (assumed to be inherently unstable, contestable, and underdetermined) are eventually made to stick, or on variations on this theme such as how "weak" claims are sometimes turned into "strong" ones.[10] In the same conceptual space I would also place discussions of how science (which is made up of many different subcultures operating according to different assumptions, methods, and practices) manages nevertheless to develop a pragmatic "unity," a kind of behavioral consensus that allows it to produce knowledge claims in the absence of a unified intellectual agreement about those very claims.[11]

Not surprisingly, sociology, social anthropology (in the United Kingdom), and cultural anthropology and ethnomethodology (in the United States) have provided much of science studies' toolbox. For the same reasons, Pierre Bourdieu's sociology of fields, and especially his concept of "habitus" have found several users in science studies (making him the most cited French thinker, after Michel Foucault). But, more frequently, it is Wittgenstein's later work that has provided the philosophical framework for science studies' group-oriented approaches.[12] ("Actor network theory" is an important exception that I'll discuss later.) But whether one talks about architecturally circumscribed spaces like laboratories, or about less physically bound entities such as schools of thought or disciplines, it often seems possible to find and talk about "language games." Debates about tacit knowledge, skill, and embodied knowledge can also be connected, in a more or less direct line, to Wittgenstein's discussion of what it means to "follow a rule."[13]

Science studies' comfortable reliance on Wittgenstein for its philosophical needs has dampened its appetite for alternatives. Its comfort level has only been enhanced by the fact that Wittgenstein is one of the few modern philosophers left largely unscathed by recent critical work—work that, instead, has inflicted substantial damage to Freud, Marx, the structuralists, and other major modern providers of comprehensive interpretive frameworks. More important, Wittgenstein's authority has been left unchallenged by both Anglophone (often analytical) philosophers as well as by French theory (which has either left Wittgenstein undeconstructed or, as in Lyotard's case, has relied on it).[14] Science studies, therefore, hasn't had to worry about having bet on a dead (or deconstructed) horse, nor has it had to defend itself from or convert to French theory.

But perhaps the main reason behind the scant interaction between science studies and French theory is that the field (contrary to the interpretation by some of its recent critics, who have branded it "postmodernist" because of its relativistic methodological assumptions) has developed a peculiar metaphysics of presence—a position that puts it at odds with several French theorists. Science studies does not attach presence to the kind of nature-related categories used by scientists or by older philosophy of science (or to the speech-like notions Derrida has discussed in the case of Western metaphysics), but rather to social structures, institutions, cultural values, networks, laboratories, trading zones, social and monetary resources, skill, tacit knowledge, and ubiquitous "practices."[15]

These categories instantiate "presence" in the sense that it is through them that science studies explains how scientific claims—claims it presents as inherently unstable—are eventually made robust and stable. But while such a metaphysics of presence is about what constitutes scientific knowledge, its mundane roots are in the academic economy in which science studies has developed and tried to establish itself. It is rooted in its relationship with the disciplines it studies and those it borrows and tries to differentiate itself from in an attempt to develop its "authorial voice."

Science studies' intellectual agenda still focuses on the age-old question of how one gets from many competing claims down to one. What differentiates it from previous philosophical traditions that have addressed these issues since the pre-Socratics is that the trajectory from "opinion" to "truth" is now usually explained as the effect of sociocultural entities (though several of them are arguably opaque or even trespassing into the occult). In its most radical expressions, science studies has turned upside down received views on the production of scientific knowledge, which presented nature itself as the ultimate arbiter of knowledge. But while placing society and not nature in the arbiter's seat, these radical revisionist moves have maintained a causal epistemological framework—one that is ultimately rooted in the nature-society dichotomy.[16] In some ways, social constructivism has done to realist philosophy of science what Marx did to Hegel. But like Marx who could not get away from the pull of dialectics, social constructivism has not been able to part with causality. In the end, it has simply inverted the direction of causality from nature to society.

Science studies in fact simultaneously criticizes and maintains the traditional dichotomy between nature and society, and the explanatory mental habits engendered by it. Although the field is vocal about the need to question the separation between nature and society, it usually ends up reinforcing such a dichotomy by casting its analyses as attempts to "bridge" it rather than to do away with a conceptualization of the problem that would then cast bridges as the natural solution. Only a handful of authors have seriously departed from this framework.[17] Most commonly, science studies still tries to bridge the gap between science and nature through a range of murky topoi such as mediation, clotting, influence, interaction, embodiment, cultural meanings, embeddedness, resonance, and through a host of optical metaphors (reflection, refraction, diffraction). That the field seems to turn a deaf ear to the opacity of these notions indicates, I believe, the extent of its commitment to a modernist, explanatory, causal ethos. Its earnest but short-lived engagement with the issues raised by the "writing culture" debate in ethnography—an engagement that has been mostly about putting the cat back in the bag as quickly as possible—is, I believe, another symptom of the field's reluctance to give up its disciplinary identity as a social "science."[18]

The stabilization of the unstable or the production of some unity out of disunity has become the field's central challenge. Science studies has reproduced, *mutatis mutandis*, the traditional distinction between the "context of discovery" and the "context of justification" and has dealt almost exclusively with the latter. Like logical empiricists who focused on the conditions under which scientific knowledge could be accepted as true while paying little attention to how new scientific claims emerged, science studies has analyzed how claims could be so-cially "blackboxed" and controversies be brought to closure, and not to how claims and beliefs keep emerging and move in different directions. While science studies is about the production of scientific knowledge, "production" tends to denote the survival of specific knowledge claims, not the proliferation of their differences. Science studies treats difference, play, and drift only as its starting point but *not* as its final result, or as processes that need analysis in and of them-selves. It assumes difference as the raw material for its analyses but then moves quickly to what it takes to be the more important stuff: the social processes through which difference is reduced, if only temporarily, to one. As a corollary, I suspect that science studies' interest in Foucault (by far the field's most cited exponent of French theory) may have been based on a selective reading of some of his notions (episteme, institutions, discipline) as objects that *constrain* (rather than produce) knowledge.

Relativistic Experts and Their Voices

I am not suggesting that science studies should reverse its interpretive priorities and dedicate itself to the joyous celebration of the proliferation of epistemological differences. That would simply flip (not undo) the polarity of the field's intellec-tual framework. What I want to point out, instead, is the strong *directionality* the field imputes to the knowledge-making process, and that such directionality sep-arates the beginning and the end of such a process not only chronologically but *analytically*. The "beginning" and the "end" become two different kinds of beasts. Not only do they attract different levels of attention, but also become the objects of different kinds of discourses and analytical constructs.

Furthermore, different values, different levels of professional reward have been attached to the study of the beginning and the end of the knowledge-making process. While most of my colleagues would argue that their analyses of the clo-sure of scientific controversies do not entail any value judgment on the claims that happened to "win" or "lose" those controversies, science studies *as a field* does attach value to closure (or cognate categories like legitimation, acceptance, canonization, etc.). More precisely, while science rewards the *results* of closure (that is, claims that are accepted by the community), science studies prizes the *explanation of the process* through which closure was achieved (or of why closure did not take place). In sum, science studies' metaphysics of presence is also re-lated to notions of disciplinary reward and "value."

The tensions produced by this metaphysics is most clear in science studies' acrobatic defenses or qualifications of its relativistic stances. The image of the field as made up of irresponsible relativists that has emerged in the recent "science wars" is something that has followed its practitioners at least since Kuhn's *Structure of Scientific Revolutions* (1962). The critics' main line has been that at best science studies flirts with the belief that "anything goes" or that at worst it fully endorses that position (or related ones, such as that scientific claims stick just because of the power of the sociopolitical interests behind them). Science studies practitioners see these critiques as misrepresentations. They respond by saying that, yes, they do believe scientific claims are underdetermined by evidence, that replication is affected by an endless logical regressus, that the choice of methodological assumptions is by no means univocal, and that communication across theoretical divides or across different experimental practices is inherently problematic. But they also say that, no, this does not amount to "anything goes." On the contrary, only a very *small* number of scientific claims do stick, and that they do so as the result of a lot of work, negotiations, and constraints.

Science studies, then, is not about arbitrariness but about how arbitrariness is made to end; it is about how consensus is established, if only temporarily. If the critics see relativism as the beginning and the end of science studies' program, its practitioners see the underdetermined nature of scientific claims only as the starting point of their work—work that then focuses almost exclusively on the intricate ways in which claims are made contingently robust despite their ever-contestable underpinnings.

While the critics equate constructivism with relativism, science studies (especially the sociology of scientific knowledge) displays a surprising scientistic ethos. Relativism is cast as a "scientific" methodology: unless you start from relativistic assumptions you will never understand how science *really* works. One starts as a relativist but ends up a social "scientist." One starts with assumptions about the inherent instability of scientific knowledge, but ends up with a (social) master narrative about how it becomes stable. In the end, we have turned ourselves into *relativistic experts*. The predicament is, I believe, telling.

The tension between relativism and normativity is particularly evident in the sociology of scientific knowledge, but it can also be found, *mutatis mutandis,* in other branches of science studies. As a result of their training in history, science historians have heard and reproduced (at least on an official level) the credo that history is about open-endedness (not determinism or normativity) and about description (not explanation). However, once they moved into science studies, historians felt that the descriptive ethos of their original discipline put them at risk of becoming epistemologically subordinated by the explanatory stances of their subject matter (science) and of their fellow travelers (sociologists and philosophers). This predicament was new to them because, in their previous incarnation as historians of social events and processes (or even as intellectual historians), they were not members of an epistemologically ambitious discipline.

This new disciplinary predicament has pushed them toward the implicit adoption of science studies' metaphysics of presence and the many tensions that go with it. For instance, they have engaged in an awkward methodological dance aimed at making "description" sound more explanatory, but not so explanatory as to undermine their disciplinary identity as historians. In some cases this has been attempted by characterizing their work as belonging to the genre of Geertz's "thick description," Ginzburg's "microhistory," or Nietzschean-Foucauldian "genealogy"—a move that is not justified so much by the theoretical and methodological clarity of such genres (which, in fact, can be quite opaque), but because they seem to give a name to the demarcation that science historians wish to draw between themselves and "merely" descriptive historians. There are also a few historians of science who proudly endorse historicism, but they usually do so not to limit the epistemological authority of their work but, on the contrary, to amplify it by criticizing the scientism and reification at the basis of the authority of philosophy and sociology of science. The result of that move is not to give up explanatory ambitions, but to defend them at the local level while undermining other disciplines, grand narratives and the explanations they produce about those same events or methodological constructs. Presence is not done away with but is rather found in local historical contexts.[19]

Disciplinary Economies

Science studies' metaphysics of presence and its scant engagement with French theory is largely a matter of how its academic genealogy framed its disciplinary kinship categories and authoritative ambitions—ambitions that cannot be severed from the logic of academic economy in which they are constituted. Science studies' epistemological stance is as hybridized as its academic predicament. The field is uneasily nested between the "two cultures," unclear about how to negotiate different kinship lines pulling it in different directions; it has emerged by rejecting previous views of the production of scientific knowledge while maintaining the same causal framework and epistemological questions of its predecessors; it brings new perspectives to old epistemological questions but imports most of its tools from other traditional disciplines (mostly social sciences) that had used them to pursue questions other than those of scientific knowledge; it tries to blend strong relativistic assumptions with an equally strong explanatory ethos; it questions the "naturalness" of science's authority but resists doing the same about its own claims; it can have a sympathetic understanding of what French theory is, but usually treats it only as a supplier of "special" tools for "special" problems because a more extensive conversation might end up destabilizing its academic position and authority.

I do not know whether, or to what extent, I mean these comments as a criticism or simply as a statement of science studies' predicament and genealogy. In fact, some of the factors behind science studies' metaphysics of presence can be quickly traced to the specific constraints deriving from its subject matter and to science's dominant role in academia.[20] As inscribed in its name, science studies is still about that thing called science, not about broader (but not necessarily less tricky) notions such as knowledge. Even if one does not think of science as an enterprise producing truth, one must acknowledge that it exists as a powerful and highly successful profession rooted in the production and reward of claims recognized by one's peers. The existence and especially the success of science (no matter what the reasons for such success) determine the subject of science studies as science studies. To a large extent, "presence" comes with the territory (or at least with *this* territory). And it is not clear to me how much science studies could move away from its subject-imposed subject without changing its name and moving into different academic niches.

Similar things could be said about science studies' commitment to an explanatory ethos. It does have costs, it does produce aporias (especially when it is coupled with relativistic assumptions about the indeterminacy of scientific claims), but then if aporias were death knells, academia would be a cemetery. Or, to put it differently, aporias may be the cost a discipline has to pay to develop and maintain its "symbolic capital" within an academic system in which rewards are ultimately tied to expertise (or expertise "effects") even though that expertise might be about aporias themselves.

One could also consider other crucial elements of the academic economy such as the "products" a discipline is expected to deliver. While we often tend to think of texts as such products, perhaps we should also focus on our role as Ph.D. producers. Academics are keenly aware of issues relating to the recruitment, funding, training, and placement of graduate students, but then for some reason we tend to bracket off those concerns and focus instead on our role as scholars and intellectuals. Once we admit that, at least in U.S. academia, the cost of a five-year graduate fellowship matches (and sometime exceeds) that of a condominium, it becomes apparent that a discipline is a peculiar industry and, as such, it would not survive for long if it failed to carefully package its students for successful placement in recognizable niches within the academic market. Science studies' metaphysics of presence, then, is also about the stabilization of academic market categories, that is, the production of disciplinary "value."

By dropping its explanatory commitments and developing closer ties to French theory, science studies would perhaps free itself from some intellectual and disciplinary constraints, but it might also change its field of authority, thereby diminishing the likelihood of its academic reproduction. By taking that direction, science studies would probably move closer to the predicament of a field like cultural studies (with all the pros and cons that move might entail). There are indications that, in some instances, this is already happening. Science studies work most explicitly informed by French theory has indeed moved toward literature and rhetoric departments or toward cross-disciplinary programs in the humanities; but by doing so it has also reduced its chances at reproducing itself as "science studies."[21]

From Boundaries to Networks

The tensions of science studies' predicament can be exemplified by the peculiar reception of Bruno Latour's work, which in some ways occupies a hybrid position between science studies and French theory.

As it does with French theory, traditional science studies sees Latour as a very important source of "suggestions," of ideas "one should think about," or of a range of "proposals" one should pick and choose from. At the same time, because it has an undeniable family resemblance with science studies, his work cannot be marginalized as French theory has been. He is perhaps the most cited author within science studies, but, at the same time, the field is far from being "Latouricized."

Latour is one of the few authors who have explicitly rejected science studies' metaphysic of presence based on the nature-society dichotomy—a position that aligns him with some of French theory.[22] And, like French theory, his work is hard to categorize in terms of disciplinary boundaries. Although it developed from empirical ethnographies of scientific laboratories, the questions it has since pursued go well beyond those of traditional science studies to the point of questioning the relevance of the fields' disciplinary identity.[23] Then, like French theory, Latour is French. This means that his work, while strongly pitched for the Anglophone market, has developed in an academic system and in disciplinary frameworks that are much closer to those of French theory than of traditional science studies. His literary style, genres, and publication venues are much closer to those of Parisian *maîtres à penser* than to American or British academic authors.[24] At the same, Latour is no friend of French theory. With the exception of the work of Michel Serres, he has had few kind words for French theory, which he has lumped in with postmodernism and then usually dismissed with little engagement.[25] While he does not place himself in the modernist camp, he also rejects the label *postmodernist* and instead defines his work as "amodern." Then, unlike French theory (but like traditional science studies) he is still strongly committed to an explanatory ethos (though one that differs from that of the traditional social sciences).

Latour's innovation hinges on his (and Michel Callon's) notion of "translation"—a notion that is quite distinct from sociocultural "mediation" (and related categories), which most of science studies sees as constitutive of scientific knowledge.[26] Translation is meant quite literally as trans-lation, that is, as spatial displacement, not as a process through which "meaning" is negotiated or reproduced. According to Latour, claims do not have sociocultural meanings, nor are they blackboxed through political, social, or professional "power." His approach is constructivist but differs radically from social constructivism in that social structures and dynamics (such as "power") are not seen as providing the containing and stabilizing framework for unstable claims. Both claims about nature and social objects are seen as symmetrically constructed through a series of spatial translations, through a long chain of dis-placements and re-alignments of hybrid entities that are neither natural nor social. The strength of scientific claims is the result of their "spatial" features—the density and length of the chains of translations of which they are part. Laboratories play a crucial role in Latour's model, but not as socially powerful institutions whose walls serve to separate expert knowledge and its legitimate practitioners from other forms of knowledge that are constructed as unscientific precisely by not being admitted in. Laboratories do not produce knowledge through socioepistemological gate-keeping, but precisely by breaking down the separation between nature and society through the construction of long, fine-textured, and dense chains of translations of which the laboratory becomes a "node."[27]

While Latour's emphasis on hybrids and displacements would seem to send him in the direction of French theory, he parts ways with the postmodernists because he does not wish his hybrids to "drift."[28] Like traditional science studies, Latour still relates knowledge to control, not proliferation. Latour's hybrids do proliferate (and the more they proliferate the better it is), but they are also "lined up" through translations and networks. He abandons science studies' social metaphysics of presence, but then immediately introduces a network-based ontology—an ontology that is neither about nature nor society but is an ontology nevertheless. In this sense, his version of "amodernity" is close to modernism.

In sum, science studies broke up the small containment vessel that traditional philosophy had built around science, and expanded the definition of science so as to include its sociocultural dimensions. But while replacing a small vessel with a larger one, it did not question the notion and role of vessel itself. The socioepistemological box that science studies constructed around science doubled as a disciplinary box for the field—a box that framed science studies' academic predicament and identity. Therefore, Latour's replacement of the nature-society dichotomy with networks of translations is not seen as just another approach to science studies but as a model that risks dissolving the field's boundaries by substituting them with interpretive networks that cut across many (perhaps all) traditional disciplinary divides. And it is not clear what kind of disciplinary boxes could accommodate the work produced through that kind of analysis. In some ways, Latour's work is like Leviticus's "abominations" studied by Mary Douglas. It doesn't have scales, but it doesn't have legs, either. And science studies can't figure out if it can eat it.

From Author Function to Discipline Function

These preoccupations are perhaps more important in the United States than in France, where, although the academic system is more rigid and less open to cross-disciplinary work than here (to the extent that fields like gender or cultural studies are given almost no academic space) there is also a sizable extrauniversity market for intellectual productions. Much of what we call French theory has developed and circulated in this market—a market that seems less concerned with disciplinary affiliations (at least in the case of those authors who manage to gain sufficient fame to operate in it).

The presence and influence of a peculiar institution such as the College de France greatly contributes to such an extrauniversity, author-based economy of intellectual products. As a highly prestigious and elitist institution that operates outside and above the normal academic system, the College can occasionally canonize remarkably hybrid authors like Barthes and Foucault (and allow them to define the titles and descriptions of their chairs). Because it embodies the state's authority—an authority that would not mean much in the U.S. academic system but is remarkably effective in France—the College can lend legitimacy to the idea that intellectual work can be almost discipline free (when done by appropriately anointed *maîtres à penser*).

These differences extend to the modalities of cultural and disciplinary reproduction. Unlike the university system, in which disciplines gain authority and reproduce themselves by placing an increasing number of their students within that very system, authors who operate in the French nonuniversity sphere tend to reproduce *themselves* (not so much their disciplines). They are more like "stars" (albeit of smallish and self-selected communities) rather that "founding fathers" of specific disciplines.

Perhaps one could say that this section of the French intellectual market is more author based, while in the United States disciplines and fields seem to dominate intellectual taxonomies and hierarchies of academic value. We even feel the need to create a discipline-like term such as "French theory" to designate something that was not seen as a discipline, field, or school in its country of origin. The coining of the term "Yale school" may reflect these dynamics. It seems, then, that in the United States the "discipline function" has taken over many dimensions of the "author function."

These two different economies of intellectual capital are inscribed in the different styles of the texts they produce. U.S. academic productions tend to follow disciplinary styles (types of narrative, footnote apparatus, standards of evidence, etc.) and are usually published by academic presses. French theory, having been articulated, published, and rewarded in a different system, tends to develop styles that are neither those of U.S. academia nor those of American academic authors who have crossed over into commercial publishing (and because of the different structure of the two intellectual fields, such a crossing carries very different connotations in the two countries).

French theory seems simultaneously too difficult and technical to be aimed at more popular, nonacademic audiences (hence the frequent critique of it as "jargony"), and too little "disciplined" to fit easily into U.S. academic taxonomies. This taxonomical puzzle informs the tendency, among sympathetic U.S. academics, to see them as providing "interesting" suggestions and ideas but not discipline-based claims and positions that the corresponding U.S. fields should feel compelled to engage with. More specifically, because academic disciplines tend to be attached to subject matters that are often defined in terms of their material features (specific natural processes, geographical areas, historical periods, kinds of texts, or categories of practices and professions), academics have a hard time figuring out what French theory's "subject matter" might be. Failing to do that, they often end up reading French theory as providing "methods," or to cast its authors in the category of "cultural commentators."

That French theory has been called contradictory names in the United States (from too radical, nihilistic, and flaky, to dangerous or even potentially Nazi friendly) suggests that we are facing a true translation problem—not translation between languages but between different intellectual economies, different "forms of life." It is also interesting that some U.S. academics seem to react to French theory the way people react to controversial artwork. Not only do some love it while others hate it, but the expression of these reactions often exceeds the vocabulary of traditional academic judgments. Unable to fit French theory into U.S. academic taxonomies, its authors are placed into the ultimate category of academic "otherness": the artist. Unable to translate the "quality" of these authors' work into categories such as expertise or knowledge, or to compare them with "the best in their field" (because it's not clear what that field might be) we end up appreciating them for their "uniqueness." They become the object of "taste."

Notes

1. I want to thank Sande Cohen, Elizabeth Lee, and Matt Jones for their comments, criticism, and help. The term *French theory* is left unspecified throughout this essay for two reasons: first, its referents change depending on the writer/reader background and disciplinary perspective; and second (and more important), I take the problems of definition of French theory to be inherent to its construction. This second issue is one of the underlying themes of this essay. In any case, the names I associate with French theory are Foucault, Baudrillard, Deleuze, Guattari, Lyotard, Derrida, and, less directly, Lacan, de Certeau, Barthes, Bourdieu, and Serres.

2. Recent surveys of the field include Sheila Jasanoff, Gerald Markle, James Petersen, and Trevor Pinch, eds., *Handbook of Science and Technology Studies* (Thousand Oaks, Calif.: Sage, 1994); Jan Golinski, *Making Natural Knowledge: Constructivism and the History of Science* (Cambridge: Cambridge University Press, 1998); and David Hess, *Science Studies: An Advanced Introduction* (New York: New York University Press, 1997). An extensive (but still partial) collection of science studies literature is in Mario Biagioli, ed., *The Science Studies Reader* (New York: Routledge, 1999). For more specific subfields see Evelyn Fox Keller and Helen Longino, eds., *Feminism and Science* (Oxford: Oxford University Press, 1996); George Marcus, ed., *Technoscientific Imaginaries* (Chicago: University of Chicago Press, 1995); Donald MacKenzie and Judith Wajcman, eds., *The Social Shaping of Technology*, (Milton Keynes: Open University Press, 1998).

3. The references to Foucault's work have increased steeply in the last five years or so. They are too numerous to be included in a note.

4. Some of the exceptions are Joseph Rouse, *Knowledge and Power: Toward a Political Philosophy of Science*, (Ithaca, N.Y.: Cornell University Press, 1987); Paul Rabinow, "Artificiality and Enlightenment: From Sociobiology to Biosociality," in Biagioli, ed., *The Science Studies Reader*, pp. 407–16; Andrew Pickering, *The Mangle of Practice: Time, Agency, and Science* (Chicago: University of Chicago Press, 1995). More examples can be found in the literature on the history of sexuality, medicine, and madness. Foucault's archaeology has been an ongoing theme in Ian Hacking's work, from *The Emergence of Probability* (Cambridge: Cambridge University Press, 1975) to *Rewriting the Soul* (Princeton: Princeton University Press, 1995).

5. The most direct engagement with semiotics is found in Brian Rotman, *Ad Infinitum . . . : An Essay in Corporeal Semiotics* (Stanford: Stanford University Press, 1993) and *Signifying Nothing: The Semiotics of Zero* (repr., Stanford: Stanford University Press, 1993). For a critical review of the uses of semiotics in science studies see Timothy Lenoir, "Was the Last Turn the Right Turn? The Semiotics Turn and A. J. Greimas," in Biagioli, ed., *The Science Studies Reader*, pp. 290–301. Some of Michel Serres's early work was on history of science, but his more philosophical positions have been taken up in Bruno Latour, *We Have Never Been Modern* (Cambridge:

Harvard University Press, 1993). See also Michel Serres and Bruno Latour, *Eclair-cissements: Cinq entretiens avec Bruno Latour* (Paris: Bourin, 1992).

6. On Deleuze and Guattari, see Richard Doyle, *On Beyond Living: Rhetorical Trans-formations of the Life Sciences* (Stanford: Stanford University Press, 1997), and espe-cially Pickering, *The Mangle of Practice*. On Derrida see Hans-Joerg Rheinberger, *Toward a History of Epistemic Things: Synthesizing Proteins in the Test Tube* (Stanford: Stanford University Press, 1997); Lily Kay, "In the Beginning Was the Word?: The Genetic Code and the Book of Life," in Biagioli, ed., *The Science Studies Reader*, pp. 224–33; Doyle, *On Beyond Living;* Rotman, *Ad Infinitum*; Roger Hart, "How to Do Things with Words: Incommensurability, Translation, and Problems of Existence in Seventeenth-Century China," in Lydia Liu, ed., *Tokens of Exchange* (Durham, N.C.: Duke University Press, forthcoming); and Mario Biagioli, "Stress in the Book of Nature: The Supplemental Logic of Galileo's Mathematical Realism," forthcoming.

7. A notable exception is Sherry Turkle, *Life on the Screen* (New York: Simon and Schuster, 1995).

8. Because this is not a review of the history and state of the field, I do not provide comprehensive references to the many authors and debates I summarize here.

9. The work of Donna Haraway is a notable exception in that, through her notion of the "cyborg," she bypasses the group-based analyses (and the nature-society di-chotomy) that tend to inform the literature on gender and science or women in sci-ence.

10. The first position, I believe, characterizes much of the sociocultural history of sci-ence and of the sociology of scientific knowledge. The second refers to the work of Latour, Callon, and the proponents of the sociology of translations and of the actor-network theory.

11. See some of the essays in *The Disunity of Science: Boundaries, Contexts, and Power*, ed. Peter Galison and David Stump (Stanford: Stanford University Press, 1996), and chapter 9 of Peter Galison, *Image and Logic* (Chicago: University of Chicago Press, 1997).

12. Given the "family resemblances" between Wittgenstein and some theoretical con-structs found in classic texts by Kuhn, Fleck, Feyerabend, Barnes, Bloor, and Collins, the filiation between Wittgenstein's work and contemporary science studies is so widespread that it is not usually recorded in explicit references. Sustained dis-cussions of the place of Wittgenstein in the sociology of scientific knowledge are David Bloor's *Wittgenstein and Social Science* (New York: Columbia University Press, 1986) as well as his *Wittgenstein, Rules and Institutions* (London: Routledge, 1997), and Michael Lynch, *Scientific Practice and Ordinary Action* (Cambridge: Cambridge University Press, 1993).

13. For a critical review of the science studies literature on tacit knowledge and skill in science studies (and Wittgenstein's place in it) see Stephen Turner, *The Social Theory of Practices* (Chicago: University of Chicago Press, 1994).

14. Jean-François Lyotard, *The Postmodern Condition* (Minneapolis: University of Min-nesota Press, 1984), but see also his *Political Writings* (Minneapolis: University of Minnesota Press, 1993). Chapter 4 of Gilles Deleuze and Félix Guattari's *A Thou-sand Plateaus* (Minneapolis: University of Minnesota Press, 1987) may be seen as a radicalization of Wittgenstein on language games. I thank Sande Cohen for some of these references.

15. I include here a few very limited pointers for those not familiar with the science studies literature. For a review of the use of "practice" in science studies, see Jan Golinski, "The Theory of Practice and the Practice of Theory," *Isis* 81 (1990): 492–505. On the role of laboratories start with Steven Shapin and Simon Schaffer, *Leviathan and the Air Pump*, (Princeton: Princeton University Press, 1985). On the relation between problems of knowledge and problems of social order (as well as on skill and tacit knowledge) see Harry Collins, *Changing Order: Replication and induction in Scientific Practice* (London: Sage, 1985). The notion of "trading zone" is developed by Peter Galison in chapter 9 of his *Image and Logic*. On "networks" see Michel Callon, "Some Elements of a Sociology of Translation," and Bruno Latour, "Give Me a Laboratory and I Will Raise the World" in Biagioli, ed., *The Science Studies Reader*. The seminal text on "interest theory" is Barry Barnes, *Interests and the Growth of Knowledge* (London: Routledge, 1977). An early but very influential discussion of science and cultural values is David Bloor, *Knowledge and Social Imagery* (London: Routledge, 1976).

16. While I believe that this framework characterizes most of contemporary science studies, it is clearest in the case of the sociology of scientific knowledge. The work of Harry Collins (starting with *Changing Order*) and his notion of "core set" is central to this school. For a critique of the causal asymmetry between nature and society, see Bruno Latour, "One More Turn After the Social Turn," in Biagioli, ed., *The Science Studies Reader*, pp. 276–89. Interesting discussions about the theoretical underpinnings of science studies and its several "schools" can be found in Andrew Pickering, *Science as Practice and Culture* (Chicago: University of Chicago Press, 1992).

17. Donna Haraway's "cyborgs" and Bruno Latour's "hybrids" have marked the beginning of this shift.

18. See the various positions proposed in Steve Woolgar, ed., *Knowledge and Reflexivity* (London: Sage, 1988). A more radical stance has been developed in Malcolm Ashmore, *The Reflexive Thesis* (Chicago: University of Chicago Press, 1989). The locus classicus of the "writing culture" debate in ethnography is James Clifford and George Marcus, eds., *Writing Culture* (Berkeley and Los Angeles: University of California Press, 1986).

19. An example of this "relentless historicism" is Lorraine Daston and Peter Galison, "The Image of Objectivity," *Representations* 40 (1992): 81–128.

20. I have sketched some of these problems in the introduction to *The Science Studies Reader*, pp. xi–xiv.

21. I would put the work of Donna Haraway, Richard Doyle, Brian Rotman, and Katherine Hayles in this group.

22. Latour, "One More Turn—After the Social Turn"; and Bruno Latour, *Pandora's Hope* (Cambridge: Harvard University Press, 1999).

23. Unlike his earlier work (*Laboratory Life* [with Steve Woolgar], *The Pasteurization of France, and Science in Action*), his more recent publications (especially *We Have Never Been Modern*) are much broader in scope and more philosophical in tone.

24. Several of his French publications are in magazines and journals (and about topics) that would not be considered "scholarly" by U.S. academic standards.

25. Latour's most explicit engagement with French theory is in *We Have Never Been Modern*.

26. Callon, "Some Elements of a Sociology of Translation"; and Michel Callon and Bruno Latour, "Unscrewing the Big Leviathans: How Do Actors Macrostructure Reality?" in Karen Knorr Cetina and Aron Cicourel, eds., *Advances in Social Theory and Methodology*, (London: Routledge, 1981), pp. 277–301.

27. Latour, "Give Me a Laboratory and I Will Raise the World," and *The Pasteurization of France*.

28. Latour, *We Have Never Been Modern*, p. 61.

Supplement A:
Research Historians and French Theory

SANDE COHEN

What does it suggest when historians, focused on the past, engage in rivalrous conflict with present modes of writing? The history of historiography shows that such rivalries are a constant of Western historical writing.[1] Given this constancy, what is the best way to pose the question of historians and their rivalries with other "representors"? Are historians *always* judges of present knowledge claims? Are historians equipped to counterclaim a "time's" necessities and accidents? If so, what strange power passes through historians?

The most pernicious charge leveled at French theory's effect in the United States has to do with the accusation that such theories are causally responsible for the waning influence of the humanities and social sciences. The distinguished historian Perez Zagorin, writing in the journal *History and Theory,* recently claimed that "postmodernism has sown a great deal of intellectual confusion in some of the humanist disciplines . . . promoting . . . politicization [of the university] . . . one of the contributory causes of the drastic and disturbing decline of the position of the humanities . . . one of the last relics of the political mood of the 1960s."[2] There is wide support for Zagorin's inaccurate statements, as can be seen in everything from book reviews in major U.S. newspapers to the most serene scholarly publications. I would like to connect the accusations leveled by historians such as Zagorin with some facts about the historical profession and then focus on some texts that castigate French theory, written out of one research history department, at UCLA. The point is to examine historians' resistance to French theory, extracting concepts drawn from that resistance; and to connect these concepts to how institutions engage in competitions for knowledge claims as compressed and volatile as the "humanities" certainly suggest.

Nationally, history departments have been shrinking since the early 1970s, at the latest. The American Historical Association has reported that for the year 1997, 954 historians were granted Ph.D.s in the United States. That is about 2 percent of doctoral awards for that same year. The humanities as a whole now comprise only 13 percent of total Ph.D.s awarded. Fewer Ph.D.s of any sort are being awarded; in 1970, for 210 million Americans, a total of thirty-two thousand Ph.D.s were granted; in 1997, with a population of about 260 million, forty-two thousand Ph.D.s were awarded, a decline relative to the growth of the population. The UCLA history department admitted, until the late 1980s, well over three hundred doctoral candidates per year; next year they will admit thirty five. There has been growth only in areas that have emerged from other disciplines, as in the addition of history of science and science studies to departments of history, and usually only at schools that can replenish positions withdrawn either through retirement or allocation of funds from the central powers that be. Doing research history is more expensive and difficult than ever, a point that many critics of the "decline of the university" often neglect, as more frequently capitalist business practices internally drive zones of research;[3] research is expensive, so the competition for resources is a palpable driving force of all academic production. Given the overall systemic shrinkage of humanities and then history departments, it is understandable that defense of research projects commands more recognition than ever. This recognition is given in the fact that UCLA's history department is now ranked sixth (by the National Research Council), "up" from twenty-fifth fifteen years ago in terms of quality of research and teaching. These rankings are crucial in signaling to funding agencies criteria of evaluation by which to support—or decline to support—research projects.

The "decline" of the humanities, and especially history departments, as raised by Zagorin and so many others, has paralleled a fierce competition in all departments of the humanities. The "top" of the profession now commands salaries of more than $100,000 per year, benefits not included; while about ten percent of the nation's faculty earn more than $80,000 per year, those earning above $100,000 make up 4.5 percent of the faculty. As the "top" has received more resources, the humanities disciplines have become more unequal—57 percent of positions in U.S. humanities departments are now nontenurable. Thus, at no research institution is it in the interests of the placeholders to sponsor more competition—especially as coming from other disciplines and intruding into a department's "home turf." One competes for entry; afterward, the goal is protection of territory, even if this means constant expansion. This internal class warfare (based on prestation and effectivity), endlessly carried on in the name of the "purity" of scholarship and historical writing, is permanent; it is indicated in the troubling fact that it now takes an average of eighteen years past the bachelor's degree to tenure—eleven years from B.A. to Ph.D., seven more to tenure—and the typical history department now has about 20 percent of its faculty "stalled" in tenure but unable to complete a second book within ten years of receiving tenure. The time it takes to produce one scholar in the humanities seems actually to be connected to a narrative of difficulty internal to every humanities division or field. In addition, the publication rates at even the best schools are mixed: the average professor with tenure at a research institution publishes two articles per year, one book every six years. Course loads in any department declaring itself to be "publicly" significant have dropped. Media-driven and scholarly reviews often revolve around "cults"—think of Stanley Fish on the cover of the *New York Times Magazine*, a picture of the scholar leaning on his motorcycle collection.

It is arguable that the "crisis" and "decline" of the humanities also has its cause in the common practice in university departments taking it on themselves to resist all the writings that might "eat into" their market share of book publishing, access to students, reproduction of "schools of thought," the vast implications of the secondary market (including citation indexes), where one's work is reviewed, and so on. Who is unaware of the ramifications of the "star system," and, in this context, is it significant that Jean Baudrillard wrote *The Mirror of Production* while teaching high school in France? The market share of French theory boomed: Baudrillard's *Simulations* has sold over twenty-five thousand copies since 1983—and not in a university press edition. Historians in America, unless picked up by the mass book market, and to that degree suffering a bit of degradation in the eyes of the research community, could hope their books would be course-adopted by their peers—not the same thing as creating a new market, which the French theorists managed to do. In short, French theory's resistance to historical representation encountered historian's resistance to a detailed examination of the language of research, the discourse of theory, the signs of interpretation, and the logics of events. It seems sheer displacement to say French theory "caused" any such decline in the humanities; it could be argued instead that French theory "saved" a decrepit and venal system from an American, yet Mandarin fate.

Now, and more specifically, one can speak of research historians, particularly modern Europeanists who were finishing degrees or starting tenure in the late 60s, as committed to not just "hard" or archival research, but also to its embedding in some story anchored to Enlightenment certitudes. Here, French theory, written by obscure intellectuals, collided with historians: French theorists shifted debates over history from the plausibility of metanarrative inclusion (and exclusions) to the *language* of plausibility, introducing *aporetics* into everything that the humanities, and especially history, thought settled. What was believed settled was the appropriateness of metanarrative to any and every human experience. French theory collided with that of modern Europeanists who refused to challenge Enlightenment notions of history, specifically the metanarratives of liberation and freedom, knowledge and understanding, reconciliation and amelioration. French theory argued that Enlightenment sense(s) of history were part of the problem and not a solution. Which problem? That the capitalization of experience had eliminated, for most people, the possibility of *making history*. The defeat of fascism and Nazism in Europe was nothing to gloat over, since capitalism soon more deeply installed than ever before a terrorism without brownshirts, the terror of subjects-in-debt or repetition, endless encodings of identity and recognition. The famous "drift" so many allude to in writings about post-everything is a red herring.

Now, the placeholders of the historian's resistance to French theory have accomplished quite a lot of writing. Zagorin's attempt to connect "confusion," "politicization," and "decline" is just one instance of the same conjunction played out repeatedly in both scholarly and popular mediums. And as the remedy against French theory is said to be research, it might be instructive to look closely at research-identified historians to see how they encode their treatments of French theory. Let's take the historians seriously at their word—that research *informs their judgments of the present.*

The UC system has produced quite a lot of writing about deconstruction, postmodernism, and French theory. There is a *public record* in which historians have made their positions clear about French theory. One of the basic expressions of the dilemma that postmodernism poses for historians has been taken up by Lynn Hunt in her essay "History beyond Social History."[4] Hunt writes on many issues relevant to the diversity of historical writing; she worries about text theory undoing social theory, the latter "a generalizable story about cause and effect." She is also concerned with not eliminating "discursive structures" as some models of history writing have done in the name of "hard data." Synthesis of "social theory" and "discursive theory" is important, if it can be done in a non-mythological way. But since social theories and discourse theories are themselves internally diverse in means or device (partly figural, partly conceptual, partly speculative, partly factual, etc.) as well as in contradiction with other theories, Hunt is unable to say that synthesis must be political—something omitted so a clear narrative line can be established. Synthesis is a political act in the end. The question becomes, Why is X synthetic theory or model given institutional and media visibility?

There is no denial by Hunt that narrative patterning is always "a strategic deployment . . . for political control over the past." Fair enough. But is "social theory" even possible within a fully capitalized social system?—that is precisely what French theory's challenge to metanarratives was all about. Crudely put, the challenge was that capitalism removes social theory, replacing it, bit by bit, with facts on the ground in its favor. The rather extraordinary conjunction in the United States of psychologism and economic behaviorism might testify to the impossibility of social theory. Hunt calls for the connection of feminism and psychoanalysis so as to make a social theory—inclusive metanarrative—to jump-start social theory. Some believe (like Roudinesco or Ravetto, in this volume) psychoanalysis to be directly repressive of social understanding, and thus incredible when used as the basis of social theory and narrative inclusion. When Hunt writes that "we will always have to tell them [stories, metanarratives]," that could be considered irresponsible: the story of humanity as told by psychoanalysis is more a mode of writing than a conduit to truth, and hardly an experimentation with sense and meaning.

So it is with some despair that one reads in Hunt, Margaret Jacob, and Joyce Appleby's *Telling the Truth About History* that American applications of French theory toward historiography are "extreme," that analysis of historical theory written out of Lyotard and company results in the death of history and historical writing, citing one critic of historiography as implying that one "ought not to write history at all or ought to admit in the end history is another form of fiction."[5] French theorists never argued that history is a form of fiction; the argument was that fictional components are mixed with aggressive figural components, syntactical modes of persuasion, political beliefs, philosophical presuppositions, and so on, that historical texts were *read* and *interpreted as* variegated semiotic machines with mixed social results. Why doesn't a research ethos extend to French theory? Hunt and colleagues make postmodernism and deconstruction mean that "all concepts are in the end illusory creatures of the moment."[6] That's a grotesque reduction. The word *extreme* comes back again to Lyotard when they write that he had reduced the West to "psychosis," a truly unacceptable metanarrative for historians. Why? Lyotard's counternarrative has the merit of saying the West was always destructive, always a slaughter bench. Through his reading of Greek philosophy and Hebraic materials, not unlike the sources Erich Auerbach worked with, Lyotard made a radical hypothesis. In the face of Enlightenment controls that do not disturb capitalist reproduction, Lyotard and others proposed that one might think of the West as a colossal *monad*, devouring the future.

Instead of facing such ideas, and the rents that accompany the sense of Enlightenment discourse as flawed, French theory is reduced to the point where "language thus stands as an insuperable barrier to truth."[7] Could research historians publicly defend the *Cratylism* implicitly supported by that statement—who or what has a direct connection to "the truth" through language said to be continuous with nonlanguage? The equation—language = barrier—was never argued by a single writer identified with French theory, so how does such an equation get made? Is it only a piece of *antiproduction* from historians?

In the volume *Knowledge and Postmodernism in Historical Perspective*, the shift from historical analysis based on documents to the proliferation of interpretive models is rendered as the slide from causality to meaning—*postmodernism* is the umbrella term for everything that smacks of cultural studies and, especially, critical theories of language joined to cultural studies. The post-modernists included in *Knowledge and Postmodernism* are featured only insofar as they do not cut the thread of "hope"; they are critics who can and have "deflate[d] the postmodern dragon," those pessimists about Enlightenment said to have abandoned the rules of representation and communication. Lyotard's writings are cited, twice in one page, and derided as "radical," this scare word standing in for any kind of systematic treatment of his ideas. Deconstruction is said to operate such that it "tears a text apart," "tears" a synecdoche for "radical," "extremist," and "violent."[8]

More of a theoretical focus can be gleaned from UCLA's history department when considering the writings of Saul Friedlander, Carlo Ginzburg, and Perry Anderson. All reject French theory in the name of psychoanalysis as well as in the name of research and documentation projects, and, for Ginzburg, by focus on the class origins of French theory. Friedlander has written that Foucault and Lévi-Strauss made arguments that counseled "gloomy forecasts" about the historical world, locating their writings in apocalyptics and antihumanism.[9] In another work, Friedlander writes that "present-day sensibilities" have been captured by an ironic mode of feeling, equated with "an abridgement of hope." While acknowledging a premise from French theory, that there can be no "closure" of the Shoah's "excess," this isn't Bataille talking, for in another place Friedlander has it that deconstruction is said to "exclude" a sense of "stable historical representation." It is opaque how the Holocaust is to remain both irreducible yet subject to "historical representation." The historian is rendered as a therapist who should be in constant "self-awareness" about representing the past, and who could disagree with that?[10]

In *Probing the Limits of Representation* (1992), Friedlander speaks of "present memory" and the "global intellectual shift" requiring adjustments in historicization. He writes that "historical relativism" and "aesthetic experimentation" of the "final solution" raise questions of the limits of representation, that an "imperative" to truth is required. Neither "imperative" nor "relativism" is defined, raising problems: if one does not deny the final solution, if one acknowledges a simple "it happened," then isn't everything else "relative" precisely once representations get going—especially as to which metanarrative(s) are the best explanatory frames? Everyone says that comedy is inappropriate as a representation of the final solution, but hasn't Benigni's film *Life Is Beautiful* demolished that restriction? If the conjunction between metanarrative giving "stable realities" and questions of truth can't be settled, shouldn't one acknowledge that disjunction—and go further with experiments in representation? In fact, shouldn't one embrace a relativism of perspectives as a starting point for historical representation? How can one insist on "truth" at the same time one claims a "feel" and "sense" that an interpretation is wrong? Friedlander says that "postmodernism" (French theory) rejects "the possibility of identifying some stable reality or truth beyond the constant polysemy and self-referentiality of linguistic constructs,"[11] but I can't think of a single text in French theory that says the final solution is nothing but polysemy and self-referentiality. But the discourse *on* the final solution is certainly polysemic and self-referential, especially after fifty-five years of historical discourse. The dualism posited between a "stable reality and truth"—it *happened*—and adherence to the polysemy of interpretations is no problem at all, for this is a difference where there isn't one, for ideological reasons. Friedlander worries that the multiplicity of interpretations might lead to "aesthetic fantasy," and hence a "stable truth" would preclude that; it simply doesn't follow, however, that production of multiple interpretations leads to "fantasy." What could be more fantastic than interpretations that derived Hitler's anti-Semitism from his bodily difficulties, notoriously documented, once quite plausible, and today thoroughly discredited? What will be said fifty years from now?

No research historian has made stronger assertions about French theory than Carlo Ginzburg. In 1986 Ginzburg went "over the top," saying, "I am deeply interested in catching the right meaning. . . . I am deeply against every kind of Derrida trash, that kind of cheap skeptical attitude . . . cheap nihilism . . . so cheap . . . silly narcissistic . . . I am deeply against it."[12] In Ginzburg's version, the historian is a connoisseur, a divinator, an intuitor par excellence, erudition put to the service of the intellectual putdown, performed in the name of leftwing empathy for the victims of history. What seems to matter is the integrity of the scholar above all else.[13] Anything skeptical of this model is dismissed or equated with fascist idealism, from Hayden White to Roland Barthes to Paul de Man and Nietzsche. Just consider Ginzburg's recent *History, Rhetoric and Proof*.

Ginzburg wants to refute skepticism or tie it to "radical" and "extreme" by insisting that an historian's relation to documentation is more important than narrative presentation. "The actuality of research" is defended—but not a single instance of "doing research" *can be presented*: to present the act of research one would have to have a *literary record of the sensations of reading and thinking about* these documents, that is, an immediate presentation that is not "research," not the vaulted act of research itself. Ginzburg insists that the historian's identity—integrity and responsibility—stems from the act of research whereas radical skepticism, soft or hard, is said to descend from "an idea of rhetoric . . . actually opposed to proof."[14] There is, then, a "good" form of rhetoric that is tied to proof and a "bad" mode of rhetoric attached to skepticism, and any deviation from "proof" leads to crimes of relativism, among others.

In *History, Rhetoric and Proof* a line of continuity is stretched from Callicles's contest with Socrates in Plato's *Gorgias* to Nietzsche on little more than allusion.

Callicles's skepticism and "haughtiness smacked enough of distinction to predispose him [to Nietzsche's] . . . *petit bourgeois* veneration" (8). Cited as "proof" for this is an 1876 letter from Rohde to Franz Overbeck—which warns of the existential danger Nietzsche exposed himself to. After this dubious linkage or skepticism's negative continuity, Nietzsche's essay "Truth and Lie" is said to have developed "relativistic implications" by severing rhetoric from truth and suturing it to "style." This allows Ginzburg to reduce Nietzsche's theory of art: "culture is art's domination over life, as occurred in ancient Greece." But *The Birth of Tragedy* made clear that art and domination are by no means synonymous, as when Nietzsche writes that domination through art is Apollonian and in that a "secondary" effect, keeping at bay the possibility of tragedy or an "abysmal and terrifying view of the world and the keenest susceptibility to suffering." Nietzsche's texts and their complicated construal of "domination" are reduced to nothing but "domination over." Nietzsche's "Truth and Lie" is reduced to making Nietzsche say that "language is intrinsically poetic, and that each word is originally a trope," but Ginzburg's reference is to a study on Nietzsche, not Nietzsche's writing. In "Truth and Lie" Nietzsche actually gives a rather complicated genealogy of language, starting with words and sounds and "nerve stimulus"; anything but language is "intrinsically poetic." Nietzsche talks about the misapplication of the principle of sufficient reason, and he is talking not about poetry as essence of language as much as he is asking about the *processes* of how language can represent truth if it is figural as well.

Ginzburg is relentless in defending "research" and tracking down to an "origin" any skeptical or radical idea, in particular Nietzsche's personal history. "Truth and Lie" was "kept secret" by Nietzsche because it was "written while he was in the grip of a crisis of moral skepticism which had led him 'to criticize and to go more deeply into his prior pessimism'" (11): an origin of radical skepticism in Nietzsche's very own life. *Proof:* Nietzsche turned from theology to philology in 1865 at Bonn; four years later, at his inaugural lecture at Basel, Nietzsche turned to classical philology and abandoned New Testament philology, cutting himself off from religion. The *Birth of Tragedy* is written in a rejection of "academic philology," hostile in fact to academia, and "Truth and Lie," an unfinished manuscript, is accounted for as "language cannot give us a satisfactory image of reality"—that proposition said to have its origin in Nietzsche's "deep friendship with Franz Overbeck." Ginzburg reduces *text* to *person*; "Truth and Lie" "echoes" its way to Luther, which in turn leads to German idealism's premise that language is spirit, spirit is life, reductions bad enough, but then taken to the penultimate reduction in Nietzsche's very own self—"Truth and Lie" was kept from publication because deep down Nietzsche "knew" the essay was an "affront to his father's memory," its radical skepticism equivalent to a denial of faith (15). "Truth and Lie" has its "origin" in Nietzsche's subjective crisis repeating Lutheran and idealist notions of "spirit." "Truth and Lie" is dismissed as reaction formation. More than one hundred footnotes document the research on this, which nonetheless tells the story of the petit bourgeois in "crisis" over an identity disorder. Vulgar yet urbanely recounted through psychoanalysis, the relegation of skepticism and relativism to an "origin" in the "lower orders" (repeated by Hunt et al. in *Telling the Truth* when they make skepticism and relativism precursors of Nazism) is unfortunately a "classic" piece of humanist aggression against anything deemed "lower."

The same thing is done to de Man in the same introduction to *History, Rhetoric and Proof*. De Man was continually duplicitous personally, and his critical theory of language is reduced to the denial of referential truth, called *antireferentiality* toward language. De Man's theory is reduced to the negative characteristics of the person, a nasty piece of work. Ginzburg does not connect de Man's Nazi-period writings to his later writings—a smart move on Ginzburg's part, but de Man's "revealed secret" (wartime writings) is the key to his supposed antireferential arguments. As with Nietzsche oedipalized, above, the same strategy on de Man muddles what is at stake and demonizes an opponent—elimination of a position. De Man's supposed antireferential position is tied to his own "existentially fragile" skepticism; Ginzburg calls it a "vacillating pendulum between truth and falsehood," this vacillation said to derive from an attempt to free himself "from the weight of history" (18). So terrible was de Man's influence that Ginzburg implies that the scholar Kofman's interest in rhetoric and skepticism led to suicide and came from the same "involvement with Nietzsche and the metaphor" as de Man's, deconstruction or French theory as such associated with "Truth . . . being liquidated in favor of an active interpretation, namely one without constrictions and limits" (19). De Man himself was awful, and the critique of referentially—where de Man *explicitly* addressed referentiality of language in saying that "difficulties only occur when it is no longer possible to ignore the epistemological thrust of the rhetorical dimension of language, that is, when it is no longer possible to keep it in its place"[15]—is reduced to "unconfessable autobiographical overtones" (19). All the proof, then, on Nietzsche and de Man is entirely allusive, reductive, Freudian (e.g., "subconscious repression" by Nietzsche and de Man [25]), about bad people producing bad theories that gum up the writing of history and monkey-wrench the whole apparatus of representation. Ginzburg even calls on the services of American journalism, citing in his essay David Lehman, who insisted that de Man was a "bad guy" because he didn't pay his rent while living in New York.

Ginzburg's erudition and use of psychoanalysis deserves a few paragraphs, especially on his method of treating and "correcting" the complex issue of intellectual influences. He has venerated his teacher, Arnaldo Momigliano, dozens of time in print. Yet Momigliano, a Jew, was a member of the Fascist Party; while a distinguished historian, he was critical of the writings of Piero Treves in the 1930s, who had refused to cooperate with the fascists and as a result lost his teaching position. But Momigliano published articles in the 1930s that one historian says are "in sympathy with the [fascist] regime."[16] In a *beiheft* in *History and Theory*, G. W. Bowersock writes that Momigliano was critical of the writings of an earlier mode of French theory, the work of Marcel Mauss, particularly his "neglect" of the Greek autobiographies and biographies in his treatment of the concept of the person, that Momigliano "had an insatiable interest in the teachers of great scholars and the academic environment . . . interested in their families, their marriages and their drinking habits" and "was at a loss to comprehend the person about whom he was writing" without knowing his "teachers, family connections, marriages and personal weaknesses." Finally, Momigliano proposed a parallel, "if not a connection, between rabbinic interpretations of personal character and Greek [character]," allergic to the French *moi*.[17] All of this is material for oedipalization, and what would it tell us?

This "unparalleled" historian/antiquarian was obsessed with the idea of *person*, as Bowersock, cited in *History, Rhetoric and Proof* as a "well-known historian," has noted. W. V. Harris writes that "Momigliano was a natural biographer" and that "in conversation, 'imbecile' was a favorite label" for the ideas of others.[18] Momigliano never completed "the book" or a sustained enterprise; his "biographical urge" (Harris's term) got in the way of completing historical projects. He never worked out a complete work of history because he could never articulate what Harris calls "the something else," a sustained historical thesis. Aren't a few of the "must have's" applied to Nietzsche and de Man applicable here? The so-called skepticism and relativism of de Man and Nietzsche reduced to bad/poor character suggests that the idealism ladled over Momigliano is subject to more protected categories of analysis—and what would a Freudian say of that?

Finally, the writings of Perry Anderson on French theory crystallize the previous discussion of research historians. Anderson is a historian of the left, of the British version of Frankfurt-style historical consciousness believed, by them, to be the key to social action and transformation. In "Arguments within English Marxism" he refers to Deleuze and Guattari's *Anti-Oedipus*, where desire has "in fact been one of the slogans of the subjectivist *Schwarmerei* [fanatics, romantic enthusiasts] that followed disillusionment with the social revolt of 1968."[19] These are the same designations that Appleby, Hunt, and Jacob use in *Telling the Truth*, especially that phrase "disillusioned" (= skeptical, = radical, = extreme). *Anti-Oedipus* is further denounced as the manifestation of "dejected post-lapsarian anarchism." These epithets have little to do with the actual writings by French theorists. Anderson's *In the Tracks of Historical Materialism* (1984) speaks of the postwar "massacre of [Marxist] ancestors" in Italy and France because of the influence of French structuralism, the "skepticism" that came with Althusser, a "loss of morale . . . in the scientific supremacy of Marxism."[20] Too many "Parisian doubts," too little interest in "agency" from French theorists, but what else is schizoanalysis in *Anti-Oedipus* but a working-up of multiple connections, working out the impasse of subject and structure? Anderson calls "exasperated" *Anti-Oedipus*'s interest in agency, (35), but his study reads as a classic Marxist attempt to purify anything on its own left. French theory is killed off through assertions that have the force of bullying—the "erasive gesture" and "dissolution of Man" of Lévi-Strauss, "subjects abolished" by Althusser, "repressors" of reference, French theory promoting "megalomania" and, through Nietzsche, a "denunciation . . . of the fixity of meaning." British Hegelian Marxism is the antidote.

Let's consider the claims about this murder of history, subject, language—French theory nastily encoded as Nazi, Nietzschean, Romantic, antihistorical and, my favorite, "nescient," or counseling ignorance (47). Consider the genealogy, similar to Ginzburg's: Lévi-Strauss's invocation of music leads to Wagner and Nietzsche, the whole of French theory reduced to "the theme of an original Dionysiac frenzy," and then back to Foucault's veneration of the "untamed" (the "mad") and Derrida's "subjectivism without a subject." French theory = Intellectual Catastrophe Number One of "our" age?

There's not enough space to do more than focus on "evidence" and "proof." First, Anderson claims French theory is responsible for an "exorbitation of language," or making language something aberrant, and for falsely extending Saussure's linguistic model to kinship, and anything else said to fall under "exchange" (40 ff.). He decries "such fundamental expansions of the jurisdiction of language." And just what is language's "jurisdiction"? Not specified here. Continuing, Anderson insists that "language is no fitting model for any other human practice" than itself—but is there some special practice of the scholar, the interpreter, the commentator, the analyst that is free from and of language? This attempt to keep language in place is accompanied by strange conjunctions. For example, in a discussion of *langue* and *parole*, utterances are said to be "free," have "no material constraint whatever . . . all other major social practices are subject to laws of natural *scarcity*" (44). Does this mean that *only* language produced by scarcity counts as language? Is scarcity a plausible concept by which to restrict language to its proper place? Following this, Anderson impugns individual speech in favor of the "relevant subjects" of the public world (political, etc.), because these subjects are potential collective agencies of social transformation—in one stroke he eliminates consideration of the ruinous discourses of such collective agencies and removes the multiplicity contained and released in any given instance of "merely subjective" discourse. Second, Anderson calls French theory's "aggrandizement of language" an *attenuation of truth* "no longer moored to any extra-linguistic reality" (45). What is the mean-ing of "moored"? *Docked?* As with other research historians, this "no longer" is threaded to French theory's "repression of the referential axis," a nasty charge without foundation. The only "proof" is to denounce Lévi-Strauss's use of a concept of the signifier, asserting, without anything else, that French theory denies "any stable intentional meaning" (46). Barthes argued that this "stable intention" is but a code with multiple effects, multiple consequences. Having put this delirium together, making theorists say things they didn't argue, all this is enthymatically routed to French theory treated as an assassin, having "severed" truth from correspondence. In point of fact, the theory of truth as correspondence is only one of many theories of truth, most argued from the ancient world out, and all French theory did to correspondence theory is to remind everyone it operates as a *code*—it is a mode of performance, a long and old one, not a concept timeless and universal. Third, all of this, in turn, is brought together as French theory's support of the *randomization of history* (48), or the challenge to the language of causality. No reference is made to an ana-lytic concept of causality. Instead, causality and sequentiality are said to be threatened, invoking Edward Said, who calls French theory's sense of history a "legislated accident." Could it be, however, that "legislated accident" is in-advertently accurate, applicable to Bosnia and Kosovo, among other places, that is, to the powers-that-be calling a halt to violence "randomly" and installing enough "legislation" to quiet the overt violence? The three negative effects of French theory are brought together as writing made "implacable and unde-cidable," which, believe it or not, *are the actual effects* for many people of read-ing all sorts of texts—especially those deemed "enlightened."

The historians discussed above directly *politicize* against French theory *from the perspective of academic "victors."* So it is a curious thing, this injunction against French theory, since it never treats the arguments of the theories with anything like intellectual responsibility—as objects of *research*. In this sense, the various de-nunciations have less to do with "doing research" than with the market share of what remains of metanarrative discourse(s). Most of these historians are "pro-gressive" Freudians and were given tenure in the mid-1970s, just as French the-ory became widely available in translation—not just Derrida, but many other writ-ers. Further studies of the discursive armature of academic writing/institution would no doubt yield many interesting results concerning the academic wars of the past thirty years or so. What seems implausible is to give less than skepticism and criticism toward the historians when they turn their weapons on present ri-vals. There is too much purification of intellectual perspectives today; the "vic-tors" act intolerant just at the moment of their "victory." But given the decline of the humanities, what do the victors now command?

Notes

1. There are too many variables about historical writing to give it anything like a "singular" or homogenous origin/function. One of the best sources on this topic is James T. Shotwell's *The History of History* (New York: Columbia University Press, 1939), pp. 51–69, who argues that monograms, titles, totemic names, the annal and chronicle, the temple-record, religious festivals (holidays), and calendars are so interwoven as to defy a singular basis for historical writing of the kind associated with the "first" Western "masters," Thucydides and Herodtous. Naming and numbering were in competition; city chroniclers made their accounts in prose (p. 170), and historiography was partially "created" in acts of skepticism against legends.

2. Perez Zagorin, "History, the Referent and Narrative: Reflections on Postmodernism Now," History and Theory 38, no. 1, (1999), pp. 22–23.

3. Every institution now has to maximize the performance of its faculty, whatever its level, rank, distinction, function.

4. Lynn Hunt, "History beyond Social History," in *The States of "Theory," History, Art and Critical Discourse*, edited and with an introduction by David Carroll (New York: Columbia, 1990), pp. 95–112.

5. Joyce Appleby, Lynn Hunt, and Margaret Jacob, *Telling the Truth about History* (New York: Norton, 1994), p. 233.

6. Ibid., p. 208.

7. Ibid., p. 213.

8. Joyce Appleby, E. Covington, D. Hoyt, M. Latham, and A. Sneider, eds., *Knowledge and Postmodernism in Historical Perspective* (New York: Routledge, 1996, p.386).

9. Saul Friedlander, G. Holton, L. Marx, and E. Sknoniloff, *Visions of Apocalypse, End or Rebirth* (New York: Holmes and Meier, 1985), p. 8.

10. Saul Friedlander, *Nazi Germany and the Jews* (New York: Harper, 1997), pp. 53, 131.

11. Saul Friedlander, Introduction to *Probing the Limits of Representation* (Cambridge: Harvard University Press, 1992), p. 4.

12. "Carlo Ginzburg: An Interview," *Radical History Review* 35 (1986), p. 100.

13. I argue this in Chapter 4 of my *Passive Nihilism* (New York: St. Martins, 1998).

14. Carlo Ginzburg, *History, Rhetoric and Proof* (Manchester, N.H.: University Press of New England, 1999), p. 2; hereafter, page numbers will be cited parenthetically in the text.

15. Paul de Man, The Resistance to Theory (Minneapolis: University of Minnesota Press, 1986), p. 14.

16. W. V. Harris, "The Silences of Momigliano," *Times Literary Supplement*, April 12, 1996, p. 8.

17. G. W. Bowersock, "Momigliano's Quest for the Person," in *History and Theory, Beiheft* 30 (1991), pp. 28–32.

18. Harris, "Silences," p. 6.

19. Perry Anderson, "Arguments within English Marxism," *New Left Review* (1980), p. 161.

20. Perry Anderson, *In the Tracks of Historical Materialism*, (Chicago: University of Chicago Press, 1984), pp. 29–30.

Supplement B:
Ecceity, Smash and Grab,
The Expanded I and Moment

CHRIS KRAUS

There is a small marker on the poet Frank O'Hara's grave in the Springs, East Hampton, New York cemetery inscribed with a single line from one of his most famous poems:

Grace to be born and live as variously as possible.

It is a sentiment that seems absolutely synonymous with the imperative rhetoric of Deleuze and Guattari about intensities and becomings. Lived experience, they insisted, implies intensities. Deleuze sought to attain and explicate the state known as *ecceity*—a moment fractured into the thousand variances and textures that compose it—emotion, thought, the air we breathe, the memory that informs it. Time as a cubist cut-up: you fracture it and recompose it. In *Dialogues*, this notion of ecceity is an expression of Virginia Woolf's expanded moment, updated, stripped of literary affect.

And yet it is interesting to note that Deleuze had true contemporaries in this project, unknown to him. The writers of the New York school of the mid-1950s were building on the work of Gertrude Stein and William Carlos Williams in their desire to found a poetics based upon transcription: transcription of the human voice, a tracing. Eileen Myles, a writer who has radicalized the tradition of the New York school by bringing it with her into lesbian fringe culture, describes the influence of Stein:

> When Stein tells us what poetry is, and what prose is, and all the journalists titter, the joke is that she's female, and an upper class bull dyke, talking like a kid about grand things. She discovered again that when language repeats itself, when you hear yourself speak and think through the actual process of words which are redundant, then language really starts to operate in a different register.

The poetry of the New York school—whose original practitioners include O'Hara, Lew Welch, Paul Blackburn, and later on Ted Berrigan, Ron Padgett, Alice Notley, Bernadette Mayer, and Anne Waldman—has all the paradoxical easiness of a Zen koan. It is flux without the rhetoric; spun on wit, the seriousness of trivia, it takes place entirely in the conversational mode. Deeply tongue in cheek, O'Hara declares *Personism* as the next poetic movement in an essay written in 1959. It is

> a movement which I recently founded and which nobody knows about, interests me a great deal, being so totally opposed to this kind of abstract removal that it is verging on a true abstraction for the first time. . . . Personism has nothing to do with philosophy, it's all art. It does not have to do with personality or intimacy, far from it! But to give you a vague idea . . . it puts the poem squarely between the poet and the person.

Wryly and offhandedly, O'Hara puts his finger on the great discovery of American poetry during the twentieth century: that poetry is living speech, transcribed (William Carlos Williams); that it is a map of a person's mind (Phillip Whalen); that it is an exchange of energy between the writer and the reader (Charles Olsen). The writer Ann Rower describes this gentle tampering with live speech as a criminal act, like breaking and entering, "smash and grab."

The work of Camille Paglia would not be so annoying if she was not so right about one fundamental thing: that in overestimating any theory, Americans ignore the fact that theory often just reformulates many tendencies already present in our culture. Theory, because it's difficult, must be serious. There is something deeply suspect about anything that's easy. And while French theory is now embedded within American academic thought, the American antiacademic tradition of poetics that shunned experimentalism in favor of live speech is rarely studied because it's considered much too marginal. Because these poets rejected a certain kind of theoretical language, people just assumed that they were dumb. Lew Welch, a minor poet of the New York School, once described poetry as glibness. You're never going to be a writer if you don't have glibness, he once said. "It's like having a tin ear. . . . The words have to be interesting. Now they have to be interesting in the way street talk is interesting, because everything else is phony."

Deleuze and Guattari's description of the body without organs, borrowed from Autonin Artaud, is not much more or less than an expanded state of alertness. Poetics, like Zen Buddhism, offers us a technology for getting there. This technology is based upon an ecceity, an inclusivity of everything that might comprise a statement: what is being said; to whom, and why; and who is saying it. In *A Thousand Plateaus*, Deleuze and Guattari look at Tantrism and schizophrenia as two mediums through which one might achieve the body without organs. In Tantrism, the withholding of ejaculation is not a question of experiencing desire as an internal lack, nor of delaying pleasure in order to produce a kind of externalizable surplus value, but instead constitutes an intensity; Deleuze and Guattari exhort the reader to shun the psychoanalytic search for self, and instead say, "Let's go further still, we haven't found our body without organs yet, we haven't sufficiently dismantled our self. Substitute forgetting for anamnesis, experimentation for interpretation. find your body without organs. find out how to make it. It's a question of life and death, youth and old age, sadness and joy. It is where everything is played out." The important thing, they say, is to find one's zone of indiscernibility—enter ecceities and the impersonality of things.

They want, as the radical mystic Simone Weil wanted, to break down the self, to disappear. And yet there's something slightly suspect in these passages from *A Thousand Plateaus*. They remind me just a bit too much of Timothy Leary and all the lesser drug-and-therapy gurus of the 1970s, advancing proscriptions for a life well lived without ever referencing themselves. Their rhetoric evades the basic question: Who are we? Is there a we? who is speaking, and to whom? Weil, a great modernist, was prepared to enact these theories on herself. In *Gravity and Grace*, she writes, "If the I is the only thing we truly own, we must destroy it. Use the I to break down I. And later on: If the body is a lever for salvation, we must use it. But how? What is the right way to use it?"

I'm amazed by the lack of correspondences acknowledged between philosophy and poetic thought. The dream of becoming everything: it seems so radical and daring when espoused by the philosophers Deleuze and Guattari, yet insignificant and trivial when poets say it. There is a tradition of antiacademic writing in America—in which O'Hara falls roughly in the chronologic center—that pivots upon the use of an impersonal I. O'Hara's *personism*, and all the contemporary poetry and writing that succeeds it, is based upon a technology through which one might achieve a public and impersonal I, and that technology is based upon the will to speak in real time, announcing the actual. O'Hara's poems read, polemically and self-consciously, like a set of bulletins, with time and place announced in the first lines and the titles. It is 4:19 in Pennsylvania Station . . .; It is 1:55 in Cambridge. In *Autobiographia Literaria*, he wryly writes, "When I was a child I played by myself in a corner of the schoolyard all alone. I hated dolls and I hated games, animals were not friendly and birds flew away. . . . And here I am, the center of all beauty! Writing these poems!" O'Hara's I is hardly psychoanalytic. It is the focal point for a tiny sliver of experience, rather than the object of investigation. It is not an I that begs for empathy. It's open; anyone can be it.

Deleuze and Guattari, for all their exhortations toward achieving a state of translucent subjectivity, never take that simple leap of identifying themselves to the reader. One is to accept the metaphysical cartography that brain is "high," body is low. In all those *milles plateaux*, we never actually see them in the room or find out what they think when they're not thinking. Great poetry, Alice Notley said, is living presence. And how does one achieve this? Notley writes about how the late Ted Berrigan worked on pace. He often said that he wanted his poems to "sound like the pace at which he walked, and many of his poems . . . are like a walk across the page." While language poetry, which explicitly pays homage to semiotic theory, has been absorbed within the mainstream of American academe, Berrigan's work is barely taken seriously. And yet his writing is exemplary of becoming because he never loses sight of what he's doing when he writes—suspending difference between poetry and prose:

> The heart stops briefly when someone dies, a quick pain as you hear the news, and someone passes from your outside life to inside. Slowly the heart adjusts to its new weight, and slowly everything continues, sane."

As Notley notes, the basis of Berrigan's practice was performance: a recognition of who is speaking, who is being spoken to. In fact, this kind of practice isn't new. It is a rediscovery over the course of some five centuries of poetry as a medium of direct address. Bragging, swooning, desperate to hold the attention of their audience, the Provençal poets were never unaware that they had one. It's no coincidence that Paul Blackburn, an influential figure within the New York school, undertook to translate them.

"I think of I as the mast of a ship," the poet Bernadette Mayer said once in an interview. If the poem's a boat, it is the writer's I that drives it. The poet Eileen Myles imagines the letter I as an illuminated character in a children's book. She says, "I see I as an inflated piece of language."

Traveling through the lineage of philosophy, Deleuze and Guattari come to a similar conclusion in *A Thousand Plateaus*, trying "to reach the point where one no longer says I, but the point where it is no longer of any importance whether one says I." And later, in *Dialogues* with Claire Parnet, Deleuze describes "style" as "managing to stammer in one's own language."

It is high irony that Deleuze, for all his celebration of the minor tendency in literature, embraces, in *Dialogues*, the American writers who wanted desperately to be major. Deleuze was also swayed by the faux sincerity of American beat writers, beloved in France as exemplary of America. Transcribing the words of a Bob Dylan song, seduced by the heroic grandiosity of Henry Miller and Jack Kerouac, Deleuze celebrates their work as the means toward a more personal life, forgetting his own and more exacting maxim: "Life is not personal." More: "lived experience," according to Deleuze and Guattari, implies intensities. And yet, because the poetry discussed here references experience, and is implicitly emotional, it is often charged with being self-indulgent, shrill. "In New York I feel like I'm a jagged bit of skin walking down the street," writes Kathy Acker in *Hannibal Lecter*. "Whenever a cock enters me every night three nights in a row, I ask myself regardless of who the cock belongs to should I let my SELF depend on this person or should I remain a closed entity. I say: I'm beginning to love you I don't want to see you again. The man thinks I'm crazy so he wants nothing to do with me."

Acker's I, though it owes a large and unacknowledged debt to the tradition of New York school writing, is a far cry from O'Hara's I in *Autobiographia Literaria*. It could be that the contemporary female I is charged with content. And yet it takes a certain cast of mind—Deleuzean, in fact—to recognize that content isn't absolute, that it can be strategic. Flipping through gossip, sickness, sex, philosophy, and posturing, Acker appreciated that French theory gave her a context and vocabulary with which to talk about her work. She said in an interview,

> French philosophies . . . gave me a way of verbalizing what I had been doing in language. I didn't really understand why I refused to use linear narrative; why my sexual genders kept changing; why basically I am the most disoriented novelist that ever existed. I just did what I did but had no way of telling anyone about it, or talking about it. And then when I read *Anti-Oedipus* and Foucault's work, suddenly I had this whole new language at my disposal. I could say, Hi! And that other people were doing the same thing. I remember thinking, Why don't they know me? I know exactly what they're talking about. And I could go farther.

The poet Alice Notley, chronicling her conflicted love for William Carlos Williams, in an essay called "Dr. Williams' Heiress," assesses the difficulty of using any kind of reflective public I when I is female. "Being woman the poet?" she asks, "Well, it's a tone of voice that people aren't used to. You have to hit these tones of voice that people are going to say are this or that, strident or shrill. And yet, You have to deal with the problem of who you are so you can be that person, talking." Real time is not continuous. It does not occur in isolation. And the body is the source of all intensities, not concepts. In *The Recorded Century*, Eileen Myles writes,

> If anybody doesn't understand a poem, the thing to remember is that it was written by a human body in real time. That's where the poem begins. If it starts and stops on the page, if there's holes in the way the words are splat-

tered on the page, you should bear in mind that the poet paused, breathed, the phone rang and she wondered if she should pick it up.

John Ashbery called this "managed chance . . . the experience of experience, a transcription of attention—the shape of a mind as it wanders all day. . . . Any piece of writing that doesn't tell you in a simple way, in this totally original American way, that the writer lived is a lie."

Supplement C:
Sokal's New Clothes (Intermezzo)

ELIE DURING

> Our goal was to show that, in some sense, the "emperor
> is naked" and that generations of students who had to
> struggle in order to understand obscure texts were some-
> times right to suspect that they were wasting their time.
>
> —*Jean Bricmont,* "Exposing the Emperor's New Clothes"

"Sokal's New Clothes" is a tale of mystification and polemics, laughter and anger, power and prestige, rigor and playfulness. A story littered with plot twists, knots, tricks, and tiffs. Some would call it the hoax of the decade (The Sokal Hoax), while others would prefer to view it as an "affair" (the *Social Text* affair, not in the romantic sense of the term, but as in the "Dreyfus affair" that tore French society apart a century ago). No matter what importance is assigned to the ensuing debate, the hoax was a hit. It became a story that the media and academia relished telling again and again.

Ever since Sokal's "Transforming the Boundaries: Towards a Transformative Hermeneutics of Quantum Gravity" was published in *Social Text*,[1] and simultaneously revealed in *Lingua Franca* by its author as a fraud, a parody "chock-full of absurdities and blatant non-sequiturs,"[2] scores of articles, conferences, and Internet chat rooms have flourished in the United States and elsewhere (particularly in France). Sokal originally intended to prove that one could easily fool the editorial board of a fashionable review of cultural studies by submitting an article that wrapped an easy relativist view of modern science in an appropriate mix of canonical postmodern quotes and theoretical rehashings, although the references to scientific content were loaded with inaccuracies and obvious nonsense. He obviously brilliantly made his point, but what does this prove?

It would be tiresome to recount all the twists and turns of the polemics sparked by Sokal's paper.[3] The debate was confused at best, but it clearly revolved around a few hotly disputed issues: the function of science studies, the strategies of epistemic relativism, the use of scientific metaphors in cultural studies, the standards of legitimate scholarship, the future of the American Left, Franco-American intellectual relations, to name but a few. Yet the story of the hoax itself is far from simple. For one thing, it is difficult to see what exactly this hoax demonstrates.[4] Each of the various actors in the Sokal controversy has his own version of the way things happened. "Our goal is precisely to say that the king is naked (and the queen too),"[5] Sokal announces in the English version of *Impostures Intellectuelles,* the book he coauthored with his Belgian colleague Jean Bricmont. A humorless extension of the original article, it supposedly emphasizes a few points at issue to carry the debate one step further. Sokal has ceased to be funny, but things are not much clearer for that. Who is naked after all, and who is playing the tricks?

Hans Christian Andersen's fairy tale "The Emperor's New Clothes" provides an interesting introduction to the narrativized ideological formations brought about by the *Social Text* affair. Those who remember the bedtime stories of their childhood know that it is essentially a tale about incompetence and vanity—the vanity that fuels the collective belief in "experts," and subsequently allows for the masking of one's personal incompetence. It raises the question of the mechanisms by which ideas diffuse in society and gain cultural legitimacy. It relies upon the blunt opposition between the illusion of institutional power on the one hand and the purity of childhood on the other. Its moral, however, is not obvious: is it to say that people should not pass themselves off as competent when they are not? Or rather is it that competence is a matter of trust, although people should not be trusted? Does the story call for more competence, or does it vindicate the virtue of incompetence? Back to our text:

> Once upon a time, in the land of Academia, there lived a vain emperor whose only worry in life was to dress in elegant clothes. He changed clothes almost every hour, following the most fashionable trends in high culture, and loved to show them off to his subjects. His wardrobe was cared for by his most devoted courtesan—known by their detractors as PoMos—who enjoyed special treatment in court. Word of the Emperor's refined habits spread over his kingdom and beyond. The discontent of certain people in the semi-autonomous region of "Hard Science" was aggravated by the general support the Emperor received from Academia; they actively voiced their disapproval of the imperial fashion by advocating allegedly more concrete and efficient means of improving the Empire. Two scoundrels had heard of the Emperor's vanity and decided to take advantage of it. One of them, no doubt a mercenary in the "Science Wars," came from the remote regions of Bel-

gium. The other came from the rich, private city-state called New York. One day, they introduced themselves at the gates of the palace with a scheme in mind. "We are two very good tailors and fabric-experts. After many years of research we have invented an extraordinary method to weave a cloth so light and fine that it looks invisible. As a matter of fact it is invisible to anyone who is too stupid and incompetent to appreciate its quality." "Just tell us what you need to get started and we'll give it to you," said the Emperor as soon as he met these dubious tailors. The two scoundrels asked for a loom, silk, gold thread and then pretended to begin working. The Emperor thought he had spent his money quite well; in addition to getting a new extraordinary suit, he would discover which of his subjects were ignorant and incompetent. Once they had taken his measurements, the two scoundrels began cutting the air with scissors while sewing with their needles an invisible cloth. They commented on their gestures, using the most sophisticated jargon. "As you can see, we're working towards a nonminimalist aesthetic of soft delirium as a response to muted, boring clothes that scream corporate culture and invisibility. Nubby metastable tweed singularities and fanciful rhizomatic signature prints provide the far-from-equilibrium conditions for the coat to create its own visual vortex. This unique piece is marked by a strategic play on the narrativization of fashion history—a combination of pre-kitsch glamour with poststructuralist hip. Your Highness, you'll have to take off your clothes to try on your new ones!" They draped the new clothes on the Emperor and then held up a mirror. The Emperor was as much baffled by the rhetoric of the tailors as he was embarassed by the situation, but since no one in the court objected, he felt relieved. He was first doubtful about showing himself naked to the people, but then he abandoned his fears. After all, no one would know about it except the ignorant and the incompetent. "All right," he said. "I will grant the people this privilege." The Emperor was paraded down the street with his court. His people had gathered in the main square, pushing and shoving to get a better look. An applause welcomed the regal procession. Everyone wanted to know how stupid or incompetent his or her neighbor was but, as the Emperor passed, a strange murmur rose from the crowd. Everyone said, loud enough for the others to hear, "Look at the Emperor's new clothes. They're beautiful! What a marvelous train!" A child named Alan, however, went up to the carriage. "The Emperor is naked," he said. The boy's remark, which had been heard by the bystanders, was repeated over and over again until everyone cried, "The boy is right! The Emperor is naked! It's true!" The Emperor stood stiffly on his carriage, while behind him a page held his imaginary mantle. The story was soon circulating around the Empire, as people told it again and again in bursts of laughter.

So the story goes. There are many other accepted versions. In some renditions, the scoundrels are not Sokal and Bricmont, but *Social Text*, and it is Sokal who takes the role of the child. In another version everyone is naked—the emperor, his court, and his people. On the contrary, some say it is the emperor who shouts that everyone is naked, as he is the only one to be dressed, or else that there was no emperor in the first place.

Others say that the tale is truncated, and that things were in fact much more complicated. The punch line of the tale itself admits many variants. Some say the child is reprimanded for his irreverent behavior, and reduced to silence for being as impolite as incompetent. Yet others say it is an expert in the manufacturing of fabric who first denounced the trickery. Other variants have it that the bystanders had a good laugh, and the emperor too, who praised the two scoundrels for their abilities as practical jokers. In yet another version the alledged tailors have to face a committee of experts and are unmasked as impostors.

Sokal himself oscillates between two readings of the tale. In one of them, he is one of the two tricksters; in the other he is the ingenuous child. It is not clear, however, who he thinks is naked—the emperor alone, or his entire court?

The ambiguous nature of the reference to the emperor's "nudity" provides a striking mirror image of the generally intricate rhetorics ensuing from the Sokal hoax. As Bruno Latour remarks in a witty and excessive article in *Le Monde*, "like any hoax, Sokal's escapes its author" ("comme toutes les farces, elle échappe à son auteur").[6] Sokal's own intentions are indeed not always transparent. At times he seems to be making a simple point about methodology and the standards of rigor required by legitimate scholarship (in this position, he has been described as a "schoolmaster" and a "cop"). Taken in this vein, his book would be an innocuous call for more rigor when using scientific notions, even if some French journalists have likened it to Kenneth Starr's report to Congress. Yet in other contexts, Sokal claims to have a more ambitious mission that borders on the prophetic: to save academia from the trends that pervert its institutions and undermine the very purpose of a university. What is at stake, then, is the search for truth, the reality of the external world, and the possibility of objective knowledge. Oddly, Sokal takes the role of a self-taught metaphysician. He finds allies in the ranks of analytic philosophers like Paul Boghossian or Thomas Nagel,[7] who applaud the vindication of what they hold as a commonsensical and healthy form of realism about truth, and who are content with the view that philosophical problems relating to science have no particular political impact.

Yet, sometimes Sokal seems to exceed the academic scope altogether. He acknowledges that he is making a political claim about the future of the academic or scholastic American Left and its present incapacity to effectively deal with concrete political issues. His arguments are curiously consonant with Rorty's, for example, although it is doubtful that he would welcome the alliance. Sokal often sounds unwittingly right wing. Despite his confessions about being an "unabashed Leftist," many adversaries of the left who would like to see the humanities purged of the "postmodernist rot" have taken sides with him.[8]

Sokal's double language and constant shift from an emancipatory mission (saving the American Left from the disease of postmodernism) to a very modest claim about standards of academic rigor blurs the issues from the outset. Quite apart from the earnest intention behind Sokal's actions, a range of characters have projected their own concerns onto the debate in order to harness the negative energy of the critical backlash to their own ends. Asking whether some writers "have become international stars for sociological rather than intellectual reasons, and in part because they are masters of language and can impress their audience with a clever abuse of sophisticated terminology" is not a real question: it already suggests its own answer.[9] There is really something disingenuous in Sokal and Bricmont's claim to have been astonished at finding themselves in the thick of a highly politicized and mediatized polemic.

Things get even more convoluted as the parties involved seem to be talking at cross-purposes. Reading French theory and contemporary science studies through the prism of problems developed in the American philosophy of science some thirty years ago (Quine, Kuhn, Feyerabend), Sokal is driven to address issues of relativism that are, ironically, foreign to his critical targets. The authors he quotes and criticizes for abusing scientific jargon (Lacan, Deleuze, or Baudrillard) are in fact not interested in scientific theories as such, nor in their capacity to describe "reality," but in the concepts they provide, and their possible reappropriation for other purposes. As Bruno Latour says, "For a French person, saying that facts are constructed is a banality. Relativism is like an infantile disease: for us who contract it in our high-school philosophy class when we are 18, it is harmless. Yet when it is transferred to the U.S., it can infect entire departments of philosophy or literature."[10] The relevance of scientific metaphors in philosophical discourse thus constantly interferes with problems that, strictly speaking, have nothing to do with it. Of course, this identifies the central problem with Sokal's perspective: it is never clear which targets he is aiming at. Is it the American postmoderns (as the original hoax may suggest), or the French masters themselves (as *Impostures Intellectuelles* seems to imply)? The French masters' entire works, or just the parts where they are drawing on scientific imagery? Theory as such or just its most bombastic varieties?

Much remains to be said about the *Social Text* affair. War, trial, epidemics: whatever metaphor is chosen to describe it, its mechanics provide an instructive case for the study of the diffusion and distortion of ideas. On a structural level, what is at stake is the power games of the university system, the ambiguous role of the media in relation to intellectual debate, the love-hate relations between American academia and French intellectuals. Circumstances allowed for a certain number of unexpected moves and tactical alliances. Yet if the debate ever winds up, it is likely that the parties involved will be even more entrenched in their positions than they were before. We will never know for sure who the tailors were, who took the role of the ingenuous child, and who was finally naked.

Notes

1. Alan Sokal, "Transforming the Boundaries: Towards a Transformative Hermaneutics of Quantum Gravity," *Social Text* 46–47 (spring / summer 1996), pp. 217–52.
2. Alan Sokal and Jean Bricmont, *Fashionable Nonsense: Postmodern Intellectuals' Abuse of Science* (New York: Picador, 1998), p. 2.
3. For a quite extensive overview, see the excellent study by Yves Jeannert, *L'Affaire Sokal ou La Querelle des Impostures* (Paris: PUF, 1998). A website from Sokal himself that was devoted to the debate (www.physics.nyu.edu / faculty / sokal) contains a useful collection of articles.
4. See Michael Lynch, in Baudouin Jurdant, ed., *Impostures Scientifiques* (Paris: La Decouverte, 1998), pp. 43–58.
5. Sokal and Bricmont, *Fashionable Nonsense*, p. 2.
6. Bruno Latour, "Y a-t-il une Science après la Guerre Froide?" *Le Monde*, January 18, 1997.
7. See Paul Boghossian, "What the Sokal Hoax Ought to Teach Us," *Times Literary Supplement*, December 13, 1996, ; and Thomas Nagel, "The Sleep of Reason," *New Republic*, October 12, 1998.
8. Heather MacDonald, "Defrocking the French Fakers," *Wall Street Journal*, November 12, 1998.
9. Alan Sokal and Jean Bricmont, "What Is This Fuss About?" *Times Literary Supplement*, October 17, 1998.
10. Bruno Latour, quoted in Nathalie Levisalles, "Le Canular du Profesor Sokal," *Libération*, December 3, 1996. Latour also describes France as a "new Colombia, a land of dealers producing hard drugs ('derridium,' 'lacanium') to which graduate students on American campuses cannot resist any better than crack." Latour, "Y a-t-il une Science après la Guerre Froide?"

Contributors

Jean Baudrillard is the author of twenty books, including *The Mirror of Production* (1970), *Simulations* (1983), and *The Ecstasy of Communication* (1988), each of which established his presence in the American scene.

Mario Biagioli is the author of *Galileo, Courtier* (1993), and the editor of *The Science Studies Reader* (1999). He teaches in the department of history of science at Harvard University, and is currently working on a volume on the author function and issues of intellectual property in contemporary science.

Sande Cohen has written *Historical Culture* (1986), *Academia and the Luster of Capital* (1993), and *Passive Nihilism* (1998). He is completing a book entitled *History and the New Prison-House of Culture*. He teaches at CalArts.

Gilles Deleuze, arguably one of the century's most important thinkers, was the author of many works, some cowritten with Félix Guattari, including *Anti-Oedipus* (1972), *A Thousand Plateaus* (1977), and *What is Philosophy?* (1994).

Jacques Derrida, the most influential French theorist in terms of American reception, and the alleged founder of the "deconstructionist school," teaches at the École Normale Superieure of Rue d'Ulm in Paris. He has published some thirty books, starting with *Of Grammatology*.

Elie During currently teaches philosophy at the University of Paris, Nanterre, and is completing his doctorate on pseudoproblems in Bergson, James, and Ludwig Wittgenstein. He is the author of two philosophical handbooks, *L'Ame* and *La Metaphysique*, as well as essays on Deleuze.

Françoise Gaillard is Professor at Paris VII, a specialist in literary theory and nineteenth- and twentieth-century literature, and is a regular visiting professor at NYU. She is the author of *Temps Denses*, among other works.

Gérard Genette has written extensively on poetics, both literary and visual. The author of many works including groundbreaking texts on narrative, figure, and mimologics, he has intensified his writing on aesthetics, including such recent works as *The Aesthetic Relation* (1999).

Alison M. Gingeras is curator for contemporary art at the Musée National d'Art Moderne at the Centre Georges Pompidou, Paris, where she is preparing exhibitions on the artists Jeff Koons and Daniel Buren. She cocurated *Invested Spaces in Visual Arts, Architecture and Design from France, 1958–98* at the Guggenheim Museum in 1998, and has written for *Parkett, Art Press*, and *Beaux-Arts Magazine*.

Chris Kraus is the author of *Aliens and Anorexia* (2000) and *I Love Dick* (1997). She produced the "Chance Event—Three Days in the Desert with Jean Baudrillard" (1996), and founded the Native Agents series at *Semiotext(e)*. She writes a column for *Art/Text*, and teaches at ArtCenter College of Design, Pasadena, California.

Julia Kristeva is the author of many works, including her pathbreaking *Recherche pour une semanalyse* (1969) and *Revolution in Poetic Language* (1974), combining critical psychoanalysis and semiotics, feminism, and more. She divides her teaching between Paris and New York.

Andrea Loselle is the author of *History's Double* (1997) and is currently writing a book on literary and photographic techniques of representation in French culture at the end of the nineteenth century. She teaches in the French department at UCLA.

Sylvère Lotringer is Professor of French and Comparative Literature at Columbia University, as well as the general editor of *Semiotext(e)*. He has authored *Antonin Artaud* (1986) and *Overexposed* (1988), as well as numerous essays in semiotics, literature, philosophy, and art.

Kriss Ravetto is the author of *The Making and Unmaking of Fascist Aesthetics* (2001). She has written many essays on cultural criticism, feminism, film theory, and literature. She teaches in the Critical Studies department at CalArts.

Élisabeth Roudinesco is the French historian of the psychoanalytic movement and the biographer of Jacques Lacan, the "French Freud" as he is known in America. She has published *Jacques Lacan and Co.: A History of Psychoanalysis in France, 1925–85* (1993) and *Madness and Revolution: The Lives and Legends of Theroisne De Mericort* (1993) among other works.

Donald F. Theall teaches at Trent University, Ontario, Canada, where he was university president from 1980 to 1987. His written work has spanned analysis of modernist literary practice, especially that of James Joyce, and sociocultural communications theory, especially that of McLuhan. He is the author, among other works, of *Joyce's Techno-Poetics* (1997), *Beyond the Word: Reconstructing Sense in the Joyce Era of Technology, Culture and Communication* (1995), and the forthcoming *The Virtual Marshall McLuhan*.

Index